International Economics

Second Edition

International Economics

Second Edition

Stephen A. Baker

For Catherine, Nick, and Alex.

Blackwell Publishers, a publishing imprint of
Basil Blackwell, Inc.
238 Main Street
Cambridge, Massachusetts   02142
USA

Basil Blackwell Ltd
108 Cowley Road
Oxford OX4 1JF
UK

Library of Congress Catalog Card Number 94–73585
ISBN 1–878975–49–8

Printed in the USA

Preface

Interest in international issues continues to grow. Discussions are frequent in the popular media, and it is now difficult to imagine a student graduating with a degree in economics who has not taken a course in international economics. Students are interested in the international issues, and interest is not confined to economics majors: most classes contain students from other disciplines, such as business, political science, and international relations. MBA courses are being revised to incorporate greater international emphasis. This, the second edition of *International Economics*, is designed to meet the need for a concise, comprehensive, up-to-date text that can be used by students with a wide range of academic backgrounds.

There are many international economics textbooks that claim to be appropriate for students with a limited economics background, and many that claim to describe fully techniques that are not usually found in principles courses. It has been my experience, however, that when the presentation of new material relies heavily on techniques with which the students are not familiar, there is a tendency to devote more time to mastering techniques than to trying to understand the relevant economic issues. Therefore, I have designed the presentation to be essentially non-mathematical, and I have used diagrams and tables to illustrate the points made in the text. Students who have taken a standard course in economics principles will be familiar with most of the techniques and diagrams used.

International Economics is divided into four sections dealing with, respectively, trade theory, exchange rates and open-economy macro–economics, historical experience, and finally, some special topics. This structure allows students to progress from learning principles to the application of those principles in economic analysis. After the principles chapters, the historical chapters offer a comprehensive critical survey of the development of the international monetary system and the history of commercial policy. Although the lessons of history are often clear, unfortunately they are often forgotten, so these chapters are designed to show how historical experience is relevant to current concerns and hence to deepen students' understanding of current issues and policies. The special topics section is a novel feature of this book; it contains an in-depth look at some issues that students find interesting: international banking, European Union, developing countries, and multinational corporations.

International Economics is structured so that instructors can cover either trade theory (Part One) or international finance and open-economy macroeconomics (Part Two) first. The history chapters and special topics are easily readable and can be used throughout the course to illustrate the principles, or they can be left until nearer the end and used selectively as time and interest permit. One of the main objectives has been to ensure that this text can be used in a wide variety of ways, to answer a wide variety of instructor needs and student backgrounds.

Please, if you would like to comment on the text, write to me. I will welcome and respond to your letters.

Acknowledgments

The second edition of this text grew out of the first, and benefitted from the many valuable comments made by reviewers of the first edition. They were: Betty Chu, San Jose State University; Denise Dimon, University of San Diego; Daniel Himarios, University of Texas at Arlington; Peter Kressler, Glassboro State College; Timothy Fries, University of Florida; Charles Engel, University of Virginia; Susan Ranney, University of Washington; Robert Stern, University of Michigan; and Henry Thompson, Auburn University. Special thanks are again due to Ed Stuart of Northeastern Illinois University who provided helpful comments on the first edition that went well beyond the call of duty.

This edition was written while I was on sabbatical in Strasbourg, France. I would like to thank Capital University for the financial support that made this possible.

Finally, I would to thank Bob Kolb, Kateri Davis, Andrea Coens, Ami Corbett, Sandi Schroeder, and Joe Rodriguez for their support and professionalism in producing this book.

Stephen A. Baker
Capital University

Contents

Part Three
Historical Experience   **253**

The Importance of International Economics

International trade is a significant and growing part of most economies. In some sectors, imported goods dominate. For example, most radios, televisions, and videocassette recorders sold in the United States are imported. Foreign brands have become familiar and popular. Could we survive without Sony's products? (Yes, but life would not be so enjoyable.) Consumers throughout the world are affected by changes in the prices of products such as coffee, wheat, and, particularly, oil. Even in sectors where imports seem unimportant, potential foreign competition can be a major influence on the prices and output of domestic manufacturers. For example, it is becoming difficult to talk about an "American" car. Even if the car is made mainly from American components, foreign products and technology have had a strong influence on the product.

International trade and investment are motivated by the same forces as domestic trade and investment. Why, if this is so, is international economics different from standard domestic microeconomics and macroeconomics? Part of the answer is that the world is divided into national markets with separate governments. Non-economics factors such as differences between languages and cultures have contributed to market separation, but there are also economic explanations of market separation. First, labor and capital have traditionally been much more mobile among regions within a country than among countries. Second, differences between national markets have been accentuated by restrictions on the movement of goods, labor, and capital. Third, people in different counties use different currencies, so international transactions can be affected by changes in the value of currencies.

How should we view the growth of international trade? Trade creates jobs in the export sector, but imported goods can also lead to the collapse of domestic firms. Is international trade a threat or a benefit? We shall see that perhaps the most important conclusion from international economics is that international trade is beneficial. (It is easy to see that individual countries have gained - the importance of international trade for the German and Japanese economies is well known, and for some newly industrialized countries in Eastern Asia, trade has been a vital part of their economic growth.)

One of the most interesting features of international trade is that countries can gain without other countries losing. The reason is that international trade increases economic efficiency. Basically, international trade is the same as trade between individuals within a country. Few people argue that trade between New York and California should be restricted, and yet trade over much shorter distances, which happens to be across a national boundary, is often a major economic and political issue. For example, the effects of freer trade between the United States and Canada continue to be a major issue in Canada.

Another issue that leads to heated debate is the effects of international capital flows. Over the last few decades improved communications and the removal of restrictions have led to increased capital mobility. We are moving toward a global capital market. Investors can and do move vast sums of money quickly from one country to another. One result has been that governments have experienced difficulty maintaining stable exchange rates in the face of large changes in the demand/supply of particular currencies.

Capital flows reduce the degree of independence countries have in setting monetary policies. Economies are so closely linked that often it is inappropriate to speak about domestic macroeconomic policy. Macroeconomic policy can no longer ignore international linkages. Countries do not all experience growth or recession at exactly the same time, but there is no doubt that, for good or ill, they move together. Capital flows also change a country's productive capability. It is difficult to talk about what a country can produce without considering which firms it can attract. Multinational corporations are increasing in importance. They produce and market goods internationally, and engage in joint ventures with other large companies. Their global activities are breaking down the traditional division of the world.

Some questions in international economics relate to whether national markets are too closely linked or too divided: Is trade really beneficial? Should international trade and capital flows be restricted? Should different countries use the same currency? Other interesting questions in international economics include: Does exchange rate variability reduce welfare? Can trade help developing countries grow? What are the effects of trade and capital flows on domestic economic policy? Are multinational corporations a threat to welfare? These are just a few of the questions we shall consider.

Part One

Principles of International Economics

One

The Causes and Effects of International Trade

Introduction

Why do countries trade? This question can be answered quite simply: Countries trade because the prices of goods and services vary across countries. Consumers find that foreign goods and services are often less expensive than domestic goods and services, while producers find that they benefit from higher foreign prices by exporting. This answer, however, does not tell us much about the effects of trade, or why some goods and services cost less in one country than another. These two basic questions will form the basis for this and the following two chapters. Although the discussion focuses on trade in goods (**merchandise trade**), the analysis could be extended to cover trade in services as well.

The Gain from Trade

If countries trade voluntarily, we might presume that they gain from trade. This presumption is correct.

The gains from trade can be shown by considering the relationship between consumption and work. It might be possible for one person to produce everything he or she needs, but it is unlikely. And even if such economic independence were possible, it would probably not be appealing to most people because they would be forced to live poorly with a narrow selection of goods. Individuals in modern economies do not try to produce exactly what they consume. Normally, people work in return for money, which in turn is used for consumption purposes. Although a person usually only helps in the production or distribution of a few goods, the range of products available for consumption is much wider; people **specialize** in the production of certain items, and obtain other goods through trade. Trade is necessary if the benefits of specialization are to be enjoyed. Even towns or regions are not completely self–sufficient; it might be technically feasible in some climates, but the people would be worse off because both the variety and total quantity of goods would be reduced if trade were prevented.

People gain by trading with one another. Hence, it is not surprising that trade takes place naturally without any deliberate action needed to encourage it. Trade also takes place naturally between countries—we would not expect the gains from trade to stop at national boundaries. The effects of trade between countries are analogous to the effects of trade between individuals: specialization increases the overall quantity of goods and trade allows countries to consume a greater quantity and variety of goods than they could without trade.

An Example of the Gain from Trade: Life in a P.O.W. Camp

A unique economics article relates R. A. Radford's true story of life in a prisoner of war camp during World War II. (Radford, 1945, pp. 189–201.) The prisoners received equal rations in the form of Red Cross parcels. However, tastes differed, and trade began naturally as a way of increasing individual satisfaction. The transit camps in which the prisoners stayed temporarily are described as being "chaotic and uncomfortable." As a result, prices were not equalized by trade, and there was scope for someone to profit from price differences. Radford mentions a padre who was said to have started a trip around the camp with some cheese and five cigarettes and ended the day with a complete parcel in addition to the original cheese and cigarettes.

Because trade was restricted, price differences reflected tastes. For example, coffee extract was cheap among the tea–drinking English, but worth much more among French prisoners. Therefore, prisoners could profit from buying coffee from the English and selling it to the French. Cigarettes were used as currency, and in more organized camps, prices were equalized by trade. The prices were sometimes listed on trading boards, and in the most highly organized camp, a non–profit shop was established. The gain from trade is what motivated commercial organization. Trade was not planned, it happened naturally, and institutions were created to help trade take place. In this example, the prisoners gained from trade, but specialization did not take place because the prisoners were not engaged in production of the goods they traded.

Before leaving this example, it is interesting to note the problem of monetary stability which arose because the prisoners used cigarettes as money. The supply of cigarettes was erratic, and a large quantity might arrive in a short period. When this happened, prices soared. Then, as the cigarettes were gradually consumed, prices would gradually fall. When there was another large delivery of cigarettes, the cycle would begin again. Radford comments that most of the economic problems in the camp were attributable to this instability.

Absolute Advantage

In this section we introduce the concept of absolute advantage. A country is said to have an **absolute advantage** in the production of a commodity if it uses fewer resources than another country to produce the commodity. This concept is used to show how a country gains through specialization when resources are moved from one sector to another and the country takes part in trade. Although the concept of absolute advantage is an imperfect explanation of the reason for trade, it is useful as a background to the concept of comparative advantage, which is examined in the next section.

Adam Smith's View

The gain from trade and specialization was recognized by Adam Smith in his book: *An Inquiry into the Nature and Causes of the Wealth of Nations*, first published in 1776.[1] His argument was as follows:

It is the maxim of every prudent master of a family, never to make at home what it will cost him more to make than to buy. The taylor does not attempt to make his own shoes, but buys them of the shoemaker. The shoemaker does not attempt to make his own cloaths, but employs a taylor. The farmer attempts to make neither one nor the other, but employs those different artificers. All of them find it for their interest to employ their whole industry in a way in which they have some advantage over their neighbours, and to purchase with a part of its produce . . . whatever else they have occassion for.

What is prudence in the conduct of every private family can scarce be folly in that of a great kingdom. If a foreign country can supply us with a commodity cheaper than we ourselves can make it, better buy it of them with some part of the produce of our own industry, employed in a way in which we have some advantage. . . .

The natural advantages which one country has over another in producing particular commodities are sometimes so great, that it is acknowledged by all the world to be in vain to struggle against them. By means of glasses, hotbeds, and hotwalls, very good grapes can be raised in Scotland, and very good wine too, can be made of them at about thirty times the expense for which at least equally good wine can be brought from foreign

---

[1] Smith's book was an attack on mercantilist views which were the basis for British economic policy at the time. Mercantilists argued that imports should be restricted so that gold would be received from foreign countries in payment for the excess of exports over imports. Increasing the stock of gold was seen as a way to increase the wealth and power of the country.

countries. Would it be a reasonable law to prohibit the importation of all foreign wines merely to encourage the making of wine in Scotland? But if there be a manifest absurdity in turning towards any employment thirty times more of the capital and industry of the country than would be necessary to purchase from foreign countries an equal quantity of the commodities wanted, there must be an absurdity, though altogether not so glaring, yet exactly of the same kind, in turning towards any such employment a thirtieth, or even a hundredth part more of either. Whether the advantage which one country has over another be natural or acquired, is in this respect of no consequence.[2]

Adam Smith's view was based on the concept of absolute advantage. In a simple economy where labor is the only factor of production, the cost of production is determined by the amount of labor used. In such a simple world, if one country uses less labor than other countries to make a good, that country is said to have an absolute advantage in making the good.

Absolute advantage is illustrated in Table 1.1. The United States has an absolute advantage in wheat because fewer hours are needed in the U.S. than in the European Union (EU) to produce 1 ton of wheat. By similar reasoning, the EU has an absolute advantage in cars in this example. What happens when trade takes place?

Introducing Trade

Let us assume that 1 car can be exchanged for 1 ton of wheat through international trade. If the U.S. gives up the production of 1 car, 300 fewer hours are needed for car production, and 1 ½ more tons of wheat can be produced instead. If the U.S. exports 1 ton of wheat and imports 1 car, it replaces the car which was given up, and still has ½ ton of wheat left. Similarly, if the EU gives up 1 ton of wheat, 400 fewer hours are needed for wheat production, and 2 extra cars can be produced. By exporting 1 car and

Table 1.1
Number of Hours per Unit of Output

	Wheat	Cars
EU	400	200
U.S.	200	300

[2]Smith, Adam, *An Inquiry into the Nature and Causes of the Wealth of Nations*, New York: Modern Library College Editions, Random House, 1985, pp. 226–28.

importing 1 ton of wheat, the EU can replace the lost wheat and still have 1 car left. In this example, each country gains by exporting the good in which it has an absolute advantage, and importing the other good.

Provided that we believe that every country is the most efficient producer of some good, we seem to have a plausible explanation of trade. Production costs differ because of differences in labor requirements among goods, and people trade in order to obtain goods at lower cost. In the example used here, more labor is required to produce cars in the U.S. than in the EU, so the U.S. imports cars from the more efficient producer. The EU imports wheat because more labor is required to produce wheat there than in the U.S.

Although this explanation seems plausible, it is too limited. It is true that countries can gain by exporting goods in which they have an absolute advantage, but a country does not need to have an absolute advantage in producing a good in order to be able to export it. This is shown in the next section.

Opportunity Cost and Comparative Advantage

The **opportunity cost** of producing a unit of a good is the amount of the other good (in our two–good model) which could have been produced using the same resources. For example, using the data shown in Table 1.1, because it takes 400 hours to produce a ton of wheat in the EU and only 200 hours to produce a car, the opportunity cost of producing a ton of wheat is 2 cars. The opportunity costs of domestic production are derived from Table 1.1 and shown in Table 1.2.

Opportunity Cost and the Incentive to Trade

Countries gain from trade because the opportunity cost of imported goods is less than the opportunity cost of domestic goods. If world prices allow the exchange of 1 car for 1 ton of wheat, the U.S. imports cars because it only gives up 1 ton of wheat for an imported car whereas the opportunity cost of

Table 1.2
Domestic Opportunity Costs

	Wheat	Cars
EU	2 cars	½ ton wheat
U.S.	2/3 car	1 ½ tons of wheat

a domestically produced car is 1 ½ tons of wheat (see Table 1.2). The EU imports wheat because the opportunity cost of wheat (1 car) is less than the opportunity cost of producing a ton of wheat (2 cars).

In this example, each country has an absolute advantage in one of the goods. What happens if one country has an absolute advantage in both goods? Is mutually beneficial trade possible?

Table 1.3 shows an example in which the U.S. has an absolute advantage in both wheat and car production. Let us continue to assume that it is possible to exchange 1 ton of wheat for 1 car through international trade. Even though the labor requirements for U.S. production in Table 1.3 are half of what they are in Table 1.1, giving the U.S. an absolute advantage in both goods, the cost of cars in terms of wheat is exactly the same as before: the U.S. gives up 1 ½ tons of wheat for each car it produces and the opportunity cost of an imported car is 1 ton of wheat. Therefore, the incentive for the U.S. to trade is the same: the opportunity cost of an imported car is less than the opportunity cost of a domestically produced car. The fact that the EU uses more labor to produce a car is irrelevant—in other words, absolute advantage is irrelevant.

The labor requirements for the EU are the same in Table 1.3 as in Table 1.1, and the incentive for the EU to trade is the same: The opportunity cost of imported wheat (1 car per ton) is less than the opportunity cost of domestically produced wheat (2 cars per ton). Therefore, both countries gain from trade.[3]

Table 1.3
Number of Hours per Unit of Output

	Wheat	Cars
EU	400	200
U.S.	100	150

---

[3]We have shown that countries benefit from international trade because the opportunity cost of imported goods is less than the opportunity cost of domestic goods. In view of this, it is not surprising that countries that have pursued liberal trade policies have usually grown faster than countries that have attempted to increase self–sufficiency by restricting imports. We examine the relationship between trade and economic growth in Chapter 18.

Comparative Advantage

The concept of opportunity cost is the basis for the concept of **comparative advantage**. A country is said to have a comparative advantage in a good if its opportunity cost of producing the good is lower than that of other countries. A country will export the good in which it has a comparative advantage. It has a **comparative disadvantage** in a good if its opportunity cost of production is higher than that of other countries. A country will import the good in which it has a comparative disadvantage.

In the preceding example, the EU has a comparative advantage in car production, and the U.S. has a comparative disadvantage, because the EU's opportunity cost of producing cars (½ ton of wheat) is less than that of the U.S. (1½ tons of wheat). Similarly, the U.S. has a comparative advantage in wheat production because the opportunity cost of producing wheat in the U.S. (2/3 car) is less than the opportunity cost of producing wheat in the EU (2 cars).

Both countries can gain from trade, because when they specialize in goods in which they have a comparative advantage, world output increases. As before, assume that the U.S. produces more wheat and fewer cars, and the EU produces more cars and less wheat. The changes in output resulting from specialization are shown in Table 1.4. It is clear that world output increases. This does not imply that all countries gain equally from trade, merely that all countries potentially gain from trade to some degree.

How much each country gains, or, in other words, how the extra output is distributed between the countries, depends on the amount of imports that a country gets for its exports. This is determined by the rate at which the goods are exchanged. The amount of one good which must be exported in exchange for imports of another good is called the **terms of trade**, and is a measure of the relative value of imports and exports.

Table 1.4
Number of Hours per Unit of Output

	Wheat	Cars
EU	−1	+2
U.S.	+1.5	−1
World	+0.5	+1

A Diagrammatic Approach

The gains from trade can be shown diagrammatically by using a **production possibility frontier** (**PPF**). This shows how much a country can produce using the limited resources it has available. Assume that the EU has 2,000 hours of labor which can be used to produce wheat or cars, and that the labor requirements are as shown in Table 1.3. If all the labor is used in wheat production and no cars are produced, 5 tons of wheat can be produced. If all the labor is used to produce cars, 10 cars can be produced. A combination of the two goods may be produced, but for every ton of wheat produced, the EU gives up 2 cars. The production possibility frontier in Figure 1.1 shows the combinations of wheat and cars that can be produced by the EU using all the labor available.

Figure 1.1
The EU's Gains from Trade

The EU has 2000 hours of labor available. This can be used to produce 10 cars or 5 tons of wheat, or any combination of cars and wheat shown by the production possibility frontier (*PPF*). For each ton of wheat produced, the EU gives up 2 cars. In the absence of trade, the EU can only consume on or below the production possibility frontier. If it specializes in car production, the EU can consume at points along the trade line (*TT*), trading cars for wheat at the rate of 1:1. For example, consumption may take place at point *C* if the EU produces 10 cars and exports 4 cars in return for 4 tons of wheat.

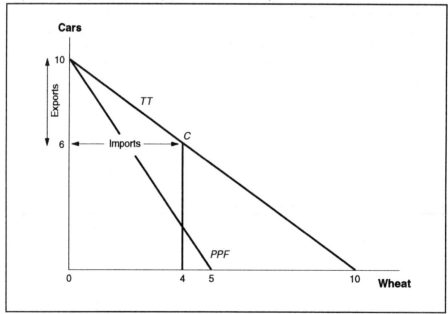

Since the slope of a line is the vertical movement accompanying a horizontal movement of 1 unit, we see that the slope of a production possibility frontier is the amount of the good represented on the vertical axis (cars) that is lost when 1 extra unit of the good represented on the horizontal axis (wheat) is produced.[4] Therefore, the slope of the EU's production possibility frontier is the opportunity cost of producing wheat. The opportunity cost of imported wheat is shown by the slope of the trade line (*TT*): for every ton of imported wheat, the U.S. must export 1 car (recall that for simplicity we assumed that 1 car is worth 1 ton of wheat at world prices).

The EU's Gain from Trade

In the absence of trade, the EU can only consume what it produces, so consumption must take place on or below the production possibility frontier. However, if the EU trades with the U.S., it is possible for it to consume more of one or both goods. For example, if the EU specializes in car production and trades 4 cars for 4 tons of wheat, it will be possible for it to have 6 cars and 4 tons of wheat. This would not have been possible without trade.

The EU can consume anywhere along the trade line by producing cars and trading cars for wheat. The trade line passes through the point on the axis showing the EU's production after specialization. For every point on the production possibility frontier, except the intercept with the vertical axis, there is a point on the trade line that represents more of both goods. Therefore, the EU must be better off if it can consume along the trade line instead of being restricted to points along its production possibility frontier. The EU gains from trade because the opportunity cost of imported wheat (the slope of the trade line) is less than the opportunity cost of domestic wheat (the slope of the production possibility frontier). If the opportunity costs were the same, the trade line and the production possibility frontier would coincide, and there would be no gain from trade.

The U.S. Gain from Trade

Figure 1.2 shows the production possibility frontier of the United States based on the data shown in Table 1.3 and using the assumption that 3,000 hours of labor are available. By producing wheat and trading wheat for cars, the U.S. is able to consume along the trade line and is clearly better off. The slope of the production possibility frontier shows the cost of wheat in terms of cars. The reciprocal of the slope shows the cost of cars in terms of wheat: the

---

[4]You may recall that slope can be defined as rise over run, that is, the vertical movement which accompanies a horizontal movement along a line or curve.

Figure 1.2
The U.S.' Gains From Trade

The U.S. has 3,000 hours of labor available. This labor can be used to produce 30 tons of wheat, or 20 cars, or any combination of cars and wheat shown by the production possibility frontier (*PPF*). For each car produced, the U.S. gives up 1½ tons of wheat. In the absence of trade the U.S. can only consume on or below the production possibility frontier. If it specializes in wheat production, the U.S. can consume along the trade line, trading wheat for cars at the rate of 1:1.

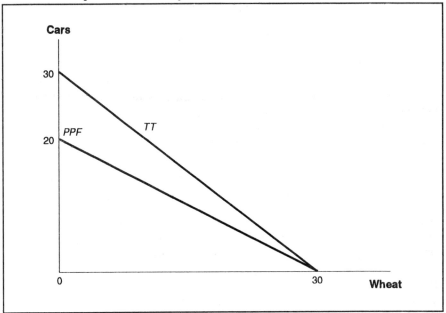

opportunity cost of imported cars. The U.S. gains from trade because the opportunity cost of imported cars (the reciprocal of the slope of the trade line) is less than the opportunity cost of domestic cars (the reciprocal of the slope of the production possibility frontier).

The gain from trade has been described as resulting from imports costing less than domestic production. Alternatively, one can say that a country gains by exporting a good when the value of the exported good in trade is higher than its domestic value. For example, the U.S. gains by exporting wheat because the foreign value of wheat (in terms of cars) is higher than the domestic value of wheat.

Table 1.5
Number of Hours per Unit of Output

	Wine	Cloth
Portugal	80	90
England	120	100

Ricardo's Example of Comparative Advantage

David Ricardo, in *On the Principles of Political Economy and Taxation* (published in 1817), was the first person to recognize the importance of comparative advantage and the irrelevance of absolute advantage. His example is worth considering to strengthen our understanding of the preceding discussion. Using Portugal and England as examples, Ricardo assumed that Portugal could produce both wine and cloth using less labor than England; thus, Portugal had an absolute advantage in producing both goods. His example is shown in Table 1.5.

In order to determine the pattern of trade, we must calculate the opportunity costs of production. The data are shown in Table 1.6. Portugal has a comparative advantage in wine production and England has a comparative advantage in cloth production. Assume that 1 unit of wine can be exchanged for 1 unit of cloth through trade. If Portugal imports 1 unit of cloth, it costs 1 unit of wine, but it would have cost 9/8 units of wine to produce a unit of clothing in Portugal, so Portugal gains from trade. Similarly, the opportunity cost of producing wine in England is 12/10 units of cloth, imported cloth costs 1 unit of wine, so England gains by importing wine. Even though Portugal has an absolute advantage in both wine and cloth, trade is beneficial for both countries.

Table 1.6
Domestic Opportunity Costs

	Wine	Cloth
Portugal	8/9 cloth	9/8 wine
England	12/10 cloth	10/12 wine

Absolute and Comparative Advantage

Obviously, some countries cannot produce goods as efficiently as other countries, and yet they still take part in international trade. For example, the U.S. has one of the highest levels of labor productivity (output per hour) in the world, yet it imports from countries such as China with much lower levels of productivity. Therefore, absolute advantage, which is based on the implicit assumption that all trading countries are world leaders in the production of their exported goods, is a less accurate explanation of trade than comparative advantage. To put it another way, although the U.S. probably has an absolute advantage in many goods over most countries, this does not mean that the U.S. exports everything. The reason is that the U.S. is better at producing some goods than others.

Absolute advantage is based on labor inputs. In passing we may note that if a country has a low labor input per unit produced, then we could say that it has high output per unit of labor, or high productivity. High overall productivity does not determine which goods are imported and which are exported, but high productivity may be of interest because high output per head implies a high real wage per head. Poor countries are basically countries with low output per head.

In the theory of absolute advantage, the cost of a good is incorrectly related to the amount of inputs (e.g., the number of hours) used to make the good. When a country imports a good, consumers do not ask what the inputs required to make the good were; they do not care whether the process used was efficient or not. The relevant question for consumers is: What is the price of the good?

Domestic Prices, World Prices, and the Direction of Trade

In a barter model, the price of one good is the amount of the other good that must be given up; therefore, the price is the opportunity cost. We have seen that trade can be explained by the difference between the opportunity costs of imported and domestic goods. Allowing for the fact that people use money instead of engaging in barter does not change the analysis. The relative prices of goods are indicators of their opportunity costs. To be precise, the opportunity cost of X in terms of Y is the ratio of the price of X to the price of Y (P_x / P_y). For example, if a radio costs \$100, and a ticket to see the Boston Celtics costs \$25, the opportunity cost of a radio is 4 tickets. Let us examine the explanation of trade in terms of relative prices.

Pre–Trade Prices and Relative Cost

In the model we have used so far, there is competition, labor is the only input, and the input requirements are fixed. In such a model, the domestic price ratio before trade takes place, the pre–trade price ratio, will be determined by and equal to the relative cost of production. For example, if it takes twice as much labor to produce cloth as it does to produce wheat, the price of cloth will be twice the price of wheat, that is, the price ratio will be 2.

To understand why, consider an example in which the price ratio is not equal to the relative cost. If the relative cost of producing cloth is 2 units of wheat, and the price ratio is 1, producers find it profitable to switch from cloth production to wheat production (cloth costs twice as much to produce as wheat, but they sell for the same amount). The decrease in the supply of cloth and the increase in the supply of wheat cause the price of cloth to rise relative to price of wheat; thus, the price ratio rises. Similarly, if the price ratio is 3, it is profitable to switch from wheat to cloth production, and the price ratio falls. Adjustment continues until the price ratio equals the relative cost of production.[5]

Price Differences and Trade

We concluded from our discussion of Table 1.1 that the U.S. gains from trade because the opportunity cost of an imported car (1 ton of wheat) is less than the opportunity cost of a domestically produced car (1 ½ tons of wheat). The domestic opportunity cost of cars equals the ratio of the domestic pre–trade price of cars to the domestic pre–trade price of wheat. The opportunity cost of imported cars is shown by the ratio of the world price of cars to the world price of wheat. Therefore, the conclusion could be reworded as follows: the U.S. gains from trade because the world price ratio differs from the domestic pre–trade price ratio.

Diagrammatically, the difference between the pre–trade price ratio and the world price ratio is shown by the difference between the slopes of the production possibility frontier and the trade line. Recall that the slope of a production possibility frontier equals the opportunity cost of the good represented on the horizontal axis (X) expressed in terms of the good represented on the vertical axis (Y). Because the opportunity cost equals the pre–trade price ratio, the slope of the production possibility frontier is also

---

[5]There is no role for demand in the determination of the price ratio because the relative cost is constant. In the next chapter we examine a model in which there are increasing costs and the price ratio is determined by the interaction of demand and supply.

equal to the pre–trade price ratio (P_x/P_y). This is a useful and important result because we can make observations about prices simply by looking at the slope: the steeper the production possibility frontier, the higher the pre–trade price ratio.

We can describe price ratios in terms of the good on the vertical axis or the good on the horizontal axis. The reciprocal of the slope is the cost of the good represented on the vertical axis expressed in terms of the good on the horizontal [$P_y/P_x = 1/(P_x/P_y)$]. As the ratio P_x/P_y rises, the ratio P_y/P_x falls; in other words, as X becomes more expensive relative to Y, Y becomes less expensive relative to X.

As an example, consider the lines in Figure 1.2. The slope of the production possibility frontier is 2/3, implying that the pre–trade price ratio of wheat to cars is 2/3 ($P_w/P_c = 2/3$). The trade line's slope is 1, thus in world markets the price ratio is 1 ($P_w/P_c = 1$). Therefore, the world price of wheat relative to cars is higher than the U.S. pre–trade price (and the U.S. gains by exporting wheat).

Alternatively, as shown above, the prices can be described in terms of the good on the vertical (cars). The pre–trade price of cars relative to wheat is 3/2, the reciprocal of the slope of the PPF [$3/2 = 1/(2/3)$]. The trade line has a slope of 1 (so the world price ratio is the same whether it is defined as P_c/P_w or P_w/P_c). Therefore, the pre–trade price of cars is relatively lower in world markets than in the U.S., and the U.S. gains by importing cars.

Price Differences and the Gain from Trade

If the world price ratio differs from the pre–trade price ratio, the slope of the trade line differs from the slope of the production possibility frontier. A country is able to gain by specializing (producing at one of the intercepts of the production possibility frontier) and then consuming at a point along the trade line. The greater the divergence between the pre–trade price ratio and the world price ratio, the greater the gain from trade. This is shown in Figure 1.3. As the world price ratio rises, the slope of the trade line increases, and the quantities of X and Y that can be consumed increase. For example, if the trade line shifts from TT1 to TT4, the quantities of X and Y consumed could increase from X1Y1 to X4Y4. Because our model does not include demand, we cannot say what the quantities consumed actually are. However, we have shown that the country could consume more of both goods, and that is sufficient for us to see that there is a gain from trade. (Recall that if the world price ratio is the same as the domestic price ratio, engaging in trade will not make a country better off because the trade line and production possibility frontier coincide.)

Figure 1.3
The Gains from Trade and World Prices

As the world price ratio (P_x/P_y) increases, the slope of the trade line (TT) increases. The gains from trade increase as the difference between the pre–trade price ratio (shown by the slope of the PPF) and the world price ratio increases. The gains from trade are shown by the increase in the quantity available of both goods. At the pre–trade prices, the country might produce and consume the combination of goods X_0Y_0. At the world price ratios shown by the slopes of TT_1, TT_2, TT_3, and TT_4, the country produces XS and could consume X_1Y_1, X_2Y_2, X_3Y_3, and X_4Y_4, respectively.

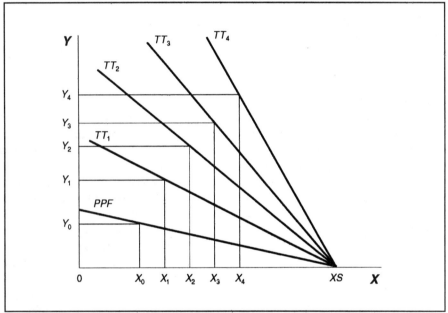

World Prices and the Direction of Trade

Using the data shown in Table 1.5 and Table 1.6, it is useful to consider what would happen if, at world prices, 2 units of wine were worth 1 unit of cloth. Cloth would be more expensive on world markets than in either country, and thus producers in both countries would find it profitable to export cloth. Similarly, wine would be cheaper on world markets than in either country and consumers would buy imported wine. In a two–country model this clearly cannot be possible. Where would the imports of wine come from, and where would the exports of cloth go?

 If world prices are such that both countries try to supply cloth, there will be an excess supply of cloth, and the price of cloth will fall (relative to wine). The price will continue falling until the excess supply is removed. This will

Table 1.7
World Price Ratios and Trade

	Price of Wine in Units of Cloth	Price of Cloth in Units of Wine
World price ratio A	1/2	2/1
Portugal's price ratio	8/9	9/8
World price ratio B	1	1
England's price ratio	12/10	10/12
World price ratio C	2/1	1/2

happen when the world price of cloth falls below the domestic price of cloth in one of the countries; that country then stops exporting cloth and exports wine instead. Similarly, consider what happens when both countries want to import wine. The price of wine (relative to cloth) will rise, and one country will begin to export wine rather than import it. Thus, the world price will change so that the two countries want to import and export different goods.

This analysis suggests that, in a two–country model, the world price ratio must lie between the two domestic pre–trade price ratios. In Table 1.7 we have extended this example by showing three world price ratios—A, B, and C. At world price ratio A, both countries will want to export cloth and import wine; the price of cloth will tend to fall relative to the price of wine. At world price ratio C, both countries will want to export wine and import cloth, and the price of cloth will tend to rise relative to the price of wine. At world price ratio B, Portugal will export wine and import cloth, whereas England will export cloth and import wine.

The difference between price ratios can be shown diagrammatically. Assuming that Portugal has 360 hours of labor available, because it takes 80 hours to produce wine and 90 hours to produce cloth (see Table 1.5), Portugal's production possibility frontier will be as shown in Figure 1.4. (with a slope of 9/8). The possible patterns of trade described in the previous paragraph can be derived by comparing the slope of the production possibility frontier with the slopes of the trade lines (TTA, TTB, and TTC) associated with the possible world price ratios (A, B, and C, respectively).

If the trade line is steeper than the production possibility frontier, the world price of cloth in terms of wine is higher than the pre–trade price. In this case the country will export cloth, as for example Portugal does when facing world price ratio A. If the trade line is flatter than the production possibility frontier, the world relative price of cloth is lower than the pre–trade price, and the world relative price of wine is higher than the

Figure 1.4
The Effect of Changing World Prices on
Portugal's Production and Trade

With 360 hours of labor available, Portugal can produce 4.5 units of wine or 4 units of cloth, or any combination of goods shown by Portugal's production possibility frontier (*PPF*). The slopes of the trade lines *TTA*, *TTB*, and *TTC* show the world price ratios *A*, *B*, and *C*, respectively, from Table 1.7. At world price *A*, Portugal produces 4 units of cloth, exports cloth, and imports wine. At world prices *B* and *C*, Portugal produces 4.5 units of wine, exports wine, and imports cloth.

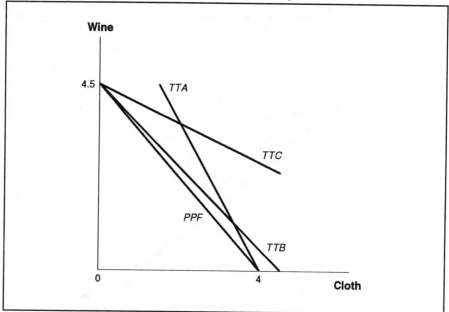

pre–trade price. In this case the country will export wine, for example, as Portugal does when facing world price ratios *B* or *C*.

Similarly, assuming that England has 600 hours of labor available, England's production possibility frontier will be as shown in Figure 1.5, with a slope of 5/6. Because the trade line *TTC* is flatter than the English *PPF*, we know that the world price of cloth is less than the English price, and that England imports cloth and exports wine. Trade lines *TTA* and *TTB* are steeper than the *PPF*, and the world price of cloth is higher than the English price, so England would produce cloth and import wine if faced by world prices *A* or *B*.

Figure 1.5
The Effect of Changing World Prices on
England's Production and Trade

With 600 hours of labor available, England can produce 5 units of wine or 6 units of cloth, or any combination of goods shown by England's production possibility frontier (*PPF*). The slopes of the trade lines *TTA*, *TTB*, and *TTC* have the same slopes as the trade lines in Figure 1.4, and show the world price ratios *A*, *B*, and *C*, respectively, from Table 1.7. At world prices *A* and *B*, England produces 6 units of cloth, exports cloth, and imports wine. At world price *C*, England produces 5 units of wine, exports wine, and imports cloth.

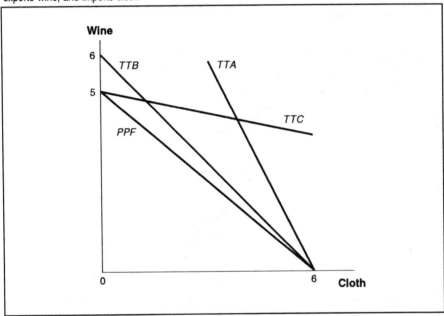

The Terms of Trade

As we have seen, world prices are important because the relationship between world prices and domestic prices is what determines which goods are exported. The world price ratio is called the **terms of trade**. The equilibrium terms of trade are those at which the quantities of goods that countries would like to trade are equal. If the actual terms of trade differ from the equilibrium terms of trade, excess demand or supply will force the terms of trade to change. Although it is clear that in a two–country model the equilibrium terms of trade must lie between the two pre–trade price ratios, we cannot say exactly what the equilibrium will be. To predict the terms of trade requires a model including both demand and supply, because the amount that a country exports or imports is the difference between domestic demand and supply. The model used so far only includes supply.

Offer Curves[6]

If we assume that we know how much a country produces and consumes at different price ratios, we can use offer curves to show how the terms of trade

Figure 1.6
The Determination of the Terms of Trade

The quantities traded by countries A and B at different terms of trade are shown by the offer curves 0AA' and 0BB'. At the point of intersection (E), the supply and demand of X and Y are equal. The slope of the line 0TE passing through E shows the equilibrium terms of trade. At different terms of trade, such as those shown by 0T₁, the demand and supply for each of the two goods would not be equal.

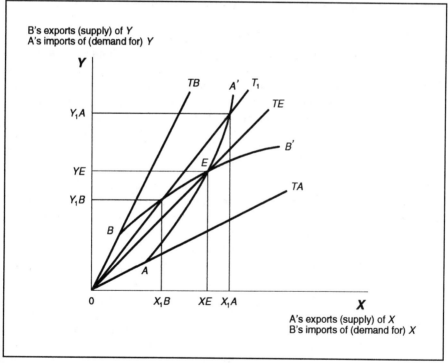

<hr>

[6]The following introduction to offer curves illustrates how demand and supply determine the terms of trade. A more rigorous analysis is presented in the next chapter.

are determined by the demand and supply of traded goods. An **offer curve** shows the relationship between the terms of trade and the quantities of exports supplied and imports demanded. In Figure 1.6, country A's supply of exports is shown on the horizontal axis, and A's demand for imports is shown on the vertical axis. The terms of trade are shown by the slope of a line from the origin to a point showing the quantities traded. For example, at point E, country A exports XE in exchange for YE, thus the world price of X in terms of Y is YE/XE, the slope of OTE. (In other words, the slope of the terms of trade line equals P_x / P_y.)

The terms of trade line, OTA, represents the terms of trade that equal country A's pre–trade price ratio. Country A is willing to trade if the terms of trade differ from this ratio, point A showing the quantities that A trades if the difference is infinitesimal. (For convenience, point A is drawn on OTA.) As the relative price of X increases, and the terms of trade line becomes steeper, country A is willing to supply more exports of X in exchange for imports of Y. For example, the amount that A is willing to trade on OT_1 (X_1A for Y_1A) is greater than on OTE (XE for YE). The curve OAA' is A's offer curve.

B's offer curve can be added to the diagram. Notice that A's exports are B's imports, and A's imports are B's exports. B's pre–trade price ratio is OTB. (Point B represents B's trade when the terms of trade differ infinitesimally from B's pre–trade price ratio.) As the relative price of X decreases, and the terms of trade line becomes flatter, the relative price of Y increases and country B exports more Y in exchange for X. B's offer curve is OBB'.

The Equilibrium Terms of Trade

The quantities that the countries want to trade are equal when the terms of trade line is OTE. If the terms of trade line is above OTE, for example at OT_1, A's supply of X (X_1A) exceeds B's demand (X_1B), and A's demand for Y (Y_1A) is greater than B's supply of Y (Y_1B). Thus, the price of X in terms of Y falls. Similarly, if the terms of trade line is below OTE, B's demand for X exceeds A's supply of X, A's demand for Y is less than B's supply, and the relative price of X rises. The important conclusion is that the terms of trade will adjust so that the supply and demand of imports and exports are equal.

Offer curves show how the terms of trade adjust to equate the demand and supply of traded goods for two countries. Obviously, in the real world there are many countries and many goods, and two or more countries may export the same good if a third country is the buyer. However, the major conclusions remain relevant: countries export goods in which they have a comparative advantage (their opportunity cost is lower than that implied by the terms of trade). When an excess demand of excess supply exists, the terms of trade change to equate demand and supply.[7]

Domestic Prices and Trade

The preceding discussion shows that a good is exported when the world price is higher than the country's pre–trade price, and imported when the world price is lower than the country's pre–trade price. However, when trade takes place, domestic prices change. Because exporters can sell their output at world prices, domestic consumers must pay world prices, so the domestic prices of exported goods goes up. Similarly, the availability of imports at world prices below pre–trade prices forces down the domestic prices of imports (from pre–trade levels). In this way prices in different countries are equalized by trade, because they all adjust toward world prices.

We have seen that trade results from differences in pre–trade prices. We would not expect post–trade prices to differ much because of the tendency for prices to be equalized through trade. In reality, prices in different countries are not exactly equal because there are numerous barriers to trade. For example, transport costs and trade restrictions prevent the free movement of goods and break the unity of the market.[8] When comparing retail prices, we must remember that marketing and distribution costs differ, and countries impose different levels of taxes on retail sales.

An interesting example of price differences exists in North America, where Canadian taxes help push up Canadian prices relative to those in the United States. The price differential acts as an incentive for cross border shopping. At peak shopping times such as Christmas, the border is extremely busy as Canadians shop abroad. There are limits on how much can be imported by individuals, although these limits have partially been relaxed as a result of the North American Free Trade Agreement (NAFTA). As cross border shopping has increased, competition from across the border seems to have pushed Canadian prices down.

---

[7]This analysis seems to suggest that the value of imports and exports must be equal. We shall see that when there are capital flows, imports and exports do not have to be equal. For example, a country can import more than it exports if it is a net borrower. As Table 7.2 shows, the United States has often been a net borrower.

[8]See the discussion of purchasing power parity in Chapter 6.

Making the Model More Realistic

The Overall Gain from Trade

The preceding section showed that there is a gain from trade because the quantity of goods available expands as a result of a more efficient allocation of resources. Not everybody gains equally, though, unless a policy of income redistribution is carried out. Consider what happens when imports suddenly become available, which is essentially what happens when an import ban is removed or a very high tariff on imports is reduced. Producers in the import–competing sector now face competition from imports. Perhaps some will go bankrupt because they cannot compete; perhaps others will experience lower profits and be forced to pay lower wages. Other sectors of the economy may also suffer because workers in the import–competing sector are customers of firms in those other sectors.

The unemployment and loss of income resulting from an increase in trade will not normally last forever; labor will move into other activities. The faster labor moves, the less significant the adverse effects of imports will be. Economists differ in their judgment of how fast the adjustment process will be; hence, there is disagreement about the size and duration of the costs to society resulting from an increase in imports. The analysis of absolute advantage and comparative advantage ignores these costs of adjustment. We would normally expect a gain from trade in the long–term, but in the short term, when the increases in imports cause job losses and lower profits in some sectors, the overall gain from trade may not be perceived by the people involved.

Specialization

The Ricardian model's prediction that countries will specialize completely is not realistic. The reason the model leads to this prediction is that the opportunity costs of the goods remain constant (because the required labor inputs per unit remain constant). If it is worth transferring one unit of labor from X production to Y production, it is worth transferring all the labor. Although the Ricardian model's prediction of the extent of specialization is unrealistic, the prediction that countries will become more specialized when trade takes place is realistic. In Chapter 2 we will see that if we assume that the costs of production increase with increased output (increasing costs), complete specialization does not necessarily result.

The Determination of Opportunity Cost

The theory of comparative advantage should not be criticized because of its simplistic approach to the determination of production costs, namely, that labor is the only input and cost is determined solely by the amount of labor used. The labor requirements are used merely to show relative production costs and relative prices so that opportunity costs can be determined. In the real world there are many different inputs, and we would expect these to influence product prices. For example, a major influence on the prices of some goods is the price of energy. The fact that many inputs are used does not change the basic analysis, though: a country's comparative advantage is determined by how much of one good is given up for another. We do not need to use inputs to derive the relative value of goods if we know market prices.

Normally we would expect the market price of a good to be influenced by both demand and supply. In the simple model presented in this chapter, supply alone determines the pre–trade price ratio, and if demand were included, it would merely determine the pre–trade quantities sold.[9] In the next chapter a more complete model is presented in which the pre–trade price ratio and the quantities produced and consumed are determined by the interaction of demand and supply.

Exchange Rates

In the domestic market, the use of a single currency leads to the unification of markets: prices in New York, Washington, Chicago, and so on are easily comparable because they are all expressed in dollars. The prices of foreign goods can be compared with the prices of domestic goods by using exchange rates to convert foreign currency prices into domestic currency. The price of a foreign good changes in domestic currency when the exchange rate changes; therefore, exchange rate changes can affect a country's comparative advantage. In Chapter 6, this issue is examined in more detail, but it can already be seen that the exchange rate is potentially of great significance to domestic producers and consumers.

The Broader Gain from Trade

Finally, it must be acknowledged that in this chapter we have taken a rather narrow view of the gains from trade. Apart from increasing the quantity and

---

[9]Chapter 2 shows how demand determines the pre–trade quantities in a model where cost is constant.

variety of goods, trade has other beneficial effects. For example, competition from imports forces domestic producers to keep prices down, produce better quality goods, and respond to the needs of the consumer. While jobs have been lost in the U.S. auto industry, competition from imports has forced domestic producers to improve. Without competition from imports, would American automobile companies have tried so hard to improve their products? It is unlikely.

Competition from imports forces domestic firms to be more efficient. One might also expect trade to lead to lower costs because trade allows companies to benefit from economies of scale by expanding sales beyond the domestic market. Domestic firms may be able to reduce their costs of production by copying some of the production methods/technology of foreign firms (as U.S. auto firms have).

Finally, although trade sometimes leads to tensions between countries, one of the benefits from trade may be that trade makes major conflicts less likely because both countries would lose from a major dispute which reduced trade. Unfortunately, trade is not a guarantee of peace: civil wars demonstrate that conflicts can arise between areas that are closely linked by trade.

Summary of Main Points

People do not usually attempt to achieve full self–sufficiency because they are able to consume a greater quantity and variety of goods by trading with other people. Similarly, countries gain from international trade because specialization increases the overall quantity of goods and trade allows countries to consume more goods and a greater variety of goods than they could consume without trade.

Adam Smith used the concept of **absolute advantage** to explain international trade. A country has an absolute advantage in a good if it uses fewer resources to produce the good than other countries. Although this explanation is still commonly used, it is flawed because absolute advantage is neither necessary nor sufficient for a country to export a product.

Ricardo provided the basis for the modern explanation of international trade using the concept of **comparative advantage**. A country has a comparative advantage in a good if the opportunity cost of producing the good is lower than in other countries.

The **opportunity cost** of producing a good is the quantity of the other good(s) that could have been produced using the same resources. In the Ricardian model, labor inputs are used to calculate the opportunity cost of a good. Market prices can also be used to derive opportunity costs because the relative prices show how much one good is worth relative to other goods.

The opportunity cost of domestic production is shown by the **pre–trade price ratio**. The opportunity cost of goods on world markets is shown by the **world price ratio**. Countries gain from international trade if the opportunity cost of domestically produced goods differs from the opportunity cost of goods on world markets, that is, if the pre–trade price ratio differs from the world price ratio.

The gains from trade can be shown diagrammatically. The pre–trade price ratio is shown by the slope of the **production possibility frontier**. The world price ratio is shown by the slope of the **trade line**. Countries gain from trade if the slope of the production possibility frontier differs from the slope of the trade line.

The price of exports relative to imports is called the **terms of trade**, which are determined by international demand and supply. The equilibrium terms of trade are where the demand and supply of traded goods are equal. If demand and supply are not equal, the equilibrium terms of trade will change.

The model presented is unrealistic because it focuses only on labor inputs, excludes money and exchange rates, the cost of production is assumed constant, and adjustment costs are ignored. The basic conclusion is that countries can be better off if they trade rather than try to produce everything domestically.

Study Questions

1. It takes 20 hours to produce X domestically, and 30 hours to produce Y. Calculate the opportunity cost of X in terms of Y. If X is available for $\frac{1}{2}Y$ on world markets, what is the saving (in terms of Y) from importing 1 unit of X?

2. Alex is a lawyer and owns a house that needs painting. Alex can paint twice as fast as a professional painter and does the same quality of work. The hourly earnings of a lawyer are three times the earnings of painters. Should Alex paint the house or have a professional painter do it?

3. a. In the following table, which country has an absolute advantage in bicycles? Which country has an absolute advantage in cars? Which country has a comparative advantage in bicycles and which in cars?
    b. If trade takes place at 6 cars per 100 bicycles, which countries export which commodities?

Number of Hours per Unit

	Bicycles	Cars
Holland	50	1,000
England	100	1,500

c. How much does each country gain if 100 bicycles are exported in exchange for 6 cars? (Express the gain to the car exporter in bicycles and the gain to the bicycle exporter in cars.)

d. Explain how the gains from specialization are shown in your answer to this question.

4. The table below shows the number of hours of labor needed to produce goods X and Y in countries A and B.

Number of Hours per Unit

	X	Y
A	5	4
B	2	3

a. Assuming that labor is paid an hourly wage equal to the amount labor produces in an hour, compare the wages in A and B expressed first in X per hour and then in Y per hour.

b. If the terms of trade (P_x /P_y) equal 1, which goods do the countries export?

c. Assuming that trade takes place, calculate the amount of imports that can be obtained from 1 hour's work. (Hint: use the terms of trade to convert the amount of exports per hour into the amount of imports per hour.) Compare this figure with the quantity of the imported good that could be produced domestically in one hour, and comment on how this illustrates a gain from trade.

5. A country has a total of 500 hours of labor that it uses to produce 100 watches and 100 shirts; it takes 2 hours to produce a shirt and 3 hours to produce a watch. Shirts are worth $4 at world prices and watches are worth $8. The country has been producing this combination of watches and shirts for some time, and the resources used in one industry cannot be used in the other industry. Does this mean that the country should not trade? If there is a gain from trade, why does it occur? Show the importance of the assumption of factor mobility (that labor can move freely from one sector to another) by considering how the gains from trade change as increased factor mobility allows the country to specialize. (Draw the production possibility frontier and the show the possibilities using appropriate trade lines.)

6. a. Why do countries trade?

b. What are the effects of trade on:
   1) consumers?
   2) domestic producers of import substitutes?
   3) producers of exports?

7.   Critically evaluate the argument that small countries cannot gain from trade by trading with the United States because the United States is large and has a technological advantage.

8.   The labor inputs from the United States and the rest of the world (ROW) are shown in the table below. Critically evaluate the argument that the rest of the world is exploited if it trades with the United States because the labor used to make the ROW's exports is greater than the labor used to make the ROW's imports from the U.S.

	Number of Hours per Unit of Output	
	Wheat	**Fruit**
U.S.	20	30
ROW	40	50

Selected References

Bhagwati, J. N., "The Gains from Trade Once Again," *Oxford Economic Papers*, 20, July 1968, pp. 137–48.

Chacholiades, M. C., *International Trade Theory and Policy*, New York: McGraw–Hill, 1978.

Chipman, J. S., "A Survey of the Theory of International Trade, Part 1, The Classical Theory," *Econometrica*, 33, July 1965, pp. 477–519.

Kemp, M. C., "Some Issues in the Analysis of Trade Gains," *Oxford Economic Papers*, 20, July 1968, pp. 149–61.

Kemp, M. C., *The Pure Theory of International Trade and Investment*, Englewood Cliffs, NJ: Prentice Hall, 1969.

Radford, R. A., "The Economic Organization of a P.O.W. Camp," *Economica*, 12, November 1945.

Ricardo, D., "On the Principles of Political Economy and Taxation," in P. Sraffa (ed.), *The Works and Correspondence of David Ricardo*, New York: Cambridge University Press, 1951.

Samuelson, P. A., "The Gains from International Trade," *Canadian Journal of Economics and Political Science*, 5, May 1939, pp. 195–205.

Smith, A. *An Inquiry into the Nature and Causes of the Wealth of Nations*, New York: Modern Library College Editions, Random House, 1985.

Two

Modern Trade Theory

Introduction

In the Ricardian model, which was discussed in Chapter 1, comparative advantage is explained solely by differences in labor productivity. In this chapter the determinants of international trade are examined in more detail. We shall see that trade can result from differences between countries' tastes for goods and from differences in their relative factor endowments. We begin by discussing how demand can be represented by indifference curves. Then we examine the role of supply. The assumption of constant costs used in Chapter 1 is replaced by the assumption of increasing costs, and the importance of factor endowments is discussed. Finally, we consider the determination of the terms of trade.

Introducing Demand

Another way of saying that there are gains from trade is to say that welfare is increased or maximized by trade. Welfare maximization for a country can be depicted using the same techniques that are used in microeconomics courses when we examine utility maximization for an individual consumer.

Consumer Indifference Curves

In consumer theory, it is assumed that a consumer's tastes can be represented by indifference curves.[1] An **indifference curve** shows the combination of two goods (X and Y) that yield a particular level of satisfaction or utility to the consumer. An indifference curve is similar to a contour line on a map, which shows points having the same height. Indifference curves, however, cannot be labelled to show the level of satisfaction because satisfaction cannot be quantified (whereas contour lines can be labelled according to the height each represents). The numbering of indifference curves, as shown in Figure 2.1 (IC_0 and IC_1) is merely for identification.

---

[1] The following discussion of indifference curves provides the minimum information needed to understand their use in international economics. A more detailed discussion can be found in any intermediate microeconomics textbook.

Figure 2.1
Consumer Indifference Curves

Indifference curves represent combinations of X and Y that yield particular levels of satisfaction or utility. They are convex and slope downward from left to right. If consumption changes from point A to point B on indifference curve IC_0, consumption of X increases (from X_0 to X_1), and consumption of Y must fall (from Y_0 to Y_1) if the level of satisfaction is to remain constant. Point C on IC_1 represents a higher level of satisfaction than points A or B because IC_1 is further from the origin than IC_0.

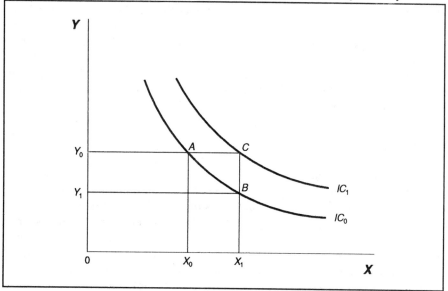

Indifference curves slope downward from left to right because, as a person's consumption of one good decreases, consumption of the other good must increase if the level of satisfaction is to remain constant. For example, in Figure 2.1, the consumer's level of satisfaction is the same at point A as it is at point B because A and B lie on the same indifference curve (IC_0). More X and less Y are consumed at point B than at point A. If the amount of Y consumed does not fall when consumption of X increases (for example, when consumption moves from point A to point C), the level of satisfaction increases, and the consumer moves to an indifference curve (IC_1) further from the origin representing a higher level of satisfaction.

Indifference curves represent different levels of satisfaction. They do not intersect because one combination of goods cannot provide two levels of satisfaction.

The amount of one good that a consumer must give up when an additional unit of the other good is consumed in order for satisfaction to remain constant is called the **marginal rate of substitution**. It is shown by the slope of an indifference curve.[2] We assume that the marginal rate of substitution declines as we move around an indifference curve; therefore, indifference curves will be convex to the origin.

The assumption of a diminishing marginal rate of substitution may be justified by the **law of diminishing marginal utility**.[3] As the quantity of X consumed increases, the consumer is willing to give up less Y for an additional unit of X for two reasons. First, additional units of X become less valuable as the quantity of X consumed increases. Second, the units of Y which are given up become more valuable as the quantity of Y consumed decreases.

There are an infinite number of indifference curves that can be drawn, representing different levels of satisfaction. (These indifference curves form an "indifference curve map.") The objective for a consumer interested in maximizing satisfaction is to consume on the highest indifference curve attainable from a given level of income.

The Budget Line

With an income (or budget) of B, the maximum amount of X a person may consume is B/P_X, provided no Y is consumed. If no X is consumed, the maximum amount of Y a person may consume is B/P_Y. The line joining these two points, as in Figure 2.2, is called the **budget line**. It shows the combinations of X and Y that cost the same amount as the consumer's income. Points below the budget line show combinations of X and Y that cost less than the consumer's income. Since satisfaction increases with spending, the consumer continues spending until all the available income is used up.[4] Thus, the consumer does not consume combinations of goods represented by goods below the budget line.

---

[2]The marginal rate of substitution is negative because Y decreases as X increases, but often the minus sign is omitted for convenience.

[3]This assumption is sufficient but not necessary. The marginal rate of substitution declines, even if the marginal utility of X increases when the consumption of X increases and the consumption of Y declines, provided that the increase in the marginal utility of Y is proportionally greater than the increase in the marginal utility of X.

[4]Saving can be considered to be a good for the purposes of this analysis.

Figure 2.2
Consumer Welfare Maximization

The maximum amounts of X and Y that can be purchased from a given income are B/P_x and B/P_y, respectively. The line connecting these points is the budget line. The consumer maximizes welfare by consuming at point C where the budget line is tangential to an indifference curve (IC_1).

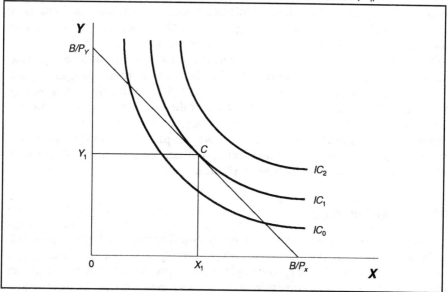

Consumer Maximization of Satisfaction

The maximum level of satisfaction is provided by the combination of goods where an indifference curve is tangential to the budget line. The indifference curve at this point is the highest that can be reached with the available income. For example, in Figure 2.2, satisfaction is maximized at point C.

Recall that the slope of an indifference curve is the marginal rate of substitution. The slope of the budget line is the price ratio (P_X/P_Y).[5] Therefore, the maximization of satisfaction leads to the equality of the marginal rate of substitution and the price ratio.

---

[5]Moving from the vertical intercept to the horizontal intercept, the vertical change divided by the horizontal change is: $-(B/P_Y)(B/P_X)$, which equals $-P_X/P_Y$. The minus sign, like the minus sign on the marginal rate of substitution, is omitted for convenience.

Social Indifference Curves

We assume that the welfare of a country can be represented by a set of **social indifference curves**, in the same way that an individual's satisfaction can be represented by a set of consumer indifference curves.[6] However, social indifference curves are not the same as consumer indifference curves in all respects. Society's welfare may be affected by changes in the distribution of income as well as by the amount of goods available. For example, we would not expect two policies to be equally attractive if one policy makes poor people poorer and rich people richer, and the other policy makes poor people richer and rich people poorer. The implication is that changes in the distribution of income may affect welfare and change the slope or position of social indifference curves. Unfortunately, if the indifference curves change, we cannot assess the effects of trade using indifference curve analysis. Therefore, for expositional convenience, we adopt the standard assumption that the income distribution is unaffected by trade, or is maintained constant by government policies which redistribute income.

Welfare Maximization

A country's welfare is maximized by consuming on the highest possible social indifference curve. The constraint a country faces is that if it does not engage in trade, it can only consume what it produces. This constraint is analogous to the income constraint a consumer faces. The quantities of X and Y available are shown by the production possibility frontier. In the Ricardian model, the production possibility frontier is a straight line resembling a consumer's budget line. In the absence of trade, the maximum welfare level is achieved at the point of tangency of the production possibility frontier and a social indifference curve.

In Figure 2.3, the pre–trade equilibrium is shown by point C_1 on the production possibility frontier (*PPF*). At this point, the slope of the social indifference curve (*SIC*$_1$) is equal to the slope of the production possibility frontier. Therefore, the marginal rate of substitution is equal to the opportunity cost of domestically produced goods.[7] Consumption at other points on the production possibility frontier would lead to a lower level of

---

[6]The assumption that society's preferences can be described by a set of social indifference curves, which do not change when trade is introduced, is discussed in more detail by Chacholiades (1978).

[7]Recall that the cost of the good on the horizontal expressed in terms of the good on the vertical is the slope of the production possibility frontier. See the discussion of Figure 1.1 in Chapter 1.

Figure 2.3
The Gain from Trade: Fixed Opportunity Costs

Before trade, consumption takes place on or below the production possibility frontier (*PPF*). Welfare is maximized at point C_1 on the social indifference curve SIC_1. When trade is introduced, by specializing in *Y* production and consuming along the trade line (*TT*), the welfare level of SIC_2 may be attained at C_2. The combination of goods consumed $(X_2 Y_2)$ when the country trades could not be achieved without trade because it lies above the production possibility frontier.

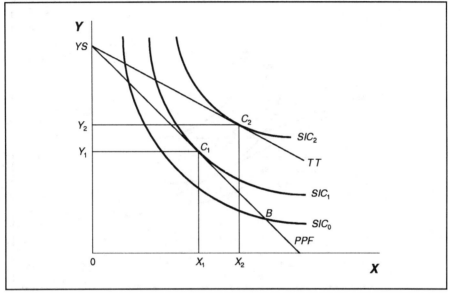

welfare, for example, consumption at point *B* leads to the level of welfare shown by indifference curve SIC_0.

The Gain from Trade: Fixed Opportunity Costs

When international trade is introduced, the country is no longer restricted to points along the production possibility frontier because consumption may take place along the terms of trade line (*TT*). Welfare is maximized when a social indifference curve is tangential to the terms of trade line. In Figure 2.3, welfare is maximized at C_2. *YS* is produced, X_2 and Y_2 are consumed, *YS* minus Y_2 is exported, and X_2 is imported. There is a gain from trade because a higher social indifference curve (SIC_2) can be reached by consuming along the terms of trade line than can be reached if consumption is confined to points along the production possibility frontier.

Figure 2.4
The Quantity of Trade and the Terms of Trade: Fixed Costs

As in Figure 2.3, the country specializes in Y production and consumes along the trade line. As the terms of trade fall, the country consumes more X. Since the country does not produce X, imports of X are shown by the amount of X consumed. The quantity of Y exported is shown by the difference between domestic production and consumption. For example, at the terms of trade shown by TT_2, the country imports X_2, produces YS and consumes Y_2, thus it exports $YS - Y_2$.

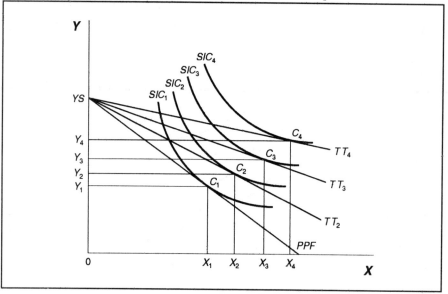

The Gain from Trade and the Terms of Trade

At the pre–trade price ratio, the country consumes C_1 in Figure 2.4. If the pre–trade price ratio is greater than the terms of trade, the country specializes in good Y and produces at point YS, the intercept of the production possibility frontier on the vertical axis. The points of consumption on the terms of trade lines are determined by the positions of the indifference curves, in other words, by the nature of the demand for goods. Post–trade consumption takes place at points C_2, C_3, and so on, depending on the terms of trade. The greater the difference between the slopes of the production possibility frontier and the terms of trade lines, the higher the indifference curve that can be reached. In other words, the greater the difference between pre–trade prices and post–trade prices, the greater the gain from trade will be.

The Ricardian offer curve, which was discussed at the end of Chapter 1, can be derived using indifference curves. The difference between domestic consumption and production is trade, and it can be plotted to form the Ricardian offer curve. For example, with the terms of trade shown by TT_2, exports of Y equal YS (the amount produced) minus Y_2 (the amount consumed). X_2 is imported because this is the amount of X consumed (and X is not produced).

The Gain from Trade and Indifference Curve Analysis

The use of indifference curves to show the gain from trade must be defended for pragmatic reasons and not because indifference curves are realistic. Indifference curve analysis is a way of illustrating the argument that there is a gain from trade, and the gain is greater the larger the difference between pre–trade prices and the terms of trade. However, the proposition that there is a gain from trade does not depend on the acceptability of the use of indifference curves. It should be remembered that the gain from trade can be shown without them. Adam Smith and David Ricardo presented persuasive demonstrations of the gains from trade over a century before indifference curves were used to make the same argument.

The discussion in Chapter 1 showed that a country gains from trade because trade increases the quantities of goods the country can consume. In other words, the consumption possibilities along the terms of trade line are greater than the consumption possibilities along the production possibility frontier (except at the point of intersection). When we introduce indifference curves into the analysis, we assume that we know what demand is like, and this allows us to determine the amount of trade at different terms of trade, and the location of the Ricardian offer curve. However, the introduction of indifference curves does not alter the reason for the gain from trade: Trade is beneficial because it increases the quantities (and variety) of goods a country can consume.

Increasing Opportunity Cost

The assumption of constant opportunity cost used in Chapter 1 implies that as labor is moved from one sector to another, the changes in the outputs of the sectors are the same for each unit of labor transferred, regardless of how large a transfer takes place. However, the labor used to produce one good may not be equally suitable for the production of other goods. Also, the capital used to produce a good may be inappropriate for the production of other goods. For example, labor skills required in the textile industry may be of little value in the automotive industry, and machines used in the construction industry may be of little use in electronics.

A more realistic assumption, reflecting the lack of homogeneity of factors of production, is that the opportunity cost of producing a good rises with the

Figure 2.5
The Gain from Trade: Increasing Costs

The production possibility frontier is bowed out from the origin because of the assumption of increasing costs. In the absence of trade, welfare is maximized when consumption and production take place at point $C_1 = Q_1$ on SIC_1. When trade is introduced, welfare is maximized if production takes place at Q_3, and consumption takes place at C_3 on SIC_3. Trade is shown by the difference between the domestic consumption and production of each good, for example, more Y is produced at Q_3 than is consumed at C_3, therefore the difference is exported.

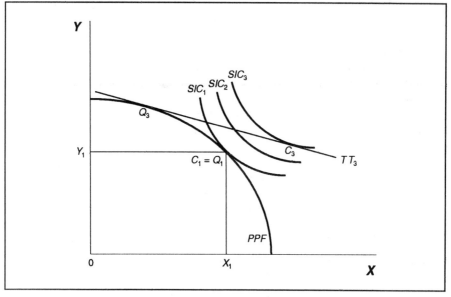

quantity of a good produced.[8] When a small quantity of X is produced, a large increase in the quantity of X can be obtained by giving up small amounts of Y, because the factors of production that increase X production most, and reduce Y production least, can be transferred from Y to X. As the production of X expands, it becomes progressively more difficult to increase X production by transferring factors of production from Y to X, and the amount of Y that must be sacrificed for each additional unit of X increases. In other words, the opportunity cost of producing a good increases as the production of the good increases. How is increasing opportunity cost reflected in the shape of the production possibility frontier? Recall that the slope of a production possibility frontier shows the opportunity cost of

---

[8]This assumption is sometimes referred to as a diminishing marginal rate of technical substitution.

domestic production. A production possibility frontier showing increasing opportunity costs is bowed out from the origin, as in Figure 2.5.[9]

The Gain from Trade Again

In the absence of trade, welfare is maximized when a social indifference curve is tangential to the production possibility frontier. In Figure 2.5, this occurs at the point $C_1 = Q_1$. When trade is introduced, the country produces more of the exported good (Y) and less of the imported good (X). Welfare is maximized when consumption takes place at C3, and production at Q_3. At these points the slope of the social indifference curve (SIC_3) and the slope of the production possibility frontier (PPF) are equal to the slope of the terms of trade line (TT_3). Therefore, welfare maximization leads to the equality of the marginal rate of substitution, the opportunity cost of domestic production, and the terms of trade.

It is interesting to note that as domestic production changes, the slope of the production possibility frontier changes, and in this way the opportunity cost is equated to the terms of trade without specialization necessarily arising. This result contrasts with that of the Ricardian model where specialization occurs because the opportunity costs of production are constant.

The Consumption Gain and the Production Gain

The gain from trade can be separated into two parts: a **consumption gain** that occurs because trade allows countries to consume at world prices rather than domestic prices, and a **production gain** that occurs because specialization increases when trade takes place. These are shown in Figure 2.6. If the level of production is fixed at Q_1, the consumption gain is shown by the increase in welfare made possible by consumption taking place at C_2 on SIC_2 rather than C_1 on SIC_1. When production changes from Q_1 to Q_3, a further increase in welfare occurs because of the benefits of increases in specialization. The production gain is shown by the movement from C_2 on SIC_2 to C_3 on SIC_3.

The division of the gain from trade into the consumption and production gains leads to an interesting and very important result: A country gains from trade even if it cannot change its production. The explanation of this result is that welfare increases if trade takes place between countries which initially (pre–trade) value the goods differently, that is, have different pre–trade price

---

[9]The slope of the production possibility frontier is sometimes called the **marginal rate of transformation (MRT)**, and an increasing opportunity cost is referred to as an **increasing marginal rate of transformation**.

Figure 2.6
The Consumption and Production Gains from Trade

Initially, production and consumption take place at C_1. If the production of X and Y does not change when trade is introduced, the gain from trade arising from the opportunity to consume at world prices is shown by the movement from SIC_1 to SIC_2 on TT_2. If production changes from Q_1 to Q_3, a further increase in welfare occurs because the country becomes more specialized. The gain from increased specialization is shown by the movement from SIC_2 to SIC_3.

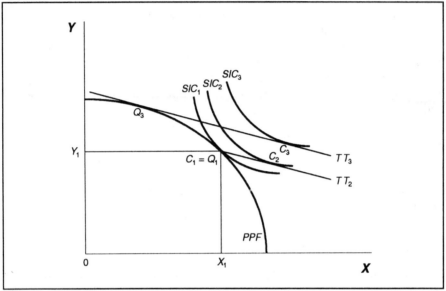

ratios. In the example shown in Figure 2.6, the gain from trade arises because other countries value Y more highly relative to X than the home country. The home country's welfare rises when it consumes less Y and exports Y, because it receives more X than is needed to maintain the initial level of welfare.

Examples of the Gain from Trade

This type of analysis may seem complicated at first sight. Essentially, the argument is very simple and can be illustrated by an example. Often neighboring families who grow vegetables swap their produce, that is, they take part in exchange. They gain from trade even in August or September when it is usually too late in the year to change their crops (production is fixed). Trade is beneficial whenever the vegetables a family would like to consume are not exactly equal to what they have. (We would expect a higher gain from trade in gardening clubs where people specialize and trade.)

In many rural and semi–rural communities people often swap produce. Usually the swap is very informal and the rate of exchange is not subject to hard bargaining, but the exchange still makes people better off. (Sometimes it appears that there is no exchange as such, produce is simply given to friends, no doubt because they return something else: friendship.)[10]

The Gain from Trade and the Terms of Trade

We can use social indifference curves to show that the gain from trade increases with the size of the disparity between the pre–trade price ratio and the terms of trade. In Figure 2.7, the terms of trade initially are slightly below

Figure 2.7
The Gain from Trade and the Terms of Trade: Increasing Costs

Initially the country produces at Q_1 and consumes at C_1 on social indifference curve SIC_1. As the terms of trade decrease from TT_1 to TT_2, the country can reach a higher social indifference curve (SIC_2). Production changes from Q_1 to Q_2, thus less X is produced and more Y. However, consumption of X increases (because a decrease in the terms of trade implies that the relative price of the imported good falls). Therefore, imports of X increase.

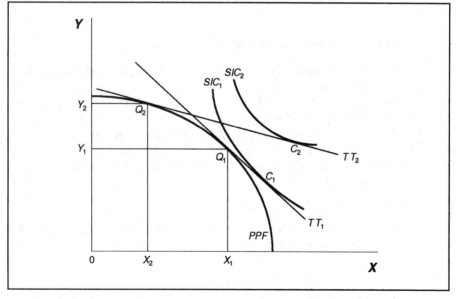

---

[10]Another example of a form of trade between friends is a "potluck" dinner where each guest brings one dish but eats a selection of dishes. Essentially, people specialize when they produce a dish, and the dish is traded for a selection of other dishes.

the pre–trade price ratio; the country imports X and exports Y. As the terms of trade line becomes flatter, production switches from X to Y (moving around the production possibility frontier), and higher social indifference curves can be reached. Also, a lower terms of trade implies that the relative price of X (the imported good) is lower, and we would expect more X to be consumed. Since the production of X falls and consumption rises as the terms of trade decrease, it is clear that imports must be increasing.[11]

The Heckscher–Ohlin Theorem

In the Ricardian model, pre–trade price differences reflect differences in labor productivity. In the Heckscher–Ohlin model, disparities between countries' pre–trade prices are caused by differences in relative **factor endowments**.

Two technical assumptions are needed to demonstrate the relationship between factor endowments and pre–trade prices. First, we assume that the pattern of demand is similar in the two countries: if the countries face the same prices, the same proportion of income is spent on each good, and this proportion does not change as income increases. Second, we assume that the production functions of the two countries are identical and do not have increasing returns to scale: if the two countries face the same input prices, the same production method will be used.

Factor Endowments and Factor Prices

Assume that there are two factors of production, labor (L) and capital (K), and two countries, A and B. If country A has more capital per unit of labor than country B (KA/LA > KB/LB), country B must have more labor per unit of capital (LB/KB > LA/KA). In this case, country A is said to be **capital–abundant** and country B is said to be **labor–abundant**. Given the assumptions of the model, factor prices will reflect the relative scarcity of the factors of production, and the ratio of the price of capital (R) to the price of labor (W) will be lower in country A than in country B (RA/WA < RB/WB).

Factor price differences lead to differences in the prices of goods. Assume that there are two goods, X and Y, and that X production requires more capital per unit of labor than Y production, in other words, X production is **capital–intensive**. If X is capital intensive, Y must be

---

[11]Increased imports do not necessarily imply increased exports. The relative price of imports is lower when the terms of trade fall, thus more imports are available for a given amount of exports. If the demand for imports is elastic with respect to the terms of trade, exports increase when the terms of trade fall. If the demand for imports is inelastic, exports decrease when the terms of trade fall. The offer curves shown are based on the assumption that the demand for imports is elastic.

labor–intensive. (If X requires more capital per unit of labor, Y must need more labor per unit of capital.) In the absence of trade, what will be the relationship between factor abundance and goods prices? If we continue to assume that country A is capital–abundant relative to country B, capital will be relatively cheap in country A, that is, the capital–labor factor price ratio (R/W) will be lower in country A than in country B. Because X production is capital–intensive, we would expect X to be cheaper relative to Y in the country which is capital–abundant: the ratio of the price of X to the price of Y (P_x/P_y) will be lower in country A than in country B. Therefore, the capital–abundant country (A) will have a comparative advantage in the capital–intensive product (X), and the labor–abundant country (B) will have a comparative advantage in the labor–intensive product (Y).[12]

One could approach the problem by emphasizing country B as follows. B is labor–abundant; therefore, in the absence of trade, the labor–intensive good (Y) will be relatively cheap in country B because labor will be relatively cheap in B. Country B will then have a comparative advantage in Y.

The Heckscher–Ohlin Theorem

The Heckscher–Ohlin theorem states that a country has a comparative advantage in the production of the good that uses the country's abundant factor intensively. This is illustrated in Figure 2.8. We assume that country A is capital–abundant and country B is labor–abundant. The countries have identical tastes, shown by a common indifference curve map. In the absence of trade, country A consumes at CA_0 and country B consumes at CB_0. When trade takes place, both consume at the same point ($CA_1 = CB_1$). Country A exports X, the capital–intensive product, and B exports Y, the labor–intensive product.

Examples of the Heckscher–Ohlin Theorem

A common example of the Heckscher–Ohlin theorem in practice is agricultural exports. When compared with most countries, the United States and New Zealand are relatively well endowed with high quality agricultural land, have suitable climates for food production, and export agricultural products. Another example is exports of labor–intensive products, such as textiles and low technology manufactured goods, from Hong Kong, Korea, and Taiwan. These countries are relatively well endowed with unskilled or

---

[12]Country B's position is derived from A's. If X is relatively cheap in A $[(P_X/P_Y)_A < P_X/P_Y)_B]$, Y must be relatively cheap in B $[(P_Y/P_X)_A > (P_Y/P_X)_B]$. (Recall that when fractions are inverted, an inequality sign must be reversed.)

Figure 2.8
The Heckscher–Ohlin Theorem with Identical Tastes

Countries A and B have the same tastes (shown by a common set of social indifference curves) and
different factor endowments (shown by the production possibility frontiers *PPFA* and *PPFB*,
respectively). Before trade, the countries produce and consume at $QA_0 = CA_0$ and $QB_0 = CB_0$
respectively. The relative price of the capital–intensive good (X) is lower in the capital–abundant
country (A), and the relative price of the labor–intensive good (Y) is lower in the labor–abundant
country (B). When trade is introduced, the countries export the good that uses intensively their
abundant factor: country A exports X and country B exports Y. They consume at the same point (CA_1
= CB_1).

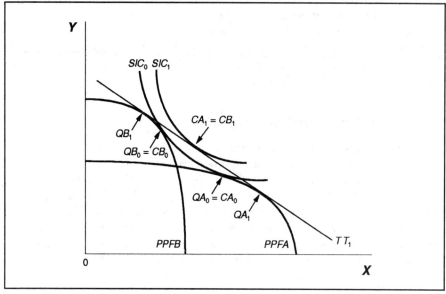

semi–skilled labor and do not have as high a level of capital and technology
as Japan and the United States.

The Potential Importance of Tastes

In deriving the Heckscher–Ohlin prediction, we assumed that tastes are
identical. Taste differences can also give rise to pre–trade price differences
and hence to trade. In Figure 2.9, even though both countries have the same
factor endowments, the same technology, and thus the same production
possibility frontiers, the pre–trade price ratios differ because tastes differ.
Country A consumes at CA_0, B consumes at CB_0, and the price ratio (P_x/P_y)
is higher in A than in B. When trade is introduced, prices are equalized, and
because the production possibility frontiers are identical, both countries

Figure 2.9
Taste Differences and Trade

Countries A and B have the same factor endowments shown by a common production possibility frontier (*PPFA* = *PPFB*). The countries' pre–trade price ratios differ because their tastes differ: the relative price of *X* is higher in country A, and the relative price of *Y* is higher in country B. When trade is introduced, country A imports *X* and exports *Y*, and country B imports *Y* and exports *X*.

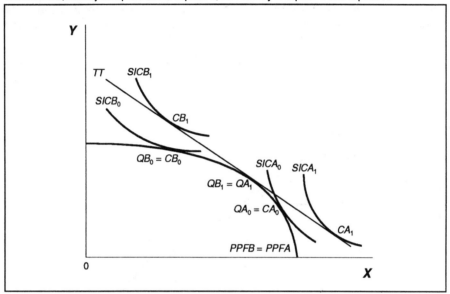

produce the same quantities of X and Y. However, they do not consume the same amounts because of the differences in tastes: country A consumes at CA_1 and B consumes at CB_1.

It is possible that differences in tastes will be large enough to offset differences in factor endowments. If a country is capital–abundant, but has a strong preference for capital–intensive goods, then these goods may be more expensive in that country than in the labor–abundant country. In this case, the pattern of trade will be the opposite of that predicted by the Heckscher–Ohlin theorem. This possibility is shown in Figure 2.10. The price of X is higher in country A than in country B because of a difference in tastes that is large enough to outweigh the effects of the difference in factor endowments.

Figure 2.10
The Heckscher–Ohlin Theorem Reversed
Because of a Difference in Tastes

Countries A and B have different factor endowments and different tastes. For simplicity the social indifference curves have not been labeled. As in Figure 2.8, country A is relatively abundant in capital and country B is relatively abundant in labor. Because of the difference in tastes, the pre–trade relative price of the capital-intensive good (X) is higher in the capital–abundant country (B). In this case, the labor–intensive country exports the capital–intensive good, and the capital–abundant country exports the labor–intensive good. Thus, the pattern of trade is the opposite of that predicted by the Heckscher–Ohlin theorem.

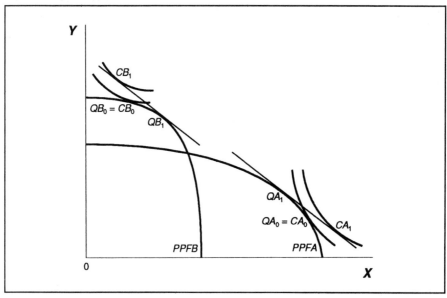

Factor Price Equalization

It has been shown that factor price differences resulting from different factor endowments can explain pre–trade price differences. Using the assumptions of the Heckscher–Ohlin model, it can also be shown that the equalization of goods prices leads to the equalization of factor prices.[13] In reality, these assumptions are not fulfilled, and we do not observe complete factor price equalization. However, we should not expect reality to correspond exactly to

---

[13]A proof of factor price equalization is beyond the scope of this text. See Chacholiades (1978).

a model. Although absolute factor price equalization does not take place, trade does generate a tendency toward factor price equalization.

If a country is labor–abundant, it exports labor–intensive goods when trade is introduced. As the output of the export industry increases, its demand for inputs increases. However, the export industry uses more labor per unit of capital than the import–competing sector. Therefore, as resources are released by the import–competing sector, insufficient labor per unit of capital is released to meet the needs of the expanding export sector. The excess demand for labor relative to capital pushes up the price of labor (the abundant factor) relative to the price of capital. The tendency toward factor price equalization is clear. In the absence of trade, the abundant factor is relatively cheap. Trade leads to an increase in the price of the abundant factor. Therefore, trade tends to equalize factor prices.

The logic may be understood by considering a simple example. The United States is well endowed with land in comparison with most countries. What would happen to the rents paid for American agricultural land if exports of agricultural produce were not allowed? Rents would probably fall because the United States has more agricultural land than is needed to supply produce for the domestic market. Therefore, trade increases the price of land (the abundant factor).

Trade and Factor Mobility

Trade can be substituted for factor mobility: trade equalizes factor prices through factor flows. Consider the case of a capital–abundant country that is next to a labor–abundant country. Labor will be relatively more expensive in the capital–abundant country than in the labor–abundant country. The capital–abundant country may choose to limit immigration, perhaps because of fears about the effect of immigration on wages: imports of labor–intensive products reduce the prices of those products and thus reduce the price of labor (assuming that labor is the factor used intensively in the import–competing sector).

An Example of Factor Price Equalization: Immigration and Trade

The effect of illegal immigrants on wages in sectors using unskilled or semi–skilled labor is often discussed. Also, one often hears complaints about unfair competition from countries with low wages. Essentially, the effect on wages of trade and immigration can be very similar. Immigration tends to reduce wages by increasing the supply of labor. As we have seen, imports of labor intensive products may also reduce wages.

The relationship between trade and factor prices has been illustrated by the discussion of the North American Free Trade Agreement (NAFTA), an agreement that has reduced barriers to trade. One result of NAFTA is that it is easier for Mexican exports to enter the United States. Some people opposed NAFTA because they believe it will reduce wages in the United States. One of the difficulties in predicting the effects of NAFTA on wages using the tools of the Heckscher–Ohlin model is that in a world with many goods, some sectors will win and some will lose. The proponents of NAFTA argued that the agreement was needed because overall it will raise both Mexican and U.S. wages.[14]

Trade and the Distribution of Income

The discussion of the relationship between factor prices and trade suggests that, because trade changes factor prices, the distribution of income will change when trade is introduced. Some people will gain from trade while others may lose. In theory, income could be redistributed in such a way as to ensure that nobody is made worse off by the introduction of trade. Without income redistribution we cannot say that there has actually been a gain from trade because the welfares of people cannot be compared. (Interpersonal comparisons of utility are impossible because welfare cannot be measured.) However, we can conclude that society is potentially better off, because specialization and trade increase the quantity of goods available for consumption.[15]

Trade and Wage Differences

Over the past two decades, the differential between skilled and unskilled labor has increased in the United States (and in many other rich countries). The 1994 Economic Report of the President considers whether trade is to blame, beginning with a description of the predictions of the Heckscher–Ohlin theorem.[16] "According to theory, when the United States trades with economies in which unskilled labor is relatively abundant, we will tend to export products requiring skilled labor and import products using unskilled labor. The relative prices of skill–intensive goods will

---

[14]NAFTA is discussed in more detail in Chapter 15.

[15]In the Ricardian model, it is assumed that opportunity costs remain constant; thus, the effect of trade on the distribution of income is not shown in this model.

[16]The following quotations are drawn from the 1994 Economic Report of the President, pp. 213–214. *The Economist* (April 2, 1994, pp. 79–80) examines the issue more broadly and in a little more detail than the Economic Report of the President, and reaches approximately the same conclusions.

therefore rise in the United States, and U.S. production will expand in export industries and contract in industries that compete with imports. Demand for skilled labor will rise, while demand for unskilled labor falls. These changes in labor demand will raise the wages of skilled workers relative to those of unskilled workers. Thus, on **a priori** grounds, one might expect an expansion of trade with developing countries to lead to greater wage inequality in the United States."

The Heckscher–Ohlin theorem does fit the facts. However, can we really blame the widening difference between wages for skilled and unskilled labor on trade? There are three reasons to be skeptical about the role of trade. First, "If increased trade with developing countries were the cause of growing wage inequality, the relative prices of goods that use highly skilled labor would be rising relative to those of goods that use unskilled labor" but "it is difficult to find any evidence of the changes in relative prices that would be required for changes in trade patterns to have altered the relative returns to different types of labor." Second, "virtually all manufacturing industries have increased their relative use of skilled labor despite growing wage differentials." This suggests that the demand for skilled labor has risen broadly throughout the economy. Third, "most U.S. trade—about 60 percent—still involves other industrialized countries whose skill levels and wages are similar to those in the United States . . . while trade is a growing part of the U.S. economy, it remains a relatively small part."

If trade is not to blame, what has caused the relative decline in unskilled wages? The answer may partly be that the demand for unskilled labor has fallen for reasons not related to trade. Machines can now do more of the basic tasks once performed by unskilled labor. Also, as technology has been introduced into many areas of work, low or falling educational standards have left unskilled workers ill-equipped for employment. (In some countries, labor unions and minimum wages have prevented wages from falling, and the result has been unemployment.) The conclusion seems to be that trade can affect wages, but that trade has not so far been the dominant influence on wage differentials.

The Determination of the Terms of Trade

Offer Curves and the Terms of Trade

Earlier we saw how imports increase and the gain from trade increases with the size of the divergence between the pre–trade price ratio and the terms of trade (see Figure 2.7). An **offer curve** can be used to show how imports and exports change with the terms of trade. For example, country A's offer curve is shown as $0A$ in Figure 2.11.

Figure 2.11
The Determination of the Terms of Trade

The equilibrium terms of trade are shown by $0TE$, which passes through E, the point of intersection of the offer curves $0A$ and $0B$. At point E, the demand and supply of X and Y are equal. If the terms of trade equal $0T_1$, B's demand for X (X_1B) is less than A's supply of X (X_1A), and the relative price of X (the terms of trade) falls. If the terms of trade equal $0T_2$, B's demand for X (X_2B), is greater than A's supply of X (X_2A), and the terms of trade rise.

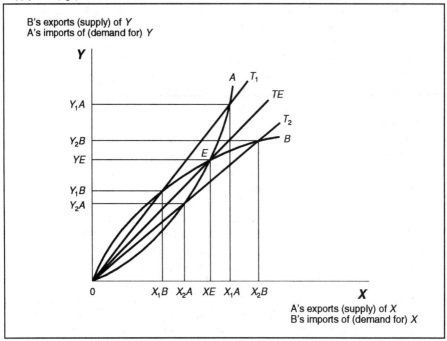

The terms of trade at a point of the offer curve are equal to the slope of a line from the origin to the point. Recall that the terms of trade may be defined as imports per unit of exports. At a point on A's offer curve, imports are given by the vertical distance while exports are given by the horizontal; thus when calculating the slope (the vertical rise divided by the horizontal run), we are also calculating the terms of trade.

An increase in the terms of trade implies that the relative price of exports is rising, or, to put it another way, that the relative price of imports is falling. The amount of trade increases as the terms of trade increase for two reasons: (1) consumption of the imported good increases and production decreases as the relative price of the imported good falls, and (2) production of the exported good increases and consumption decreases (as the relative price of the exported good rises). If the terms of trade were equal to the pre–trade price ratio, production and consumption would not change and there would be no trade. (This is what is shown by the offer curve passing through the origin.)

The offer curve for another country (country B) is included in Figure 2.11. In a two–country model, the exports of one country are the imports of the other country, and the axes are labelled accordingly. B's offer curve bends the opposite way from A's because the axes are reversed. Assuming that the pre–trade price ratio for country B differs from that of country A, the slopes of the offer curves at the origins differ. At the origin, the slope of country A's offer curve is less than the slope of country B's offer curve; thus we can conclude that the pre–trade price ratio is lower in country A than in country B.

The Equilibrium Terms of Trade

The equilibrium terms of trade are the terms of trade at which the quantities supplied by the two countries are equal. In Figure 2.11, the equilibrium terms of trade are shown by the line $0TE$. If the terms of trade are below $0TE$, the quantity of imports of X demanded by country B exceeds the quantity of exports of X supplied by country A, and the relative price of X in terms of Y, the terms of trade, will rise. If the terms of trade are above $0TE$, the quantity of imports of X demanded by country B is less than the quantity of exports of X supplied by country A, and the terms of trade will fall. (The equilibrium could have been described in terms of good Y.)

Export–Led Growth and the Terms of Trade

In general, the terms of trade will change if the underlying demand or supply of goods changes. For example, if a country is large enough to influence world prices, an increase in the demand for imports will raise the relative price of imports. A similar effect occurs if technological progress in the export sector increases the supply of exports, because the relative price of exports will fall (which is equivalent to an increase in the relative price of imports). The effects of an increase in the supply of exports (or an increase in the demand for imports) are shown in Figure 2.12. When the offer curve of country A moves from $0A_1$ to $0A_2$, the terms of trade change from $0T_1$ to $0T_2$.

When a country's supply of exports increases, the country experiences two conflicting forces: welfare tends to increase because the quantity that can be produced increases, and welfare tends to fall because the relative price of exports tends to fall. It is possible that the country may even lose from growth of the export sector because of the price effects of an increase in the supply of exports. This possibility is referred to as immiserizing growth and is shown in Figure 2.13. Growth shifts the production possibility frontier from

Figure 2.12
Export–Led Growth and the Terms of Trade

If A's supply of exports increases, the quantity of exports offered per unit of imports increases, and the offer curve moves outward from $0A_1$ to $0A_2$. The deterioration of the terms of trade is shown by the shift in the terms of trade line from $0T_1$ to $0T_2$.

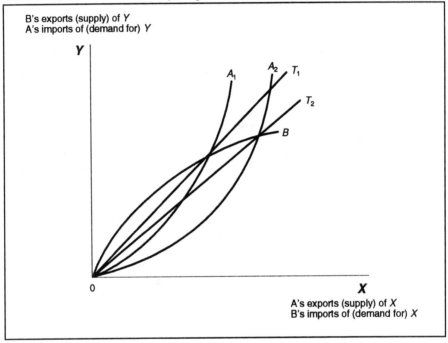

PPF_1 to PPF_2. Initially, the level of welfare is shown by social indifference curve SIC_1. At constant terms of trade, the country would clearly be better off after growth, because social indifference curve SIC_2 could be reached. However, the decline in the terms of trade, shown by the shift in the terms of trade line from TT_1 to TT_0, means that welfare falls to the level shown by social indifference curve SIC_0.

Examples of Immiserizing Growth

The price effects of supply changes can be illustrated by the experience of the Organization of Petroleum Exporting Countries (OPEC). In 1973 and 1979, OPEC found that by restricting exports, members were better off than if they sold all they could. (This experience is essentially the mirror image of immiserizing growth. Some countries have become poorer from increased

Figure 2.13
Immiserizing Growth

Growth is shown by the outward movement of the production possibility frontier from PPF_1 to PPF_2. If the terms of trade are constant and shown by the terms of trade line TT_2, which is parallel to $\overline{TT}_1$, welfare would increase from the level shown by social indifference curve SIC_1 to that shown by SIC_2. However, because growth is concentrated in the export sector, there is a decline in the terms of trade. This is shown by the shift in the terms of trade line from TT_1 to TT_0. The lower level of welfare resulting from the decline in the terms of trade is shown by SIC_0.

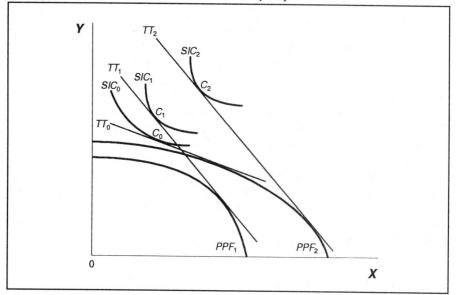

exports.) In the 1970s, OPEC members became richer from lower exports. Later, as more nations became oil producers, the supply of oil increased faster than the demand for oil, and the world price fell in the early 1980s. Recently, oil exporters have been forced to adjust to much lower oil revenue.

The general point is that when countries' exports consist of a limited range of products, the effects of demand and supply changes may be very significant. This possibility is particularly important for less developed countries, as is shown in Chapter 18.

The Effect of a Fall in the Demand for Imports

A decrease in demand for imports (or a fall in the supply of exports) has the opposite effect from an increase in the supply of exports. If the demand for imports falls, the terms of trade tend to improve. Diagrammatically, this is shown by an inward movement of the offer curve. The fall in demand for imports could be caused by an import restriction. The beneficial terms of trade effect has been used as an argument for tariffs, and this is discussed in Chapter 5.

Small Countries and Large Countries

In drawing the offer curves in this chapter we have implicitly assumed that both countries are large enough to influence the terms of trade: movements of either countries' offer curve will change the equilibrium terms of trade. Let us assume for a moment that country A is small and cannot affect world prices, whereas country B is large. In this case, while A's offer curve will have the normal shape, from A's point of view, B's offer curve will be a straight line from the origin. This means that, if A's demand or supply changes, and A's offer curve moves, A will always face the same terms of trade, as given by the slope of the straight line offer curve it faces. Even though country A cannot affect the terms of trade, it gains from trade provided that world (B's) prices differ from A's pre–trade domestic prices.[17] (The gain from trade for a small country can be shown by a diagram such as Figure 2.5.)

If world prices resemble the pre–trade prices of a large country, the implication is that the large country will gain less from trade than a small country. The reason is that countries benefit from the difference between domestic prices and world prices. The closer world prices are to domestic prices, the less the country gains from trade.

Summary of Main Points

A country's welfare can be represented by a set of **social indifference curves**. These are convex and do not intersect. The further a social indifference curve is from the origin, the higher the level of welfare it represents. In the absence of trade, countries are restricted to consuming at points along the production possibility frontier. Introducing trade allows consumption to take place along the terms of trade line and a higher level of welfare (shown by a higher social indifference curve) can be reached.

The gain from trade can be separated into a **consumption gain**, from being able to consume at world prices, and a **production gain**, from specialization. The consumption gain implies that a country will gain from trade even if it cannot change its output.

---

[17]If a country cannot affect the terms of trade, the possibility of immiserizing growth (shown in Figure 2.13) is removed.

The Heckscher–Ohlin theorem explains the difference between pre–trade and post–trade prices, that is, comparative advantage, in terms of differences between countries' **relative factor endowments**. The theorem predicts that a country will have a comparative advantage in the good that requires intensive use of the country's **abundant** factor. A country is relatively well endowed with labor (labor–abundant) if it has more labor per unit of capital than the other country (the capital–abundant country). The reason that the labor–abundant country has a comparative advantage in the labor–intensive good is that the price of labor relative to the price of capital will be lower in the labor–abundant country.

The Heckscher–Ohlin theorem is based on the assumption that tastes are similar across countries. Differences in tastes can be a cause of international trade (and can offset the influence of factor endowments on trade). It is also assumed that countries have the same production functions.

An interesting prediction of the Heckscher–Ohlin theorem is that trade will tend to equate relative factor prices. As the output of the export sector expands, the relative price of the factor used intensively in the export sector (the abundant factor) will increase. Since this factor was relatively cheap before trade took place, trade tends to equalize factor prices.

Trade is the difference between production and consumption. Indifference curves can be combined with production possibility frontiers and terms of trade lines to show how much countries consume and produce at different terms of trade. This information can be used to plot **offer curves**, representing the demand for imports and the supply of exports at different terms of trade. The equilibrium **terms of trade** are those at which the demand and supply of traded goods are equal. This equilibrium is shown by the intersection of the offer curves.

An increase in the supply of exports (or an increase in the demand for imports) shifts the offer curve outward and causes a deterioration in a country's terms of trade. It is possible that the deterioration in the terms of trade will more than offset the benefits of growth in the export sector and that the country's welfare will fall, a possibility known as **immiserizing growth**. A tariff reduces a country's demand for imports and shifts the offer curve inward. In this case the terms of trade improve.

Study Questions

1. Assume that country A is labor–abundant, country B is capital–abundant, production of good X is labor–intensive, and production of good Y is capital–intensive. What is the pattern of trade?
2. Using the assumptions of the previous question, describe how and why there will be a tendency toward factor price equalization.

3. Using the assumptions of Question 1, discuss how factor flows can lead to factor price equalization in the same way as trade. In the Heckscher–Ohlin model, what would happen if factors were completely mobile?

4. Assuming increasing costs (a concave PPF), show the gains from trade diagrammatically for a country that imports Y and exports X. Split the gain into the consumption and production gains.

5. Using social indifference curves, show that an improvement in the terms of trade increases welfare even if production is fixed.

6. Critically examine the view that, if all factors of production are fully employed before trade, world output cannot increase when trade begins, and there cannot be a gain from trade.

7. Country A faces a straight–line offer curve from country B. What does this imply? Can A gain from trade? Explain.

8. Why does the Ricardian model predict that countries will be completely specialized and the Heckscher–Ohlin model predict that specialization will increase without complete specialization necessarily arising?

9. Critically evaluate the view that, because developed countries have more factors of production than less developed countries, mutually beneficial trade is not possible.

Selected References

Bhagwati, J. N., "The Pure Theory of International Trade," *Economic Journal*, 74, March 1964 pp. 1–84.

Caves, R. E. and H. G. Johnson, (eds.), *Readings in International Economics*, Homewood, IL: Richard D. Irwin, 1968.

Chacholiades, M. C., *International Trade Theory and Policy*, New York: McGraw–Hill, 1978.

Chipman, J. S., "A Survey of the Theory of Intentional Trade: Part 3, The Modern Theory," *Econometrica*, 34, January 1966, pp. 18–76.

Clement, M. O., R. L. Pfister, and K. J. Rothwell, *Theoretical Issues in International Economics*, New York: Houghton Mifflin, 1967.

Ellis, H. S. and L. A. Metzler, *Readings in the Theory of International Trade*, Homewood, IL: Richard D. Irwin, 1949.

Krauss, M. B., *A Geometric Approach to International Trade*, New York: Halstead–Wiley, 1979.

Meade, J. E., *A Geometry of International Trade*, London: Allen and Unwin, 1952.

Three

Qualifications and Extensions of Trade Theory

Introduction

In this chapter we discuss some qualifications and extensions of trade theory. The object is not to challenge the value of standard theory, but rather to extend the analysis to show that many factors can influence trade. All economic models are simplifications of reality; one model cannot be expected to explain every possibility. Different models are useful because they yield different insights and because they are appropriate in different circumstances.

We begin by examining some empirical tests of the Heckscher–Ohlin theorem which have stimulated other explanations of trade.

Empirical Tests of the Heckscher–Ohlin Theorem

The Pattern and Growth of World Trade

The Heckscher–Ohlin theorem is a static explanation of trade because comparative advantage results from factor endowments, which it is assumed do not change. Although the approach may be appropriate for the study of trade in primary products (where endowments of natural resources are clearly of vital importance), factor endowments are not always an adequate explanation of trade in manufactured products. For example, the emergence of Southeast Asian countries as major exporters of manufactured goods in the last two decades, the recent dramatic increase in exports from mainland China, and the decline in the relative importance of Western countries in world trade, cannot be explained easily using the Heckscher–Ohlin model.

The Heckscher–Ohlin model leads us to expect that there will be a high degree of trade between countries with dissimilar factor endowments. For example, we would expect a large amount of trade between developed countries and less developed countries because less developed countries have more labor per unit of capital than developed countries. Also, less developed countries often have natural resources, whereas developed countries have better manufacturing skills and more advanced technology.

Table 3.1 shows that trade between developed countries is much greater than trade between developed countries and less developed countries. This

Table 3.1
The Structure of World Trade (1992)

	Percentage of Exports from		
	Developed economies	Developing economies	Eastern Europe and former USSR
Going to			
Developed economies	75.0	58.1	61.6
Developing economies	22.4	38.9	17.6
Eastern Europe and former USSR	2.5	2.3	19.1

Note: Totals may not sum to 100% because of rounding errors and omissions.
Source: Calculated using data from United Nations *Monthly Bulletin of Statistics,* June 1993.

pattern of trade cannot be explained by factor endowments, because although the factor endowments of developed countries are not identical, the endowments of developed countries usually have a closer similarity with each other than with the endowments of less developed countries.

Geographical proximity is an important part of the explanation of the pattern or trade. Canada is the most important single destination for U.S. exports, and the United States is the most important destination for Canadian exports. Also, to a large degree, members of the European Union and EFTA trade with other members of the two groups. Trade barriers also play a role: North America and Europe have free trade agreements under which trade between countries in each area is subject to fewer taxes and restrictions than trade with countries outside the areas. However, geographical proximity and trade barriers cannot fully explain the degree of trade between developed countries. For example, as Table 3.2 shows, a quarter of U.S. exports go to Europe, and over a quarter of Japanese exports go to the United States.

Although the Heckscher–Ohlin model may not explain all trade, most economists would not object to the proposition that factor price differentials resulting from factor endowments can be a cause of trade. Whether factor endowments alone are actually an adequate explanation of trade flows is a question that has been the subject of many empirical studies. One of the most influential studies was undertaken by Wassily Leontief.

Table 3.2
Trade Between Some Major Trading Areas (1992)

	Canada	European Union	EFTA[a]	Japan	USA
		Percentage of Exports from			
Going to					
Canada	—	0.6	1.1	2.2	19.8
European Union	7.1	62.4	61.1	18.4	23.1
EFTA	1.4	9.9	12.2	2.8	2.4
Japan	4.6	1.8	2.4	—	10.9
USA	78.0	5.8	6.7	28.1	—

[a]Most of the members of the EFTA have now joined the European Union. (See Chapter 17.) The high degree of trade between EFTA members and the EU was one of the reasons for joining.
Source: Calculated using data from United Nations *Monthly Bulletin of Statistics*, June 1993.

The Leontief Paradox

Leontief (1953) tested the Heckscher–Ohlin theorem by comparing the labor and capital needed by the United States to produce $1 million worth of exports and $1 million worth of import substitutes. He found that American export production used more labor per unit of capital than the production of import substitutes. Assuming that import substitutes are produced in the same ways as imports, it appeared that the United States imported capital–intensive goods and exported labor–intensive goods. This finding was not what was expected: casual empiricism suggests that the United States is capital abundant and, if the Heckscher–Ohlin theorem is valid, American exports should be more capital intensive than American imports.

Leontief's first test used 1947 data. Similar results were obtained with 1951 data by Leontief (1956) and with 1962 data by Baldwin (1971). Maskus (1985) also found evidence of paradoxical outcomes for the United States. Studies of the capital–labor ratios of other countries' imports and exports yielded more paradoxes. For example, Tatemoto and Ichimura (1959) found that Japan exported capital intensive products, even though Japan in the 1950s was one of the most labor–abundant industrial countries. However, Japan's trade with the United States was consistent with the predictions of the Heckscher–Ohlin model. Bharadwaj's (1962) investigation of Indian trade showed that India, a labor abundant country, exported labor–intensive products as we would expect, but India's exports to the United States were capital–intensive. Wahl (1961) found that Canada, a capital abundant country, exported capital intensive goods to the United States, but since most of Canada's trade is with the United States (which is perhaps better endowed with capital than Canada), this result does not clearly support the Heckscher–Ohlin theorem. Finally, in a study of 35 countries, Baldwin (1979) found that paradoxical outcomes were common.

These studies cast doubt on the general validity and relevance of the Heckscher–Ohlin theorem. We shall consider some of the explanations of the Leontief paradox as a way of examining the foundations of the Heckscher–Ohlin theorem in more detail. This discussion also serves as a useful introduction to other explanations of trade that are discussed in the following sections.

Labor Productivity

Leontief explained the paradox himself by arguing that American workers are more productive than foreign workers. To be specific, he suggested that American labor is three times more productive than foreign labor. In effect, this would triple the U.S. labor force. He did not attribute this difference in productivity to differences in the quality of labor, but rather to American "entrepreneurship, superior organization, and a favorable environment." However, Leontief's explanation cannot be accepted without reservation. Although these factors might increase the productivity of labor, they might also increase the productivity of capital. This explanation is only acceptable to the extent that labor productivity is increased more than the productivity of capital.

One of the basic assumptions of the Heckscher–Ohlin model is that labor is homogeneous (the same in all counties). Leontief's explanation suggests that homogeneous labor may produce different amounts in different countries. The paradox can easily be explained if we drop the assumption that labor is homogeneous. For example, it has been suggested that American workers are more productive because they are more skilled. Thus, one explanation of the paradox is that the United States is relatively abundant in skilled labor and exports products that use skilled labor intensively. This explanation suggests that the emphasis on labor and capital as the only factors of production is unwarranted and that the role of training and education should also be considered.

Research and Development

Training and education are particularly important for research and development. Research and development expenditures have been found to be positively associated with a sector's export performance. The explanation of Leontief's findings is that the United States has a comparative advantage in technologically advanced products, and the high labor cost in export industries is due to the use of highly educated labor needed for research and development. Baldwin's (1971) study, which shows that workers are more highly educated in the export sector than in the import–competing sector, supports this explanation.

Natural Resources

The Leontief paradox has been attributed to the importance of trade in natural resources. The United States is a large importer of natural resources and the extraction of natural resources uses a large amount of capital. Therefore, the paradox can be explained by differences in the type of natural resources with which countries are endowed. This explanation seems to be supported by the evidence. Leontief (1956) found that when natural resources are excluded for the data, the paradox was removed, and Baldwin (1971) found that the size of the paradox was reduced. However, the outcome depends on which industries are excluded, and the selection of the industries to be excluded is inevitably arbitrary.

Identical Production Functions

It is assumed in the Heckscher–Ohlin theorem that production functions are identical. If production functions are not in fact identical, Leontief's methodology for testing the predictions of the Heckscher–Ohlin theorem was not appropriate. Leontief's data were drawn from the input–output table for the United States. He assumed that the inputs used by other countries when they produced America's imports were the same as the inputs used by import–competing firms in the United States. If the production functions are not identical, these American input data are not an indication of the factors actually used when the goods were produced in other countries. While the United States used capital–intensive methods to produce its import–competing goods, the production of the imports in other countries may have been labor–intensive, as the Heckscher–Ohlin model predicts. Or it could be that the imports were produced using capital–intensive methods. The point is simply that, with different production functions, we cannot tell from American data alone.

Factor Intensity Reversals

The Heckscher–Ohlin theorem is based on the assumption that factor intensities are not reversible: if a good is produced by a labor intensive method at one set of factor prices, it is not produced by a capital–intensive method at another set of factor prices. A detailed discussion of factor–intensity reversals is beyond the scope of this text. It is sufficient to note that in deriving the Heckscher–Ohlin result we assumed that one good is capital intensive and one is labor intensive. The Heckscher–Ohlin theorem leads us to expect that countries will export goods that use their abundant factors intensively. If one country uses a country's abundant factor intensively at one factor price ratio, and a different good uses the abundant factor intensively at another factor price ratio, the simple relationship between factor abundance and comparative advantage is lost.

Factor intensity reversals can explain the Leontief paradox: at pre–trade factor prices the United States may want to import a labor–intensive good; at post–trade prices (when the good is imported) the same good may be produced by a capital intensive method. Attempts to assess the significance of factor intensity reversals have given conflicting results, in part because different types of production functions have been used in empirical work. Unfortunately, trade theory does not specify the appropriate form of production function.

Taste Differences

We have seen that taste differences can be responsible for trade, and may be sufficiently strong to override the influence of factor endowments on pre–trade prices.[1] For tastes to be used as an explanation of the Leontief paradox, it must be assumed that the United States has a much stronger preference for capital–intensive goods than other countries. However, this explanation is not supported by the evidence. Empirical work suggests that taste differences are not great between countries with similar income levels, and as we have seen, trade is higher between developed countries (which have similar levels of income) than between developed and less developed countries.

Barriers to Trade

Another explanation of the Leontief paradox is that it arises because of tariffs. There is evidence to suggest that American imports of labor–intensive products are restricted. These restrictions reduce the tendency toward the

---

[1]See Figure 2.10.

result which would be expected from the Heckscher–Ohlin theorem, and may be part of the explanation.[2]

Summary

The preceding discussion shows that the basic Heckscher–Ohlin theorem does not explain the trade of individual countries, or the structure of world trade. As the explanations of the Leontief paradox show, factor endowments are not the only influence on trade. Indeed, factor endowments may not even be a particularly important influence on trade. We now turn to the examination of theories that have offered other explanations of trade.

The Preference Similarity Hypothesis: Tastes and Product Development

Tastes and Trade

Linder (1961) explains the pattern of trade in manufactured goods by the effect of tastes on the type of goods produced and traded. He argues that for a country to export a commodity, it is necessary that there also be a domestic demand for the product. Linder gives three reasons to support his argument. First, producers have a greater awareness of profit opportunities in their domestic market; the profits from exporting will only be obvious after a considerable period of producing for the home market. Second, research efforts are aimed at satisfying the most obvious needs, which, he suggests, are the needs of the domestic market. Third, even if entrepreneurs recognize the need for a product in a foreign market, it is expensive to develop and adapt a product to fit an unfamiliar market.

This reasoning leads Linder to the view that the range of products a country might export is a subset of the range of products it consumes. The potential range of imported products includes all the products the country consumes. (Whether a particular product is actually imported depends on the price of the import in relation to the price of domestic goods.) Thus, Linder argues, the range of goods that are potential exports is equal to, or is a subset of, the range of goods which may be imported. Linder's argument would lead us to look for similarities between countries' tastes rather than differences between countries' factor endowments. The greater the overlap between countries' consumption patterns, the greater the potential for trade. This result is very different from that of the Heckscher–Ohlin theorem.

---

[2]See Baldwin (1971).

Linder explains the high degree of trade between countries with similar income levels by pointing to the correlation between incomes and tastes. Countries with similar income levels consume similar goods, and since countries trade the same types of goods that they consume, we should expect trade between countries with similar levels of income to be high, which it is.

Examples of the Preference Similarity Hypothesis

It is not difficult to think of examples of goods which are produced for the domestic market and exported to countries with similar incomes. Automobiles are an obvious example: German cars are produced and consumed in Germany, but one often sees German cars in the United States. Clearly some Americans have the same tastes in cars as Germans. Italians like nice clothes, and it is not surprising that Milan has become one of the leading fashion exporting centers of the world. People in other countries also like Italian clothes. France has a well–deserved reputation for good food and wine: French wine is produced and consumed in France, but there is also a large export market. Le Creuset high quality enamel cookware from France is sold in rich countries throughout the world. The United States makes films primarily for the tastes of the domestic market, but film exports are a very big business because people in other countries also like the films.

Primary Products

Before turning to a discussion of the usefulness of Linder's theory of trade in manufactured goods, we must note that Linder offers a different explanation of trade in goods that are known as **primary products** (agricultural products, metals, minerals, and fuels). The basic nature of primary products implies that the potential for their export is easily recognized, and little adaption of the product is needed. However, it is often foreign entrepreneurs who begin to export primary products, perhaps because they are more aware of the demand for primary products in their home countries.

Limitations of the Preference Similarity Hypothesis

Although Linder's model explains the pattern of trade shown in Table 3.1, supply conditions are virtually ignored, just as demand is ignored in the Heckscher–Ohlin model. In the long run, the assumption that a country's natural advantages in some types of manufactured goods remain unexploited because of a limited domestic market seems unrealistic.

We have only to consider the case of Hong Kong to see the limitations of Linder's argument. Hong Kong produces a vast range of products quickly and cheaply using an educated mobile pool of labor. Many of these products are exported even though they are often not consumed in significant amounts in Hong Kong itself (artificial Christmas trees are an example). Even if Hong Kong producers are not fully aware of all the marketing possibilities in the West, Western importers and retailers looking for low–cost sources of supply may seek out efficient foreign producers. The rapid growth of exports from mainland China aimed at Western markets is another example where exports do not appear to result from an established domestic market.

Linder recognizes that foreign entrepreneurs can exploit natural resources, but doesn't develop the same argument for manufactured goods. Where manufacturing is undertaken by foreign entrepreneurs, Linder says that the reason is often to increase exports to countries with similar demand structures. However, demand is not always the reason for developing production in another country. For example, Mexican production for the American market is clearly based on Mexico's low costs of production, not on the similarity of Mexican and American tastes. The preceding qualifications do not imply that Linder's model is wrong; like all models, it is not a complete explanation of trade. Another factor that determines the goods a country exports and imports is the availability of technology in the country.

The Product Cycle Model

Some countries have access to better technology than other countries, and this gives them a comparative advantage in the production of certain goods. The goods may be technologically advanced, or the production technology may be advanced. For example, it is clear that Japan has a comparative advantage in the production of some types of electronic equipment and in automobiles. Countries that do not possess the same technology cannot compete effectively.[3]

The **product cycle model**, which was put forward by Vernon (1966), suggests that trade in manufactured products may be the result of the development and application of new technology. Vernon's work was an extension of earlier work by Linder which focused on domestic demand as a necessary condition for a good to be exported. Although Vernon accepts the commonly held view that access to technological developments is similar in advanced countries, he argues that producers are more aware of the possibilities of using technology in their home markets. For example, he suggests that the characteristics of the United States (higher labor costs and greater availability of capital than in most other countries) have led American

---

[3]Japan is now second only to the United States in the export of high–tech products.

producers to specialize in products that allow capital to be substituted for labor.

Stages in the Product Cycle

Vernon divides the development and marketing of a product into three stages: new product, maturing product, and standardized product. He suggests that initially a product will be produced and marketed mainly in the domestic market. This enables the producer to test the product and perfect production techniques.

During the maturing product stage, the product becomes standardized and mass production becomes possible. Product standardization does not mean that product differentiation ends: variety may increase as producers recognize the characteristics that appeal to consumers. At this stage the product is marketed internationally. Producers look for similar markets in other advanced countries as potential export markets. Also, as foreign consumption of the product increases, producers begin to consider other countries as possible locations for production.

The third stage occurs when the product is at an advanced stage of standardization. Production and transport costs are important factors influencing the location of production at this stage. It becomes possible for exports from third countries to be made from foreign facilities rather than from the United States, and for the American market to be supplied with imports. Production and exports by the United States tail off as foreign competition develops. At this stage, production may shift to less developed countries.

Figure 3.1 shows the stages of development and marketing of a good. The division of the cycle into stages is for expositional convenience; the stages will vary with different products.

The Product Cycle and the Heckscher–Ohlin Theorem

Vernon's model leads us to expect that a country will export products that are at a certain stage of the product cycle. Through time, a country will develop and export different goods. Different countries may produce and export the same good as the good moves through its product cycle. This view of trade is very different from the Heckscher–Ohlin model in which the assumptions of constant technology, standardized products, and complete knowledge ensure that technology, marketing, and product development have no role.

If the term **factor endowment** is interpreted loosely enough, and is taken to include the ability to develop or produce new goods, then Vernon's model has similarities to the Heckscher–Ohlin model. However, such an

Figure 3.1
Stages in the Product Cycle Hypothesis

During the first stage the product is developed and sold mainly in the United States. In the second stage, the product becomes more standardized, the United States dominates the export market, and foreign production begins. In the final stage, foreign competition increases, the United States begins importing the product, and American production declines. (Adapted from Vernon, 1966.)

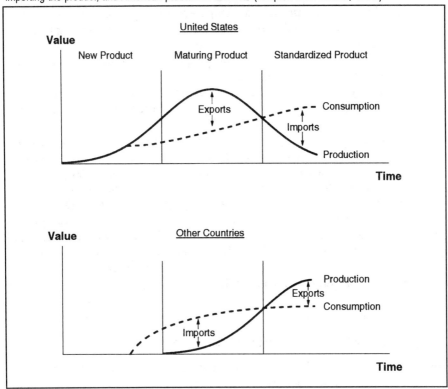

interpretation does not seem to be consistent with the static nature of the Heckscher–Ohlin model.

Vernon used his model to explain the Leontief paradox. As we have seen, the model suggests that the United States exports products that are in the early part of the product cycle. Because the degree of standardization of these products is low, mass production is not possible. However, the United States imports products that are at an advanced stage of standardization, and thus can be produced using capital intensive methods.

Examples of the Product Cycle

The product cycle theory is often used to explain early Japanese–American trade. The United States had a technological advantage that gave it a comparative advantage in the early stages of production, whereas Japan was able to produce goods more efficiently than the United States after the initial development had been completed. More recently, it is less clear that American technology and product development are superior, and many new products are being developed in Japan. While Japan has been moving toward the development stage, other countries, such as Korea, Taiwan, and mainland China, have been able to compete in the production of standardized goods which do not use the latest technology.

The market for color television receivers is an example of the product cycle. Color broadcasting began in 1954 in the United States. In the early years, domestic producers dominated the market for receivers. In 1967, imports were equal to 6 percent of the market. By 1970, imports had grown to 19 percent, and over 90 percent of those imports came from Japan. However, Japan did not simply copy American products. Japanese firms adopted all–solid–state components before American firms, thus improving the quality of their sets, and they concentrated on smaller sets. (American producers were less interested in smaller sets because of the lower profit margin.) Also, Japanese firms benefitted from lower costs of production. As the technology grew older and the product became standardized, production spread to other countries. The share of Japan in American imports decreased to 80 percent in 1977 and 50 percent in 1978, while imports from Taiwan and Korea increased.[4]

The Product Cycle Theory's Relevance Today

Vernon himself has questioned the usefulness of the product cycle theory in helping to explain modern trade. The theory was based on the view that national markets were separate and that producers responded to domestic market conditions. The importance of the product cycle has been reduced by the growth of multinational companies that cater to a global market by producing in more than one country and marketing goods internationally.

Although its importance has diminished, the theory still has some relevance. The international trade of small firms that engage in research and development may conform to the product cycle theory. Such firms may begin

---

[4]A more detailed description of the market for color television receivers, and the protection given to American producers, is contained in Organization for Economic Co–Operation and Development (1985).

by developing goods for the domestic market because they do not have the network of foreign subsidiaries needed to produce and market goods internationally. Also, the trade of developing countries may follow the predictions of the theory because domestic market conditions give some countries technological advantages in certain areas. However, the model no longer provides as convincing an explanation of American trade with the rest of the world as it did when it was first put forward.

Policy Relevance

An important conclusion for economic policy that emerges from this analysis, and which continues to be relevant, is that it may be unwise for countries to attempt to stay competitive in particular products. The notion that a country was, and therefore should remain, a world leader in the production of one product is the antithesis of the product cycle approach. If a country wants to maintain or increase the value of its exports, the answer may be for it to accept its natural role, either as a producer or developer of some types of goods, and not try to maintain a degree of competitive power in particular goods.

One of the key elements determining a country's degree of success in international trade may be the ease with which resources can be moved from one sector to another. The greater the degree of flexibility, the easier it is for an advanced country to produce new products continuously, or for a less advanced country to take over the production of standardized goods.

Intra–Industry Trade: Other Influences on Trade

So far we have mainly assumed that countries import and export different goods, but in fact countries often export and import the same products, or to be more precise, products that are classified as the output of the same type of industry. This phenomenon is called **intra–industry trade**. An explanation of intra–industry trade is an interesting exercise for its own sake, and is useful because it serves as a background against which other influences on trade can be considered.

The existence of intra–industry trade seems to contradict the Heckscher–Ohlin model. Firms in an industry produce similar products and might be expected to use similar factors of production. On the basis of the Heckscher–Ohlin model, we would expect the firms in an industry to have the same comparative advantage or disadvantage because of the similarity between their use of factors of production. We shall examine explanations of intra–industry trade in order to enhance our understanding of the causes of international trade.

The Classification of Goods and Industries

Industries are often classified according to the goods produced, not the factors of production used. Although firms producing the "same" goods might use the same factors of production, we cannot guarantee that this will be the case. For example, furniture may be made with many different materials, such as wood, plastic, and metal. Another example where the same product may be produced using different factors of production is the textile industry: the methods used to make nylon cloth have little similarity to the methods used to make cotton cloth. Manufacturers using different factors of production cannot be expected to face the same costs or the same competitive pressures.

In part, the simultaneous import and export of goods produced by one industry, and the use of different factors of production by firms in the same industry, reflect too high a degree of aggregation in our classification of industries. If we were to specify goods more carefully, different industries might be distinguished.

Industries may be classified using the *Standard International Trade Classification* (SITC). The more digits used to classify an industry, the more specific the classification. For example, SITC code 7 represents machinery and transport equipment; 78 represents road vehicles (including air cushion vehicles); 782 represents motor vehicles for the transport of goods and special purpose motor vehicles; 782.21 represents crane lorries.[5]

Grubel and Lloyd (1971) examined Australia's trade and found that the degree of intra–industry trade diminishes as the criteria for defining an industry becomes more stringent. To be specific, they found that intra–industry trade fell from 20 percent of total trade at the three–digit SITC level to 6 percent of trade at the seven–digit SITC level. Since intra–industry trade is found even at the lowest level of aggregation used in compiling trade statistics, the seven digit level, this suggests that the level of aggregation is not an adequate explanation of intra–industry trade. In theory, more stringent criteria could be used, but there are other explanations of intra–industry trade that lead us to expect that such trade will be found at very low levels of aggregation.

Entrepôt Trade

The problem of defining products is illustrated by the trade of countries that are engaged in entrepôt trade. These countries provide services, such as

---

[5]*Standard International Trade Classification, Revision 3*, New York: United Nations, 1986.

storage, blending, and packaging, that do not alter the goods sufficiently for the classification of the goods to be changed; it appears that the same goods are being imported and exported. Hong Kong and Singapore are examples of countries engaged in entrepôt trade.

Transport Costs

Intra–industry trade can be explained by the existence of transport costs. Because of transport costs, it may be cheaper to import a product from a firm just over a nearby national border than it is to purchase the product from a firm located on the other side of the home country. To put it another way, national boundaries have not usually been drawn for economic reasons, and we would not expect potential market areas determined by transport costs to be confined neatly within national boundaries. Grubel and Lloyd suggest that transport costs can only explain intra–industry trade in a limited range of products, for example, perishable foods, building materials, and electricity.

Temporary Differences Between Supply and Demand

Fluctuations in production or consumption can give rise to international trade. For example, the growing season for agricultural products often differs between different countries. Although agricultural products can sometimes be stored, it maybe cheaper to import agricultural products than to try and store domestic output. Electricity can also be stored, but some European countries find that, because peaks in demand do not coincide, it is cheaper to satisfy peak demand partly by importing electricity than it is to have the production and/or storage capacity needed to meet the demand for electricity at all times of the day.

Economies of Scale and Product Differentiation

Finally, intra–industry trade can be explained by **economies of scale** and by **product differentiation**. If firms concentrate on the domestic market and attempt to produce a broad range of products, they may not be able to benefit from economies of scale. International trade allows firms to specialize in a narrower range of products and produce more than can be sold domestically. In this way, they may achieve economies of scale by using large plants and longer production runs. One reason why producers in different countries choose to produce slightly different versions of the same good is that their domestic markets differ. For example, if there is a high concentration in one area of people with incomes of a certain level, producers in that area may specialize in goods consumed by this group. Although the same good may be produced in different areas, differences in average per–capita incomes could give rise to different qualities of the same good being produced.

The automobile industry is an example of an industry where the minimum–sized efficient plant is quite large, and producers specialize in different versions of the same product. In this case, intra–industry trade is substantial. Intra–industry trade is also found in the aircraft and weapons industries, where long production runs are needed to recoup research and development costs, and international orders are very important.

Summary of Main Points

The Heckscher–Ohlin theorem does not explain all trade. In particular, the high degree of trade between developed countries that appear to have similar factor endowments and the emergence of Southeast Asian nations as important exporting countries cannot easily be explained using a model focusing on differences in factor endowments.

Empirical testing of the Heckscher–Ohlin model also casts doubt on the general validity of the model. Leontief tested the Heckscher–Ohlin model using data for the United States and found that more capital per unit of labor was needed to produce imports than was required to produce exports. This result is called the **Leontief paradox** because it contradicted the presumption that the United States is capital–abundant and would export capital–intensive products.

Various explanations of this paradox have been offered. These include differences in labor productivity, labor skills, research and development expenditures, endowments of natural resources, production functions, and tastes, and the roles of barriers to trade and factor intensity reversals. These explanations helped to identify other causes of international trade.

Linder's model, the **preference similarity hypothesis**, predicts that trade will take place between countries that have similar tastes. The reasons Linder offers are that producers are more aware of profit and marketing possibilities in the home market, and adapting a product to sell in another country is expensive. Thus, goods are normally designed for the domestic market and then exported to similar markets. Linder's model explains the high degree of trade between developed countries because countries with similar incomes appear to have different tastes.

In the **product cycle model** Vernon suggests that the goods in which a country has a comparative advantage are influenced by the technology the country possesses. In particular, he suggests that the United States has access to higher technology than other countries and has a comparative advantage in products during the early stages of a product's development when research and development play an important role. Production later moves to lower–cost countries after the product and technology have been standardized. This model is interesting because it predicts that the products in which a country has a comparative advantage will change as the products mature. The development of multinational firms that produce and market goods internationally casts doubt on the importance of demand and supply conditions in the home market.

In practice, countries often appear to import and export the same good. This may occur for a number of reasons, including the use of too broad a classification of goods, transport costs, temporary differences between demand and supply, economies of scale, and product differentiation.

Study Questions

1. The Heckscher–Ohlin theorem is plausible but cannot explain trade in all goods or the pattern of trade between all countries. Discuss.
2. What is the Leontief paradox? Discuss three possible explanations of the paradox.
3. How can the product cycle hypothesis be used to explain the Leontief paradox and the structure of world trade shown in Tables 3.1 and 3.2?
4. How can transport costs act both as a barrier to trade and a cause of trade?
5. How can tastes and economies of scale be used to explain the existence of intra–industry trade?
6. How can Linder's model be used to explain the fact that developed countries trade more with each other than with less developed countries?
7. Economies of scale lead to a production possibility frontier that is concave from below (it bends inward rather than outward as shown in the Heckscher–Ohlin diagrams). Show that in this case international trade results in complete specialization. Explain this result with reference to the reason for the difference between the degree of specialization in the Ricardian and Heckscher–Ohlin models.
8. Discuss the view that the different theories of international trade presented in this chapter highlight different aspects of trade, and that one theory is no more true than another.

Selected References

Baldwin, R. E., "Determinants of the Commodity Structure of U.S. Trade," *American Economic Review*, 61, March 1971, pp. 126–46. Reprinted in Baldwin and Richardson, 1981.

Baldwin, R. E., "Determinants of Foreign Trade and Investment: Further Evidence," *Review of Economics and Statistics*, 61, February 1979, pp. 40–48.

Baldwin, R. E. and J. D. Richardson, *International Trade and Finance*, 2e, Boston: Little Brown, 1981, 3e, 1986.

Bharadwaj, J., "Factor Proportions and the Structure of Indo–U.S. Trade," *Indian Economic Journal*, 10, October 1962, pp. 105–16.

Chacholiades, M., *International Trade Theory and Policy*, New York: McGraw–Hill, 1978.

Grubel, H. G., "The Theory of Intra–Industry Trade," in I. D. McDougall and R. H. Snape, (eds.), *Studies in International Economics*, Amsterdam: North Holland, 1970. Reprinted in Baldwin and Richardson 1981.

Grubel, H. G. and P. J. Lloyd, "The Empirical Measurement of Intra–Industry Trade," *Economic Record*, 47, December 1971, pp. 494–517.

Krugman, P., "New Theories of Trade Among Industrial Countries," *American Economic Review*, 73, May 1983, pp. 338–42. Reprinted in J. Adams, (ed.), *The Contemporary International Economy*, 2e, New York: St. Martin's Press, 1985.

Leontief, W. W., "Domestic Factor Proportions and Foreign Trade: The American Position Re–examined," *Proceedings of the American Philosophical Society*, 97, September 1953, pp. 332–49. Reprinted in H. G. Johnson and R. E. Caves, (eds.), *Readings in Intentional Economics*, Homewood IL: Richard D. Irwin, 1968.

Leontief, W. W., "Factor Proportions and the Structure of American Trade: Further Theoretical and Empirical Analysis," *Review of Economics and Statistics*, 38, November 1956, pp. 386–407.

Linder, S. B., *An Essay on Trade and Transformation*, New York: Wiley, 1961. An excerpt is reprinted in Baldwin and Richardson, 1981.

Maskus, K. E., "A Test of the Heckscher–Ohlin Vanek Theorem: The Leontief Commonplace," *Journal of International Economics*, 19, 1985, pp. 210–12.

Organization for Economic Co–Operation and Development, *Costs and Benefits of Protection*, Paris: OECD, 1985.

Posner, M. V., "International Trade and Technical Change," *Oxford Economic Papers*, 13, October 1961, pp. 323–41.

Stern, R. M., "Testing Trade Theories," in P. B. Kenen, (ed.), *International Trade and Finance*, Cambridge: Cambridge University Press, 1975.

Tatemoto, M. and S. Ichimura, "Factor Proportions and Foreign Trade: The Case of Japan," *Review of Economics and Statistics*, 41, November 1959, pp. 442–46.

Vernon, R., "International Investment and International Trade in the Product Cycle," *Quarterly Journal of Economics*, 80, May 1966, pp. 190–207. Reprinted in Baldwin and Richardson. 1981.

Vernon, R., "The Product Cycle Hypothesis in a New International Environment," *Oxford Bulletin of Economics and Statistics*, 41, November 1979, pp. 255–67.

Wahl, D. F., "Capital and Labor Requirements for Canada's Foreign Trade," *Canadian Journal of Economics and Political Science*, 27, August 1961, pp. 349–58.

Wood, A., "Give Heckscher and Ohlin a Chance," *Weltwirtschaftliches Archiv*, Band, 130, 1994, pp. 20–49.

Four

Barriers to Trade

Introduction

In this chapter we examine the economic effects of barriers to trade. We begin by examining the economic effects of a tariff. While tariffs have become less important, tariff levels having fallen over the past few decades, tariffs are still common. Also, an analysis of the effects of tariffs is useful because it provides a background against which we can consider the effects of other trade barriers. Our discussion leads to the conclusion that, in general, trade barriers are economically inefficient. When government intervention is justified to achieve an objective, there is usually an alternative policy that is more efficient and does not require restricting trade.

The Economic Effects of Tariffs

What Are Tariffs?

Taxes on traded goods are known as **tariffs** (or import duties). They are one of the most common forms of trade barrier. When tariffs are applied, evasion must be prevented, that is, action must be taken to prevent smuggling. This is one reason why countries maintain guarded borders and why people travelling between countries are occasionally stopped and searched. Most goods enter a country through a small number of ports, and usually it is not difficult or expensive for taxes to be levied on a good as it moves from one country to another.

Tariffs can be imposed on an **ad valorem** basis (as a percentage of the value of the good), on a **specific** basis (a certain amount of money per unit of the good imported), or on a **compound** basis (a combination of ad valorem and specific). Tariffs can be applied narrowly, to one or two goods, or generally, to all imports or to imports of certain types of goods (for example, agricultural goods). The method of fixing the tariff need not concern us because the basic effects of the different types of tariffs are the same.[1]

---

[1]One difference between ad valorem and specific tariffs is that when the price of a good rises because of inflation, a specific tariff falls as a percentage of the value of the good whereas an ad valorem tariff rises since its percentage is unaffected.

The effects of a tariff can be classified as follows:
1. Consumption Effect
2. Production Effect
3. Import Effect
4. Revenue Effect
5. Redistribution Effect
6. Terms of Trade Effect
7. Balance of Trade Effect
8. Income and Employment Effects

Each of these effects is briefly described below. The effects are examined in more detail when we discuss the welfare effects of a tariff in the following section and as part of our discussion of arguments for protection in the next chapter.

Consumption Effect

The effect of a tariff on consumption is clear: tariffs increase import prices, which tends to reduce consumption of imports, and increase consumption of domestic substitutes. As consumers switch from imports to domestic substitutes, the increase in demand for domestic goods pushes up their prices. Since the prices of both imported goods and domestic substitutes rise, total consumption of these goods declines.

Production Effect

Tariffs lead to an increase in the demand for domestic goods, as consumers switch to domestic substitutes for imported goods. This is one reason why domestic producers sometimes lobby for tariff protection. Domestic producers will respond to an increase in demand for their output by increasing the price and output of domestic goods. The size of the increase in output—the production effect—is determined by the initial size of the import–competing sector, and the response of domestic supply to the increase in demand caused by the tariff (the elasticity of supply). Some sectors are more able to expand their output than others, and the potential for increased output is often used as an argument for tariff protection. We return to this question when we discuss the infant–industry argument for tariff protection in the next chapter.

Import Effect

Tariffs increase the price of imports, and this leads to a fall in the quantity demanded. The size of the import effect is determined by the consumption and production effects. For example, if the quantity demanded of a good does not change very much as its prices rises, and domestic production of the good does not increase, imports will not change greatly. However, if there is a significant fall in the quantity demanded and a large increase in the quantity of domestic substitutes supplied, there will be a large fall in the quantity of imports. In other words, the larger the elasticities of demand and supply, the larger the import effect.

Revenue Effect

Tariffs generate revenue for the government. Tariffs levied primarily to raise revenue are called revenue tariffs. For ad valorem tariffs, the amount of tariff revenue equals the percentage tariff rate multiplied by the post–tariff value of imports. For specific tariffs, the revenue equals the per unit tariff multiplied by the post–tariff quantity of imports. Obviously, if a tariff on a good is so high that no imports enter the country, there will be no revenue; in this case the tariff is said to be **prohibitive**. Clearly, when generating revenue is one of the main reasons for imposing a tariff, the government must consider the change in the quantity of imports as well as the revenue per unit. A high tariff may generate a lot of revenue per unit, but if very few imports enter the country, little revenue will be collected.

Redistribution Effect

The discussion so far has shown that tariffs redistribute money: consumers pay more, domestic producers of import substitutes receive higher prices, and the government receives tariff revenue. The redistribution of income can itself be considered an effect of the tariff. We shall examine the overall welfare effects of a tariff in a moment, but when discussing the actual effects of a tariff we should always remember that, in practice, tariffs lead to gains and losses for different groups.

Terms of Trade Effect

The **terms of trade** may be defined as the ratio of the price of exports to the price of imports. A favorable change in the terms of trade occurs if the price of exports rises in relation to the price of imports. Tariffs can lead to a favorable change in the terms of trade. When a country imposes a tariff on a good, the country's demand for imports of the good normally falls. The world price of the good may fall in response to the fall in the country's demand if the country accounts for a significant percentage of the total demand for the good.[2] To the extent that the world price of the imported good falls while the price of exports remains the same, there is a favorable change in the terms of trade.

Balance of Trade Effect

The **balance of trade** is the difference between the values of exports and imports. The balance of trade tends to increase when tariffs are imported because of the import effect, and this increase is sometimes used as an argument in favor of tariffs. For example, countries experiencing unemployment may find an increase in the balance of trade desirable because the demand for domestic goods increases. (The conditions under which tariffs increase domestic employment are discussed in the next section.) Countries that have fixed exchange rates sometimes use tariffs because an increase in the balance of trade from lower imports reduces the demand for foreign exchange, and this may help a country maintain its chosen exchange rate.

Although the balance of trade effects seem simple, there are many factors that may reduce the overall effect of tariffs on the balance of trade: although imports of the goods that bear tariffs normally decrease, consumption of other imported goods may increase, and export production may be adversely affected by an increase in the cost of imported inputs that are used in the export sector. The balance of trade effects of a tariff are discussed in more detail in Chapter 5. For the present it is sufficient to note that the overall effect of tariffs on the balance of trade may be much smaller than might appear at first sight.

Income and Employment Effects

Finally, to the extent that there is an increase in the balance of trade, the demand for domestic goods (**aggregate demand**) increases. An increase in aggregate demand caused by tariffs will affect national income and employment in basically the same way as an increase in government spending. The income and employment effects of an increase in aggregate demand depend on the condition of the economy when the tariff is imposed. If there is full employment, an increase in aggregate demand will not lead to an increase in output because the economy cannot produce any more; inflation will be the only result. In this case, although the monetary value of national income will go up, output will not, and therefore real income will stay the same. Unemployment is a necessary condition for tariffs to increase

---

[2]Recall that a fall in the demand for imports moves a country's offer curve inward. If the country is large, the terms of trade increase. See Chapter 2.

Figure 4.1
The Effects of a Tariff Levied by a Small Country

Domestic demand and supply are shown by DD and SS, respectively. At the world price of P_0, QD_0 is demanded, QS_0 is supplied domestically, and imports equal $QD_0 - QS_0$. A tariff (t) raises the domestic price of imports to P_1. The quantity demanded falls to QD_1, the quantity supplied rises to QS_1, and imports fall to $QD_1 - QS_1$. Consumer surplus falls by P_0P_1ef, producer surplus increase by P_0P_1ba, and tariff revenue of $cbed$ is collected. The net loss from the tariff equals $abc + def$.

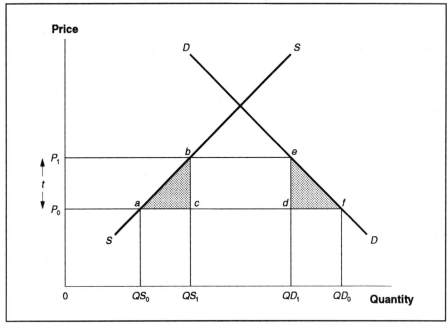

real income and employment.[3] If there is unemployment and aggregate demand increases, then output, employment, and prices may rise together.[4]

A Diagrammatic Approach

The first five effects of a tariff are shown in Figure 4.1. Assuming that the importing country cannot affect the world price (the supply of imports is

---

[3]This condition is similar to the condition for a devaluation to be effective. See Chapter 9.

[4]Economists who believe that the economy tends naturally toward full employment often doubt the usefulness of tariffs to reduce unemployment.

perfectly elastic), the country will be able to consume all it wants at the world price P_0. The domestic supply of the good is shown by the supply curve SS, and the domestic demand is shown by the demand curve DD. The initial price is P_0, domestic producers supply QS_0, and domestic consumption is QD_0. The difference between domestic consumption and domestic production, $QD_0 - QS_0$, is made up by imports.

When a tariff is imposed, the price of imports rises from P_0 to P_1. The consumption effect is the fall in consumption from QD_0 to QD_1. The production effect is the increase in production from QS_0 to QS_1. As consumption falls and domestic production rises, less is imported. The import effect is the fall in imports from $QD_0 - QS_0$ to $QD_1 - QS_1$. The difference between P_0 and P_1 is the amount of the tariff the government collects on each unit of the good. The area of the triangle $cbed$ is thus equal to the total revenue collected because the area equals the amount of the tariff per unit multiplied by the quantity imported, that is, $(P_1 - P_0) \times (QD_1 - QS_1)$. This is the revenue effect. Finally, the diagram shows that consumers pay higher prices and consume less, while producers (of import substitutes) receive higher prices and produce more. Thus, tariffs reduce the welfare of consumers and increase the welfare of producers. This is the redistribution effect.

The Welfare Effects of a Tariff

The welfare effects of a tariff can be shown using **consumer surplus** and **producer surplus**.[5] Consumers experience a loss of consumer surplus when the price rises, which is represented in Figure 4.1 by the area of the trapezoid P_0P_1ef. There is an increase in producer surplus, which is represented by the area of the trapezoid P_0P_1ba. The tariff revenue gained by the government is represented by the area of the rectangle $cbed$. If the gains to producers and the government are deducted from the loss to consumers, we are left with two triangles: abc and def. These triangles represent the net loss to society resulting from the tariff.

This result was derived using the implicit assumption that one dollar yields the same amount of welfare whether it accrues to consumers, producers, or the government. Clearly, this is a strong assumption. However, the undesirability of tariffs can be shown without this assumption.

---

[5]Consumer surplus is shown by the area above the price line and below the demand curve. It represents the difference between consumers' valuation of successive units of the good, and the price paid. Producer surplus is shown by the area below the price line and above the supply curve. It represents that difference between the marginal cost of successive units of the good and the price received.

The Allocation of Resources

We saw in Chapter 1 that there are gains from trade. If trade is reduced, we would expect those gains to be reduced. This is what happens when a tariff is imposed. A tariff leads to economic inefficiency because a tariff–levying country produces more of a good instead of buying from countries that can produce the good at a lower (opportunity) cost. In other words, inefficiency is shown by the increase in domestic production that results from the higher market price that a tariff generates.

Domestic producers of import substitutes gain (because they are able to sell more at the higher price), so why do we say tariffs are inefficient? An example will illustrate the answer. Canada could be self–sufficient in peaches by imposing a tariff that raises the price of peaches so much that domestic production becomes profitable and imported peaches become so expensive that no one buys them. Most people would agree that such a policy would be ridiculous because of the country's climate. However, this example is simply a more extreme case of the general argument that countries should import from other countries if other countries can produce a product at a lower cost.[6]

The Tariff Viewed as a Consumption Tax and a Producer Subsidy

Rather than use a tariff to support an industry, we could tax consumption of the good the industry produces and use the tax revenue to subsidize producers of the good. The effects of this joint policy would be basically the same as the effects of a tariff, that is, a tariff is in effect a tax on consumers that finances a subsidy to producers. A tariff acts like a tax because consumers pay more for the goods they buy, and a tariff acts like a subsidy because domestic producers receive more (in the form of a higher price) for the goods they sell.[7] Therefore, when tariff protection is given to an industry, it is as though consumers are taxed to support the industry. This may not be obvious because the tax on consumers and the subsidy to producers occur in the form of a higher market price, and do not result from an explicit tax–subsidy program. But this way of viewing the effects of a tariff highlights the gains and losses imposed by a tariff.

---

[6]This example is similar to that used by Adam Smith in his argument in favor of free trade. See Chapter 1.

[7]If the tariff is not prohibitive, tariff revenue is collected. This revenue shows that the additional consumer expenditure caused by the tariff is greater than the amount received by producers. Producers do not benefit from the higher prices consumers pay for imports; the government receives tariff revenue instead.

An Example of the Inefficiency of Tariffs

For example, tariffs on imported food have basically the same effects as a policy of taxing food and using the revenue to subsidize farmers. The European Community uses tariffs on food to support farmers, but food taxes accompanied by farm subsidies would be politically unacceptable. (One objection would be that taxing food, a necessity for life, would hurt poor people who spend a high percentage of their incomes on food.) But the policies have the same effects. It is simply that the true cost of tariff protection of farmers is obscured.

Tariffs versus Subsidies for Support of Domestic Production

If a country decides that it wants to support domestic production of a good in order to increase employment in a particular sector, a tariff is rarely if ever the best way to do it. A tariff supports producers of a particular good by taxing consumers of the same good. An alternative policy with the same effect on output and employment is for governments to subsidize domestic producers by the amount that the market price would have risen with a tariff.

The Advantages of Subsidies Over Tariffs

This policy of **subsidies** may be preferred to tariff support for four reasons. First, a subsidy may be financed from general taxation in a manner consistent with income distribution objectives. It does not need to be financed by taxing only consumers of the good. Thus, a subsidy can typically be financed more equitably than a tariff. Second, because consumers do not have to pay a higher price for the imported good, they will consume more of the good than if a tariff were imposed. To the extent that consumption of the good from a low–cost source (other countries) is maintained, the subsidy will be less inefficient than the tariff. Third, subsidies are less likely to induce foreign retaliation. Fourth, whereas tariffs redistribute income from consumers to producers in an implicit way, subsidies are explicit redistributions. The amount of support given to domestic producers by subsidies is subject to public scrutiny, whereas subsidies given through tariffs are not so clear, although no less real. For people who favor an open society, subsidies are therefore preferable to tariffs.

In Figure 4.2 the effects of a subsidy are shown: a subsidy of s per unit gives producers the same revenue as they receive from the tariff shown in Figure 4.1, that is, P_0 and P_1 are the same in both diagrams and $P_0 + s = P_1$. The domestic quantity supplied (QS_1) is the same under the subsidy as it is under the tariff because producers receive the same revenue per unit. The

Figure 4.2
Subsidies versus Tariffs

The initial position is the same as in Figure 4.1. A subsidy shifts the domestic supply line from SS to S_1S_1, and raises output from QS_0 to QS_1. The monetary cost of the subsidy is P_0P_1bc and producer surplus rises by P_0P_1ba, thus the net cost of the subsidy is abc. The subsidy is preferable to a tariff that raises domestic output by the same amount, because a tariff would cause an additional welfare loss equal to def.

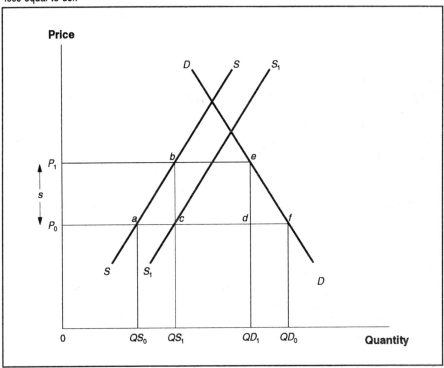

financial cost of the subsidy is the amount of the subsidy (s) multiplied by the number of units subsidized (QS_1), the area of the rectangle P_0P_1bc. Producers experience an increase in producer surplus equal to P_0P_1ba. Thus, there is a net welfare loss to society equal to the area of the triangle abc. There is no change in consumer surplus because the market price does not change. The subsidy is therefore a less costly way of increasing domestic production than a tariff.

Why then would tariffs ever be adopted rather than subsidies? One reason is that producers may prefer tariffs to subsidies precisely because the support is less obvious. Who wants to be seen to be dependent on government handouts? Another reason is that tariffs generate government revenue, whereas subsidies must be financed; thus, tariffs appear to cost less. However, once it is recognized that tariffs are in effect producer subsidies financed by consumption taxes, the fact that the government must levy taxes to finance subsidies is not a valid argument in favor of tariff support.

Problems of Financing Subsidies

In discussing the relative merits of tariffs and subsidies as alternative ways of providing support to an industry, we implicitly assumed that the country has a developed tax system. However, in some developing countries, tariffs may be necessary to raise revenue for government activities because other forms of taxation are not available. This does not mean that tariff support of industries is justified. Even if tariffs are needed to raise money, supporting industries through the use of subsidies is still preferable to tariff support.

In the absence of a developed tax system, the fundamental problem is how to finance the subsidies. General tariffs, covering a wide range of goods, are more efficient revenue raising devices than tariffs levied solely on the goods that the industries produce. Therefore, if financing subsidies from general taxation is not possible, subsidies financed from general tariffs should be used. In general, tariff support of specific industries is neither necessary nor desirable, even in developing countries.

Although revenue raising is best achieved by general tariffs, other considerations may lead developing countries to apply higher tariffs to some goods than to others. For example, it might be argued that tractors are more important for economic development than luxury motor cars. Even if the resulting tariff structure is economically inefficient, developing countries face many problems, and economic efficiency maybe of less importance to them than other objectives (such as a higher rate of economic growth). However, it is interesting that the countries attempting to increase economic growth by restricting trade have usually grown more slowly than the countries pursuing policies that have encouraged greater international trade.[8] We shall examine some of the special problems of developing countries in Chapter 18.

Non–Tariff Barriers

Tariffs have decreased in importance over the last four decades, in part because of international agreements within the General Agreements on Tariffs

---

[8]See the World Bank's *World Development Report 1987*, New York: Oxford University Press, 1987.

and Trade.[9] However, in recent years there has been an increase in the importance of non–tariff barriers. Non–tariff barriers have been used for some time in the textiles, clothing, and steel industries, but recently the coverage has also included industries such as automobiles, machine tools, microchips, and consumer electronics.[10]

Non–tariff barriers to trade can be classified into four types:

1. Restrictions on the quantity of goods.
2. Government procurement biases.
3. Taxes or subsidies to particular industries.
4. Administrative obstructions that make international trade unnecessarily difficult or expensive.

Quotas

A restriction on the quantity of imports or exports is known as a **quota**. Quotas may be applied as a limit on the absolute amount of goods that can be imported, or defined in terms of a share of the domestic market. The quota can be divided among a group of countries, or a global quota may be applied in which case the origin of the goods is not taken into consideration.

If a global quota is applied, the producers who are first in line will supply the market, but they will not necessarily be the producers that the government or consumers would prefer. Rather than allow supply to be determined on a first–come, first–served basis, governments typically issue licenses to importers or foreign suppliers. The division of the quota is inevitably somewhat arbitrary. For example, if the division is made using historical market shares, new or growing firms will be penalized. Assessing firms according to criteria such as product quality, efficiency, price, and so on, is likely to be expensive, and the allocation will still be arbitrary because officials must interpret the different criteria and reach an overall conclusion. In some countries, the discretionary power wielded by officials leads to corrupt practices.

The Economic Effects of Quotas

Quotas reduce the supply of imports of a good and cause prices to rise (because of the decrease in supply). Higher prices cause a fall in

---

[9]The history of commercial policy, including the formation and principles of GATT, is discussed in Chapter 15.

[10]These developments are discussed in Organization for Economic Co–Operation and Development (1985), in the International Monetary Fund's annual report: *Exchange Arrangements and Exchange Restrictions*, and in Kelly (1988).

consumption, but domestic production increases. Quotas are therefore similar to tariffs in their effects on consumption, production, and trade. The main difference between quotas and tariffs lies in their effects on government revenue. Whether or not revenue is generated by quotas depends on how the quotas are imposed.

Fees may be charged for the quota license, in which case the government receives some of the increase in the price of the good that occurs because of the decrease in supply caused by the import restriction. Quota licenses may be auctioned competitively. In this case it does not matter who holds the quota license, tariffs and quotas are very much alike. Producers bidding against each other will bid away any large profits that possession of a license might have yielded, and the government receives license revenue instead of tariff revenue. However, in practice, competitive auctions are not held, and quotas do not generate as much revenue for the government as tariffs. Instead, quotas generate profits for the holders of import licenses.

If the quota licenses are held domestically, quotas generate profits for domestic firms. Charging for the licenses merely redistributes income from quota holders to the government. In this case tariffs and quotas have the same overall effect on welfare, although they have different effects on the distribution of income. If the quota licenses are held by foreign firms, quotas reduce national welfare more than tariffs because quotas generate profits for foreign firms rather than government revenue.

The economic effects of a quota are shown in Figure 4.3. To allow easy comparison to be made, the quota shown in Figure 4.3 equals the amount that is imported under the tariff shown in Figure 4.1, that is, $QD_1 - QS_1$. The market supply (S_1S_1) is obtained by adding the quota to the domestic supply curve (SS). The equilibrium price (P_1), the domestic quantity supplied (QS_1), and the amount of trade ($QD_1 - QS_1$) are the same as in the tariff case. Also, the effect on producer surplus (P_0P_1ba) and consumer surplus (P_0P_1ef) are the same. The difference is that the area $cbed$, showing the money earned by quota holders buying at world prices (P_0) and selling at domestic prices (P_1), does not automatically accrue to the government as tariff revenue. Whether this area represents a further welfare loss beyond that caused by the tariff depends on whether fees are charged for quota licenses and on whether licenses are held by domestic or foreign firms.

Tariffs versus Quotas

Although in many respects tariffs and quotas are similar, tariffs may be preferable to quotas because tariffs generate government revenue rather than profits for quota holders. A second reason for preferring tariffs to quotas arises from the way in which quotas are applied: discrimination among suppliers is inevitable, so some are favored with licenses and some are not. This discrimination is a source of inefficiency and possible corruption.

Figure 4.3
The Effects of a Quota

The initial position is the same as in Figure 4.1. A quota is imposed that limits imports to $QD_1 - QS_1$, the post–tariff quantity shown in Figure 4.1. The total supply (S_1S_1) equals domestic supply (SS) plus the quota. (The country cannot consume imports at less than the world price, P_0, thus S_1S_1 does not extend below P_0.) The price effect $(P_1 - P_0)$, the loss of consumer surplus (P_0P_1ef), and the gain to producers (P_0P_1ba) are the same as in the tariff case. The rectangle *cbed* is the quota holders profit. If the quota licenses are held domestically, the net loss is the same as in the tariff case: *abc + def*.

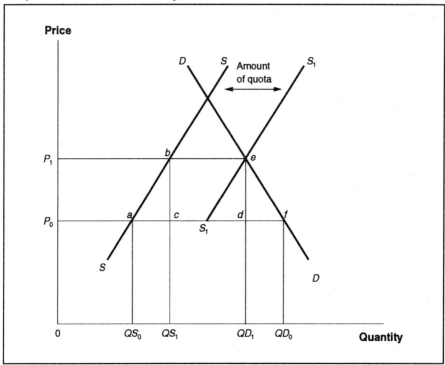

However, if a stable domestic price is desired for a good, and the world price is unstable, a quota may be preferable to a tariff. In the case of a tariff, the domestic price changes as the world price changes. A quota breaks the link between the domestic price and the world price: the domestic price is determined by domestic demand and domestic supply augmented by the quota.

One reason why domestic producers may prefer quota to tariff protection is that an appreciation of domestic currency or escalating costs may offset the protective effects of a tariff, but quotas will continue to provide protection from foreign competition.[11] Another reason why domestic producers may prefer quota protection is that the amount by which a tariff raises the price of imports is obvious, while the protective effect of quotas is less clear.

Voluntary Export Restraints

Recently quotas have been adopted by foreign exporters. These are known as **voluntary export restraints (VERs)** or **orderly marketing agreements (OMAs)**.[12] It would be more correct to say that VERs have been imposed by importing countries because, despite their name, VERs were not usually adopted by exporters. Rather, foreign producers were induced to restrict exports by the threat that, if they did not do so, importing countries would impose tariffs or quotas. A notorious example of a VER is the agreement by Japanese automobile producers to limit exports to the United States. Another example is the agreement by the European Union to limit steel exports to the United States. The Multifiber Agreement, which restricts trade in textiles, is an example of an OMA. During the recession in world trade of the early 1980s, such agreements were popular with exporters worried about maintaining access to markets, and with governments concerned that imports might already increase high rates of unemployment.

Some people may find this type of policy undesirable in a democratic society, because VERs impose losses on one group (consumers) in order for another group (producers) to gain, without the VER necessarily being approved or discussed by the legislature. There is little doubt that one of the attractive features of VERs for politicians is that they can claim they support free trade while at the same time negotiating VERs to benefit important groups. Not only are VERs politically undesirable, but they are also economically nonsensical, as we will see.

The Economic Effects of VERs

VERs have almost the same effects as quotas, and Figure 4.3 could represent either a quota or a VER. However, in the case of VERs, the government cannot share in the profits arising from an increase in the value of the good caused by the fall in supply (shown in the diagram by *cbed*). The foreign supplier or domestic importer benefits from the higher price. To the extent that VERs benefit mainly foreign suppliers, they are inferior to tariffs (which

---

[11]This may be why some domestic manufacturers have argued for protection in the form of voluntary export restraints.

[12]VERs are negotiated informally, whereas OMAs are formal agreements with all the major exporters of a product.

raise government revenue) or quotas (which may raise government revenue or generate profits for domestic license holders).[13] However, it is not surprising that foreign suppliers would rather restrict their exports voluntarily than be subject to tariffs or quotas.

Government Procurement Biases

Government purchases are a significant percentage of spending in most countries. Although some of this government spending finances the purchase of services that are not traded internationally, government spending on goods is significant. **Government procurement biases** are a form of discrimination against foreign producers. Most governments appear to have a policy of favoring domestically produced goods, although it is not usually stated explicitly. In the United States, the Buy American Act of 1933 (amended in 1954) required agencies to buy American goods provided that imports were not more than 6 percent cheaper than domestic goods (but rising to 25 percent in some sectors and 50 percent in the case of defense).

Taxes and Subsidies

If domestic producers pay lower taxes or receive higher subsidies than foreign producers, domestic producers will have a competitive advantage. Export production, or the production of goods that compete with imports, can be encouraged through the tax system. Policies that help domestic producers engaged in foreign trade make it more difficult for foreign firms to compete and are therefore another form of trade barrier. Alternatively, higher taxes can undermine the competitive position of domestic firms. For example, in North America, it is often claimed that the higher taxes in Canada, needed to finance government programs like health care, create problems for Canadian firms trying to compete with firms from the United States.[14]

---

[13]A VER for one product may also lead to increased imports of other products, because foreign producers can use the profits generated by the VER to finance moves into other areas not subject to controls. See Organization for Economic Co–Operation and Development (1985).

[14]The Commission of the European Community has proposed that taxes be harmonized to strengthen the unity of the community market. Little progress has been made, but the proposal shows recognition of the problems raised by differences between national taxes and subsidies.

Administrative or Regulatory Obstructions

Administrative obstructions may be imposed to discourage trade or make trading unnecessarily difficult or expensive. A famous example was the 1982 decision by the French government to require all imports of videocassette recorders to enter France through a single customs post (Poitiers). This type of regulation increases the cost of goods by creating delays at customs posts. The British government was able to exclude French turkeys from the Christmas market in 1982 by insisting on excessive inspection of imported poultry, thus making imported turkeys more expensive.

Regulations may be introduced for legitimate reasons, such as health, safety, environmental considerations, or labelling information. If such regulations were uniform across countries, they would have little effect on trade. There are, however, many differences among countries' regulations regarding the production, nature, and marketing of goods, and such regulations can be used to restrict imports.[15] There are sometimes arguments over whether a country's law is designed to prevent trade, or whether it merely reflects national preferences.

In December 1988 there was a dispute when a European Community ban on the sale of meat containing artificial hormones was extended to cover imported meat. The United States complained that this was a restriction of trade because most American beef contains artificial hormones, and there was no health hazard. The Commission of the European Community took the position that the ban on hormones was not a trade restriction because it covered all meat sold in the European Community, and it was a response to widespread public concern. The European view was that the hormone ban resembled the United States' regulation prohibiting imports of cheese made with unpasteurized milk (a product that France could export to the United States). Such disputes are bound to occur occasionally between countries with different regulations.[16]

Some regulations adversely affect the competitive position of domestic producers. For example, domestic producers may face higher production

---

[15]This is why the Commission of the European Community has introduced legislation to harmonize regulations between member states. However, the Community is a special case where members generally support laws that will reduce barriers between countries, thereby creating a "single market."

[16]In the summer of 1993, following some cases of foot and mouth disease in Eastern Europe, the European Community banned all imports of meat from the area, even imports from countries where no cases had been found. Was it just a coincidence that the Community had a massive stock of pig–meat in storage (which was bought in an effort to keep up Community prices)?

costs because they are required to maintain higher standards for health and safety in factories or because of tighter pollution controls. Administrative trade barriers are probably as important as other types of trade barriers, but their importance is much more difficult to assess. Also, like VERs, they are not subject to close scrutiny by the democratic process.

Compliance Costs

In addition to the enforcement costs, compliance costs are born by private individuals who must comply with the regulations. Initially, a firm must identify the tariffs and regulations its product is subject to, and this can be expensive in itself. Changing a product or its packaging to meet the regulations is also expensive, as is the preparation of documentation necessary for a good to enter a country. These costs may be significant and should not be ignored when discussing any actual trade policy.[17]

Summary of Main Points

Tariffs are taxes on traded goods. Tariffs reduce the welfare of a country by reducing the gains from trade. Although tariffs raise revenue for the government and producers of import substitutes benefit from tariff protection, the overall level of welfare falls because the loss to consumers is greater than the sum of the gain to producers and the revenue generated. When support of an industry is justified, tariff support is less desirable than support from **subsidies** that can be financed from general taxation, do not reduce the gains from trade, do not invite foreign retaliation, and provide support in a manner that allows public scrutiny. A tariff has similar effects to a consumption tax on a particular good, which is used to generate revenue and finance subsidies to producers of the same good. It would be surprising if the best way to raise revenue to finance a subsidy to an industry were to be a tax on consumers of the good that the industry produces.

A **quota** limits the quantity of a good that can be imported. Quotas and tariffs have similar effects on consumers and producers, but quotas do not normally raise as much revenue as tariffs. Instead, quotas generate profits for holders of quota licenses. If the license holders are domestic residents, tariffs and quotas are similar except that they have different effects on the distribution of income. If the license holders are foreign, quotas reduce national welfare more than tariffs.

---

[17]The Organization for Economic Co–Operation and Development (1985) cites studies showing that the average international transaction may require 35 documents and 360 copies, and cost in excess of 1 percent of the value of shipments. This cost is large when compared with the profit margins arising from international trade.

Non–tariff barriers include: quotas, **voluntary export restraints** (VERs) and **government procurement biases**. Also, policies that are not explicitly directed at international trade may affect the competitiveness of firms, for example, differences between **taxes** and **subsidies**, or **regulations** setting standards for such things as labeling, packaging, and health and safety in factories.

Study Questions

1. Briefly explain what is meant by:
    a. tariffs
    b. quotas
    c. voluntary export restraints
2. In what ways are a tariff and a quota similar and in what ways do they differ?
3. Evaluate the desirability of voluntary export restraints with reference to alternative policies to support domestic industries.
4. Using a diagram, show the welfare effects resulting from the imposition of a tariff.
5. Using diagrams, compare the welfare effects of tariffs and subsidies as alternative policies to achieve an increase in domestic production.
6. If a tariff were placed on imported steel, who would gain and who would lose? Would you expect the efficiency of the steel industry to improve in the long–run if it were given more protection?
7. Why do economists say that barriers to trade cause economic inefficiency?

Selected References

Baldwin, R. E., *Non–Tariff Distortions of International Trade*, Washington D.C.: Brookings Institution, 1970.

Corden, W. M., *Trade Policy and Economic Welfare*, Oxford, Oxford University Press, 1974.

Johnson, H. G., "The Standard Theory of Tariffs," *Canadian Journal of Economics and Political Science*, 2, August 1969, pp. 333–52.

Kelly, M., et al., *Issues and Developments in International Trade Policy*, International Monetary Fund Occasional Paper No. 63, Washington, D.C.: IMF, December 1988.

Michaely, M., *Theory of Commercial Policy*, Oxford: Phillip Allan 1977.

Organization for Economic Co–Operation and Development, *Costs and Benefits of Protection*, Paris: OECD, 1985.

Stern, R. M., "Tariffs and Other Measures of Trade Control: A Survey of Recent Developments," *Journal of Economic Literature*, 11, September 1973, pp. 857–88.

Five

Commercial Policy

Introduction

In this chapter we critically examine the arguments for protection. We shall see that most of the arguments do not stand up to close scrutiny. Although the discussion focuses on tariffs, it applies equally to non–tariff barriers. We also consider the effects of customs unions and effective protection.

Support for Domestic Industries

The Infant Industry

The oldest argument for tariff protection is the **infant industry argument**. It was advanced by Alexander Hamilton in 1791, writing about the need to protect early American industries from established industries in Europe. List writing in Germany in 1841 expanded on Hamilton's work. The argument is that young industries should be protected from international competition and allowed to grow and become efficient through experience, in other words, by learning by doing. Without protection, it is argued, output will be lower than it could be, or a new industry will not be able to become established.

The first problem that arises with infant industry tariffs is how to decide which industries should be protected. Since almost any industry will grow if protected, the potential for growth alone is not sufficient justification for protection. A more stringent criterion is called the **Bastable test**: in order for an industry to merit protection, an industry must grow and become so efficient that it will be able to compensate society for the losses incurred by society by protecting it through its infancy. (By way of analogy, an infant must be able to grow and earn enough to repay the costs of his or her education.) The benefits arising from the growth of an infant may go totally to firms within the industry, in which case they are said to be internal, or to people and firms outside the industry, in which case they are said to be external. These cases must be examined separately.

Internal Benefits

If the benefits are internal, and the industry is expected to become so efficient that protection is called for by the Bastable test, protection is unnecessary: the industry's expected future growth and future profitability will induce private investors to support it through its infancy. If private funds are not forthcoming, even though the industry is a good investment opportunity, the first step in considering a request for government intervention should be to decide why the private market is not willing to support the infant through the learning period. Having done this, steps can be taken to ensure that investment funds become available.

The reason why private funds are not forthcoming may be that investors do not believe the firm will grow. In this case, if the government has superior information, it could choose to make the information available and allow private investors to finance the growth of the industry and reap the rewards. Another possibility is for the government to make the investment more attractive to private investors by providing subsidized loans or a favorable treatment of investors. (This is often done for agriculture.) There are many policies that can be used to increase investment in an industry and that are preferable to protection. If attempts to encourage private investment were to fail, this would still not be a justification for tariff protection: the government could make the investment and reap the benefit on behalf of society.

It is worth remembering that the fact that the government believes an industry will grow is not sufficient reason for government intervention. There is little reason to believe that the government is any better at picking winners than the private market. But even if it is, this would not imply that supporting infant industries by tariffs is justified. It has been shown that tariffs are unnecessary and undesirable because other policies can be chosen that do not distort trade.

External Benefits

In the case of external benefits, the size of an industry may be suboptimal because investors in one firm do not take account of the benefits gained by other people. They consider their own private return, not the total return to society. For example, the development of a new production technique may be of benefit to society, but private investors will not provide funds to pay for the development of new techniques if the profits accrue to all firms. Patent law, which seeks to give producers sole rights over the use of a technology for a certain period, is one answer to this problem. Alternatively, research and development may be subsidized. Tariff protection is not justified under such circumstances. Protection would increase the returns to investors in the industry, and the industry would grow, but there is no guarantee that increased research and development would be undertaken. The reason is that the fundamental problem would remain: knowledge has characteristics that make if difficult for firms to maintain ownership of it.

Another argument based on the existence of external benefits is that when an infant industry grows, other industries benefit as well because workers and firms in the protected industry are customers of firms in other industries. There are two reasons why this is not a valid argument for tariff protection. First, the argument ignores the costs borne by consumers of the protected product. Second, it is likely that the growth of any industry will have some positive effects on other industries. Thus, the potential for external benefits is not by itself sufficient to justify protection.

Do Protected Infants Become Efficient?

Whether the benefits are internal or external, the infant industry argument is an argument for temporary protection. Eventually, the industry is supposed to become efficient. (The Bastable test incorporates this basic requirement.) In practice, one of the strongest arguments against tariff protection of an infant industry is that the protected infant has little incentive to grow up. When an industry is exempted from competitive pressure, why should it become more efficient? There is no need to reduce wages or adopt the most efficient technology when the industry is safe from competition. One of the benefits of trade is that competition from imports increases the efficiency of domestic production. This benefit is lost when industries are protected.

The reply to the infant industry argument can be summarized as follows. Infant industry arguments may be valid arguments for government intervention. However, tariffs are not justified in such cases because, even if intervention is justified, industries can be supported more efficiently through policies which maintain competitive pressures and do not distort trade.

Other Arguments for Protection

The infant industry argument is only one example of many arguments used to justify protection to support domestic industries. For example, it is argued that barriers to trade are justified to support industries needed for national security. Other examples of industries facing competition from imports that are often put forward as deserving cases include traditional craft–based industries, or industries that are important employers in particular areas of the country. It is usually claimed that protection is necessary to help these industries continue producing because they would otherwise be wiped out by cheap imports.

Such arguments assume that all firms are equally inefficient. It is true that competition from imports may force some inefficient firms to close, but this does not mean that a domestic industry will be wiped out. The better domestic firms may well prosper because resources, such as skilled labor, are released by the closure of inefficient firms, and with fewer domestic firms the sales of the efficient domestic firms can increase. Support for the remaining domestic firms may be unnecessary. However, the real weakness of the argument for support relates to the type of support proposed.

Although tariff protection certainly does help industries, it does so at an unnecessarily high cost to society. The same degree of support can be provided openly, and at a lower cost to society, through a subsidy. Tariffs are neither necessary nor desirable as a means of supporting domestic production. In general, the reasons given for supporting an industry are irrelevant and do not affect the validity of the argument against the use of tariffs as a means of giving support. Put simply, if an industry merits support, a tariff is not the best way to provide the support.

The Terms of Trade Argument

An argument for the use of tariffs by large countries can be made resting on a favorable change in the terms of trade. A rise in the terms of trade is an improvement because the country gets more imports for a given amount of exports. Tariffs may cause a beneficial movement in the terms of trade of sufficient size to outweigh the net cost arising from a less efficient allocation of resources. On the supply side, a similar case arises when a large country, or a group of countries, restricts its exports to force up the price as OPEC did with the price of oil in 1973 and 1979. Curtailing exports does not make sense unless the price of exports can be affected.

When a tariff is imposed, the fall in the country's demand for the imports leads to a reduced world demand for the product. If the country is large, the world price falls in response to the restricted demand, and the decline in the price of the import improves the country's terms of trade. In theory, it is possible for a country to receive an overall net gain when it imposes a tariff. To show this, let us consider an extreme case where the terms of trade improve by so great an amount when a tariff is imposed that domestic prices do not change.[1] Consumers and producers are unaffected if prices do not change, yet the country gains tariff revenue, so the country must have gained. If domestic prices rise by a small amount, the loss to consumers from the price increase will exceed the gain to producers.

---

[1]This is an extreme case which arises if the supply of imports is perfectly inelastic. In this case, a fall in the country's demand for imports (caused by a tariff) will lead to the same quantity of imports being supplied and consumed. The domestic price will remain unchanged because the price paid for imports will fall by the amount of the tariff. One can use offer curves to show this extreme case. When A imposes a tariff, its offer curve moves inward. If B's supply is perfectly inelastic, B's offer curve is flat over the relevant range, A's imports (B's exports) remain constant, while A's exports fall, and A's terms of trade improve.

However, the country may still gain because of the revenue effect, provided that the price rise is not too big.

The Welfare Effects of a Tariff for a Large Country

The possibility of a large country gaining from a tariff is shown in Figure 5.1. When a tariff is imposed the domestic price of imports rises from P_0 to P_1, the quantity imported falls from $QD_0 - QS_0$ to $QD_1 - QS_1$, and the world price

Figure 5.1
The Effects of Tariff Levied by a Large Country

The large country's demand and supply are shown by DD and SS, respectively. The initial price is P_0. When a tariff (t) is imposed, the domestic price rises from P_0 to P_1, the world price falls from P_0 to P_2, and the quantity of imports demanded falls from $QD_0 - QS_0$ to $QD_1 - QS_1$. Consumer surplus falls by P_0P_1ef, and producer surplus rises by P_0P_1ba, giving a net loss of $abef$ from the effects on producers and consumers. Tariff revenue of $gbeh$ is gained. Deducting $cbed$ from both $abef$ and $gbeh$ (because $cbed$ is common to both), the overall effect of the tariff is seen to depend on the relative sizes of $gcdh$ and the triangles abc and def.

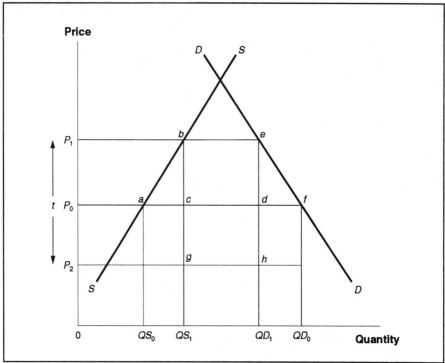

falls from P_0 to P_2. Consumer surplus falls by P_0P_1ef, and producer surplus rises by P_0P_1ba. The area *abef* represents the loss arising from the effects of the higher price on consumers and producers. In order to obtain the overall welfare effect, we must take tariff revenue into account. The country gains tariff revenue equal to *gbeh*. To help us compare the relative sizes of the areas representing the gain in tariff revenue (*gbeh*) and the loss to producers and consumers (*abef*), we can deduct *cbed* from both areas.[2] Doing this leaves a gain of *gcdh* and losses of *abc* and *def*. It is possible that the sum of *abc* and *def* is less than *gcdh*, and that a large country will gain from a tariff. If the domestic price does not change when the tariff is imposed, as in the above example, *abc* and *def* are zero; thus, the country clearly gains from a tariff. The more elastic the country's demand for imports, and the less elastic the foreign supply of the good, the more likely a gain from a tariff is.

Evaluating the Terms of Trade Argument

The terms of trade argument is only valid for large countries because small countries cannot affect world prices. However, even large countries cannot always expect to gain, because if other countries retaliate, a country may end up worse off than it was initially. Most economists believe that although the terms of trade argument is theoretically interesting, it is largely irrelevant for international economic policy because no single country has the necessary market power. Similarly, export quotas are only feasible if a significant portion of supply can be controlled. Although exporters may be able to influence prices in the short run by collusive agreements, experience casts doubt on their ability to do so in the long run.[3]

Unfair Competition

Dumping

Allegations of unfair competition are often made by groups who stand to gain from protection. One example of this type of argument for tariffs arises when goods are sold in foreign markets at a price below cost, a procedure

---

[2]In effect, *cbed* is a transfer of money from consumers to the government because the tariff forces consumers to pay a higher price for the good.

[3]Most collusive agreements between exporters of primary products have collapsed or become ineffective. The experience of the early 1980s showed that even the power of the Organization of Petroleum Exporting Countries (OPEC) to fix prices is not unlimited. See Chapter 14.

known as **dumping**. Dumping can take various forms, but allegations of two kinds are common: 1) the price of the good may be low because of a government subsidy; or 2) an exporting firm may attempt to establish a market, or take over a market completely, by charging a price below the cost of producing the good (**predatory dumping**). In both cases the problem created by dumping arises because the low price is not permanent. Firms in the affected market may go bankrupt, and then, when the foreign government subsidy is withdrawn, or the foreign firm's market share has increased, consumers are faced with higher prices. Clearly, bankrupting domestic firms for a short period of cheap imports is undesirable. (Note that foreign subsidies are not a problem if they are permanent: if foreign governments are kind enough to subsidize our imports, why should we not accept?)

The difficulty in evaluating dumping complaints lies in distinguishing between dumping and normal international competition. In the case of what appears to be predatory dumping, the foreign firm may simply be more efficient and able to sell at a lower price than domestic firms permanently. No producer likes to admit that foreign producers are more efficient, so allegations are often made that foreign producers receive an unfairly high degree of government support. Since the treatment afforded by governments to exporting firms inevitably differs, these allegations are usually difficult to prove or refute. However, cases do arise where the price of imports appears to be artificially low and cannot be expected to remain so. In these cases, since the problem arises from a temporarily low price for imports, the best solution may be to raise the price of imports by a temporary tariff. Permanent protection is not justified. Unfortunately, temporary protection has a way of becoming permanent.[4]

Cheap Labor

It is sometimes argued that foreign producers rely on cheap labor, hence tariffs should be used to prevent competition from these producers. This argument has been used often by critics of the North American Free Trade Agreement. There are two fundamental errors in this argument. First, the reasons why a good is produced at lower cost are irrelevant unless a possible case of dumping is being examined. If labor is cheap because of foreign coercion, there may be a moral argument for protection, but we should try

---

[4]There is another answer to the dumping argument: firms that fear short–run price volatility maybe able to protect themselves through the use of futures markets for their products, or by storing the product.

to keep moral arguments separate from economic arguments.[5] Provided that the supply of low–cost imports is likely to continue, there is no economic argument for protection. However, labor may be cheap because of a government subsidy, and in this case, if there is a danger that the subsidy will be removed and the price of imports will rise, an argument can be made for protection because this is an example of dumping.

The second error arises because it is forgotten that labor is only one of the inputs used in the production process: we do not hear the argument that tariffs should be applied because land is cheaper in one country than in another. If we used tariffs to make all goods cost the same by applying tariffs to offset differences in input prices, there would be no point in trade. Tariffs imposed to equalize costs are sometimes called **scientific tariffs**, a term suggesting a degree of rationality in their formulation. In fact, such tariffs would destroy world trade. International trade flourishes because of differences in the prices of goods, which are often caused by differences in input prices. Differences in input prices should be welcomed and not used as an excuse for protectionist measures.

Foreign Trade Practices

Foreign barriers to trade impede exports and result in lower domestic welfare. Such barriers are often cited as a justification for domestic barriers to imports. There are two weaknesses in the argument that tariffs should be imposed on imports from countries that have high trade barriers. First, the domestic economy gains from free trade even if other countries maintain trade barriers. Foreign barriers that reduce exports do reduce domestic welfare, but retaliating to foreign trade barriers by imposing domestic trade barriers reduces domestic welfare still further. Second, the argument ignores the possible effects on world trade. All countries restrict trade, but they do so in different ways. If each country were to increase barriers whenever foreign barriers exceeded domestic barriers, there would be a global increase in trade barriers and welfare would fall. There may be a case for threatening to impose tariffs unless foreign markets are opened up, but if negotiations fail and domestic tariffs are used, the result is undesirable. Therefore, foreign trade practices are seldom likely to be a justification for domestic trade barriers.

A related argument is that trade barriers should be imposed when imports from one country exceed exports to that country. Each country trades with many other countries and there is no need for trade between two

---

[5]This does not mean that moral arguments should be ignored when commercial policy is formulated. Perhaps through careful use of trade sanctions, some countries can be induced to change their behavior.

countries to balance: a country may import more from one country than it exports to it, but it will often export more to other countries than it imports from them. Tariffs that sought to balance trade between areas would lead to retaliation and the welfare of all countries would fall.

The Petition of the Candlemakers

Frederic Bastiat, a French economist, ridiculed the protectionist position in "The Petition of the Candlemakers." He based his fictitious case on the unfair competition argument and on the external benefits argument. Even today, after 150 years, his satirical parody resembles modern arguments for protection.

> "We are subjected to the intolerable competition of a foreign rival, who enjoys, it would seem, such superior facilities for the production of light, that he is enabled to inundate our national market at so exceedingly reduced a price, that, the moment he makes his appearance, he draws off all custom for us; and thus an important branch of French industry, with all its innumerable ramifications, is suddenly reduced to a state of complete stagnation. The rival is no other than the sun.
>
> Our petition is, that it would please your honorable body to pass a law whereby shall be directed the shutting up of all windows, dormers, skylights, shutters, curtains, in a word, all openings, holes, chinks, and fissures through which the light of the sun is used to penetrate into our dwellings, to the prejudice of the profitable manufactures which we flatter ourselves we have been enabled to bestow upon the country; which country cannot, therefore, without ingratitude, leave us now to struggle unprotected through so unequal a contest.
>
> We foresee your objections, gentlemen; but there is not one that you can oppose to us which you will not be obliged to gather from the works of the partisans of free trade. We dare challenge you to pronounce one word against our petition. . . .
>
> Do you tell us, that if we gain by this protection, France will not gain because the consumer must pay the price of it?
>
> We answer you: You no longer have any right to cite the interest of the consumer. For whenever this has been found to compete with that of the producer, you have invariably sacrificed the first. You have done this to encourage labor, to increase the demand for labor. The same reason should now induce you to act in the same manner. . . ."

In support of his case, Bastiat used the benefits that would accrue to other sectors of French society, saying that the candlemakers will "buy large quantities of tallow, coals, oil, resin, wax, alcohol, silver, iron, bronze, crystal, for the supply of our business; and then we and our numerous contractors having become rich our consumption will be great, and will become a means of contributing to the comfort and competency of the workers in every branch of national labor."[6]

The Balance of Trade, Income, and Unemployment

The **balance of trade** is the difference between the values of exports and imports. The balance of trade effect tends to be positive because of the import effect, that is, imports of the good bearing the tariff will decrease. However, there are five reasons why we might expect the overall effect on the balance of trade to be less than the import effect. First, if the United States were to impose tariffs, other countries might retaliate by imposing tariffs on American exports. Second, unless there are unemployed resources, an increase in domestic production in the import–competing sector will attract resources away from other sectors, including the export sector. Thus, exports may be harmed. Third, as the import–competing sector expands, it will use more inputs. Some of the inputs may be imported or incorporate imported materials. Fourth, if tariffs are applied to a narrow range of goods, or imports from particular countries, consumers may switch from one imported good to another imported good rather than to a domestically produced good. Finally, under flexible exchange rates, a reduction in the demand for imports will tend to increase the value of the dollar, and reduce the competitiveness of exports.[7]

Even if the balance of trade effect is significant, tariffs are not usually a suitable policy for increasing the balance of trade. Selective policies, such as barriers to trade, inevitably single out some groups of people for special treatment. This may be viewed as an advantage; for example, imports can be reduced by penalizing consumers of imported luxuries. However, this attribute can also be viewed as a disadvantage in that some people are discriminated against because their economic freedom is reduced. Many considerations are relevant to whether it is ever justifiable to single out particular groups for special treatment. These might include one's own political views, the economic problems of the country, which groups gain or lose, the nature of the good, and so on. However, one generalization is valid:

---

[6]Abridged from, Frederic Bastiat, *Economic Sophisms*, New York: G.P. Putnam's Sons, New York, 1922.

[7]The relationship between trade and the exchange rate is discussed in Chapter 6.

selective policies are likely to be less effective than general policies, for instance, devaluation or lower government spending, simply because selective policies affect fewer people than general policies.

The Danger of a Collapse of World Trade

To the extent that there is a favorable balance of trade effect, tariffs tend to switch domestic demand from imports to domestic goods and increase the demand for domestic goods. Therefore, tariffs are likely to be popular when there is domestic unemployment. Unfortunately, tariffs do not cure unemployment so much as export it, because unemployment is created in the foreign country's export sector. The foreign country will face increased pressure from some of its own producers to impose tariffs, and it may well do so. This may create unemployment in the export sector of the country that initially imposed the tariff.

During world recessions there is a very real danger that countries will attempt to solve their domestic unemployment problems at the expense of other countries. If this happens, the level of world trade will fall and everyone will be worse off. Although some economists feel that tariffs are useful in certain special circumstances, there is general agreement that an escalation of trade barriers should be avoided. Also, once tariffs are in place, their removal will probably be opposed by the people they benefit; introducing tariffs may be easier than removing them.

Alternative Ways to Increase Unemployment

Tariffs are not the only type of policy that influences unemployment. If unemployment is common throughout all sectors of the economy, there is normally a better policy available, at least for developed countries. General policies, such as reducing taxes or increasing government spending, have more widespread effects, do not disrupt trade, and do not invite foreign retaliation. If unemployment is a problem in particular sectors, policies such as investment subsidies or retraining grants may be helpful. The argument against tariffs to increase employment in particular sectors was given in Chapter 5: barriers to trade reduce welfare and are unnecessary because the same employment effects can be obtained by a more efficient policy, such as production subsidies.

Figure 5.2
The Effects of a Customs Union

Initially a country has a nondiscriminatory tariff and imports $QD_0 - QS_0$ from C at \$35 (\$20 plus a 75% tariff). When A and B form a customs union, A imports $QD_1 - QS_1$ from B at \$30. Consumer surplus increases by P_1P_0be, and producer surplus falls by P_1P_0af, thus the gain from the combined effect on producers and consumers equals the area *fabe*. Tariff revenue of *dabc* is lost. Therefore, the net effect of the formation of the customs union is determined by the relative sizes of *fabe* (a gain) and *dabc* (a loss).

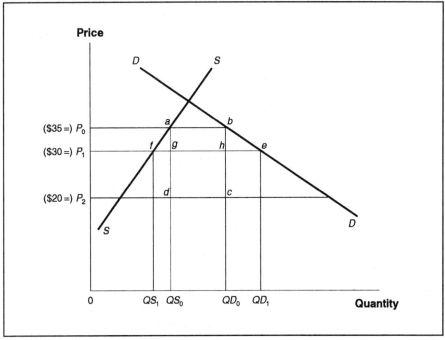

Customs Unions

In a **customs union** there is free trade between the members, and a common tariff barrier is maintained for imports from nonmember countries.[8] The formation of a customs union may seem a step toward free trade, and as such, something which should be welcomed because it will increase welfare. Unfortunately, the truth is a little more complicated. Although trade between members is liberalized, the common tariff adopted may be the highest of the

---

[8]The policies of the European Union (EU) include a customs union agreement. This and other policies of the EU are discussed in Chapter 17.

members' pre–union tariffs because each country resists a lowering of its own tariffs when a customs union is formed. This would not be a step toward freer trade. Even if the average level of union tariffs is not significantly higher than the pre–union rates of the members, the discrimination against nonmembers entailed in a customs union agreement may be a source of inefficiency.

The economic effects of the formation of a customs union are shown in Figure 5.2. There are three countries—A, B, and C. Countries B and C sell a good (X) for $30 and $20, respectively. Initially, A has a nondiscriminatory tariff of 75 percent, and imports $QD_0 - QS_0$ from country C at a cost of $35. If country A forms a customs union with country B, imports from country B can enter freely, but imports from country C still bear a tariff of 75 percent. Country A will import $QD_1 - QS_1$ from country B at a cost of $30.

Trade Creation and Trade Diversion

Country B is a higher cost producer than country C, and the only reason that country A imports from country B is that there is unequal tariff treatment of countries B and C. A shift in production from a low–cost source to a high–cost source is called **trade diversion**, and it leads to lower economic efficiency. The displacement of imports from country C by imports from country B is an example of trade diversion. A shift in production from a high–cost source to a low–cost source is called **trade creation**, and it leads to an increase in economic efficiency. The displacement of domestic production by lower–cost imports, shown in the diagram by the movement from QS_0 to QS_1, is an example of trade creation. The abolition of all tariffs would increase welfare because there would be trade creation and no trade diversion.

The Welfare Effects of Customs Unions

The effect of a customs union on welfare can be derived by adding together the effects on consumers, producers, and tariff revenue. The fall in price $P_0 - P_1$ leads to an increase in consumer surplus of P_1P_0 be and a (smaller) fall in producer surplus of P_1P_0 af. Before the union, country A received tariff revenue on imports from country C, but after the union, country A's imports from B do not generate revenue. The loss of tariff revenue is shown in the diagram by the area of the rectangle *dabc*. A customs union between countries A and B will lead to an increase in welfare if the area of the trapezoid *fabe* is greater than the area of the rectangle *dabc*, that is, if the gain to consumers minus the loss to producers is greater than the loss of tariff revenue. The more elastic are demand and supply, and the smaller is the price difference between the partner country and the most efficient producer, the more likely it is that a customs union will increase welfare.[9]

What the overall effect on country A will be we cannot say. Even if country A gains, whether world welfare is increased depends on the effects of the union on countries B and C. The ambiguity arises because a trade agreement that leads to free trade between some countries but excludes other countries is not a clear step toward free trade. The effect on nonmembers is generally negative because they face a common external tariff and cannot compete on equal terms with firms inside the customs union.

So far we have only considered the short–run effects of customs unions. The long–run effects are more difficult to quantify but are potentially much more important. As a result of the removal of tariffs between members, competition between firms within the union will increase as firms look beyond their home markets to markets in other member countries. This competition between firms within the union may lead to significant gains in efficiency. Also, as firms expand and produce for a larger market, economies of scale may be enjoyed. Finally, there may be an inflow of foreign investment from foreign firms wishing to avoid the common external tariff by producing within the customs union. These long–run effects will increase the welfare of members of the customs union.[10]

Effective Protection

Tariffs may be applied to goods that are used as inputs by domestic producers. If domestic producers have to pay more than world prices for imported inputs because of these tariffs, they will be at a competitive disadvantage relative to foreign producers. However, domestic producers benefit if tariffs are levied on the goods they produce. For example, a tariff on imported steel will worsen the competitive position of domestic automobile producers relative to foreign producers who can use lower–cost steel, but a tariff on imported cars will benefit domestic automobile producers.

---

[9]Since *gabh* is part of *fabe* and *dabc*, we can deduct *gabh* from both, in which case a customs union is beneficial if $(fag + hbe) > dghc$.

[10]These long–run benefits were important in persuading members of the European Community to go beyond the removal of tariffs by eliminating other barriers to trade in an attempt to create a single European market. The case for the single market is described in P. Cecchini, *The European Challenge, 1992, The Benefits of a Single Market*, Aldershot, England: Wildwood House, 1988. Critics of the policy claim that it is becoming difficult for firms outside the Community to compete with firms within the market, and they have dubbed the policy "Fortress Europe."

Calculating Effective Protection

The **effective rate of protection** is a measure of the overall degree of protection given to domestic producers, taking into account the tariffs levied on inputs and the tariff on the final good. The formula for calculating the effective rate of protection (e_t) when there is one input is:

$$e_t = (T - at)/(1 - a)$$

where T is the tariff on the final good, t is the tariff on the input, and a is the cost of the input as a fraction of the cost of the final good. If T is equal to t, the effective rate of protection is equal to the **nominal rate of protection** (the rate on the final good). If T is larger than t, the effective rate of protection is greater than the nominal rate of protection. If T is smaller than t, the effective rate of protection is less than the nominal rate of protection. It is quite possible for the effective rate of protection to be negative if T is small and t is large. (The example given of automobile producers being adversely affected by a tariff on steel is an example where e_t is negative, because T = 0 and $t > 0$.)

Value Added and Effective Protection

An understanding of what is meant by **value added** is necessary for us to understand the concept of effective protection more fully. Value added is the difference between the value of a final product and the cost of inputs used in its production. When the price of the final good rises relative to the cost of the inputs, value added rises. Domestic producers benefit from tariffs on the final products because their value added rises when the price of the final product rises. However, because domestic producers are only responsible for part of the value of the good, their value added increases by a larger percentage than the tariff. For example, if a domestic producer is responsible for half of the value of a good, and the good rises in price by 10 percent, the value added of the producer rises by 20 percent, providing that the quantity and prices of the inputs remain the same.[11] The effective rate of protection is a measure of the increase in value added per unit caused by a tariff structure. This is the reason that the effective and nominal rates of protection can differ.

---

[11]Assume that a good costs $100 and the cost of inputs is $50. If the price increases by $10, value added increases by $10, that is, the value added increases by 20 percent (from $50 to $60).

An Example of Effective Protection

Let us assume that a domestic producer of bicycles uses imported tubing, the bicycles retail for $400, and the tubing costs $300. The producer's value added is $100 under free trade. If a 30 percent tariff is imposed on bicycles and no tariff is imposed on tubing, the effective rate of protection is:

$$e_t = (30\% - 0.75 \times 0)/(1 - 0.75) = 120\%$$

The price of bicycles is $520 after the tariff, thus the producer's value added is $220. The effective rate of protection is 120 percent because the value added rises by 120 percent. Let us assume that the 30 percent tariff on bicycles is retained, and consider the effects of a tariff on tubing. A 30 percent tariff imposed on imported tubing will result in an effective rate of protection equal to 30 percent. However, if the tariff on tubing is 40 percent, the effective rate of protection is zero. If the tariff on tubing exceeds 40 percent, the effective rate of protection will be negative. In the last case, the producer would be better off under free trade.

The Importance of Effective Protection

The concept of effective protection is useful when analyzing commercial policy. For example, in tariff negotiations, by reducing tariffs on inputs more than tariffs on final goods, countries can claim to be liberalizing trade while actually increasing effective protection. It is difficult to compare levels of protection in different countries because ideally we would want to examine effective rates of protection, not just nominal rates. In practice, tariffs often increase as a percentage of the value of goods, the nearer the goods are to the final stage of production. This is not surprising if, as seems likely, domestic producers bargain for positive effective protection. Tariff escalation is seen by some less–developed countries as a barrier to their development. They argue that the growth of their manufacturing sectors (which have the potential to export to developed countries) is prevented because developed countries' markets are protected by "high" rates of effective protection.

Tariff escalation was a concern in the last GATT agreement, the Uruguay round.[12] Table 5.1 shows the tariffs before and after this agreement for a number of product categories which are important to developing countries. Notice that the tariffs are often higher on manufactured goods than on raw materials. This escalation results in higher effective rates of effective protection for manufacturers in developed countries than is suggested by the tariff on the finished product. Table 5.2 shows some examples of how the

---

[12]The Uruguay round is discussed in Chapter 15.

**Table 5.1
Tariff Escalation in Selected Product Categories
Before and After the Uruguay Round**

Product Category by Stage of Processing	Weighted Average		
	Pre	Post	Reduction
Hides, skins and leather			
Raw	0.1	0.1	0
Semi–manufacturers	4.6	3.6	22
Finished products	8.7	7.0	20
Rubber			
Raw	0.1	0.0	100
Semi–manufactures	5.5	3.3	40
Finished products	5.1	3.6	30
Wood			
Wood in the rough	0.0	0.0	0
Wood based panels	9.4	6.5	31
Semi–manufactures	0.9	0.4	50
Wood articles	4.7	1.6	67
Paper			
Pulp and waste	0.0	0.0	0
Paper and paperboard	5.3	0.0	100
Printed material	1.7	0.3	83
Paper articles	7.3	0.0	100
Jute			
Fibers	0	0	0
Yarns	5.4	0.1	98
Fabrics	5.7	3.2	43
Copper			
Unwrought	0.9	0.7	30
Semi–manufactures	4.3	3.1	28
Finished products	1.7	1.2	29
Nickel			
Unwrought	0.5	0.3	40
Semi–manufactures	2.6	1.0	63
Aluminum			
Unwrought	0.5	0.3	40
Semi–manufactures	5.9	4.8	17
Lead			
Unwrought	2.4	1.3	45
Semi–manufactures	4.5	2.8	37
Zinc			
Unwrought	2.1	1.8	17
Semi–manufactures	4.7	2.9	38
Tin			
Unwrought	0.1	0.0	100
Semi–manufactures	3.9	1.8	53
Tobacco			
Unmanufactured	14.7	11.5	22
Manufactured	22.1	9.2	58

Source: GATT, Increases in Market Access Resulting from the Uruguay Round, News of the Uruguay Round, April 1994, p. 14.

Table 5.2
Escalation of Tariff Protection by Stage of Processing in the EEC, Japan, and the United States

Production Process	EEC		Japan		United States	
	Nominal	Effective	Nominal	Effective	Nominal	Effective
Groundnut oil						
Groundnuts, green	0.0	—	0.0	—	18.2	—
Groundnut oil, crude and cake	7.5	92.9	7.6	93.7	18.4	24.6
Groundnut oil, refined	15.0	186.4	10.1	324.8	22.0	64.9
Paper and paper products						
Logs, rough	0.0	—	0.0	—	0.0	—
Wood pulp	1.6	2.5	5.0	10.7	0.0	−0.5
Paper and paper articles	13.1	30.2	5.9	17.6	5.3	12.8
Wood products						
Logs rough	0.0	—	0.0	—	0.0	—
Sawn wood	1.9	4.9	0.7	2.0	0.0	0.0
Wood manufactures	7.4	10.7	9.8	15.3	7.4	8.4
Dairy products						
Fresh milk and cream	16.0	—	0.0	—	6.5	—
Condensed and evaporated milk	21.3	44.3	31.7	154.8	10.7	30.1
Cheese	23.0	58.8	35.3	175.6	11.5	34.5
Butter	21.0	76.6	45.0	418.5	10.3	46.7
Wool fabrics						
Raw wool	0.0	—	0.0	—	21.2	—
Wool yarn	5.4	16.0	5.0	9.3	30.7	62.2
Wool fabrics	14.0	32.9	14.7	35.1	46.9	90.8
Cotton fabrics						
Raw cotton	0.0	—	0.0	—	6.1	—
Cotton yard	7.0	22.8	8.1	25.8	8.3	12.0
Cotton fabrics	13.6	29.7	7.2	34.9	15.6	30.7
Leather products						
Bovine hides	0.0	—	0.0	—	0.0	—
Leather	7.0	21.4	6.2	20.2	17.8	57.4
Leather goods excluding shoes	7.1	10.3	10.5	15.8	22.4	32.5
Jute products						
Raw jute	0.0	—	0.0	—	0.1	—
Jute fabrics	21.1	57.8	20.0	54.8	0.0	−0.9
Jute sacks and bags	15.3	9.8	34.3	75.2	2.8	7.3
Palm kernel oil						
Palm nuts, kernels	0.0	—	0.0	—	0.0	—
Palm kernel oil, crude and cake	7.0	87.1	6.4	79.1	4.2	52.3
Palm kernel oil, refined	14.0	195.9	8.0	79.2	3.4	6.1
Chocolate						
Cocoa beans	5.4	—	0.0	—	0.0	—
Cocoa powder and butter	13.6	76.0	15.0	125.0	2.6	22.0
Chocolate products	12.0	−6.8	30.6	36.3	5.7	10.3

Source: A. J. Yeats, "Effective Tariff Protection in the United States, the European Community, and Japan," *Quarterly Review of Economics and Business*, 14, Summer 1974, p. 47. Reproduced with permission of the publisher: Bureau of Economic and Business Research, College of Commerce and Business Administration, University of Illinois.

nominal and effective rates of protection varied across stages of production (for an earlier period). As the goods move toward the final stages of production, the nominal rate of protection increases, and as a result, the effective rate of protection increases at each stage of production.

Summary of Main Points

The **infant industry argument** is one of the oldest arguments for tariff protection of industries. The argument is that protection allows new industries to grow and become efficient. Arguments have also been made for protection of industries that are major employers or for industries that are needed for national security. These are not valid arguments for tariff protection because, even though government support of some industries may be justified, tariffs are less efficient than subsidies as a way of providing this support.

The **terms of trade argument** for tariffs is that if a large country imposes a tariff, the fall in the country's demand for the import may cause the world price of the good to fall. If so, it is possible that there will be an overall increase in the welfare of the country when the gain from the improvement in the terms of trade is taken into consideration. This argument is theoretically valid but has little practical significance because single countries do not usually dominate the world market for particular products.

Allegations of unfair competition are often made by groups that will benefit from protection. In general, such arguments do not justify the use of tariffs because the economic benefits from access to cheap imports do not depend on why the goods are cheap. A possible exception arises in the case of **dumping**, where firms are charging an artificially low price that cannot be expected to remain low. The problem with dumping is that the supply of low–cost imports is not permanent. In such cases, temporary protection may be justified. However, in assessing cases of alleged dumping, it is often difficult to ensure that allegations of dumping are not attempts to restrict normal international competition.

Tariffs raise the domestic price of imports and lead to a fall in the consumption of imported goods. This effect leads some economists to suggest that tariffs can be used to switch domestic demand from imports to domestic goods, increasing the balance of trade, domestic income, and employment. This argument is often overstated because it does not take into account the effects of tariffs on other sectors of the economy, in particular the export sector. Also, importantly, there is the danger that other countries will retaliate and the country will end up worse off.

Countries forming a **customs union** agree to eliminate tariffs on trade between members of the group and the establishment of a common external tariff on imports from nonmember countries. The effect on the welfare of the members may be positive or negative. To the extent that trade between members increases and production moves from member countries with high costs to member countries with low costs, the welfare of members will increase.

The **effective rate of protection** measures the protection given to an industry taking into account tariffs levied on products that it uses. It is possible for the effective rate of protection to be positive or negative. In practice, the tariffs of developed countries give domestic industries positive rates of effective protection, and this may act as a barrier to exports of manufactured goods from developing countries.

Study Questions

1. Explain the assertion that the infant industry argument may justify government intervention but does not justify tariff support.
2. If the United States were to impose a tariff on imported oil, why might the fall in welfare per head of population be smaller than if the same policy were enacted by a small country like Luxembourg? (Assume that the only significant difference between the two countries is their size.)
3. What is dumping? What problems are there in identifying cases of dumping that merit the use of tariffs?
4. Distinguish between the nominal and effective rates of protection. Comment on the importance of the concept of effective protection.
5. The composition of value added (under free trade) in American bicycle manufacturing is as follows:

Cost of imported steel tubing	$100
American value added	$100
Total Price	$200

   a. What is the effective rate of protection given by a 10 percent tariff on imported steel tubing when there is no tariff on bicycles?
   b. What is the effective rate of protection given by a 10 percent tariff on both imported steel tubing and imported bicycles?
   c. What is the effective rate of protection given by a 10 percent tariff on imported bicycles when there is no tariff on steel tubing?
6. Draw a diagram showing the welfare effects from the imposition of a tariff by a large country. Using the diagram, explain why a large country may gain when it imposes a tariff.

7. Define trade creation and trade diversion. Draw a diagram showing the welfare effects from the formation of a customs union. Using the diagram, explain how a customs union will reduce members' welfare if trade diversion exceeds trade creation.

8. The cost of producing butter in Britain is as follows:

Quantity (million of pounds)	Cost (pence per pound)
1	50
2	100
3	150
4	200
5	250
6	300

Butter is available in unlimited amounts from New Zealand at 100 pence per pound and from France at 150 pence per pound. Initially, Britain has a nondiscriminatory tariff of 100 percent, and consumes 5 million pounds.
   a. Where is the butter that Britain consumes produced?
   b. Britain forms a customs union with France, retains a 100 percent tariff on imports from New Zealand, and continues to consume 5 million pounds. What is the new pattern of trade?
   c. How are trade creation and trade diversion illustrated by this example?

9. In the long-run, tariffs are more likely to increase than decrease unemployment. Discuss.

10. If a country faces unfair trade practices, should it retaliate by using tariffs itself?

Selected References

Adams, J., (ed.), *Tariffs, Quotas, and Trade: The Politics of Protectionism*, San Francisco: Institute for Contemporary Studies, 1979.

Baldwin, R. E. and A. O. Krueger, *The Structure and Evolution of Recent U.S. Trade Policy*, Chicago: University of Chicago Press, 1984.

Bastiat, F., *Economic Sophisms*, New York: G. P. Putnam's Sons, New York, 1922.

Bhagwati, J. N., "The Generalized Theory of Distortions and Welfare," in J. N. Bhagwati et al., (eds.), *Trade, Balance of Payments and Growth*, pp. 69–90, Amsterdam: North Holland, 1971.

Corden, W. M., *The Theory of Protection*, Oxford: Oxford University Press, 1971.

Corden, W. M., *Trade Policy and Economic Welfare*, Oxford: Oxford University Press, 1974.

Grubel, H. G., "Effective Tariff Protection: A Non–specialist Guide to the Theory, Policy, and Controversies," in R. E. Baldwin and J. D. Richardson, (eds.), *International Trade and Finance*, Boston: Little Brown, 1974.

Johnson, H. G., "Optimal Trade Intervention in the Presence of Domestic Distortions," in R. E. Baldwin, et al., (eds.), *Trade Growth and the Balance of Payments*, pp. 3–34, Amsterdam: North Holland, 1965.

Johnson, H. G., "A New View of the Infant Industry Argument," in I. A. McDougall and R. H. Snape, (eds.), *Studies in International Economics*, Amsterdam: North Holland, 1970.

Krauss, M. B., "Recent Developments in Customs Union Theory: An Interpretative Survey," *Journal of Economic Literature*, 10, June 1972, pp. 413–36.

Yeager, L. and D. G. Tuerck, *Foreign Trade and U.S. Policy: The Case for Free International Trade*, New York: Praeger, 1976.

Part Two

Exchange Rates, The Balance of Payments, and Open–Economy Macroeconomics

Six

Foreign Exchange Markets

Introduction

An **exchange rate** defines the value of one currency relative to another and allows us to convert prices expressed in one currency into prices in another currency. Exchange rates are important because they determine the relationship between the domestic and foreign prices of goods, services, and assets. Changes in the exchange rate can affect the flows of goods, services, and capital between countries.

In this chapter we examine the foreign exchange market and the determination of exchange rates. Two exchange rates are considered in detail: the spot rate and the forward rate. Both are determined by demand and supply. In order to understand the determination of exchange rates and why exchange rates change, we examine why people buy and sell foreign currency.

Exchange Rates and the Foreign Exchange Market

The foreign exchange market is the largest market in the world; the daily turnover is now about one trillion dollars per day. We refer to a single market (even though the market is based in many centers around the world) because the centers are so closely linked that at any time there is a single world price for a currency. The countries with the highest average daily turnovers in 1992 were: the United Kingdom ($300 billion), the United States ($192 billion), and Japan ($126 billion).

The reason that the United Kingdom (London) has the highest market share is that most of London's business is with people in other countries, not domestic residents. As a result, sterling transactions account for less than a quarter of London's business. In fact, London accounts for a higher percentage of the market in dollars (26 percent) than the United States (18 percent), and a higher percentage of the market for deutsche marks (27 percent) than Germany (10 percent).[1] Other centers include: Singapore, Switzerland, Hong Kong, Singapore, and Germany. Trading continues 24 hours a day because as markets close, other markets to the west open up.

---

[1]Bank for International Settlements (1993), p. 15.

Spot and Forward Defined

Foreign exchange may be purchased **spot** or **forward**. When a spot transaction is made, the delivery of the currency is taken at the time of purchase. Spot transactions are the type of foreign exchange transactions most people are familiar with. For example, the purchase of foreign exchange at an airport or a bank is a spot transaction. Spot transactions account for about just under half the turnover of the foreign exchange market. Forward transactions are now a very close second.

When a **forward transaction** is made, a price is fixed for a delivery date some time in the future. Once a forward contract is agreed upon, the price of the foreign currency in that contract remains the same regardless of what happens to the spot exchange rate. (Penalty clauses ensure that the contract is honored.) Forward contracts may be negotiated for various dates in the future. Most contracts are for periods up to one year, although contracts are available for much longer periods.[2]

Published Exchange Rates

Table 6.1 is a facsimile of the table of exchange rates published by *The Wall Street Journal*. Although nearly every independent country has its own currency, only the rates of the currencies of the most important trading nations are usually quoted.[3] Note that the rates of exchange quoted are for amounts of $1 million or more. The exchange rates quoted are similar to wholesale prices; the price for purchases of foreign exchange is higher for small amounts.

The spot and forward exchange rates are shown in two forms: as the number of dollars per unit of foreign currency, and as the number of units

---

[2]There are also **futures** and **options** markets in foreign currencies, but together they only account for about 6 percent of the market. Futures contracts are traded on futures markets, for example the International Money Market in Chicago. In order to facilitate trading, futures contracts are available for standardized amounts (about $50,000, depending on the currency) and expire on particular dates, for example the third Wednesday of March, June, September, or December. In contrast, forward contracts are for much larger minimum amounts, say over $5 million, and the date is fixed according to the needs of the customer. Speculators are major users of the futures market. In a sense, forward contracts are tailor made and futures contracts are "off the peg." Options in foreign exchange resemble other financial options; they are a right to buy or sell, not an obligation. Naturally, the cost of buying an option is much higher than the cost of futures or forward contracts.

[3]Not all independent countries have their own currency. For example, Belgium and Luxembourg use the same currency, the franc, while retaining separate governments.

Table 6.1

CURRENCY TRADING

EXCHANGE RATES

Friday, November 4, 1994
The New York foreign exchange selling rates below apply to trading among banks in amounts of $1 million and more, as quoted at 3 p.m. Eastern time by Bankers Trust Co., Dow Jones Telerate Inc. and other sources. Retail transactions provide fewer units of foreign currency per dollar.

Country	U.S. $ equiv. Fri.	Thurs.	Currency per U.S. $ Fri.	Thurs.
Argentina (Peso)	1.01	1.01	.99	.99
Australia (Dollar)	.7510	.7425	1.3316	1.3468
Austria (Schilling)	.09365	.09352	10.68	10.69
Bahrain (Dinar)	2.6539	2.6539	.3768	.3768
Belgium (Franc)	.03207	.03201	31.18	31.24
Brazil (Real)	1.1848341	1.1848341	.84	.84
Britain (Pound)	1.6145	1.6155	.6194	.6190
30-Day Forward	1.6137	1.6147	.6197	.6193
90-Day Forward	1.6129	1.6139	.6200	.6196
180-Day Forward	1.6098	1.6108	.6212	.6208
Canada (Dollar)	.7369	.7357	1.3570	1.3592
30-Day Forward	.7369	.7357	1.3571	1.3593
90-Day Forward	.7371	.7359	1.3566	1.3588
180-Day Forward	.7365	.7353	1.3578	1.3600
Czech. Rep. (Koruna)				
Commercial rate	.0362345	.0363702	27.5980	27.4950
Chile (Peso)	.002501	.002501	399.77	399.77
China (Renminbi)	.115221	.115221	8.6790	8.6790
Colombia (Peso)	.001194	.001194	837.21	837.21
Denmark (Krone)	.1684	.1680	5.9389	5.9522
Ecuador (Sucre)				
Floating rate	.000442	.000442	2265.01	2265.01
Finland (Markka)	.21430	.21409	4.6662	4.6709
France (Franc)	.19231	.19194	5.2000	5.2100
30-Day Forward	.19225	.19188	5.2016	5.2116
90-Day Forward	.19231	.19194	5.2000	5.2100
180-Day Forward	.19237	.19200	5.1982	5.2082
Germany (Mark)	.6596	.6583	1.5160	1.5190
30-Day Forward	.6596	.6583	1.5160	1.5190
90-Day Forward	.6604	.6591	1.5143	1.5173
180-Day Forward	.6617	.6604	1.5113	1.5143
Greece (Drachma)	.004283	.004273	233.50	234.05
Hong Kong (Dollar) ...	.12937	.12937	7.7300	7.7300
Hungary (Forint)	.0092533	.0092920	108.0700	107.6200
India (Rupee)	.03211	.03211	31.14	31.14
Indonesia (Rupiah)	.0004606	.0004606	2171.03	2171.03
Ireland (Punt)	1.5996	1.5974	.6252	.6260
Israel (Shekel)	.3298	.3298	3.0320	3.0320
Italy (Lira)	.0006429	.0006410	1555.43	1560.01

Country	U.S. $ equiv. Fri.	Thurs.	Currency per U.S. $ Fri.	Thurs.
Japan (Yen)	.010251	.010230	97.55	97.75
30-Day Forward	.010274	.010253	97.33	97.53
90-Day Forward	.010336	.010315	96.75	96.95
180-Day Forward	.010424	.010403	95.93	96.13
Jordan (Dinar)	1.4767	1.4767	.6772	.6772
Kuwait (Dinar)	3.3681	3.3681	.2969	.2969
Lebanon (Pound)	.000602	.000602	1661.00	1661.00
Malaysia (Ringgit)	.3902	.3905	2.5630	2.5607
Malta (Lira)	2.8169	2.8169	.3550	.3550
Mexico (Peso)				
Floating rate	.2920134	.2913328	3.4245	3.4325
Netherland (Guilder) ..	.5885	.5873	1.6992	1.7028
New Zealand (Dollar) .	.6193	.6150	1.6147	1.6260
Norway (Krone)	.1512	.1508	6.6128	6.6312
Pakistan (Rupee)	.0327	.0327	30.58	30.58
Peru (New Sol)	.4591	.4591	2.18	2.18
Philippines (Peso)	.04065	.04065	24.60	24.60
Poland (Zloty)	.00004291	.00004324	23304.00	23128.00
Portugal (Escudo)	.006461	.006438	154.77	155.32
Saudi Arabia (Riyal) ..	.26667	.26667	3.7500	3.7500
Singapore (Dollar)	.6803	.6800	1.4700	1.4705
Slovak Rep. (Koruna) .	.0324675	.0324675	30.8000	30.8000
South Africa (Rand)				
Commercial rate	.2842	.2851	3.5185	3.5078
Financial rate	.2442	.2445	4.0950	4.0901
South Korea (Won)	.0012567	.0012549	795.75	796.90
Spain (Peseta)	.007921	.007905	126.25	126.50
Sweden (Krona)	.1367	.1358	7.3177	7.3634
Switzerland (Franc) ...	.7890	.7877	1.2675	1.2695
30-Day Forward	.7898	.7885	1.2662	1.2682
90-Day Forward	.7921	.7909	1.2624	1.2644
180-Day Forward	.7955	.7943	1.2570	1.2590
Taiwan (Dollar)	.038388	.038388	26.05	26.05
Thailand (Baht)	.04011	.04011	24.93	24.93
Turkey (Lira)	.0000277	.0000278	36118.01	35984.01
United Arab (Dirham)	.2723	.2723	3.6725	3.6725
Uruguay (New Peso)				
Financial	.185874	.185874	5.38	5.38
Venezuela (Bolivar) ...	.00590	.00590	169.57	169.57
- - -				
SDR	1.47767	1.48215	.67674	.67470
ECU	1.25610	1.25400	....	....

Special Drawing Rights (SDR) are based on exchange rates for the U.S., German, British, French and Japanese currencies. Source: International Monetary Fund.
European Currency Unit (ECU) is based on a basket of community currencies.

of foreign currency per dollar. The two forms give the same information, one is simply the reciprocal of the other. For example, if the dollar–sterling exchange rate is 1.6, the sterling–dollar rate is 1/1.6 or 62.5 cents.

Unless stated otherwise, a reference to the exchange rate in this book refers to the number of dollars per unit of foreign currency.[4] This form of presentation allows us to think of the exchange rate as the price of foreign currency. For example, if the dollar–franc rate of exchange is 0.19, the price

---

[4]The reader should note that current practice in the foreign exchange market is normally to refer to the number of foreign currency units per dollar.

of 1 franc is 19 cents. Thinking of the foreign exchange rate as the price of
foreign currency helps us understand how the exchange rate is determined
and the causes of exchange rate changes. The exchange rate responds to
changes in demand and supply in the same way as any market price. If the
demand for foreign exchange rises, or the supply falls, the exchange rate
increases. If the demand for foreign exchange falls, or the supply rises, the
exchange rate decreases.

Appreciation and Depreciation

A rising exchange rate indicates that the value of foreign currency has
increased relative to the dollar, and may be referred to as an **appreciation** of
foreign currency or as a **depreciation** of the dollar. Similarly, a decrease in
the exchange rate indicates a fall in the value of foreign currency relative to
the dollar, and may be referred to as a depreciation of foreign currency or as
an appreciation of the dollar.

Devaluation and Revaluation

Monetary authorities sometimes maintain a **fixed** exchange rate, that is, they
declare a value for their currency and buy or sell foreign currency in order
to maintain that value. The terms appreciation and depreciation can be used
to describe market–induced changes, and the terms **devaluation** and
revaluation are sometimes reserved to describe the decrease or increase
(respectively) in the value of a currency resulting from a change in an
officially declared and maintained exchange rate. However, in the present
international monetary system, the distinction between official and
market–induced exchange rate changes is not very useful, because even
though fixed exchange rates have been abandoned by many countries, most
governments have unofficial target rates and intervene in the foreign
exchange market. The present system is known as **dirty floating.** (A **clean
float** is a system in which a currency's value is determined by the market
and there is no official intervention.) Current exchange rate arrangements are
summarized in Table 6.2.

Arbitrage in the Spot Market

Communication between financial centers throughout the world is virtually
instantaneous, and at any given time the exchange rates in financial centers
around the world are equal. If they were not equal, **arbitrage** would occur.
Arbitrage is the act of buying in one market and selling in another in order
to profit from a difference in market prices. For example, if the dollar–sterling
rate in London is 1.2 and the rate in New York is 1.5, it is possible to make
30 cents profit on each pound bought in London and sold in New York.

Table 6.2
Exchange Arrangements
(as of September 30, 1993)

Currency pegged against	Number of countries
U.S. dollar	20
French franc	14
Russian ruble	5
Other	7
SDR	4
Other currency composites	26
Flexibility limited against a single currency	4
Cooperative arrangements (EMS)	9
More flexible	
According to a set of indicators	4
Other managed floating	27
Independently floating	52
Total	172

Source: IMF, International Financial Statistics, March 1994.

However, as people buy sterling in London and sell it in New York, the London price tends to rise and the New York price tends to fall. Thus, the opportunity for profit is removed by the arbitrage it stimulates. In practice, minute discrepancies between exchange rates would be sufficient to trigger large flows of funds because transaction costs are very low and the profit from arbitrage would be realized almost immediately.

Table 6.1 does not show all possible exchange rates; only the value of currencies against the dollar is shown. This is partly to save space: with 50 currencies, there are 2,450 exchange rates that might be quoted.[5] Also, quoting the rates between other currencies is unnecessary because the rate of exchange between two currencies can be calculated from the value of the two currencies against the dollar.[6] For example, if the dollar–sterling rate is 1.5, and the dollar–mark rate is 0.5, the sterling–mark rate is 0.5 divided by 1.5, that is, 0.33.

---

[5]If there are n currencies, there are $n - 1$ possible exchange rates for each currency, thus $n(n - 1)$ exchange rates might be quoted. In fact, there are well over 100 currencies; therefore, the table of all possible exchange rates would be large.

[6]If there are n currencies, there are only $n - 1$ "independent" exchange rates, in the sense that if the $n - 1$ exchange rates are known, the values of all other possible exchange rates can be calculated.

Cross Rates and Triangular Arbitrage

The rate of exchange between two currencies, calculated from the values of the two currencies against a third currency, is called the **cross rate**. For example, the number of units of *A* per unit of *B* can be calculated as follows:

$$A:B = (\$:B)/(\$:A)$$

How can we be sure that the market rate, the rate that actually exists between two currencies, will correspond to the cross rate? The answer is that excellent communication links between centers and the potential for **triangular arbitrage** ensure that cross rates and market rates are always equal.

Triangular arbitrage is the process of switching funds between three currencies in order to profit from differences between market rates and cross rates. For example, assume that the dollar–sterling rate is 1.5, the dollar–mark rate is 0.5, and the sterling–mark rate is 0.25. A person could convert $15 to £10, covert the £10 to 40DM, convert the 40DM to $20, and make $5 profit.[7] Life is not so simple, unfortunately. In our example, triangular arbitrage would lead to one or more of the following effects: 1) as people buy sterling with dollars, the dollar–sterling rate increases; 2) as people buy marks with pounds, the sterling–mark rate increases; 3) as people buy dollars with marks, the mark–dollar rate increases. The inequality between cross rates and market rates, and thus the opportunity for profit, could be removed by any of these effects.

We cannot predict which exchange rates will change, or by how much. However, one thing is certain: disparities between market rates and cross rates do not last. There are three characteristics of the foreign exchange market that allow us to be confident that triangular arbitrage would take place if cross rates were not equal to market rates, and that the flows of funds from triangular arbitrage would be so great as to remove any discrepancies between cross rates and market rates:

1. the potential number of market participants is very large,
2. transactions costs are insignificant for large sums, and
3. information can be obtained quickly and inexpensively.

---

[7]It is easy to see how the arbitrager will act. Comparing the cross rate and the market rate we see that in the market the mark is cheap if bought with sterling, because the market rate (£:DM) is less than the cross rate. So, the arbitrager will buy marks with sterling. To make a profit, the arbitrager starts and ends with dollars, so the process is: $ –> £ –> DM –> $.

Real Exchange Rates

When the value of a currency rises or falls, this changes a country's competitive position. The effect of exchange rate changes may be offset by changes in the prices of goods. For example, a 10 percent appreciation tends to make exports less competitive, but if domestic prices are stable and foreign prices are rising by 15 percent, exports are actually becoming more competitive. **Real exchange rate** indexes show the change in the value of one currency relative to other currencies taking into account differences between countries' inflation rates. Such indexes are useful when we want to assess the possible effects of exchange rate changes on international trade flows.

Effective Exchange Rate Changes

A currency may rise against some currencies while falling against others. If we wanted to assess the likely effects on a country's overall competitive position of a change in a currency's value, we might calculate the average change in value against all other currencies. However, this simple average is not very helpful because countries trade more with some countries than with others. Changes in a currency's value against the currencies of major trading partners are more significant than changes in relation to less important trading partners. For this reason, **effective exchange rate indexes** are sometimes calculated.

Effective exchange rate indexes are weighted averages of exchange rates, the weights being chosen to reflect the importance of countries' trade. There are many types of effective exchange rate index. **Bilateral exchange rate indexes** take into account the importance to one country of trade with each other country. The rational is that the importance of changes in the value of domestic currency against another country's currency is higher the greater the amount of trade with the country is.

A **multilateral trade–weighted effective exchange rate index**, as published in the *Federal Reserve Bulletin*, uses the importance of countries in world markets. The rationale in this case is that a country faces competition from major trading countries in world markets, even if it does not trade with those countries to a significant extent. The **multilateral exchange rate model index** (MERM), published by the International Monetary Fund, goes one step further by taking into account the sensitivity of trade flows in response to changes in exchange rates. This index is designed to show the impact of exchange rate movements rather than merely describe the movements themselves.

The Determination of the Spot Rate

The spot rate is determined by the demand and supply of foreign currency. The demand and supply of foreign currency result mainly from international trade and capital flows. In the following discussion, we begin with a model that excludes capital flows, showing how the demand and supply of foreign currency resulting from international trade determine the exchange rate. Then capital flows are discussed. This order of presentation is adopted for ease of exposition, and not because international trade is a more important influence on the exchange rate than capital flows. The relative importance of trade and investment varies, and we cannot say which will be more important at any given time.

Exports and the Supply of Foreign Exchange

Let us consider the case of an American exporter selling to a French importer. When the French importer sells American goods in France, the sales revenue is in French francs. Assuming that the American exporter wants to be paid in dollars, French francs must be converted into dollars. Therefore, American exports lead to sales of foreign currency, in other words, a supply of foreign exchange. Sometimes we find references to the foreign exchange earned by exporting firms. This is another way of saying that exports lead to a supply of foreign exchange.

The quantity of foreign currency supplied changes with the exchange rate. Assume for simplicity that the prices of American exports are fixed in dollars. As the exchange rate rises, the value of the dollar falls in relation to the franc, the foreign currency prices of exports decrease, and the quantity of American exports demanded increases. If the demand for exports is elastic, the foreign currency value of exports increases when the foreign currency prices of exports fall. Thus, the quantity of French francs to be converted into dollars (the quantity of foreign currency supplied) increases when the exchange rate rises. This is why the supply curve for foreign currency shown in Figure 6.1 slopes upward from left to right.

Imports and the Demand for Foreign Currency

Imports lead to a demand for foreign currency. The revenue from selling French goods in the United States is in dollars, but French exporters want payment in francs; therefore, dollars must be converted into francs. In other words, American imports lead to a demand for foreign currency.

The quantity of foreign currency demanded varies with the exchange rate. As the exchange rate rises, if the prices of American imports from France are fixed in French francs, the dollar prices of the goods rise (as the

Figure 6.1
The Demand and Supply of Foreign Exchange

The equilibrium exchange rate is S_E, the rate at which the demand and supply of foreign exchange are equal.

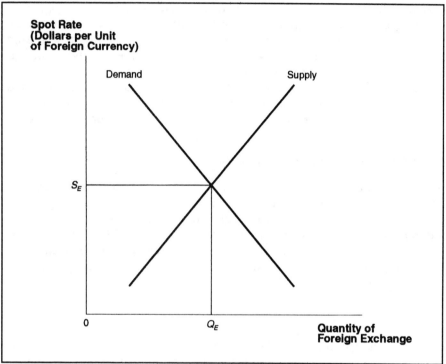

dollar becomes less valuable). When the prices of imports rise in domestic currency, we would expect the quantity of imports demanded to fall. Thus, the quantity of foreign currency demanded falls when the exchange rate rises, as shown in Figure 6.1.

The Equilibrium Exchange Rate

If we think of foreign currency as a good, Figure 6.1 is simply a standard supply and demand diagram. As the price of foreign currency rises, the quantity of foreign currency demanded decreases, and the quantity of foreign currency supplied increases. The equilibrium exchange rate is determined by the intersection of the demand and supply curves. If the exchange rate is above the equilibrium rate, the excess supply of foreign currency leads to a decrease in the exchange rate. The excess supply is removed in two ways.

First, as the exchange rate falls, the quantity of foreign currency demanded rises (because the prices of imports in domestic currency fall and more imports are demanded). Second, the quantity of foreign currency supplied decreases (because the quantity of American exports demanded decreases as export prices rise in foreign currency). Similarly, an excess demand for foreign currency is removed by an increase in the exchange rate.

People buying foreign currency offer domestic currency in exchange, thus the demand for foreign currency is equal to the supply of domestic currency in the foreign exchange market. Similarly, the supply of foreign exchange can be thought of as a demand for domestic currency. The basic analysis is the same regardless of whether the determination of the exchange rate is described in terms of the demand and supply of domestic currency on the foreign exchange market, or the demand and supply of foreign currency.[8]

Asset Markets and the Exchange Rate

Consideration of the return from international investment provides another reason for the downward slope of the demand for foreign exchange.[9] The expected return (r) to an investor from a foreign investment is made up of two parts: the expected return on the foreign asset (i_f) and the expected gain (or loss) from an increase (or decrease) in the value of foreign currency relative to domestic currency during the life of the investment. The total expected gain can be expressed as:

$$r = i_f + (ES - S)/S$$

where S is the current spot rate and ES is the spot rate that is expected to exist when the investment matures.[10] For example, if an investment in France pays 10 percent, and the franc is expected to appreciate by 5 percent ($ES = 0.21$ and $S = 0.20$), the total expected return from an investment in France would be 15 percent. This is the return expected; the actual return may be more or less, depending on how accurate investors' predictions are.

---

[8]Note that the supply of domestic currency in the foreign exchange market is not the same as the domestic money supply. The domestic money supply is the total stock of domestic money. The supply of domestic currency in the foreign exchange market is only the amount of domestic money which people would like to convert into foreign currency.

[9]We assume in this section that the investment is not covered in the foreign exchange market. Covered investments are described later.

[10]This equation is an approximation. The exact return is: $i_f (ES/S) + (ES - S)/S$.

Let us consider how the quantity of foreign exchange demanded responds to a change in the exchange rate. As the spot rate falls, other things equal, the return from a foreign investment increases. The reason is that a fall in the spot rate leads to a higher expected appreciation (or lower depreciation) of foreign currency. In other words, as S falls, the value of $(ES - S)/S$ rises if ES remains unchanged. Therefore, a fall in the spot rate tends to increase the quantity of foreign assets demanded by domestic residents. Foreign investment leads to a demand for foreign currency; thus, the quantity of foreign currency demanded increases as the exchange rate falls. In other words, the demand for foreign exchange slopes downward as shown in Figure 6.1.

The same approach can be used to explain why the quantity of foreign exchange supplied increases as the exchange rate rises. The total return (r') to a foreigner investing in the domestic market is:

$$r' = i_d - (ES - S)/S$$

where i_d is the domestic interest rate.[11] As the spot rate rises, the foreigner's expected return increases, and, as a result, the quantity of domestic assets demanded tends to increase. Thus the supply curve of foreign currency slopes upward.

Which Is More Important, Trade or Capital Flows?

It has been shown that exchange rate determination can be explained using the demand and supply of foreign exchange resulting from either international trade or capital flows. The relationship between trade flows and the exchange rate is often useful for explaining long–term exchange rate fluctuations, but it cannot explain the dramatic short–term exchange rate changes that have been observed since the move away from fixed exchange rates in 1973. Flows of goods do not change so quickly. Models that focus on asset markets and capital flows are often more useful for explaining short–term exchange rate changes. The large exchange rate changes sometimes associated with the collapse of fixed exchange rate systems seem to be the result of speculative capital flows. The possibility of an exchange rate change of a few percent in the near future may be enough to trigger massive flows of funds. We examine speculation and other causes of exchange rate changes in the next section.

---

[11]This equation is an approximation. The exact return is: $(S/ES)(i_d - (ES - S)/S)$.

Figure 6.2
An Increase in the Demand for Foreign Exchange

When the demand for Japanese imports increases, the demand for yen increases, and the dollar–yen exchange rate rises from S_0 to S_1. Such a change might also be caused by an increase in the American demand for Japanese assets.

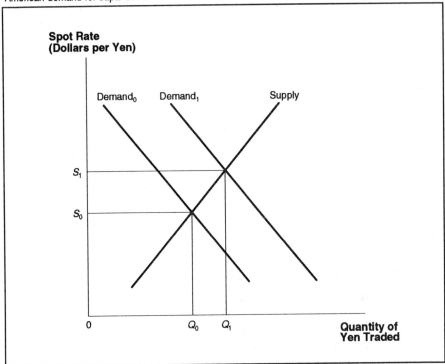

Changes in the Demand and Supply of Foreign Currency

Changes in the Demand or Supply of Traded Goods

Imports lead to purchases of foreign exchange and exports lead to sales of foreign exchange. Thus, changes in the demand for imports or exports can lead to changes in the exchange rate. An increase in the demand for imports will lead to a depreciation of domestic currency. For example, an increase in the American demand for imports from Japan will increase the demand for yen, and the dollar–yen exchange rate will rise. This is illustrated in Figure

6.2. Similarly, an increase in the supply of exports will lead to an increase in the supply of foreign exchange and an appreciation of domestic currency.[12]

Changes in Domestic Income and Consumption

An increase in national income will normally lead to higher consumption and an increase in the demand for imports, simply because some of the goods consumed are imported. As we have seen, an increase in the demand for imports tends to decrease the value of domestic currency (Figure 6.2). The government may be able to influence the value of a currency by using aggregate demand to change the level of income, and thereby change the level of imports. For example, if the government reduces aggregate demand, this will tend to decrease the level of imports (along with the levels of income and consumption).

Increasing income is not always associated with a depreciating currency. A country may be fortunate enough to be benefitting from export led growth: the level of national income may be increasing in response to higher exports. Increasing exports increase the supply of foreign exchange, and although imports increase as national income increases, the overall effect will be an appreciation of the currency. Japan is an obvious example of a country which has benefitted from rising exports. One of the reasons that Japan was able to be such a successful exporter over the last few decades is that productivity in Japan increased dramatically. This meant that Japanese exports remained competitive even though the yen appreciated.

Inflation and Relative Price Changes

We would normally expect that a country with above–average inflation would have a currency that is declining in value. The reason is that when a country experiences inflation in excess of that in other countries, its exports become less attractive and imports more attractive. Therefore, the demand for foreign currency increases and the supply of foreign currency decreases. This is shown in Figure 6.3 by the shift of the demand curve for foreign currency to the right, and the shift of the supply of foreign currency to the left. As a result, the exchange rate rises (domestic currency depreciates). The

---

[12]We assume that the country is not large enough to affect world prices. If the country is large enough to affect world prices, export prices will fall as the supply increases. In this cases, the quantity of foreign exchange supplied will only increase if the demand for exports is elastic (because when demand is elastic the percentage increase in the quantity of exports is greater than the percentage fall in the price of exports).

Figure 6.3
The Effect of Inflation on the Exchange Rate

If domestic inflation exceeds world inflation, the demand for foreign exchange increases (as imports become less expensive relative to domestic goods), and the supply of exports decreases (as exports become more expensive relative to foreign goods). As a result, the exchange rate increases from S_0 to S_1.

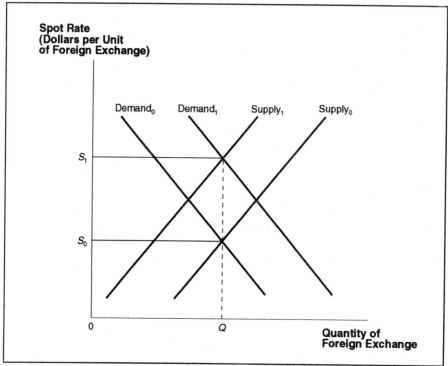

relationship between inflation and the exchange rate is called **purchasing power parity** and is examined in more detail later in the chapter.

Assets and the Exchange Rate

The demand for assets depends on many factors, for example, the rate of return paid to holders of the asset, the default risk on the asset, and the possibility of capital gain (either through an increase in the value of the asset or an increase in the value of the currency in which the asset is valued). Changes in the demand for assets are thought to be one of the major reasons for short–term fluctuations of the exchange rate.

Figure 6.4
An Increase in the Supply of Foreign Exchange

When the supply of foreign exchange increases, the exchange rate decreases (from S_0 to S_1). Such a change might be caused by an increase in the foreign demand for American assets or an increase in the foreign demand for American exports.

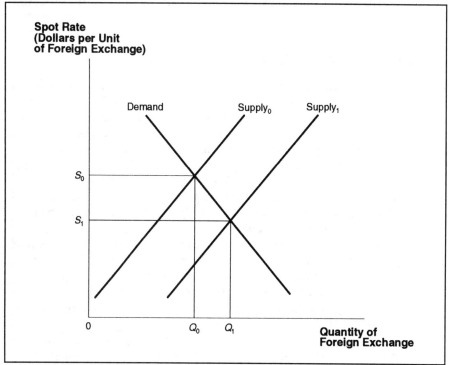

As an example, assume that an increase in American interest rates leads to an increase in the demand for American assets by foreigners. There will be an increase in the supply of foreign currency as foreigners buy the dollars needed to make investments in the United States. The same effect would occur if foreigners increase their investments in the U.S. stock market (because they expect share prices to increase). An increase in the supply of foreign currency is shown in Figure 6.4. When the supply of foreign currency increases, the equilibrium exchange rate falls. Thus, an increase in the demand for American assets erodes the competitive position of American producers because it leads to an appreciation of the dollar. This example resembles what happened in the early 1980s when the dollar increased in value because of an inflow of foreign capital.

It should be remembered that the demand and supply of foreign currency must be equal. Therefore, if there is a net supply of foreign currency from investors, there must be a net demand from other market participants. Another way of saying this is that the net purchase of American assets by foreigners is financed by a net transfer of goods to the United States. We shall see in the next chapter that this would be recorded in the balance of payments as a capital account surplus accompanied by a current account deficit.

Government Intervention in the Foreign Exchange Market

When the government fixes the exchange rate, it intervenes in the foreign exchange market to ensure that the demand and supply of foreign currency are equal at the chosen exchange rate. For example, if the demand for foreign currency exceeds the supply, the government can increase the supply of foreign exchange and prevent the exchange rate from rising, as shown in Figure 6.5. Similarly, the government can prevent an exchange rate from falling by increasing the demand for foreign currency. Governments can also intervene to change an exchange rate. If the government thinks the exchange rate is too low (or too high), it can buy (or sell) foreign currency to push the exchange rate in the desired direction.

The stocks of foreign currency that governments hold for intervention in the foreign exchange market are called **international reserves**. These stocks are limited, so a government cannot indefinitely continue selling foreign currency to maintain an exchange rate below the market equilibrium rate. In contrast, if the market rate is above the official value, a government can intervene to reduce the value of its currency for a longer period because the country can add the foreign currency to its international reserves. The domestic currency needed for purchases of foreign currency can be printed, or domestic currency can be obtained by sales of Treasury bills. Which method is used depends on the objectives of the monetary authorities.

Speculation in the Spot Market

We can **speculate** in the spot market by buying currencies that we expect to go up in value, and selling currencies we expect to go down in value.[13] Normally, speculators do not hold currency, just as domestic savers do not

---

[13]**Speculation** is a technical term referring to the activity pursued. To be precise, if a person has an open position in foreign currency, that is, if the person's assets and liabilities in foreign currency are not equal, that person is speculating. The term does not imply that the person's actions are harmful or wrong in any sense. In fact, as the discussion shows, speculation may have beneficial effects.

Figure 6.5
Official Intervention

There is an excess demand for foreign exchange at the chosen exchange rate (S_0). Sales of foreign exchange by the monetary authorities increase the supply of foreign exchange and prevent the exchange rate from rising.

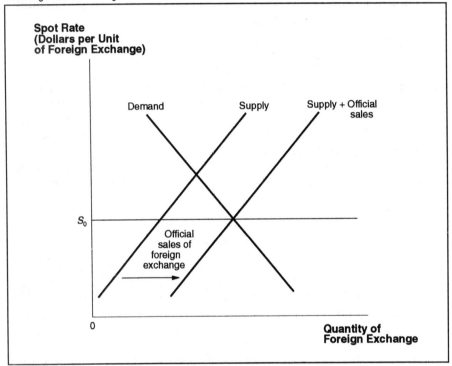

hold currency. Instead, they hold interest–bearing assets such as bank accounts. For simplicity, let us assume that the speculator's time horizon is short, so that differences between the interest rates that can be earned on assets in different currencies are not important. In this case, the rules for speculation in the spot market are:

$S > ES$	sell foreign currency
$S = ES$	do nothing
$S < ES$	buy foreign currency

where *S* and *ES* denote the current spot rate and the expected spot rate, respectively. For example, if a speculator expects the dollar–sterling exchange rate to rise from 1.2 to 1.5, it is profitable to buy pounds now and sell them after the exchange rate has risen. If the speculator's prediction is correct, a profit of 30 cents is earned on each pound bought and sold. (Transactions costs must be deducted, but these are trivial for large amounts.) Of course, if the prediction is wrong, there may be no profit or even a loss. Therefore, speculators in the foreign exchange market attempt to make profits in the same way as speculators in other markets: by buying low and selling high.[14]

Speculators' actions tend to move the exchange rate toward the expected exchange rate. If speculators expect a fall in the exchange rate, their sales of foreign currency make a fall more likely. Similarly, purchases of foreign currency by speculators expecting a rise in the exchange rate make a rise more likely. If speculators predict the future equilibrium exchange rate accurately, by buying currency when the exchange rate is low and selling when the exchange rate is high, their actions will tend to move the exchange rate toward the long–run equilibrium rate. In other words, profitable speculation will stabilize the exchange rate by pushing the rate toward the long–run rate.

Stabilizing and Destabilizing Speculation

Whether speculation is normally stabilizing or destabilizing, in the sense of moving the exchange rate toward or away from the long–run equilibrium exchange rate, has been a topic for continuous debate. One view is that under flexible exchange rates, destabilizing speculation is not likely to be the norm because speculators would make losses in the long run. The reasoning is as follows. If speculators are to push the exchange rate away from its equilibrium value, they must buy when the exchange rate is already high and sell when it is low. This behavior would lead to losses. Therefore, destabilizing speculation cannot continue. However, destabilizing speculation is clearly possible at times, even if it is not the norm.

Destabilizing speculation may be more likely under fixed exchange rates, or dirty floating, because speculators may speculate that an officially supported exchange rate will be changed or abandoned, and there is very little danger of significant losses if their expectations are incorrect. For example, assume that an excess demand for foreign exchange is being offset by official intervention (sales of foreign currency by the monetary authorities). Some speculators might believe that government intervention

---

[14]One does not have to have an initial holding of a currency in order to sell the currency. A speculator can borrow a currency, sell it, buy it back after it has fallen in value, repay the loan, and be left with a profit.

Figure 6.6
Official Intervention and Speculation

There is an excess demand for foreign exchange at the chosen exchange rate (S_0). Sales of foreign exchange by the monetary authorities increase the supply of foreign exchange and initially prevent the exchange rate from rising. However, speculators buy foreign exchange because they expect it to appreciate. Their purchases of foreign exchange increase the demand for foreign exchange. The result is that the amount of intervention needed to maintain the chosen exchange rate increases.

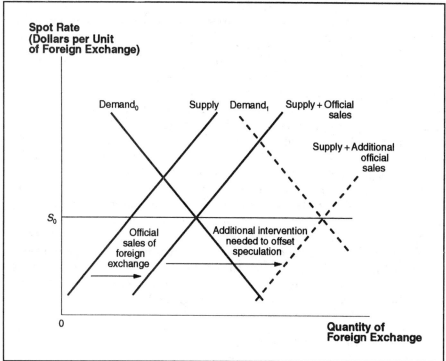

will not last, and speculate by buying foreign exchange. If the government does stop intervening, and the exchange rate rises, they will be rewarded with a capital gain. If the exchange rate does not change, the foreign exchange can be sold at the original exchange rate. Speculators only lose the transactions costs incurred, which are minute in comparison with the possible gain. (A fall in the exchange rate is very unlikely if initially there is an excess demand for foreign exchange.)

We have seen that speculators make the expected rise in the value of foreign currency more likely because their purchases add to the excess demand for foreign exchange. This is shown in Figure 6.6. Faced with an increase in the demand for foreign currency, if the monetary authorities want to maintain the exchange rate, they can meet the additional demand for foreign currency by running down reserves. Speculators may buy foreign currency because they anticipate that official intervention will not last and that foreign currency will appreciate. Purchases of foreign currency by speculators increase the demand for foreign exchange and shift the demand curve to the right. The monetary authorities can either increase their sales of reserves or abandon the chosen exchange rate.

Exchange Market Stability and the Role of Elasticities

The discussion in the previous section leads to the conclusion that exchange rate changes will bring about equality between the demand and supply of foreign currency. However, if the supply of foreign currency is downward sloping and flatter than the demand curve, exchange rate changes will not lead to equilibrium in the foreign exchange market. Under such conditions, exchange rate changes will increase rather than decrease differences between the demand and supply of foreign exchange. This section explores the relationship between exchange rate changes and trade, and examines the possibility of the foreign exchange market being unstable.

Earlier we saw that the demand and supply of foreign currency are related to flows of imports and exports, respectively. Ignoring capital flows, equality between the demand and supply of foreign exchange may be brought about by the effects of exchange rate changes on the quantities of imports and exports. The changes in the quantity of foreign currency demanded and supplied depend on the elasticities of demand and supply of imports and exports with respect to changes in their prices. Let us begin by examining imports and the demand for foreign exchange.

The Demand for Foreign Exchange

Assuming for simplicity that import prices are fixed in foreign currency, the prices of imports in domestic currency rise when the exchange rate rises. If the demand for imports is not perfectly inelastic, which seems a reasonable assumption, the quantity of imports falls, and the quantity of foreign exchange demanded declines.

Incidentally, although the demand for some products may be inelastic, this does not mean that the demand for imports in general is inelastic. The demand for imports in general is more elastic than the average of the elasticities of demand for individual commodities. The reason is that an increase in the prices of imports in general reduces consumers' real incomes, whereas the effects of an increase in the price of a single good on consumers' real incomes is comparatively small. Therefore, the consumption of an imported good declines more when its price rises as part of a general increase in import prices (caused by depreciation) than when an increase in its price is not part of a general increase in import prices.

The Supply of Foreign Exchange

Although we can be confident that depreciation will reduce the quantity of foreign currency demanded, it is less certain that the quantity of foreign currency supplied will rise. Assuming that export prices are fixed in domestic currency, depreciation lowers the foreign currency prices of exports. If the demand for exports is not perfectly inelastic, the quantity of exports demanded increases. The quantity of foreign currency supplied tends to increase because more exports are sold, but the lower price means that each unit of exports generates less foreign currency. Which effect will dominate?

In the short run, it is quite conceivable that the quantity of exports demanded will not increase significantly, and that the quantity of foreign currency supplied will decrease when a currency depreciates. This would be shown by a supply curve of foreign currency that slopes downward from left to right. This can lead to instability in the foreign exchange market. To see this, assume that initially there is an excess demand for foreign currency. Foreign currency will tend to increase in value relative to domestic currency; in other words, domestic currency will depreciate. If the supply curve is downward sloping and flatter than the demand curve, depreciation increases the excess demand for foreign currency. This possibility, shown in Figure 6.7, is the opposite of what we might normally expect.

Many international economists doubt the importance of this theoretical possibility for three reasons. First, the result requires the supply of exports to be both downward sloping and flatter than the demand for foreign currency. Although it is possible that the quantity of foreign currency supplied will not increase, or may even decrease with a depreciation, it is less likely that the quantity of foreign currency supplied will decrease more than the quantity of foreign currency demanded.

Second, even if the foreign exchange market is unstable in the short run, it is more likely to be stable in the long run because the elasticities of demand for imports and exports will normally be greater in the long run than in the short run.

Third, the effects of capital flows must be considered. We saw that the demand and supply of foreign currency resulting from capital flows leads to demand and supply curves with normal slopes. Also, we have seen that if the exchange rate departs from its equilibrium value, and speculators predict the equilibrium value correctly, stabilizing capital flows will tend to restore the exchange rate to its equilibrium value. These effects may offset the instability which tends to arise from the short–run inelasticity of demand for traded goods.

Figure 6.7
An Unstable Foreign Exchange Market

In this case the foreign exchange market is unstable because the supply curve is downward sloping and flatter than the demand curve. If the exchange rate is below the equilibrium rate (S_E), there is an excess supply of foreign exchange, and the exchange rate falls, moving away from equilibrium. If the exchange rate is above S_E, there is an excess demand for foreign exchange and the exchange rate rises. Therefore, the exchange rate tends to move away from equilibrium, not toward it.

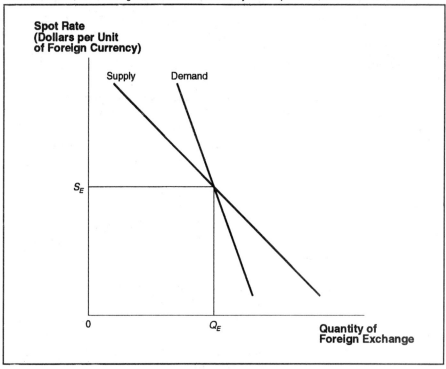

Exchange Rate Overshooting

The possibility that elasticities will be smaller in the short run than in the long run implies that the exchange rate change needed to remove an excess demand or supply of foreign currency may be larger in the short run than in the long run.[15] This possibility is shown in Figure 6.8. In the short run,

---

[15]The relationship between the balance of payments and the exchange rate is discussed in Chapter 9. It is shown that it takes time for the balance of trade to respond to a change in the exchange rate. This delayed response is consistent with the demand for goods being less elastic in the short run than in the long run.

Figure 6.8
Exchange Rate Overshooting

The short–run supply of foreign exchange is less elastic than the long–run supply of foreign exchange. Assume that the demand for foreign exchange increases. In the short run the exchange rate rises to S_1, on the short run supply curve. In the long run, because the supply is more elastic, the equilibrium exchange rate is lower (S_2). Therefore, an increase in the demand for foreign exchange leads to a rise, then a fall, in the exchange rate. In other words, the exchange rate temporarily "overshoots" its long–run value.

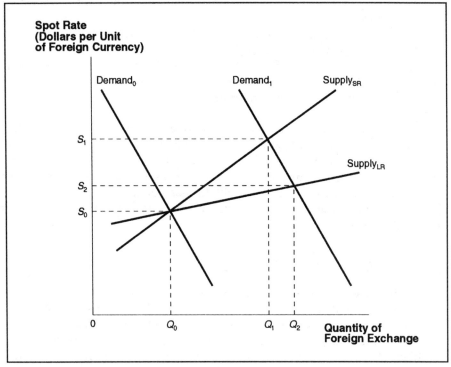

when the demand for foreign exchange increases, the exchange rate rises from S_0 to S_1. The long–run equilibrium exchange rate (S_2) is lower because the long–run supply of foreign currency is more elastic than the short–run supply. Therefore, because of inelasticity, the exchange rate overshoots the long–run equilibrium rate. Some economists have suggested that this model helps explain why exchange rates have been so unstable since fixed exchange rates were abandoned in 1973.[16]

---

[16]Another explanation of overshooting is discussed in Chapter 10.

Purchasing Power Parity

The **purchasing power parity** theorem suggests that exchange rate changes reflect differences between countries' rates of inflation. The theorem can be expressed in the form of an equation:

$$P_{US} = P_W + \dot{S}$$

where P_{US}, P_W, and $\dot{S}$ represent the rate of inflation in the United States, the world inflation rate, and the change in the exchange rate, respectively. If the U.S. inflation rate (P_{US}) is greater than the world rate (P_W), the theorem predicts the dollar will depreciate $(\dot{S} > 0)$, that is, the dollar price of foreign currency will increase. If U.S. inflation is below the world rate, the theorem predicts that the dollar will appreciate $(\dot{S} < 0)$. The purchasing power parity theorem suggests that inflation rates must be similar if exchange rates are to remain stable.

Purchasing power parity may be brought about by the effects of inflation on the demand and supply of foreign exchange. If a country experiences inflation above that of the rest of the world, domestic consumers will switch from domestic goods to imported goods as domestic goods become relatively more expensive. Also, export sales will decrease as the prices of exports rise. As a result, the demand for foreign exchange will decrease, and the exchange rate will increase.

Does Purchasing Power Parity Hold?

There are three reasons why we might not expect exchange rate changes to conform exactly with purchasing power parity. First, transport costs and barriers to trade reduce the free movement of goods. The prices of goods in other countries are unimportant if imports are prevented by official controls or high transport costs. Second, not all goods and services are traded internationally. For example, we would not expect the prices of houses or haircuts to be equalized by trade. Third, trade is not the only influence on the exchange rate. For example, investment and speculation lead to capital flows which may cause the exchange rate to depart from purchasing power parity.[17]

Although we might not expect exchange rate changes to equal inflation rate differentials exactly, it is equally unlikely that prices in different

---

[17]In addition, because countries' patterns of consumption and production differ, price indexes include different goods, or different weights are attached to the same good. Therefore, inflation rates are not strictly comparable.

countries will diverge continuously. If inflation rate differences are not reflected in the exchange rate, the incentive to trade will increase as prices diverge. The greater the divergence between inflation rates or the longer the period we consider, the more likely it is that exchange rate changes will be related to inflation rates. For example, if inflation is higher in Canada than in the U.S. and the exchange rate initially does not change, Canadian imports from the U.S. will become progressively cheaper relative to Canadian goods, and Canadian exports to the U.S. will become progressively more expensive in the U.S. Eventually, we would expect rising Canadian imports and falling exports to lead to a fall in the value of the Canadian dollar relative to the American dollar.

It is not surprising that empirical studies have shown that purchasing power parity helps explain long–run changes in exchange rates and also exchange rate changes between countries with very different inflation rates. However, purchasing power parity is not useful for predicting short–run exchange rate changes between countries with broadly similar inflation rates.[18]

Some Examples of Purchasing Power Parity

Table 6.3 shows the average rates of inflation of a few large countries, and the changes in the value of their currencies against the dollar over the period 1963–92. The two nations with the highest rates of inflation, Italy and the United Kingdom, experienced the greatest decline in the value of their currencies. Canada and France had rates of inflation that were similar to that of the United States, and over the 30–year period their currencies changed by small amounts against the dollar. Germany and Japan had lower inflation rates and their currencies increased in value. The appreciation of the yen over the period was larger than we would expect from purchasing power parity. The reason is probably that Japanese productivity increased dramatically over the period, thus adding to Japanese competitiveness, and the value of the yen increased.

Table 6.4 shows that rapidly rising prices in Argentina and Brazil over the period 1983–86 were accompanied by similar increases in the amount of national currency needed to pay for a dollar. More recently, from 1990 to 1992, Brazil's consumer price index increased by 5,350 percent and the number of cruzeiros per dollar rose by 6,500 percent. The relationship between prices and exchange rates is not perfect, but we would not expect exact correspondence. (Purchasing power parity is not exact, and measurements of price changes during hyper–inflation are not very accurate.)

---

[18]Officer (1976) reviews the theory of purchasing power parity and empirical studies of the relationship between exchange rates and purchasing power parity.

Table 6.3
Inflation and Exchange Rates: 1963–92

	Average Annual Inflation Rate[a]	Overall Percentage Appreciation (–) Depreciation (+)[b]
Germany	3.4	–59
Japan	5.1	–65
United States	5.2	—
Canada	5.7	+18
France	6.4	+12
United Kingdom	8.0	+46
Italy	9.0	+136

[a]The average annual change in the consumer price index.
[b]Percentage change in the number of units of currency per U.S. dollar.
Source: IMF *International Financial Statistics Yearbook* 1993.

The results indicate that purchasing power parity is a useful approximate guide to long–run exchange rate changes.

Table 6.4
Inflation and Exchange Rates for Argentina and Brazil

	Consumer Price Index (1980 = 100)	Exchange Rate Index[a] National Currency per U.S. Dollar (1980 = 100)
Argentina		
1983	2,403	5,850
1986	256,300	523,906
% change	10,566	8,856
Brazil		
1983	984	1,160
1986	23,436	27,320
% change	2,282	2,255
United States		
1983	127	
1986	146	
% change	15	

[a]Exchange rate index calculated by the author.
Source: IMF *International Financial Statistics Yearbook*, 1988.

Forward Exchange Rates

The forward exchange rate is determined in the same way as the spot rate—by demand and supply. However, the reasons for buying and selling foreign exchange in the spot market differ from the reasons for buying and selling in the forward market. One of the major reasons for buying and selling forward is to remove exchange risk from international trade and investment.

Exchange Risk and International Trade

When goods are traded, there is normally a delay between a price being agreed upon and payment being made. Companies with contracts for future payments or receipts in foreign currency face **exchange risk**, the risk that the value in domestic currency of future payments or receipts will change as a result of a change in the exchange rate. By using the forward market, companies can fix the value of these contracts in domestic currency. For example, an American importer who has contracted to pay £1 million in three months time faces the risk that an increase in the dollar–sterling exchange rate will increase the dollar value of the liability. The risk can be removed by "covering forward": by buying sterling in the forward market the importer fixes the exchange rate that will be paid for the currency. In general, companies that have to make future payments in foreign currency can cover by buying the currency forward, and companies that expect to receive foreign currency can sell the currency forward.

It might be that a company that uses the forward market would have been better off if it had not covered. For example, a company which has bought sterling forward may later find that sterling has depreciated, and if it had waited it could have bought the sterling at a lower price in the spot market. This does not mean that the decision to cover was wrong. We can never be absolutely certain what the future spot rate will be, and if forward cover is not taken, the company is speculating. The company might win or lose from such speculation. Many importers and exporters choose to avoid exchange risk by using the forward market.

Exchange Risk and International Trade and Investment

International investors are important forward exchange market participants. Through a process called **covered interest arbitrage**, they are largely responsible for the determination of the forward rate. When comparing the rates of return between assets within a country, investors do not need to worry about exchange rates. International investment is not so simple, however, because forward cover must be taken if the investor wants to ensure that the values of international investments are not affected by exchange rate movements.

Covered Interest Arbitrage

Assume that a person is considering investing in New York or London in an asset that has virtually no risk of default, for example, Treasury bills. At maturity, the value (V_n) of an investment of X dollars in New York is:

$$(\$V_n) = X(1 + NR)$$

where NR is the rate of interest expressed as a decimal. For example, if the rate of interest is 10 percent, the investor will receive $1.10 for each dollar because $1.10 = $1(1 + 0.1)$.

Calculating the yield from an investment in London is slightly more complicated because we must consider exchange rates. X dollars converted into pounds gives $X(1/S)$ pounds, where S is the spot exchange rate. At maturity, the sterling value ($£V_l$) of an investment in London is:

$$(£V_l) = X(1/S)(1 + LR)$$

where LR is the rate of interest in London (again expressed as a decimal).

The dollar value of the London investment is uncertain because the sterling from the investment must be converted back into dollars at whatever the spot rate happens to be at the end of the period. This uncertainty can be removed by covering forward. In this case, the investor would sell sterling for dollars in the forward market. If a forward contract is taken, the dollar value of the investment is not affected by changes in the spot rate.

Assuming that forward cover is taken, each pound sold in the forward market yields F dollars, where F is the forward rate. Therefore, the dollar value (V_l) of an investment X in London is:

$$(\$V_l) = X(F/S)(1 + LR)$$

The investments in London and New York are now comparable because the returns are expressed in dollars and the investment in London is not subject to exchange risk. We can compare the return per dollar invested by dropping the X from each equation; thus we compare $(1 + NR)$ with $(F/S)(1 + LR)$. If the return in New York $(1 + NR)$ is greater than the return in London $[(F/S)(1 + LR)]$, we would expect Americans to invest in New York; if the return in London is greater than the return in New York, we would expect Americans to invest in London. (We shall see in a moment that covered interest arbitrage tends to equalize the returns in the two centers.)

We have described the problem in terms of the returns to an American investor. The problem can also be described in terms of the returns to a British investor. The yield in sterling per pound invested in London ($£Y_1$) is:

$$£Y_1 = (1 + LR)$$

A covered investment in New York has a yield per pound of:

$$£Y_n = (S/F)(1 + NR)$$

For the British investor, comparing the yields in London and New York, the problem is whether $(1 + LR)$ is greater or less than $(S/F)(1 + NR)$. Multiplying both yields by (F/S), we see that the British investor could compare $(F/S)(1 + LR)$ with $(1 + NR)$. Therefore, the British and American investors face what amounts to the same decision, and other things being equal, they will invest in the same place.

Interest Parity

Suppose that the covered rate return in London is greater than the return in New York. When making an investment in London, American investors buy spot sterling and sell sterling forward. Therefore, the spot rate tends to rise and the forward rate tends to fall. As the forward rate tends to fall relative to the spot rate, the covered rate of return on an investment in London falls. Therefore, covered interest arbitrage tends to equalize the rates of return in the two centers. Similarly, if the covered rate of return in New York is greater than the return in London, British investors in New York sell sterling in the spot market and buy sterling in the forward market. The forward rate tends to rise relative to the spot rate, and the covered rate of return on an investment in New York falls. Again, covered interest arbitrage equalizes the rates of return. When the covered rates of return are equal in the two centers, that is, when:

$$(1 + NR) = (F/S)(1 + LR)$$

the forward rate is said to be at **interest parity**.

The **forward premium** (p) is equal to the difference between the spot rate and the forward rate divided by the spot rate:

$$p = (F - S) / S$$

If a currency is worth more in the forward market than it is in the spot market, it is said to be at a **premium** in the forward market. Conversely, if a currency is worth less in the forward market than it is in the spot market, it is said to be at a **discount**. If the forward rate is at interest parity, it can be shown that the forward premium is approximately equal to the interest differential:[19]

$$p \approx NR - LR$$

In practice, the forward rate is normally at interest parity, and the forward premium is (approximately) equal to the interest rate differential when we compare the rates of return on similar assets. The reason is that covered interest arbitrage is free of exchange risk, thus divergences from interest parity potentially generate very significant capital flows. Large investors, banks, and corporations engage in this type of activity. However, there are a number or reasons why interest parity does not always hold exactly.

Departures from Interest Parity

Investors face transactions costs when buying or selling securities or foreign currency. The costs of purchasing domestic or foreign securities may be similar, in which case interest parity will not be affected. However, the cost of buying and selling foreign exchange only affects foreign investments and can be responsible for small departures from interest parity. The shorter the period of the investment, the more significant transactions costs are likely to be in relation to the yield on the investment. While a small deviation from interest parity is possible, transactions costs cannot explain large deviations because investors from third countries face the same foreign exchange transaction costs on alternative foreign investments, and their actions will tend to drive the forward rate to interest parity.

Government policies can lead to departures from interest parity. For example, foreign governments may impose controls that prevent the repatriation of funds held abroad, or the funds may even be confiscated. The risk that government policies will prevent an investment yielding the expected return is called **political risk**.

---

[19] The definition of the forward premium $[p = (F - S)/S]$ yields:

$p = (F/S) - (S/S) = (F/S) - 1.$

$\Rightarrow (F/S) = p + 1$

The definition of interest parity is:

$(1 + NR) = (F/S)(1 + LR)$

Substituting $(p + 1)$ for (F/S), yields:

$(1 + NR) = (p + 1)(1 + LR)$

Solving for p we obtain:

$p = NR - LR - pLR$

Since pLR is small, $p \approx NR - LR$ is a useful approximation.

Another reason for departures from interest parity is that the rate of return on an investment reflects the degree of default risk on the investment: we would not expect the rate of return on investments with different degrees of default risk to be the same. Conformity to covered interest parity is strong on investments in government securities in the Eurodollar market because there are no capital controls in this market, and the investments are similar in the sense that the degree of default risk is negligible.

Finally, under certain circumstances speculators may influence the forward exchange rate. Flows of arbitrage funds are potentially very large; therefore, for speculators to exert an influence on the forward rate there has to be a substantial degree of certainty about what the future value of the spot rate will be relative to the forward rate. Because speculators cannot usually be sure about the future spot rate, the effects of speculation will usually be offset by flows of arbitrage funds.[20] Let us examine how speculation takes place in the forward market.

Speculation in the Forward Market

We can speculate in the forward market by buying foreign currency in the forward market when we expect the future spot rate to be higher than the present forward rate. If the expectations prove to be correct, the foreign currency bought at the forward rate can be sold at the higher spot rate. Similarly, if we expect the future spot rate to be lower than the present forward rate, we can sell forward. If correct, foreign currency can be purchased in the spot market and sold at a higher price to meet the forward contract. The rules for speculation in the spot market are:

$F > ES$	sell foreign currency in the forward market
$F = ES$	do nothing
$F < ES$	buy foreign currency in the forward market

where F and ES denote the current forward rate and the expected spot rate, respectively.

---

[20]To be more precise, if the supply of arbitrage funds is perfectly elastic, any tendency for the forward rate to diverge from the forward rate consistent with covered interest parity induces a flow of arbitrage funds that ensures that covered interest parity is maintained.

Speculation in the forward market can lead to capital flows. Assume that initially the forward rate is equal to the spot rate (because interest rates in New York and London are identical). If speculators begin selling sterling forward because they expect a fall in the dollar–sterling spot exchange rate ($F > ES$), the dollar–sterling forward rate will fall. A fall in the forward rate tends to reduce the covered return on a London investment relative to an investment in New York; therefore, we would expect capital to flow out of Britain. This capital outflow puts downward pressure on the spot value of sterling. Under fixed exchange rates the government may have to intervene to prevent sterling from falling in value.

Government Intervention in the Forward Market

The return on investments in London can be increased, and the capital outflow prevented, by raising interest rates in London. However, the British monetary authorities may be reluctant to tighten British monetary policy to raise interest rates. Such a policy tends to reduce the level of national income, and if the authorities feel (hope) that the speculative pressure is temporary, changing monetary policy would be undesirable. An alternative is for the British monetary authorities to intervene directly in the forward market, buying sterling forward. This policy would reduce the capital outflow by increasing the forward rate.

At the time of intervention in the forward market, the government does not need any international reserves. This is one of the advantages of intervening in the forward market rather than the spot market. However, forward intervention may lead to increased speculation that sterling will fall in value, and eventually the authorities must meet their forward commitments.

The cost of meeting forward commitments, the monetary cost of forward intervention, depends on whether sterling falls in value as the speculators predicted. Recall that we assumed that the spot rate and the forward rate were equal initially. When the forward contracts mature, if sterling has not fallen in value, the British monetary authorities can honor their obligations to buy sterling without any loss of reserves. Using dollars, they buy sterling from contract holders for the same price at which sterling can be sold for dollars in the spot market. However, if sterling has fallen in value, the British monetary authorities must pay more for sterling from contract holders than they receive when they sell the sterling on the spot market; therefore, the authorities lose reserves. If intervention in the forward market is large, forward exchange market intervention can be very costly.

Summary of Main Points

Exchange rates specify the value of one currency relative to another. Exchange rates are important because they determine the relationship between the domestic and foreign prices of goods, services, and assets. The **spot exchange rate** may be thought of as the domestic (dollar) price of foreign currency. The **forward exchange rate** is the price used for foreign currency to be delivered in the future.

The spot rate is determined by the demand and supply of foreign exchange. Payments to foreigners for imports, or American purchases of foreign assets, lead to a demand for foreign exchange. Receipts from foreigners for exports, or foreign purchases of domestic assets, lead to a supply of foreign exchange.

An increase in the exchange rate is a **depreciation** of the dollar, and a decrease in the exchange rate is an **appreciation** of the dollar. Exchange rate changes are caused by changes in the demand or supply of foreign currency. A depreciation of the dollar may be caused by an increase in the demand for foreign currency or a fall in the supply of foreign currency. Similarly, an appreciation of the dollar can be caused by a decrease in the demand for foreign currency or an increase in the supply of foreign currency. The government can also influence the exchange rate by adding to the demand or supply of foreign currency.

Speculators may attempt to profit from differences between the current spot rate and the expected future spot rate. Speculators buy currencies that they expect to increase in value and sell currencies that they expect to fall in value. In doing this they tend to push the value of the currency in the expected direction. Speculation may be stabilizing or destabilizing, depending on whether the expected exchange rate is an accurate prediction of the future spot rate.

The effect of exchange rate changes on the demand and supply of foreign currency is likely to be greater in the long run than in the short run, because the demand for traded goods is more elastic in the long run. In the short run, it is possible that depreciation will lead to a lower value of exports (if the percentage decrease in the foreign currency price of exports is greater than the percentage increase in the quantity of exports). This possibility is less likely in the long run when demand is more elastic. Also, the exchange market may be stabilized by capital flows.

Purchasing power parity suggests that exchange rate changes will reflect differences between inflation rates. If domestic inflation exceeds foreign inflation, the demand for imports tends to increase, the foreign demand for exports to decrease, and the dollar tends to fall in value. Small inflation differentials may be offset by other influences on the exchange rate, such as capital flows. Purchasing power parity is most likely to be a useful guide to long–run exchange rate changes or to short–run changes when inflation differentials are large.

The forward exchange market can be used to avoid exchange risk: people who will receive foreign currency in the future can sell the currency forward, and people with future foreign currency payments can buy foreign currency forward. The forward exchange rate is mainly determined by **covered interest arbitrage**. An American investing in the London market can avoid **exchange risk** by selling sterling in the forward market. Using the forward market, investors can compare the rates of return on domestic and foreign investments. **Covered interest parity** is established when the forward premium is approximately equal to the interest differential:

$$p = (F - S) / S \approx NR - LR$$

When covered interest parity is established, the returns from domestic and foreign investment are equal:

$$(1 + NR) = (F/S)(1 + LR)$$

The forward rate is usually close to the rate consistent with covered interest parity, but divergences from interest parity can be caused by transactions costs, political risk, and speculation. Speculation in the forward market takes place when the forward rate and the expected future spot rate are different.

Study Questions

1. Why does the demand for foreign currency slope downward and the supply of foreign currency slope upward? What factors determine the slopes of the curves?
2. Under what conditions will the supply of foreign currency slope downward from left to right?
3. Using the exchange rates given below, calculate the return on $30 from triangular arbitrage assuming that the arbitrager begins and ends with dollars.

sterling–franc rate	= 0.1
franc–dollar	= 6.0
dollar–sterling rate	= 1.5

Why will this profit opportunity disappear?

4. What is the likely effect on the dollar–sterling exchange rate of:
   a. an increase in American investment abroad?
   b. an increase in American imports?
   c. the British discovery of North Sea oil reserves?
   d. a fall in the world price of wheat?
   e. an across–the–board tariff on British imports?
   f. an expected fall in the value of sterling (and a consequent fall in the dollar value of British assets held by Americans)?
5. Show how the Bank of England can intervene in the foreign exchange market to maintain the sterling–dollar exchange rate when there is an excess demand for dollars. (**Hint:** the demand for foreign currency in this case is a demand for dollars.) Show how speculators may help or hinder the effort to maintain the exchange rate, depending on the exchange rate they expect.
6. Assuming that there is no speculation in the forward market, show how the forward rate is determined by covered interest arbitrage. What factors may cause a departure from covered interest parity?
7. The dollar–sterling spot exchange rate is 1.50. The interest rates in New York and London are 8 percent and 4 percent, respectively. What is the dollar–sterling forward rate? What is the forward premium? Is sterling at a premium or a discount?
8. If the rate of inflation in Argentina is 200 percent and the rate of inflation in the United States is 5 percent, is it possible for the Argentinean monetary authorities to maintain a constant austral–dollar exchange rate? Explain using diagrams showing the effects of inflation on Argentina's demand and supply of foreign currency. (Use the demand and supply of dollars as functions of the austral–dollar exchange rate.)
9. Assume that German interest rates are higher than U.S. rates, and the DM is at a discount in the forward market relative to the dollar. If speculators start selling DM, the DM will tend to fall. However, arbitragers will buy DM, thus preventing the fall. Why?

Selected References

Bank of England, "The Market in Foreign Exchange in London," Press Notice, 20, August 1986.

Bank for International Settlements, *Central Bank Survey of Foreign Exchange Market Activity in April 1992*, Basle: BIS, March, 1993.

Bergstrand, J. H., "Selected Views of Exchange Rate Determination After a Decade of Floating," *New England Economic Review*, May/June 1983, pp. 14–29.

Crystal, K. A., "A Guide to Foreign Exchange Markets," *Federal Reserve Bank of St. Louis Review*, 66, March 1984, pp. 5–18.

Federal Reserve Bank of New York, "Summary of Results of Foreign Exchange Market Turnover Survey," New York: Federal Reserve Bank of New York, August 1986.

Fieleke, N. S., "The Rise of the Foreign Currency Futures Market," *New England Economic Review*, March/April 1985, pp. 38–47.

Fleming, J. M. and R. A. Mundell, "Official Intervention in the Forward Exchange Market: A Simplified Analysis," *IMF Staff Papers*, 11, March 1964, pp. 1–19.

Gaillot, H. J., "Purchasing Power Parity as an Explanation of Long–term Changes in Exchange Rates," *Journal of Money, Credit, and Banking*, 2, August 1970, pp. 348–57.

Kubarych, R. M., "Foreign Exchange Markets in the United States," Revised Edition, New York: Federal Reserve Bank of New York, 1983.

Levi, M., *International Finance*, 2/e, New York: McGraw Hill, 1990.

Officer, L. H., "The Purchasing Power Parity Theory of Exchange Rates: A Review Article," *IMF Staff Papers*, 23, March 1976, pp. 1–59.

Organization for Economic Co–Operation and Development, *Exchange Rate Determination and the Conduct of Monetary Policy*, Paris: OECD, 1985.

Rhomberg, R. R., "Indices of Effective Exchange Rates," *IMF Staff Papers*, 23, March 1976, pp. 88–112.

Walmsley, J., *The Foreign Exchange and Money Market Guide*, New York: Wiley, 1992.

Seven

The Balance of Payments

Introduction

This chapter describes what the balance of payments is and examines the principles used in compiling the balance of payments: the concept of double–entry bookkeeping and the classification of transactions into credits and debits. The meaning and significance of balance of payments deficits and surpluses, the relationship of the balance of payments to national income, and the level of international indebtedness are also considered. The focus is on the balance of payments of the United States, but most of the discussion is equally applicable to other countries.

Balance of Payments Accounting

The **balance of payments** is a statistical record of the transactions by the residents of one country with the residents of other countries over a period of time (usually a quarter or a year). The data for the United States are compiled by the Department of Commerce and published in the *Survey of Current Business*. Data for other countries may be found in *International Financial Statistics* or the *Balance of Payments Yearbook*; both are published by the International Monetary Fund.

Credits and Debits

Table 7.1 shows a summary of the balance of payments of the United States using broad groupings of transactions. Some of the entries are positive in value and some are negative. The principle used when the balance of payments is compiled is that **credit** entries, those that are positive in value, record transactions that normally lead to receipts from foreigners and thus a supply of foreign exchange. For example, exports appear as a credit because they lead to receipts from foreigners and a supply of foreign exchange. (In cases where exports are donated to other countries or are bartered for imports, they are still classified as credits. The reason is that if the decision to export were not related to other transactions or considerations, exports would lead to receipts from foreigners.) **Debit** items, those that are negative, record transactions that normally lead to payments to foreigners and thus a demand for foreign currency. For example, imports appear as a debit because

Table 7.1
The Balance of Payments of the United States in 1992

		Millions of Dollars
1	Exports of goods, services, and income received	730,460
2	Merchandise exports	440,138
3	Service exports	179,710
4	Income receipts on investments	110,612
5	Imports of goods, services, and income paid	−763,965
6	Merchandise imports	−536,276
7	Service imports	−123,299
8	Income payments on investments	−104,391
9	Unilateral transfers	−32,895
10	U.S. assets abroad net change [increase/capital outflow (−)]	−50,961
11	U.S. official reserve assets	3,901
12	Other U.S. government assets abroad	−1,609
13	U.S. private assets	−53,253
14	Foreign assets in the United States net change [increase/capital inflow (+)]	129,579
15	Foreign official assets	40,684
16	Other foreign assets	88,895
17	Allocations of special drawing rights	—
18	Statistical discrepancy	−12,218
	Some Important Balances	
19	Merchandise balance (lines 2 and 6)	−96,138
20	Balance of goods and services (lines 19, 3, and 7)	−39,727
21	Current account balance (lines 1, 5, and 9)	−66,400
22	Current account plus net private capital flows (lines 21, 12, 13, 16, and 18, or lines 11, and 15)	−44,585

Source: Department of Commerce, Survey of Current Business, December 1993.

they lead to payments to foreigners and a demand for foreign exchange. The use of positive and negative entries does not mean that the positive entries are good and the negative entries are bad.

Merchandise Trade, Services, and Investment Income

In Table 7.1, the sections of the balance of payments (lines 1 and 5) showing exports and imports of goods and services, and investment income/

payments, are the largest. Merchandise trade is trade in goods. The United States exports and imports a wide range of goods. Some of the most important exports are: aircraft, agricultural produce, automotive vehicles and parts, chemicals, computers and electronic equipment, and machinery. Some of the major imports are: automotive vehicles and parts, computers and electronic equipment, machinery, petroleum and petroleum products, and various types of consumer goods. The most important examples of services are: travel and transportation, royalties, and license fees. Finally, the United States receives revenue from U.S. assets abroad (line 4), and payments are made to owners of foreign assets in the United States (line 8).

Unilateral Transfers

The entry for unilateral transfers (line 9) records transfers of funds (such as pensions) that are not related to sales of goods or assets, and net gifts of goods and services to foreigners by Americans. The entry is needed to comply with the principles of double–entry bookkeeping described in a later section.

Capital Flows

Capital flows are shown by the change in the stock of U.S. assets abroad (line 10) and the change in the stock of foreign assets in the United States (line 14). These entries are sometimes jointly known as the **capital account**. An increase in U.S. assets abroad, a **capital outflow**, is recorded as a debit item because the acquisition of foreign assets involves a payment to foreigners. For example, an increase in U.S. assets takes place when an American company buys a German factory.[1] An increase in foreign assets in the United States, a **capital inflow**, is recorded as a credit item because foreigners make payments to Americans when they invest in the United States. For example, an increase in foreign assets in the United States takes place when a Japanese firm buys an American factory.

Official Reserves

Changes in international reserves (line 11) are included as a capital flow. The accumulation of international reserves is analogous to the accumulation of foreign capital assets. When the United States buys foreign exchange (or gold), it makes payments to foreigners and adds to the demand for foreign

---

[1] It may help to think of a capital outflow as the import of a piece of paper, the paper being a claim to a foreign asset.

exchange; thus, the accumulation of international reserves is a debit entry. Similarly, an increase in foreign governments' reserves of American dollars (line 15) is recorded as a credit because foreign monetary authorities increase the supply of foreign currency when they purchase dollars.

Special Drawing Rights

Special Drawing Rights are an asset issued by the International Monetary Fund.[2] When special drawing rights are allocated, they are added to the stock of international reserves and the increase in reserves is shown as a debit. A credit item of an equal amount, recording the allocation of special drawing rights, is added to the balance of payments to comply with the principles of double–entry bookkeeping (line 17). Special drawing rights are not allocated every year. The last allocation was in 1981.

The Statistical Discrepancy

Finally, the statistical discrepancy is calculated and added to the balance of payments (line 18). Since the balance of payments is based on the principle of double–entry bookkeeping, it should always sum to zero. However, it is impossible to identify and record all transactions perfectly. The statistical discrepancy is a reflection of omitted transactions and imperfect valuation. For instance, unrecorded capital flows are thought to be one of the main reasons for the statistical discrepancy. The discrepancy can be large—in 1982 the statistical discrepancy was over $40 billion.

The last four lines in Table 7.1 show measures of net trade with the rest of the world. The significance of measures such as these is discussed in the following sections.

Measurement Problems

The data on trade flows are obtained from customs declarations. The data are quite reliable in the sense that most goods are recorded. However, the value of the goods may not always be accurate because companies sometimes have an incentive to overcharge or undercharge for goods, perhaps to avoid taxes or as a way of transferring capital between countries.[3] Another problem is that goods are not necessarily paid for at the time they are shipped. Thus, in an accounting period, there can be a difference between the value of

---

[2]Special Drawing Rights (SDRs) are described in Chapter 13.

[3]See the discussion of transfer pricing in Chapter 19.

merchandise trade and the value of payments associated with the trade. Under certain circumstances, such as when a currency is expected to increase or decrease in value, transactions may be brought forward or delayed. For example, if an American company has to make a payment in French francs, and the company expects the franc to depreciate, the company may delay payment because the dollar cost of the payment will be less after the franc has fallen. Leads and lags in payments may be another major factor responsible for the statistical discrepancy.

Data relating to international transactions by the government are reasonably complete, with the exception of the data on military and security operations. Most of the remaining data making up the balance of payments are obtained from surveys. Data on services are obtained from surveys of banks and financial corporations. Tourist expenditures are calculated from surveys of a small number of tourists. Data on fees and royalties are obtained from surveys of trade organizations. Data on capital flows are obtained from surveys of major institutions dealing in international investment. Although efforts are made to ensure that the surveys are accurate, some degree of error is inevitable. Imperfect measurement of capital flows is thought to be a major reason for the statistical discrepancy.

Double–Entry Bookkeeping

The balance of payments is drawn up using **double–entry bookkeeping**. This method uses the principle that every transaction has two sides: the transfer of whatever is sold (goods, services, or assets) and the payment. One side of the transaction leads to a credit, and the other side leads to a debit. Therefore, when one side of an international transaction is recorded as a credit or debit item, there is always an accompanying debit or credit, respectively, of an equal amount showing the other side of the transaction. In other words, the balance of payments must sum to zero because double–entry bookkeeping is used. This is a very important conclusion.

The concept of double–entry bookkeeping is perhaps best illustrated by examples.

1. An American company exports a machine and is paid with a check drawn on the New York bank account of a French company.

    The export of the machine is recorded as a credit because exports normally lead to receipts from foreigners. The reduction in size of the French company's American bank account is recorded as a debit showing a reduction in foreign assets in the United States. The reason is that if the reduction in the French company's account had taken place independently (instead of being a payment for American goods), the American bank would have made a payment to the French company.

2. An American firm imports champagne from France and pays with a check drawn on its bank account in France.

   The imported champagne appears as a debit under merchandise imports because imports normally lead to payments to foreigners. The reduction in the size of the American firm's bank account in France is recorded as a credit showing a decline in U.S. assets abroad. The reason is that if the reduction in the American firm's account had taken place independently (instead of being a payment for French goods), the French bank would have made a payment to the American company.

3. An American company uses a check drawn on a New York bank to pay for a factory in Britain, and the check is deposited in the New York account of a British firm.

   The purchase of the British factory is recorded as a debit, showing an increase in U.S. assets abroad, because the purchase entails a payment to foreigners. The increase in the British firm's New York bank account is recorded as a credit, showing an increase in foreign assets in the United States. The reason is that if the increase in the British firm's bank account had taken place independently, the British firm would have made a payment to an American bank.

4. An American company reduces the size of its foreign bank account and repatriates the funds.

   The decline in the American company's foreign bank account is recorded as a credit showing a reduction in U.S. assets abroad. The amount of dollars held by foreigners declines when an American firm repatriates its funds. This is recorded as a debit, showing a decline in foreign assets in the United States, because buying dollars (assets) from foreigners entails making payments to foreigners.

5. The American government gives $100 million cash to a developing country which holds the money in a New York bank account.

   The gift is shown as a debit under unilateral transfers because it is a payment to foreigners. A credit records an increase in foreign assets in the United States because if the increase in the foreign government's bank account had taken place independently, the foreign government would have made a payment to the American bank.

Deficits and Surpluses

An understanding of the principles of balance of payments accounting is important as a background to the concepts of surplus and deficit in the balance of payments. There are two important conclusions which follow from the preceding discussion. First, since the balance of payments must sum to zero, it follows that there can only be a surplus or deficit on part of the balance of payments. In other words, there is no such thing as an overall surplus or deficit. When reference is made to a balance of payments surplus or deficit, it is the structure of the balance of payments that is being referred to, not the overall value. Second, we should not assume that a balance of payments surplus is necessarily good and a deficit bad. A surplus on part of the accounts is always matched by a deficit on the rest of the accounts.

Balance of Payments Equilibrium

It is inevitable that, at any given time, some parts of the accounts will be positive in total and some parts will be negative. Economically, the terms "surplus" and "deficit" are often used to imply more than just that the total of some parts of the balance of payments is positive or negative. Surpluses and deficits are often defined as balance of payments positions that are not sustainable: in other words, the terms can be used to indicate the existence of disequilibrium balance of payments positions. For example, large net borrowing from abroad may indicate a long–run disequilibrium position because a country cannot borrow or run down its holdings of foreign assets continuously. (This is true under fixed or flexible exchange rates.)

Under fixed exchange rates, balance of payments equilibrium often takes on a more specific meaning, that is, surpluses and deficits are positions that are not consistent with the maintenance of a stable exchange rate. For example, assume that international reserves are being depleted (because the monetary authorities are intervening in the foreign exchange market to prevent domestic currency from falling in value). This is not an equilibrium because the stock of reserves is limited. Eventually, the monetary authorities will be forced to stop selling foreign currency, and domestic currency will fall in value.[4]

---

[4]In Chapters 9 and 10 the expression "balance of payments equilibrium" denotes positions where the demand and supply of foreign currency are equal at the existing exchange rate without intervention by the monetary authorities.

The Balance of Payments and the Foreign Exchange Market

The foreign exchange market and the balance of payments are closely related. In the foreign exchange market, the amount of foreign currency sold must obviously be equal to the amount of foreign currency bought. Foreign exchange is not created or destroyed in the market, it is transferred from one holder to another. The balance of payments can be thought of as a record of all of the possible reasons for purchases and sales of foreign currency. Therefore, it would seem that the balance of payments must sum to zero because the supply and demand for foreign currency must be equal. Unfortunately, it is not quite so simple.

The correspondence between the balance of payments and the foreign exchange market is not perfect because the balance of payments also includes records of transactions that do not lead to foreign exchange transactions. Gifts of goods and barter trade are obvious examples. Another example of a transaction that does not lead to a foreign exchange transaction is an export by a Japanese company to the United States that is paid for by transferring ownership of a dollar deposit in New York. The balance of payments would record the acquisition of U.S. assets by foreigners and the sale of exports to foreigners, but in this case neither would be accompanied by a foreign exchange transaction. Also, recall that the balance of payments is not a completely accurate record of international transactions (hence the need for the statistical discrepancy).

A problem which arises when using balance of payments statistics as a guide to the motives underlying foreign exchange transactions is that the balance of payments does not distinguish between transactions that are undertaken independently (for their own sake) and transactions that result from the financing of independent transactions. For example, an increase in foreign assets in the U.S. may occur because Japanese investors want to invest in the United States, or an increase may reflect a temporary use of funds received by Japanese firms for goods that have been sold to the United States (as in the preceding example).

Accounting Balances

Various accounting balances have been used to measure balance of payments surpluses and deficits. As countries have moved toward more flexible exchange rates, an exchange rate policy has become less important, and the importance of these accounting balances for current policy has decreased. Therefore, we shall only discuss the concepts briefly. The purposes of this discussion are to illustrate the principles of balance of payments accounting, to set the background for the analysis of balance of payments adjustments in the following chapters, and to facilitate the historical analysis in Part Three.

Definitions of accounting balances within the balance of payments reflect three distinctions: 1) between real and financial transactions, that is, between trade in goods and services, and capital flows; 2) between short–term capital flows and long–term capital flows; and 3) between official transactions carried out by the monetary authorities and other international transactions.

The Current Account and Net Foreign Assets

The **current account** records trade in goods and services, and unilateral transfers. In a sense, the current account measures the extent to which a country lives within its means. Ignoring unilateral transfers, a deficit in the current account indicates that an economy is spending more on imports of goods and services than it is earning from exports of goods and services. Why is this unsustainable?

Recall that the balance of payments must sum to zero. Therefore, the current account is equal to the (negative) value of the rest of the balance of payments. In other words, a current account deficit will be accompanied by a surplus on the rest of the balance of payments. If a country spends more than it earns on goods and services, it must be running down its stock of foreign assets, and/or increasing its debt to foreigners. A current account deficit implies falling net foreign assets. This cannot go on forever because the country's stock of foreign assets is limited, and there is probably a limit to how much foreigners will be willing to lend to one country.[5] Therefore, a current account deficit may be an indication of balance of payments disequilibrium.

The current account is also of interest because it is part of a nation's national income accounts. As such, it represents the contribution to aggregate demand resulting from trade. For example, a current account surplus implies that foreign trade adds to aggregate demand because foreigners are purchasing more of a country's output than domestic residents are buying abroad. However, the effects of capital flows on economic activity are not shown by the current account. (In the absence of official intervention, a current account surplus is accompanied by a capital account deficit, implying that more capital is flowing out of the country than is flowing into the country.)

---

[5]How much a country may borrow probably depends on what the borrowing is used for. We return to this topic when we discuss the sectoral balance later in this chapter.

The Basic Balance

The **basic balance** adds long–term capital movements to the current account balance. The basic balance is supposed to show the underlying long–term balance of payments position of a country. The proposition is that trade and long–term capital flows do not fluctuate in response to temporary economic disturbances but reflect long–term forces. For example, one might expect trade to change slowly in response to changes in a country's competitive position, and long–term capital flows to reflect long–term investment based on the returns to capital (not short–run speculation).

How does the basic balance relate to the concept of balance of payments equilibrium? The reasoning behind the basic balance is that the amount of short–term capital that a country can attract is limited, and the stock of reserves is limited; therefore, a country cannot finance a deficit on the rest of the balance of payments by incurring short–term debt or running down reserves.

As a theoretical concept, this measure of the balance of payments may have some appeal, but in practice the measure is much less attractive because capital flows cannot be classified unambiguously into short–term and long–term flows. For example, some holders of American companies' stocks, which are classified as long–term investments, may be prepared to liquidate those investments at short notice. Many supposedly short–term investments follow long–term trends. Whether an investment is short–term or long–term depends as much on the investor's intentions as on the nature of the asset. Thus, the distinction between short–term and long–term investments is not particularly useful. Doubts about the importance or validity of the basic balance led the U.S. Department of Commerce to stop publishing the basic balance in 1977.[6] The IMF continues to publish the basic balance (for example, in *International Financial Statistics*).

The Current Account Balance Plus Net Private Capital Flows

An indication of the net demand or supply of foreign exchange from the private sector is provided by the sum of the current account and net private capital flows. The remaining items in the balance of payments are changes in U.S. and foreign official assets; therefore, this balance shows official transactions. The balance may be of interest if there is a possibility that a currency will be devalued. For example, a deficit on the sum of the current account and net private capital flows must be equal to sales of foreign

---

[6]The reasons for changing the presentation of balance of payments data are discussed in "Report of the Advisory Committee on the Presentation of Balance of Payments Statistics," *Survey of Current Business*, June 1976, pp. 18–27.

currency by the monetary authorities. If the monetary authorities stop intervening (because they are running out of reserves), the exchange rate will change, and the structure of the balance of payments will change. In the absence of official intervention, the exchange rate will change to ensure that the current account and capital accounts sum to zero (because the balance of payments will always sum to zero). To put it another way, when there is no official intervention, the exchange rate changes to equate the demand and supply of foreign currency from private transactions.

Unfortunately this balance does not clearly indicate the likely change in an exchange rate. We cannot be sure how the domestic or foreign monetary authorities will react because the present international monetary system has no clear rules defining if or how an exchange rate should be maintained. For example, it is quite possible that one government may be attempting to increase an exchange rate while another government is trying to reduce the same exchange rate.

Summary

It is clear from this brief discussion of balance of payments accounting that because there are many possible ways of defining balance of payments deficits or surpluses, unqualified references to "the" balance of payments surplus or deficit are meaningless. We must specify which part of the balance of payments we are referring to.

National Income and the Balance of Payments

Gross domestic product is equal to the value of goods and services produced in an economy over a period of time.[7] The increase in gross domestic product is often used as an indicator of improvements in economic welfare. In an economy without trade, the value of output is equal to the sum of three different types of spending in an economy: consumption (C), investment (I), and government spending (G).[8] The value of output is sometimes called

---

[7]Gross national product is equal to gross domestic product plus net factor receipts (mainly investment income) from the rest of the world.

[8]In this chapter I refers to actual investment. In the following chapter a distinction is made between planned and actual investment.

national income (Y) because the value of goods and services produced is equal to the sum of incomes earned in the production process.[9] Thus:

$$Y = C + I + G \tag{1}$$

This is an identity because any output not sold to consumers or the government is by definition part of investment, that is, the accumulation of inventories is classified as part of investment.

Net Exports Add to the Demand for Goods and Services

If we want to calculate the gross domestic product of an economy that engages in trade, there are two additional considerations. First, because output may be sold abroad as well as at home, the value of exports (X) must be added to domestic spending. Second, the value of imports (M) must be deducted because some domestic spending may be on imported goods and services rather than domestic goods and services. Therefore, the expression for national income in an open economy is:

$$Y = C + I + G + X - M^{10} \tag{2}$$

Alternatively, we can express national income as the total value of spending or **absorption** (consumption, investment, and government spending) plus the current account (net exports of goods and services):

$$Y = A + X - M \text{ (where } A = C + I + G) \tag{3}$$

In this form the relationship between spending, net exports (X − M), and national income is clear. If national income exceeds absorption (Y > A), net exports will be positive. If absorption exceeds national income (A > Y), net exports will be negative. This presentation leads to an important conclusion: net exports can only increase if income rises relative to absorption. If income does not increase, absorption must fall if net exports are to increase. Recalling

---

[9]The value of goods and services is equal to spending on goods and services. Since every cent spent on goods and services accrues to someone as income in some form, if all sources of income are identified, income equals output.

[10]This expression gives gross domestic product. We must add net factor income (net investment income) from abroad to get gross national product. Then, if the country receives gifts (transfers) from other countries, these must be added to gross national product to give national income. For simplicity, we assume zero net investment income and transfers.

that national income is a measure of national output, it is clear that for a country to have a positive trade balance, it must produce more than it uses (absorbs) domestically. We shall return to the role of absorption in the following chapters.

Sectoral Balance

Income can be spent on consumption (C), saved (S), or taken as taxes (T). Therefore:

$$Y = C + S + T \qquad (4)$$

The allocation of income must be equal to the level of income earned, thus, Equations 2 and 4 must be equal. Combining these equations, subtracting C from both sides, and moving M to the right, yields:

$$I + G + X = S + T + M \qquad (5)$$

Equation 5 is derived from national income accounting and must hold because of the way in which the variables are defined in the national income accounts. Although it has no behavioral implications, this equation can be used to yield insights into the relationship between components of national income by sector. For example, Equation 5 can be rewritten:

$$(I - S) + (G - T) + (X - M) = 0 \qquad (6)$$

In this form the equation shows that the difference between private sector investment and saving $(I - S)$, the government deficit $(G - T)$, and the current account balance $(X - M)$, must add up to zero. The difference between private investment and saving shows net borrowing by the private sector. The difference between government spending and taxation is government borrowing. Also, recall that the current account balance is equal to net foreign investment, that is, net investment by the home country in foreign countries.[11] Thus, Equation 6 shows that net borrowing by one sector must be matched by net lending in other sectors.

Sectoral Balance and the Current Account

In the discussion of balance of payments equilibrium, it was suggested that a current account deficit may be an indication of disequilibrium, because

---

[11]Recall that the balance on the current account is equal to the (negative) value of the rest of the balance of payments.

foreigners may not be willing to increase investments in a country continuously, and the stock of foreign assets which can be sold is limited.[12] Let us examine this issue a little more carefully.

The willingness of foreigners to invest in an economy may be influenced by the possibility of long–term real growth. Using the sectoral balance Equation 6, it is clear that a current account deficit must be accompanied by an excess of private investment over savings or an excess of government spending over taxes. Since government spending (in the form of public investment) or private investment may increase the long–run income of an economy, under some circumstances an inflow of foreign investment can continue. Perhaps the inflow of capital will dry up most quickly if the current account deficit is reflected in government spending that finances current consumption rather than public investment. (Unfortunately, most government spending in the United States is consumption, not investment.)

The Balance of Payments of the United States

An illustration of the sectoral balance is shown in Table 7.2. During the 1970s, changes in the government deficit were mainly reflected in the disparity between investment and saving. This relationship held during the first years of the 1980s: net foreign investment was not significantly affected even when the federal deficit caused the overall government deficit to explode in 1982. Significant American borrowing from abroad began in 1983, and by 1984 the government deficit was mainly reflected in large net borrowing from abroad. Later, in 1991 and 1992, lower net inflows of capital meant that the government deficit was again reflected in the difference between saving and investment.

When, as in 1984, a government deficit is accompanied by a trade deficit of roughly the same amount, borrowing from abroad is approximately equal to the government deficit. However, the temptation to say that foreign countries lend to the government and finance government spending should be avoided. Foreign funds entering the domestic market may be invested in the private sector, while domestic funds are loaned to the government.

Some economists have suggested that the growth of the federal deficit in the 1980s was responsible for the current account deficit (capital account surplus). The argument is that government borrowing combined with a tight monetary policy led to a high real interest rate in the United States. Investors were attracted by American rates of return, and an increased demand for dollars from foreign investors, as well as a reduced demand for foreign

---

[12]If international reserves finance the current account deficit, the fall in reserves is recorded as a fall in U.S. assets abroad. International reserves cannot finance a current account deficit continuously because the stock of international reserves is finite.

Table 7.2
The United States Sectoral Balance

	I–S	G–T	Net Foreign Investment	Other Factors[a]
1970	−15.5	11.5	4.9	0.9
1971	−16.7	19.2	1.3	3.8
1972	0.7	3.9	−2.9	1.8
1973	−2.3	−6.9	8.7	−0.5
1974	−10.2	4.5	5.1	−0.6
1975	−80.3	64.8	21.4	6.0
1976	−36.7	38.3	8.8	10.4
1977	3.3	16.8	−9.2	10.9
1978	21.2	−2.9	−10.7	7.6
1979	22.3	−9.4	2.0	14.9
1980	−32.0	35.3	11.5	14.8
1981	−27.9	30.3	9.5	12.0
1982	−113.5	108.6	−2.5	−7.4
1983	−94.6	139.8	−35.0	10.2
1984	−23.8	108.8	−94.0	−9.0
1985	−21.2	125.3	−118.1	−13.9
1986	−3.8	146.8	−141.7	1.2
1987	18.6	111.7	−155.1	−24.8
1988	−8.7	98.3	−118.0	−28.4
1989	12.9	77.5	−89.3	1.1
1990	−52.2	138.4	−78.5	7.8
1991	−193.0	196.2	6.4	9.6
1992	−190.4	269.1	−55.1	23.6

[a]Includes the statistical discrepancy and allocations of SDRs.
Source: *Economic Report of the President*, 1994, p. 302.

currency (supply of dollars) from American investors, pushed up the value of the dollar. The result was that net exports fell as the dollar increased in value. When increased government spending leads to a fall in private spending, the change is sometimes described as **crowding out**. In this case, increased government spending crowded out net exports through the effects of the budget deficit on interest rates and the value of the dollar.

The Balance of International Indebtedness

The net capital inflow into the United States over the last decade is reflected in the international investment position of the United States shown in Table 7.3. The decline in the net investment position of the United States after 1983 occurred because American investment abroad (shown by the increase of U.S.

Table 7.3
The Net Investment Position of the United States

	1984	1986	1988	1990	1992
U.S. Assets Abroad					
At current cost	1,178.9	1,410.7	1,698.0	1,924.8	2,003.4
At market value	1,083.1	1,508.2	1,860.9	2,018.4	2,113.3
Foreign Assets in the U.S.					
At current cost	944.7	1,391.5	1,838.3	2,216.7	2,524.7
At market value	905.9	1,398.6	1,398.6	2,288.0	2,724.8
Net Position					
At current cost	234.2	19.2	−140.3	−291.9	−521.3
At market value	177.3	109.7	5.4	−269.7	−611.5

Source: *Economic Report of the President*, 1994, p. 385.

private assets abroad) was smaller than foreign investment in the United States (shown by the increase of foreign assets in the U.S).

The Net Credit Position of the United States

A word of caution is appropriate at this point. The data showing assets are not accurate enough to make precise statements about the size of a country's net external assets. In particular, U.S. investments abroad made many years ago are undervalued when they are recorded at cost (rather than market value). The figures showing the market value of assets are estimates because market value is not certain unless the assets are actually sold. However, there is no doubt that the United States is now a large net debtor. An indication of this net debt position is that in the third quarter of 1987, payments on foreign–owned assets in the United States exceeded receipts from assets abroad for the first time in recent U.S. history.[13] Since then, the United States has added to its debts because outflows of capital have been less than inflows.

The significance of being a net debtor is that servicing the debt to foreigners is a drain on national income. Therefore, the rate at which the United States is accumulating foreign debt may lead us to be concerned about the effects on future U.S. prosperity. An inflow of foreign capital adds to the funds which are available in the United States. The effects on future income depend on how the funds are used. If borrowing from abroad finances additional productive investment (public or private), it will lead to higher future real income. Under these conditions, the accumulation of net debt may

---

[13]See *Economic Report of the President*, 1988, p. 99.

Table 7.4
Rates of Investment as a Percentage of GDP

	1975–79	1980–84	1986	1988	1990	1992
United States	20.1	19.6	19.1	18.4	16.9	15.5
Japan	31.8	29.9	27.8	30.6	32.8	30.8
European Community	22.4	20.5	19.3	20.7	21.1	—

Source: IMF World Economic Outlook, October 1992, p. 169, and IMF, International Financial Statistics Yearbook, 1993.

not be a source of concern, and the debt may even decline in relation to national income (as income grows).

Table 7.4 shows total investment (public and private) as a percentage of national income. The data suggest that the capital inflow of the 1980s merely allowed the United States to continue investing at a mediocre or falling rate. To put it another way, the United States appears have borrowed to maintain low investment while government spending or consumption increased. Unfortunately, the United States has not borrowed to finance increasing investment. International comparisons between countries' rates of investment are imperfect because of differences between the ways countries measure investment. However, the data do suggest that the United States is investing less than other countries. Japan has a particularly high level of investment, which is one of the reasons that the Japanese economy has grown so rapidly.

Japan and the United States

It is interesting to compare the American and Japanese economies. One of the striking differences between the two economies is the level of saving. Japan has enjoyed a high level of private savings (between 20 and 24 percent of GDP). The large amount of funds available domestically has kept Japanese interest rates down and encouraged Japanese investment. Private savings have not been gobbled up by government borrowing. Although public investment has been around 7 percent of GDP, the budget deficit of the central government has been kept under control, and the overall government sector (local and central) has often been in surplus. The funds available from the private and official sectors have been so great that Japan has been able to invest in other countries. Low Japanese interest rates helped keep the value of the yen down, which has helped Japanese exporters. Therefore, the overall result has been a current account surplus and a capital account deficit (net capital outflow).

The position of the United States is almost exactly the opposite. The funds available from a low domestic private savings rate have been reduced by large government deficits which have kept interest rates up and resulted in low levels of private investment. Government spending has largely financed current public consumption, not public investment, so the overall investment rate (private plus public) has been low. The value of the dollar has been pushed up by the inflow of funds borrowed from abroad. As a result, the current account has been in deficit, and the capital inflow has turned the United States into a net debtor.

One policy option is to push down the value of the dollar. While this may help reduce the current account deficit, if the current account is balanced, then we know from the principles of balance of payments accounting that the United States will no longer be borrowing from abroad. But the United States needs the inflow of foreign capital if domestic investment is to be maintained. Without foreign capital, the funds available in the United States would be even lower, and borrowing by the government to finance the budget deficit would leave even less for private investment. And investment is needed for growth. A solution to the overall problem seems to require both increased private saving and lower government borrowing. But will the government have the courage to cut spending or increase taxes, and introduce policies which penalize consumption and encourage saving?

Summary of Main Points

The **balance of payments** is a record of the transactions of the residents of one country with residents in other countries. **Debit** items reflect transactions that would normally lead to payments to foreigners, for example, purchases of imports or American investment abroad. **Credit** items reflect transactions that would normally give rise to receipts from foreigners, for example, exports or foreign investment in the United States.

The major parts of the balance of payments show imports and exports of goods and services, American purchases of foreign assets, and foreign purchases of American assets. The final entry is the statistical discrepancy, which reflects valuation errors and transactions that are not recorded.

The balance of payments must sum to zero because it is based on **double–entry bookkeeping**. Since the balance of payments must sum to zero, a surplus or deficit can only exist on part of the accounts.

The balance of payments shows why people buy and sell foreign currency. Credit items might be expected to lead to a supply of foreign currency and debit items to a demand for foreign currency. The demand and supply of foreign currency are equal, and the balance of payments must sum to zero. Thus, the relationship between the balance of payments and the foreign exchange market appears close. However, some balance of payments entries reflect transactions where there were no corresponding transactions in the foreign exchange market. Also, some international transactions (particularly capital flows) go unrecorded.

Balance of payments equilibrium refers to the structure of the balance of payments, that is, to the relative values of different types of international transaction. A disequilibrium balance of payments position is one that is not sustainable; for example, a country may not be able to continue borrowing large amounts. When the exchange rate is fixed, a disequilibrium balance of payments position is one that is not consistent with maintaining the chosen exchange rate. For example, a country cannot support a fixed exchange rate by running down its holdings of foreign exchange reserves continuously.

Various measures of the balance of payments have been used. One of the objectives historically has been to indicate whether the position was likely to make exchange rate changes more likely. The concept of balance of payments equilibrium was more important under fixed exchange rates than it is now.

One balance of payments measure that is still published is the **current account** balance showing the balance of exports and imports of goods and services, and unilateral transfers. It is of interest because the current account is a measure of the extent to which a country is spending more than it earns: the current account balance is equal to the change in net foreign assets held by the country, that is, a country with a current account deficit must have falling net foreign assets.

The United States has had large current account deficits since the early 1980s. These have been reflected in a fall in America's net foreign assets. The United States is now the world's largest debtor.

The sectoral balance equation:

$$(I - S) + (G - T) + (X - M) = 0$$

can help us analyze the American experience. During the 1970s, the government deficit was reflected mainly in the balance between investment and saving. From 1984 until about 1990, the government deficit was reflected mainly in current account deficits, that is, net borrowing from abroad.

Study Questions

1. Explain what is recorded in the current account and the capital account. Using examples for each account, explain the principles used to determine whether a transaction is recorded as a debit or a credit.
2. How are the following transactions shown in the balance of payments?
   a. An American company exports a good and is paid with a deposit into a bank account it holds in a foreign country.
   b. An American company exports a good and allows three months before payments must be made.

    c. An American import is financed by a payment into the New York account of a foreign exporter.

    d. An American factory is purchased by a Japanese company using a check drawn on the Japanese company's account in New York.

    e. An American tourist pays a British hotel bill with dollars.

3. Explain what is meant by **double–entry bookkeeping**. If this method is used, why is there a statistical discrepancy? How can there be a balance of payments deficit or surplus if double–entry bookkeeping is used and the balance of payments must sum to zero?

4. Why might a current account deficit be both undesirable and unsustainable? Why does no one seem to worry about current account surpluses?

5. If saving is greater than investment, and government spending equals taxation, explain how we can deduce whether the current account or capital account is in surplus.

6. Using the sectoral balance equation, discuss reasons for the decline of the American trade balance from 1980 onward.

7. Why might we be concerned about the long–term effects of a prolonged American trade deficit?

8. Using data from the IMF publication, *International Financial Statistics*, compare the balance of payments of Germany, Japan, and the United States for 1980 and 1992. What are the major changes which have taken place?

9. In the October 1992 *World Economic Outlook* (p. 29), the IMF predicted that cutting government spending and increasing taxes in the United States would lead to higher investment and higher real net exports. Using the sectoral balance equation, explain why this prediction seems reasonable.

Selected References

Cooper, R. N., "The Balance of Payments in Review," *Journal of Political Economy*, 74, August 1966, pp. 379–95.

International Monetary Fund *Balance of Payments Manual*, 4e, Washington, DC: IMF, 1977.

Kemp, D. S., "Balance of Payments Concepts—What Do They Really Mean?" *Federal Reserve Bank of St. Louis Review*, July 1975, pp. 14–23.

Kindelberger, C. P., "Measuring Equilibrium in the Balance of Payments," *Journal of Political Economy*, 77, December 1969, pp. 873–91.

Stern, R. M., et al, "The Presentation of the U.S. Balance of Payments: A Symposium," in *Essays in International Finance*, No. 123, Princeton, NJ: Princeton University Press, 1977.

Yeager, L. B., *International Monetary Relations*, 2e, New York: Harper and Row, 1976.

Appendix: The Liquidity Balance and Official Settlements Balance

Under fixed exchange rates, one of the main issues was the sustainability of the chosen exchange rate. Various balance of payments definitions were used.

The Liquidity Balance

The **liquidity balance** was designed to show the possible pressure on American reserve assets (in particular, gold). The balance distinguishes between liquid and nonliquid short–term capital flows, and is defined as the sum of changes in U.S. reserves and changes in U.S. liquid liabilities to foreigners (private and official).[14] The distinction between liquid and nonliquid liabilities is that liquid liabilities are easily transferable whereas nonliquid liabilities are not. For example, trade financing loans with a duration of less than three months made by foreign banks to U.S. corporations are not transferable and are recorded as short–term nonliquid liabilities.

The justification for this balance of payments definition is that a liquidity balance deficit is not an equilibrium position—either the stock of reserves is falling or the stock of U.S. liquid liabilities to foreigners is increasing. A deficit cannot be permanently financed by reserves because the stock of reserves is limited, and increasing U.S. liabilities to foreigners are inconsistent with the maintenance of a fixed exchange rate. If foreigners suddenly chose to sell the American assets they held, the American monetary authorities would be obliged to intervene in the foreign exchange market, and American reserves would fall.

The liquidity balance suffers from serious flaws. Although liquid liabilities to foreigners are considered, American holdings of foreign liquid assets are not considered. This asymmetrical treatment means that the balance is of dubious significance. For example, if an American bank and a British bank agreed to increase their deposits with each other, the liquidity balance of payments deficit would increase because U.S. liquid liabilities are part of the U.S. deficit, but U.S. claims are ignored. Also, the liquidity balance does not show what it is supposed to show—the vulnerability of American reserves—because the balance of payments records changes in the stocks of reserves and U.S. liquid liabilities, not the sizes of the stocks. (The size of the

---

[14]The liquidity balance should not be confused with another balance the reader may encounter, the **net liquidity balance**. This equals the change in reserve assets plus the difference between liquid private claims on foreigners and liabilities to foreigners.

stock of U.S. liquid liabilities relative to the stock of reserves may be an indicator of the vulnerability of American reserves.) Finally, as shown in the discussion of the basic balance, it is impossible to distinguish clearly between short–term and long–term capital flows.

The Official Settlements Balance

The **official settlements balance** is a modified version of the liquidity balance. A distinction is drawn between official and private U.S. liquid liabilities, and the balance is defined as the sum of official liquid liabilities to official foreigners (central banks) and changes in reserves. The official settlements balance has similar flaws to the liquidity balance: it measures changes in the stocks and not the stocks themselves, and U.S. liquid assets are ignored.

Under the Bretton Woods system (see Chapter 13) the official settlements balance was supposed to show the vulnerability of American gold reserves because dollars held by foreign central banks (liquid liabilities to official foreigners) could be used to buy gold from the United States. When the option to buy gold ended in August 1971, the official settlements balance ceased to be significant.

Eight

The Determination of Income in an Open Economy

Introduction

In this chapter we examine the factors that determine the level of national income in an open economy. We begin with a simple model of a closed economy (no foreign trade) with fixed prices and without a government sector. Using the assumption that the exchange rate is fixed, the model is extended to include a government sector and international trade. Finally, the assumptions of the model are relaxed and the effects of inflation and exchange rate changes are considered. At first the model may seem unrealistic, but it is developed to incorporate the elements needed to show the role of international trade in determining income, and to identify reasons why income may change. The model also shows how the incomes of different countries are linked through trade. The model is "Keynesian" in that it concentrates on aggregate demand as the determinant of income.

The Determination of Income in a Closed Economy with No Government[1]

Gross national product (GNP) is the value of goods and services produced in an economy over a period of time. GNP is often referred to as **national income** because the value of goods and services produced is equal to the sum of incomes earned in the production process. (The value of goods and services produced is equal to expenditure on the goods and services because every dollar spent ends up as income to someone if all sources of income are identified. Thus, income is always the same as output.)

The value of national income (Y) in a closed economy with no government is equal to the value of consumption (C) plus investment (I):

$$Y = C + I \qquad (1)$$

---

[1]Readers who are familiar with the standard model of income determination presented in principles of macroeconomics courses may want to skip (or skim through) this section.

Because income is the value of goods and services produced, it is also called **aggregate supply**.

The Equilibrium Level of Income

The **equilibrium level of income** is the level of income at which aggregate demand is equal to aggregate supply. In an economy with no government or foreign trade, **aggregate demand** (D) is composed of the demand for consumption goods and services (C) and the demand for investment goods or planned investment (I_p):

$$D = C + I_p \qquad (2)$$

Initially we shall assume that there are unemployed resources in the economy and that the level of income (aggregate supply) can increase without the price level rising. We will see that in this case the equilibrium level of income is determined solely by aggregate demand. We begin by examining consumption because it plays an important role in income determination.

The Consumption Function

Consumption is the largest single type of spending in aggregate demand. The consumption function helps us to predict what will happen to consumption as income changes. We would normally expect consumption to increase with the level of income. In our model we assume that the relationship between consumption (C) and income (Y) is:

$$C = C_a + cY \qquad (3)$$

where C_a represents a particular level of consumption that does not change with income (**autonomous consumption**), and c is the amount of each extra dollar of income that is consumed (the **marginal propensity to consume**). Autonomous consumption can be thought of as a level of consumption determined by habits, wealth, and past income levels. If income increases, autonomous consumption does not change. Total consumption does increase with income, though, and the amount of the increase is determined by the marginal propensity to consume. For simplicity we assume that the marginal propensity to consume is constant.

The marginal propensity to consume is less that one because people use increases in income to finance saving as well as consumption. The amount of each extra dollar that is saved is the **marginal propensity to save** (s). Since each extra dollar is allocated between consumption and saving, the sum of

Figure 8.1
The Consumption Function and the Level of Aggregate Demand

The consumption function ($C = C_a + cY = 100 + 0.67Y$) shows how consumption increases with the level of income. For example, at an income level of 1200, consumption equals about 900. Aggregate demand (D) is obtained by adding planned investment ($I_p = 200$) to consumption.

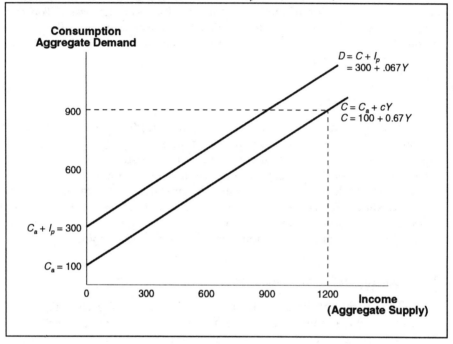

the marginal propensity to consume and the marginal propensity to save equals one, that is, $c + s = 1$.

For example, if the consumption function is:

$$C = \$100 + 0.67Y$$

then autonomous consumption equals $100, the marginal propensity to consume is 0.67, and the marginal propensity to save is 0.33. If income equals $1,200, consumption equals about $900 ($100 + 0.67 × $1,200).

The consumption function is shown in Figure 8.1. The vertical intercept represents autonomous consumption, and the function slopes upward showing that consumption increases as income increases. The slope is the increase in consumption per dollar increase in income, that is, the slope of the consumption function is the marginal propensity to consume (0.67).

Investment

We assume that investment demand, or planned investment, is determined **exogenously**, in other words, by factors outside of the model. This assumption does not imply that the potential effects of changes in planned investment on the level of income are ignored. These effects are examined after the determination of the level of income has been discussed. The main purpose of the assumption is to simplify the analysis: we treat the level of planned investment as constant while the basic model of the determination of income is developed.

Aggregate Demand

Recall that aggregate demand equals consumption plus planned investment. If planned investment equals 200, the line representing aggregate demand in Figure 8.1 ($D = C + I_p$) is a line 200 above the consumption function. The intercept of 300 on the vertical axis shows the total amount of autonomous expenditure, the level of demand that is independent of the level of income. The intercept represents the sum of planned investment (200) and autonomous consumption (100). As income increases, the level of aggregate demand increases because consumption increases with income.

The Equilibrium Level of Income

The determination of the equilibrium level of income is shown in Figure 8.2. The horizontal axis shows income, or aggregate supply, and the vertical axis shows aggregate demand. Points at which aggregate demand and supply are equal are shown by the 45–degree line. The equilibrium level of income ($Y_E = 900$), where demand and supply are equal, is the income level at which the aggregate demand line crosses the 45–degree line.

If the level of income differs from the equilibrium level, the excess aggregate demand or supply is reflected in firms' inventories of goods, beginning a process that leads to equilibrium. For example, below the equilibrium level of income, aggregate demand is greater than aggregate supply. Firms find that their inventories are falling (because demand exceeds supply), they respond by increasing production, and the level of income rises. Similarly, above the equilibrium level of income, aggregate demand is less than supply. Firms find that their inventories are rising, they decrease production, and the level of income falls.

Figure 8.2
The Determination of the Equilibrium Level of Income

Aggregate demand and aggregate supply are equal at the equilibrium level of income $Y_E = 900$. At income levels below Y_E, aggregate demand exceeds aggregate supply, inventories are falling, firms respond by increasing output, and income rises. For example, when the level of income (aggregate supply) is at $Y_1 = 600$, aggregate demand equals 700. At income levels above Y_E, aggregate supply exceeds aggregate demand, inventories are rising, firms respond by decreasing output, and the level of income falls. For example, at $Y_2 = 1200$, aggregate demand equals 1100.

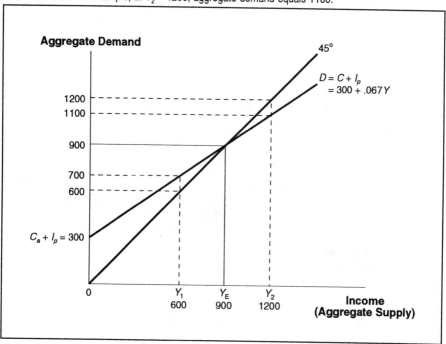

Saving and Investment

The equilibrium level of income was defined as the income at which aggregate demand and aggregate supply are equal. The equilibrium level of income can also be defined as the level of income at which saving and planned investment are equal. To show this, consider how people can use their income.

People can use their income to finance consumption or saving:

$$Y = C + S \tag{4}$$

Setting aggregate demand equal to income, we obtain:

$$C + I_p = C + S$$

or more simply:

$$I_p = S \qquad\qquad (5)$$

If the level of income is greater than aggregate demand, saving is greater than planned investment. ($Y > D$ implies that $C + S > C + I_p$, thus $S > I_p$.) If income is less than aggregate demand, saving is less than planned investment. ($Y < D$ implies that $C + S < C + I_p$, thus $S < I_p$.)

Figure 8.3
The Equality of Saving and Planned Investment
at the Equilibrium Level of Income

Saving and planned investment are equal at the equilibrium level of income $Y_E = 900$. At income levels below the equilibrium level of income, planned saving is less than planned investment. For example, at $Y_1 = 600$, saving equals 100 ($Y - C = 600 - 500$) and planned investment equals 200. At income levels above the equilibrium level, planned investment is greater than saving. For example, at $Y_2 = 1200$, saving is 300 ($Y - C = 1200 - 900$) and planned investment is 200.

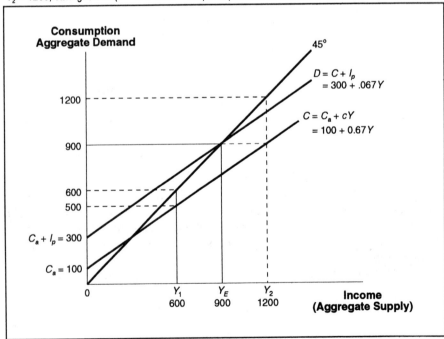

In Figure 8.3 the level of saving is shown by the vertical distance between the consumption line and the 45-degree line. The level of planned investment is shown by the vertical distance between the aggregate demand line and the consumption function. At the equilibrium level of income (Y_E), saving and planned investment are equal. Below Y_E, saving is less than planned investment, and above Y_E saving is greater than planned investment.

To investigate the relationship between planned investment and saving in more detail, we must introduce the **saving function.**

The Saving Function

The difference between income and consumption equals saving:

$$S = Y - C \tag{6}$$

Substituting Equation 3 (the consumption function) into Equation 6 we obtain:

$$S = Y - C_a - cY \tag{7}$$

which can be written as:

$$S = -C_a + (1 - c)Y \tag{8}$$

or more simply as:

$$S = -C_a + sY \tag{9}$$

where s is the marginal propensity to save ($s = 1 - c$).

For example, if the consumption function is:

$$C = 100 + 0.67Y$$

the saving function is:

$$S = -100 + 0.33Y$$

The saving function is shown in Figure 8.4. The slope of the saving function is the marginal propensity to save: in this case the slope (the vertical change per unit change in the horizontal) is the change in saving per dollar increase in income.

When planned investment is added to the diagram, the level of income (Y_E) at which saving and investment are equal can be determined. Below Y_E, planned investment exceeds saving, thus aggregate demand is greater than

Figure 8.4
Saving and Planned Investment

Saving is negative at zero income (because savings finance autonomous consumption). As income rises, the level of saving rises. The equilibrium level of income $Y_E = 900$ is the level at which planned investment and saving are equal.

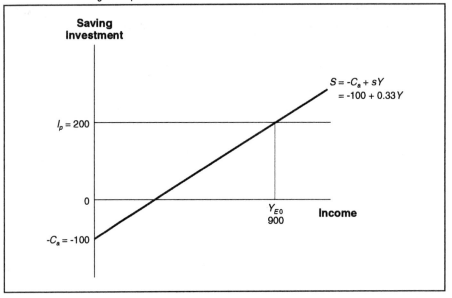

income (aggregate supply). Figures 8.2 and 8.4 are different ways of showing the same relationship.

Although planned investment and saving may differ, it should be noted that in this model, with no government or international trade, actual investment and saving are always equal. Recall that income is the value of goods and services produced, the sum of consumption and actual investment (Equation 1), and that income can be used for consumption or saving (Equation 4). Putting Equations 1 and 4 together, it is clear that:

$$S = I \tag{10}$$

Investment and Income

Having set up the basic model of income determination, we can use the model to examine how changes in the level of planned investment lead to changes in the level of income. If planned investment rises at the initial level of income, aggregate demand exceeds supply, and income rises. See, for

Figure 8.5
The Effects of an Increase in Planned Investment

If planned investment increases from 200 to 300, the equilibrium level of income increases from $Y_0 =$ 900 to $Y_1 = 1200$. The slope of the saving function between points a and b is the marginal propensity to save ($s = 0.33$), and is equal to the change in investment divided by the change in income (dI_p/dY). The multiplier (k) is the change in income divided by the change in investment (dY/dI_p), thus the multiplier is the reciprocal of the slope [$k = (1/s) = (1/0.33) = 3$].

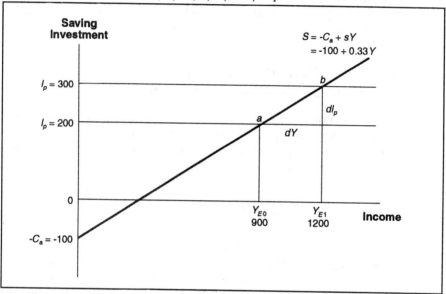

example, Figure 8.5. When planned investment increases from 200 to 300, the equilibrium level of income rises from 900 to 1,200. (The same result could be shown by moving the aggregate demand line upward in Figure 8.2.) Clearly, a fall in investment leads to a fall in income.

The Multiplier

The size of the increase in income caused by an increase in investment is determined by the **closed–economy multiplier**. To be specific, the change in income equals the change in planned investment multiplied by the multiplier. The multiplier for a closed economy with no government is $1/(1 - c)$, where c is the marginal propensity to consume. Because $1 - c$ is the marginal propensity to save (s), the multiplier can also be defined as $1/s$. For example, if the marginal propensity to consume is 0.67, the multiplier is 3 [because $3 = 1/(1 - 0.67)$]. In this case, if planned investment rises by 100, the level of income rises by 300.

The multiplier can be derived from Figure 8.5. The multiplier (k) is defined so that the change in income (dY) is the multiplier times the change in planned investment (dI_p):

$$dY = kdI_p$$

Therefore, the multiplier is equal to dY/dI_p. Figure 8.5 shows that the slope of the saving function, the marginal propensity to save (s), is equal to dI_p/dY. Therefore, the multiplier is the reciprocal of the slope of the saving function, that is, $k = 1/s$. In the example shown, $k = 1/0.33 = 3$.

The Determination of Income in an Open Economy with a Government

The determination of income in an open economy with a government sector is slightly more complicated than in the preceding discussion, but the method is basically the same. In an open economy with a government sector, the level of aggregate demand (D) is made up of consumption (C), planned investment (I_p), government spending (G), and net exports ($X - M$):

$$D = C + I_p + G + X - M \tag{11}$$

The equilibrium level of income is the income level at which aggregate demand and income (aggregate supply) are equal. The determination of the equilibrium level could be portrayed in the same way as show in Figure 8.3. The aggregate demand curve for an open economy resembles that shown in Figure 8.3, and the equilibrium level of income would be the intersection of the aggregate demand line and the 45–degree line. In this section an alternative method of presentation is used because we can show the balance of trade as well as the level of income.

Equilibrium in an Open Economy with a Government Sector

Income may be used to finance consumption (C), saving (S), and taxes (T):

$$Y = C + S + T \tag{12}$$

(Equation 12 is similar to Equation 3. The addition of a government sector means that some income is taken by taxes.) If aggregate demand equals aggregate supply, Equations 11 and 12 are equal:

$$C + S + T = C + I_p + G + X - M \tag{13}$$

Equation 13 can be rearranged to give:

$$I_p + G + X = S + T + M \tag{14}$$

This equation is the equilibrium condition for our model of the determination of income in an open economy with a government sector.[2]

The terms on the left are called **injections** and the terms on the right are called **withdrawals**. Thus, the equilibrium level of income can be defined as the income level at which injections and withdrawals are equal. Income increases if injections increase or withdrawals decrease, and income falls if injections decrease or withdrawals increase. It is clear how trade can affect income: imports are one of the withdrawals, thus increased imports tend to reduce income; exports are one of the injections, thus increased exports tend to increase income. In order to explore the determination of the equilibrium level of income in more detail, the determination of the levels of injections and withdrawals must be considered.

Injections

Initially we assume that injections are constant because they are determined exogenously, that is, they are not directly related to the level of domestic income. For example, the level of investment may be determined by interest rates and expectations, exports by the levels of income in other countries and by relative prices, and government spending by political considerations. Because injections are exogenously determined, injections are also sometimes called **autonomous expenditures**. The response of income to changes in injections is considered after the determination of the level of income has been examined.

Withdrawals

The relationship between saving and income is basically the same in this model as in the simple closed economy model with no government, that is,

---

[2]Equation 14 is very similar to Equation 5 in Chapter 7. The difference is that, since Equation 14 is an equilibrium condition, planned investment is used in the equation rather than actual investment. When actual investment is used in the equation, as in Chapter 7, the equation always holds because of the way in which the variables are defined in the national income accounts.

Figure 8.6
Injections, Withdrawals, and the Equilibrium Level of Income

The equilibrium level of income is the income level at which injections equal withdrawals. Above Y_E, injections are less than withdrawals, and the level of income falls. Below Y_E, injections are greater than withdrawals, and the level of income rises.

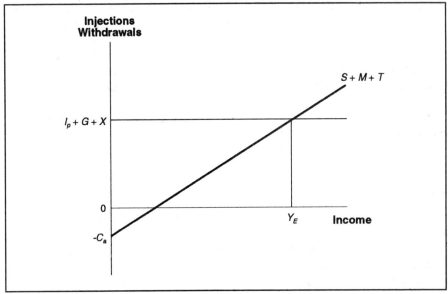

saving increases with income.[3] For simplicity, we assume that imports are a constant proportion of income, that is, $M = mY$, where M and m denote total imports and the **marginal propensity to import**, respectively. When income increases, imports increase along with the general income–induced increase in consumption. (If we were to draw the import function, with income on the horizontal axis and imports on the vertical axis, it would slope upward from the origin, the slope being the marginal propensity to import). Finally, we assume that total tax revenue (T) is also a constant proportion (t) of income, that is, $T = tY$. Thus, total tax revenue, like total imports, rises with income.

---

[3]When there are no taxes, saving increases by $1 - c$ when income increases by 1. There is a slight difference when taxes are present because saving is financed out of disposable income. If income increases by 1, disposable income increases by $1 - t$ (where t is the tax rate), and saving increases by $(1 - c)(1 - t)$.

Equilibrium

Figure 8.6 shows the determination of the equilibrium level of income, the level of income where injections and withdrawals are equal. If the level of income is above the equilibrium level of income, withdrawals exceed injections, and the level of income falls. If the level of income is below the equilibrium level of income, injections exceed withdrawals, and the level of income rises.

The Balance of Trade and the Level of Income

An alternative presentation of the determination of the level of income is useful for our purposes because the balance of trade $(X - M)$ at the equilibrium level of income can be shown.

Equation 14 can be rearranged to give:

$$X - M = S + T - I_p - G \tag{15}$$

If we plot $X - M$, as in Figure 8.7, the line slopes downward because imports increase with domestic income while exports do not change (because exports are determined by incomes in other countries). The slope of the line showing $X - M$ is equal to the marginal propensity to import multiplied by -1. The line showing $S + T - I_p - G$ slopes upward because saving and taxes increase with income, while planned investment and government spending do not change. The slope of $S + T - I_p - G$ is equal to $1 - c(1 - t)$.[4] The equilibrium level of income is the intersection of the $X - M$ line and the $S + T - I_p - G$ line. The balance of trade (B) at this income level can be read from the vertical axis.

Absorption and Trade

Domestic **absorption** (A) is total domestic spending, that is, the value of consumption, investment, and government spending:

$$A = C + I_p + G \tag{16}$$

---

[4]The slope is given by the sum of the increases in savings and taxes when income increases by one dollar. Saving increases by $(1 - c)(1 - t)$ and taxes increase by t, thus the slope is equal to $1 - c(1 - t)$.

Figure 8.7
The Balance of Trade and the Equilibrium Level of Income

By rearranging the variables that make up injections and withdrawals, the equilibrium level of income, the level at which injections equal withdrawals, can be expressed as the income level at which $X - M = S + T - I_p - G$, or $X - M = Y - A$. This presentation allows us to read the trade balance (B) from the vertical axis. In the example shown, the country has a trade deficit at the equilibrium level of income Y_E.

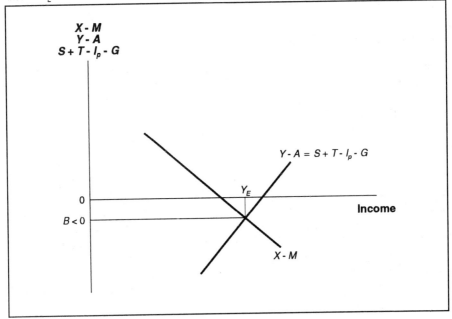

The line showing $S + T - I_p - G$ indicates the difference between income and absorption:[5]

$$S + T - I_p - G = Y - A \qquad (17)$$

Recall that $S + T - I_p - G$ also shows the trade balance (Equation 15). Combining Equations 15 and 17 shows that the trade balance is equal to the difference between domestic income and absorption:

---

[5]From Equation 12:
$$S + T = Y - C$$
Deducting $I_p + G$ from both sides gives:
$$S + T - I_p - G = Y - C - I_p - G = Y - A$$

$$X - M = Y - A \qquad (18)$$

When the balance of trade is expressed in this form, it is clear that, if the level of output (Y) is fixed, the balance of trade can only increase if the level of domestic absorption falls. The three components of absorption (C, I, and G) generate welfare; therefore, if income is constant, lower welfare is the price that must be paid for increasing the balance of trade. This is a sobering conclusion for a country with limited growth prospects seeking to increase its balance of trade. This formulation also shows why the International Monetary Fund sometimes recommends lower domestic spending (an "austerity program") for countries which have balance of payments difficulties. Lower spending, or what we have called absorption, is needed for the balance of trade to increase, but when a country already has a very low level of income, it is easy to see why the recommended policy meets with resistance.

An Increase in Planned Investment or Government Spending

An increase in planned investment or government spending increases the demand for domestic goods and services and leads to an increase in the equilibrium level of income. The effects are shown in Figure 8.8. The $S + T - I_p - G$ line shifts downward and the level of income increases. Note that, as income increases, the balance of trade decreases because of an income–induced increase in imports. The size of the change in the balance of trade is determined by the marginal propensity to import: The larger the marginal propensity to import, the larger the decrease in the balance of trade for a given change in income.

The size of the marginal propensity to import also helps determine the effects of changes in government spending and investment on the level of income. For a small, very open economy such as that of Luxembourg, increases in government spending have a small impact on aggregate demand; as the level of income increases, there is a large increase in the demand for imports. This reduces the overall effect on domestic demand and income. (Diagrammatically, the $X - M$ line is steeply sloped for Luxembourg, thus, when the $S + T - I_p - G$ line shifts downward, the change in income is small.) For a country such as the United States, the income–induced increase in imports is much less significant, and government spending has a greater impact on income. (The $X - M$ line is much flatter for the United States than it is for Luxembourg.)

Figure 8.8
The Balance of Trade and Changes in Domestic Spending

An increase in investment or government spending shifts the line showing $X - M = S + T - I_p - G$ downward. The level of income increases from Y_0 to Y_1 because the demand for domestic goods and services increases. The balance of trade (B) changes from an initial zero balance to a deficit of B_1 because the level of imports increases with the increase in income.

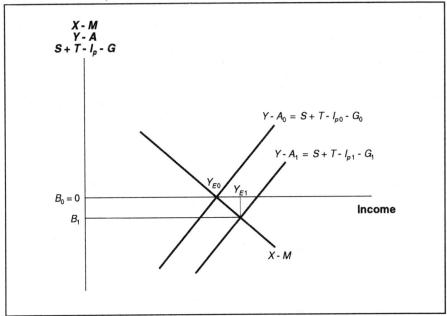

An Increase in Exports

Figure 8.9 shows the effects of an increase in exports. An increase in exports shifts the $X - M$ line upward and leads to an increase in the equilibrium level of income. The reason for this is that an increase in exports, like an increase in government spending or investment, increases the demand for domestic goods and services.

The balance of trade increases when exports increase, but an income–induced increase in imports partially offsets the positive effect on the balance of trade. In Figure 8.9, if income had remained unchanged at Y_0, the balance of trade would have changed from B_0 to B_2. However, because income increases from Y_0 to Y_1, the balance of trade only increases to B_1.

Figure 8.9
The Effects of an Increase in Net Exports

An increase in net exports shifts the line showing $X - M$ upward. The equilibrium level of income increases because the demand for domestic goods and services increases and the balance of trade increases. If income remained at the initial level, the balance of trade (B) would increase from B_0 to B_2 when exports increase. However, the balance of trade only increases to B_1 because imports increase as the level of income rises from Y_0 to Y_1.

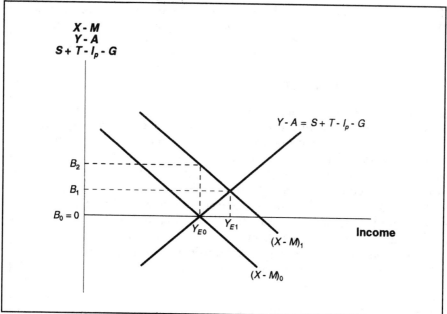

Devaluation

Devaluation has a similar effect on income as an increase in exports. When a country devalues, the domestic prices of imports increase and the foreign prices of exports decrease. As a result, we would expect the quantity of exports to increase and the quantity of imports to fall. Both effects tend to push up the level of income.[6]

As income rises there is an income–induced increase in imports that tends to reduce the effects of the devaluation. Therefore, to ensure that the effect of the devaluation on the balance of trade is maximized, a cut in

---

[6]We assume that the demand for traded goods is elastic, so that the value of imports in domestic currency decreases when the currency falls in value.

government spending or increased taxes may accompany the devaluation. If the government cuts spending or increases taxes, absorption is reduced, the level of income does not increase, and the full effect of devaluation on the balance of trade is maintained.

A devaluation shifts the $X - M$ line in the same way as the increase in exports shown in Figure 8.9. To show the effects of lower government spending or higher taxes, we could add a new $Y - A = S + T - I_p - G$ line to Figure 8.9 which would intersect the post–devaluation balance of trade line $(X - M)_1$ at the initial level of income Y_0 but at a higher balance of trade B_2. (The reader may want to experiment and check this result by adding a line above and parallel to $Y - A = S + T - I_p - G$ in Figure 8.9.)

The Open Economy Multiplier

The amount by which income changes when autonomous spending (C_a, I_p, G, or X) increases is determined by the **open economy multiplier**. The multiplier for an open economy is slightly more complicated than the multiplier derived for a closed economy with no government. The multiplier for an open economy with a government sector is $1/[1 - c(1 - t) + m]$. The multiplier can be derived from Figure 8.6 using the same method used to derive the closed economy multiplier from Figure 8.5.[7] Note that the open economy multiplier is smaller than the closed economy multiplier. The reason is that some income now finances imports and taxes rather than consumption. The larger the marginal propensity to import, and the larger the tax rate, the smaller the open economy multiplier will be.

The Foreign Trade Multiplier

When income rises, imports increase. These imports are the exports of other countries; therefore, other countries experience an increase in injections and the income levels increase. As other countries' incomes increase, they will increase their imports, and the home country's exports will increase. Therefore, we would expect growth in one country to spill over to other countries, and increasing trade and economic growth to occur together. This is in fact what has happened during most of the period since World War II. World trade and incomes have grown together. Countries have grown at different rates, and growth has not been perfectly smooth, but the fact that many countries experience growth or recessions at roughly the same time shows their interdependence.

---

[7]The slope of the withdrawals line showing $S + M + T$ is equal to $1 - c(1 - t) + m$. The multiplier equals the reciprocal of the slope of the withdrawals line.

Table 8.1
The Effects on Real Income of an Increase in Government Spending
(of 1 percent)

| Effect on | Year | Country Increasing Spending | | |
		United States	Europe	Japan
United States	1	1.5	0.1	0.1
	2	1.0	0.1	0.1
	4	0.2	—	—
Europe	1	0.2	1.2	—
	2	0.3	1.1	0.1
	4	0.3	0.5	0.1
Japan	1	0.4	0.1	1.2
	2	0.5	0.1	1.4
	4	0.3	0.1	0.8

Source: IMF *World Economic Outlook*, April 1986, p. 79.

An Example of the Multiplier in an Open Economy

The international effects of an increase in income that results from a 1 percent increase in government spending are shown in Table 8.1. The figures show the level of income after a number of years relative to the level of income in the base period. The impact of one country on another country is determined partly by the domestic multipliers of the countries and partly by the amount of trade between them. For example, the effect on Europe of an increase in American income is much greater than the effect of an increase in Japanese income because Europe exports far more to the United States than it does to Japan (see Table 3.2).

Income, Inflation, and Trade

Inflation

When the effects of changes in autonomous spending (C_a, I_p, G, or X) were discussed earlier, we assumed that domestic prices were constant. However, if the economy is at or near full employment, the rate of inflation tends to increase as aggregate demand increases. As firms attempt to increase production, their demand for labor increases, but if the economy is at full employment, then employment cannot increase. The excess demand for labor leads to higher wages and inflation. Labor is not the only input that may increase in price. As firms increase their demand for inputs in general, the prices of inputs increase, and costs increase.

Inflation and Trade

If the economy is at or near full employment, the effects of an increase in autonomous spending on income may be offset by falling net exports (caused by rising domestic prices). Assume that the country begins with balanced trade and stable prices, and income is at the full employment level. An increase in autonomous spending, for example government spending, will tend to increase the level of income (the $S + T - I_p - G$ line shifts downward). However, as producers increase output and unemployment falls, inflationary pressures may build up and erode the country's competitive position: inflation pushes up the prices of exports and makes imports more attractive. The result is that net exports fall, and income tends to fall back toward the original level. (Inflation shifts the $X - M$ line downward, reducing the balance of trade, and reducing the level of income.) In other words, as the economy approaches full employment, increases in government spending may "crowd out" net exports.

Exchange Rates, Trade, and Income

Exchange rate changes can also change a country's competitive position. When a country's currency rises in value, its exports become more expensive in foreign markets and imports become more attractive to domestic consumers. The change in relative prices brought about by appreciation is similar to the change in relative prices that would be caused by domestic inflation above the world rate. Diagrammatically, the effects of inflation and currency appreciation are the same: the $X - M$ line shifts downward.

We have shown that government spending crowds out net exports if inflation increases. Government spending may also lead to lower net exports because increasing government spending tends to increase interest rates, and domestic currency appreciates.[8]

Devaluation has the effect of shifting the $X - M$ line upward because net exports increase. The level of income increases because an increase in net exports increases aggregate demand. However, if devaluation takes place in a country that is at or near full employment, then as the level of income tends to rise, prices rise. The result may be that inflation offsets the effect of

---

[8]Interest rates increase because government spending tends to increase income, which increases the demand for money, and because of increased borrowing to finance the government spending.

devaluation on the country's competitive position; the $X - M$ line shifts back downward because of inflation. This suggests that devaluation alone may not be sufficient to improve a country's competitive position. Deflationary policies may be needed to make a devaluation "work," that is, to prevent domestic inflation from eroding the gain in competitiveness brought about by devaluation. We return to the price effects of devaluation in Chapter 9.

An Example: The American Economy in the 1980s

This model can be used to explain the behavior of the American economy during the 1980s. During this period the size of the budget deficit increased dramatically. This is shown in the model by a downward shift of the $S + T - I_p - G$ line. However, in the first half of the 1980s, the dollar increased in value, which would be shown by a downward shift of the $X - M$ line. Our model would lead us to expect that the trade balance would decline. This is exactly what happened. (The model does not predict whether income will rise or fall. This depends on the relative strengths of the two effects.) During the second half of the 1980s, the budget deficit continued and American saving remained low, thus the trade deficit continued (because the $S + T - I_p - G$ line stayed down).

As always, when using any model, we must be careful not to claim that this is all that happened. One factor that is omitted is an explanation of why the dollar rose in value until 1985, and fell back thereafter. (To explain this behavior we need to consider interest rates as well as exchange rates, income, and prices.) However, the model does provide important insights into the recent behavior of the American economy. Also, the model highlights the choices facing American policymakers today. The most pleasant way to achieve an increase in the American balance of trade might be an increase in exports and real income (which would increase saving and tax revenue). But, if the growth of exports and real income are insufficient, an improvement in the trade balance can only occur if domestic absorption falls.

Which components of absorption should the American government encourage to fall if it wants to reduce the trade deficit? Investment is not high in the United States when compared to other countries, and investment is needed for growth, so investment spending should be maintained or even increased. Therefore, lower absorption implies lower government spending or lower consumption. The government directly controls taxes and government spending, and taxes can be used to reduce consumption, so one might say that the policy choice is really between higher taxes and lower government spending. Which should be chosen is a political decision beyond the scope of our model.

Summary of Main Points

Gross national product or **national income** is the value of goods and services produced in a country over a period of time. In a fixed–price model (with unemployment), the level of national income (**aggregate supply**) is determined by the level of aggregate demand. In a closed economy model with no government sector, **aggregate demand** is made up of consumption plus planned investment.

The **equilibrium level of income** can be defined as the level of income at which aggregate demand equals aggregate supply, or the level at which saving and planned investment are equal. An increase in investment leads to a multiple increase in income, with the **closed economy multiplier** being $1/(1 - c)$.

In an open economy with a government sector, aggregate demand is made up of consumption, planned investment, government spending, and the balance of trade. The equilibrium level of income is where aggregate demand and aggregate supply are equal. This equilibrium can also be defined as the income level at which **injections** $(I_p + G + X)$ equal **withdrawals** $(S + M + T)$.

The equilibrium level of income can be shown as the point at which the trade balance $(X - M)$ is equal to the difference between income and **absorption** $(Y - A)$. (Absorption equals the sum of consumption, investment, and government spending.) This form of presentation shows that an increase in the balance of trade can only be achieved by an increase in income relative to absorption. If income cannot grow, absorption must be reduced if the balance of trade is to increase.

The equilibrium level of income can also be defined as the level at which the difference between income and absorption $(Y - A)$ is equal to $S + T - I_p - G$. This form of presentation is useful because we can examine the effects on income and the balance of trade of changes in injections and withdrawals.

The effect on income of changes in injections is shown by the **open economy multiplier** $[1/(1 - c(1 - t) + m)]$. Increases in government spending or investment lead to higher income, but a lower balance of trade, because imports increase as income increases. An increase in exports increases both the level of income and the trade balance; however, the trade balance increases by less than the increase in exports because imports increase as the level of income rises.

Inflation tends to reduce net exports because the prices of domestic goods rise relative to foreign goods, and this leads to a lower level of income (as the $X - M$ line shifts downward). Appreciation of domestic currency has a similar effect to inflation: domestic goods become relatively more expensive. Depreciation increases net exports and leads to an increase in income (as the $X - M$ line moves upward).

As the level of income approaches the full employment level, increases in injections (which tend to increase income) may be offset by inflation. For example, if a country devalues when income is at full employment, inflation may offset the effect of devaluation. Thus, policies to reduce absorption may be needed if the trade balance is to increase at the full employment level of income.

Study Questions

1. If the marginal propensity to import is 0.25, how large a change in income is needed to remove a deficit of $300? If the marginal propensity to consume is 0.66, and the tax rate is 0.25, how large a change in government spending would be needed to produce the desired change in income?

2. Calculate the level of income and the balance of trade in each of the cases shown below:

	c	Ca	Ip	t	G	m	X
a.	0.660	50	100	0.25	50	0.25	100
b.	0.660	100	300	0.25	100	0.25	100
c.	0.750	200	100	0.20	100	0.10	200
d.	0.800	100	100	0.25	100	0.10	100
e.	0.875	100	100	0.20	100	0.50	100

3. Using the information given in the table above, show the composition of the equilibrium condition $(S + M + T = I_p + X + G)$ at each of the equilibrium levels of income.

4. What is the value of the multiplier in a closed economy with no government sector when the marginal propensity to consume is 0.75? If a foreign sector is introduced, but there is still no government sector, what is the value of the multiplier if the marginal propensity to import is 0.25? Why is the multiplier for an open economy less than the multiplier for a closed economy?

5. Discuss the effects of a cut in government spending on the level of income and the balance of trade. What are the factors which determine how large a cut in government spending is needed to remove a given trade deficit?

6. Discuss why the level of income in one country may fall if the levels of income in other countries fall. What are the implications for international economic policy?

7. If an economy has above–average inflation, why might we expect the level of real income to fall if the exchange rate is stable? How can exchange rate changes alter the situation?
8. Describe the conditions under which the effectiveness of devaluation may be reduced by:
   a. increasing income
   b. inflation

Selected References

Alexander, S. S., "Effects of a Devaluation on a Trade Balance," *IMF Staff Papers*, 2, April 1952, pp. 263–78.

Dornbusch, R., *Open Economy Macroeconomics*, New York: Basic Books, 1980.

Rivera–Batiz, F. L. and L. Rivera–Batiz, *International Finance and Open Economy Macroeconomics*, New York: Macmillan, 1985.

Stern, R. M., *The Balance of Payments: Theory and Economic Policy*, Chicago: Aldine, 1973.

Nine

Balance of Payments Adjustment

Introduction

In this chapter we examine balance of payments adjustment under fixed and flexible exchange rates. Two themes run throughout the discussion. First, balance of payments adjustment imposes costs on an economy, no matter how it takes place. Second, although balance of payments adjustment processes may appear to be based on different variables, there are strong similarities between the adjustment processes.

Given that fixed exchange rates have been abandoned by many developed countries, it may seem strange to begin a chapter on balance of payments adjustment by examining adjustment under fixed exchange rates. The reason we do so is that governments continue to intervene in the foreign exchange markets to influence the values of their currencies. To the extent that exchange rate flexibility is constrained, balance of payments adjustment under the present system of limited exchange rate flexibility (dirty floating) resembles adjustment under fixed exchange rates. Also, the assumption of fixed exchange rates is useful because it allows us to focus on particular aspects of the adjustment process that are relevant to adjustment in both fixed and flexible exchange rate systems.

Our discussion concentrates on the removal of a balance of payments deficit because the pressure on deficit countries to adjust is much stronger than the pressure on surplus countries. In Chapter 7 we saw various ways of measuring deficits and surpluses in the balance of payments. Throughout this chapter the term **deficit** implies an excess demand for foreign exchange and the term **surplus** implies an excess supply of foreign exchange. A balance of payments deficit is shown in Figure 9.1.

Monetary Adjustment Under Fixed Exchange Rates

When the monetary authorities intervene in the foreign exchange market to maintain a chosen exchange rate, they buy or sell foreign currency. When they buy foreign currency, they sell domestic currency, and when they sell foreign currency, they buy domestic currency. Thus, intervention in the foreign exchange market affects the domestic money supply. Let us examine the monetary effects of foreign exchange market intervention in more detail.

Figure 9.1
A Balance of Payments Deficit

A balance of payments deficit exists at the initial exchange rate S_0 because there is an excess demand for foreign currency. If the monetary authorities want to maintain S_0, they must sell foreign currency (equal to $QD_0 - QS_0$) from the stock of international reserves. In the long run, financing a deficit from reserves is not possible because the stock of reserves is limited. In the long run the choice is between an exchange rate increase, or the adoption of policies that decrease the demand for foreign currency or increase the supply of foreign currency.

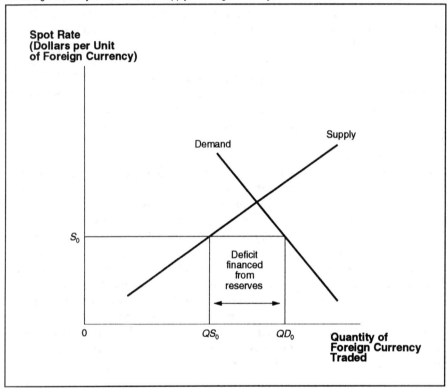

Intervention and the Money Supply

If a country has a balance of payments deficit, the excess demand for foreign exchange at the maintained exchange rate is met by sales of foreign currency from the stock of international reserves held by the monetary authorities. Sales of foreign currency reduce the money supply because the central bank receives domestic currency in return for the foreign currency it sells. (Some domestic currency is taken out of circulation.) Similarly, if a country has a balance of payments surplus, the monetary authorities buy foreign currency to maintain the exchange rate. Since the foreign currency is purchased with domestic currency, the money supply increases. Essentially, the monetary effects of sales (or purchases) of foreign exchange is identical to the effects of sales (or purchases) of Treasury bills by the monetary authorities.

If the monetary authorities do not offset the effects of foreign exchange market intervention on the money supply, an adjustment process will begin that will eventually restore balance of payments equilibrium.[1] The monetary adjustment process includes changes in domestic prices, the interest rate, and national income, as shown in Figure 9.2. Let us examine each in turn.

The Price Effect

A deficit reduces the supply of money, and domestic prices tend to fall as a result. In the domestic market, imports become less attractive relative to domestic goods as the prices of domestic goods fall. The demand for foreign currency falls as people switch from buying imports to buying domestic goods. Similarly, the home country's exports become more attractive to foreign consumers, and the supply of foreign currency increases as exports increase. Therefore, an excess demand for foreign currency tends to be removed by changes in both the demand and supply of foreign currency.

The relationship between the price level, the money supply, and the balance of payments was recognized by David Hume more than two hundred years ago. He suggested that an increase in the money supply would lead to an increase in the domestic price level and a balance of payments deficit. Over a longer period, the balance of payments deficit reduces the money supply, the domestic price level falls to its initial level, and balance of payments equilibrium is restored. Hume's argument is interesting because it suggests that persistent balance of payments deficits are caused by persistent monetary growth—a view many economists still hold.

The Interest Rate Effect

The price effect of monetary adjustment was discussed first for historical reasons. In fact, when the money supply falls because of a balance of payments deficit, the most important initial effect may be a rise in the rate of interest. A higher domestic interest rate encourages foreign investors to invest their funds in the home country, and also encourages domestic investors to invest at home rather than abroad. Therefore, an increase in the rate of interest tends to remove an excess demand for foreign currency in two ways:

---

[1]It is often said that monetary adjustment is automatic in the sense that adjustment does not require an explicit policy decision. Adjustment is not inevitable because the monetary authorities can prevent or alter the speed of adjustment.

Figure 9.2
Monetary Adjustment

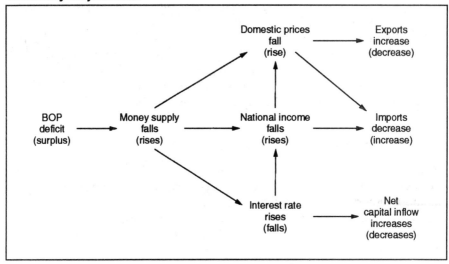

first, by increasing the supply of foreign currency from foreign investors, and second, by decreasing the demand for foreign exchange from domestic investors.[2]

The size of the capital flow depends on the degree of capital mobility, that is, the responsiveness of capital flows to the difference between the interest rate in one country and another. If there is a high degree of capital mobility, an interest rate differential will induce large capital flows. If there is a low degree of capital mobility, capital flows will be small. Clearly, when considering whether to use interest rates to influence the demand/supply of foreign exchange, the degree of capital mobility is important. In passing, it is worth noting that the degree of capital mobility is also an important determinant of the degree of domestic monetary autonomy, because capital flows tend to remove differences between interest rates.[3]

---

[2]When a country raises its interest rate to reduce an excess demand for foreign exchange, it does so by reducing the money supply. Interest rate policy and monetary policy are the same thing. It is interesting that people often refer to using the interest rate to influence the balance of payments (or the exchange rate); this shows how strong the interest rate effect is.

[3]See Chapter 10.

The Income Effect

A higher interest rate leads to a fall in aggregate demand because some expenditures are sensitive to interest rates and fall as the interest rate rises. For example, an increase in the interest rate may lead to lower investment by firms or a fall in purchases of consumer durables such as cars and televisions. The level of aggregate demand may also fall because of the cash balance effect. When there is a balance of payments deficit, people find that the amount of cash they have available falls (because the central bank's purchases of domestic currency takes money out of circulation). They may respond by reducing expenditure in order to replenish their cash balances.

A lower money supply tends to reduce aggregate demand, and as aggregate demand falls, the level of national income tends to fall. The balance of payments deficit decreases as the level of national income falls, because the demand for imports declines with income. This is the income effect of monetary adjustment.

Foreign Adjustment

A domestic balance of payments deficit must be accompanied by a surplus in other countries. Whereas a balance of payments deficit reduces the money supply, a surplus increases the money supply. Therefore, monetary adjustment tends to be two–sided because the monetary effects experienced domestically are felt in reverse in foreign countries.

The Cost of Monetary Adjustment

It has been shown that monetary adjustment leads to the removal of balance of payments deficits (and surpluses). However, like other forms of the adjustment, monetary adjustment entails real adjustment costs. In the short run, removal of a balance of payments (BOP) deficit through a contraction of the money supply leads to a higher interest rate, lower real income, and lower employment. In the long run, as inflation falls and people revise their expectations of inflation, we might expect lower monetary growth to be reflected in a lower interest rate and lower wage demands, and the level of income should return to its natural rate. However, at least in the short run, there are real adjustment costs.

Lags in the Adjustment Process

The effect of the money supply on the balance of payments is not immediate. There are two important lags in the monetary adjustment mechanism. First, the effect of changes in the money supply on domestic income and prices is subject to long and variable lags. Second, the response of the balance of trade to changes in relative prices, whether caused by monetary contraction or by devaluation, is not immediate.[4] The interest rate effect of monetary contraction may not be subject to significant lags, provided that capital flows are sensitive to interest rate changes. However, if capital does not flow freely between countries, or is prevented from doing so, this mechanism cannot be relied on. For some countries, for example, where the risks to investors are high because the countries are heavily in debt, capital inflows may not take place. In these cases, other policies are needed to reduce a balance of payments deficit, at least in the short run.[5]

The Monetary Approach to the Balance of Payments

Proponents of the **monetary approach to the balance of payments** hold the view that the balance of payments is essentially a monetary phenomenon. They argue that balance of payments deficits reflect an excess supply of money, and surpluses reflect an excess demand for money. Two assumptions are common: first that purchasing power parity tends to hold (in the long run); second, that interest rates tend to be equalized by capital flows. Monetary growth above that in other countries leads to higher inflation and lower interest rates than in other countries, and a balance of payments deficit develops because both the current account and capital account fall in value.

The balance of payments is seen as a mirror of domestic monetary conditions. If the supply of money exceeds the demand for money, a balance of payments deficit develops. If the demand for money exceeds supply, a balance of payments surplus develops. The balance of payments not only reflects differences between the demand and supply of money, under fixed exchange rates the demand and supply of money are equalized by the monetary effects of intervention to maintain the exchange rate. When there is a deficit, the excess supply of money is reduced as the authorities sell foreign currency (buy domestic currency) to maintain the exchange rate. When there is a surplus, the money supply rises as the authorities buy foreign currency (sell domestic currency).

---

[4]See the following discussion of the J–curve effect.

[5]The delay in balance of payments adjustment may mean that the monetary authorities run out of reserves before the balance of payments deficit is removed. If so, waiting for automatic monetary adjustment is clearly not possible if the monetary authorities want to maintain a fixed exchange rate. This, Johnson (1958) suggests, is an argument for increased international reserves.

Sterilization

We have seen how a balance of payments deficit leads to adjustment through a fall in the money supply. A country may decide that monetary adjustment is undesirable, perhaps because of the adjustment costs. In this case, the effect on the money supply of sales of foreign exchange can be offset by an increase in the money supply through open market operations. The central bank buys Treasury bills from the public, increasing the public's holding of domestic currency (to offset the fall in the money supply that would otherwise result from official sales of foreign currency). When offsetting open market operations take place, the monetary effects of the balance of payments are said to be **sterilized**. However, if the exchange rate is to be maintained, sterilization alone is not a long–term option because eventually the monetary authorities will run out of international reserves. Sterilization merely stops the monetary adjustment mechanism from working. Having prevented monetary adjustment, other policies must be adopted to bring about balance of payments equilibrium. Let us examine how fiscal policy affects the balance of payments.

Fiscal Policy and the Balance of Payments

Traditionally, when analyzing the effects of fiscal policy on the balance of payments, economists have focused on income–induced changes in net exports. We follow this approach, leaving a discussion of capital flows and fiscal policy until the next chapter. In this section we show that a balance of payments deficit can be reduced by an increase in the balance of trade. This may be induced by a deflationary fiscal policy, that is, a reduction in government spending or an increase in taxes.[6] A reduction in government spending or an increase in taxes are referred to as deflationary policies because they lead to lower income and prices.

The Income Effect of Fiscal Policy

Lower government spending leads to lower income because cuts in government spending reduce the level of aggregate demand. Assuming that the level of exports is exogenously determined (by relative prices and the levels of income in other countries), a reduction in the level of income increases the balance of trade by lowering the demand for imports. If the

---

[6]You may find it useful to review the effects of changes in the levels of government spending and taxation on income and the balance of trade. These are discussed in the previous chapter.

marginal propensity to import (the amount spent on imports out of one extra dollar of income) is denoted by m, the demand for imports (M) is:

$$M = mY \qquad (1)$$

where Y represents the level of income. The balance of trade (B) is:

$$B = X - mY \qquad (2)$$

where X represents the exogenous level of exports.

It is clear that a reduction in income increases the balance of trade. The larger the proportion spent on imports, the smaller the change in income that is needed for a given change in the balance of trade. For example, an increase

Figure 9.3
Fiscal Policy and the Balance of Payments

If government spending is cut from G_0 to G_1, the line showing $Y - A = S + T - I_p - G$ moves upward. The equilibrium level of income falls and the balance of trade increases from B_0 to B_1 (because imports fall as the level of income falls). The greater the marginal propensity to import, the steeper the $X - M$ line, and the greater the increase in the balance of trade for a given reduction in government spending.

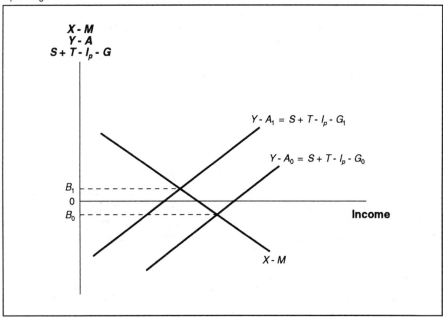

of $10 billion in the balance of trade can be achieved by a cut in income of $50 billion if the marginal propensity to import equals 0.2, but if the marginal propensity to import equals 0.1, income must fall by $100 billion. This approach to the balance of payments adjustment is called the **income approach** for obvious reasons.

The effects of a fall in the level of income brought about by a cut in government spending are shown in Figure 9.3.[7] The line showing $S + T - I_p - G$ shifts upward when G falls, and the equilibrium level of income decreases. The change in the balance of trade is shown on the vertical axis. The larger the marginal propensity to import, the steeper the $X - M$ line, and the greater the effects of fiscal policy on the balance of payments.

The Price Effect

When aggregate demand falls, the price level tends to fall. The (short–run) price effect resulting from a deflationary fiscal policy is similar to that which might result from a deflationary monetary policy: the demand for domestic goods decreases and the price level falls. Balance of payments adjustment takes place because domestic goods become more attractive relative to foreign goods. Diagrammatically, the price effect of deflationary fiscal policy on the balance of trade could be shown by an upward movement of the $X - M$ line. The price and income effects of deflationary fiscal policy are summarized in the chart in Figure 9.4.

The Costs of Adjustment

The main cost of adjustment incurred when reducing a balance of payments deficit by lowering income is the reduction in expenditure that does not fall on imports. The larger the proportion spent on imports, the smaller the cost of adjustment, because a smaller change in income will be needed to achieve a given change in imports. An indication of the difference in adjustment costs

---

[7]The derivation of this figure was described in Chapter 8. Recall that the equilibrium condition for an open economy is $S + T + M = I_p + G + X$. This can be rearranged to give $X - M = S + T - I_p - G$. The line showing $X - M$ slopes downward because imports increase with income. The line showing $S + T - I_p - G$ slopes upward because S and T increase with income. The $S + T - I_p - G$ line also shows $Y - A$, where $A = C + I_p + G$.

Figure 9.4
Fiscal Policy and the Balance of Payments

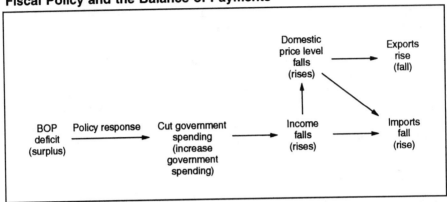

across industrial countries is given by Table 9.1.[8] The table also shows that trade has grown relative to national income.

The income approach leads to the conclusion that a balance of payments deficit can be removed by a fall in the level of income. It is not surprising that this policy is not always popular, especially in poor countries where the level of income is low to begin with. A policy of reducing income to increase the balance of trade is sometimes called an austerity program. The International Monetary Fund is often criticized for recommending this policy. However, there is usually more to IMF recommendations than austerity. When a government adopts an austerity program, it is usually part of a package of policies to achieve economic stability and correct a balance of payments deficit. For example, we shall see in the next section that if devaluation and deflationary fiscal policy are combined, the fall in income need not be so great as when the only policy instrument used is a cut in government spending.

Foreign Repercussions

One country's imports are another country's exports. If one country reduces its income level in order to reduce imports, the level of income will fall in other countries as their exports fall. If a number of countries pursue

---

[8]Ideally, we should use the marginal propensity to import. We assume that the average propensity to import is equal to the marginal propensity to import. If the marginal propensity to import is larger than the average propensity, the table overestimates the costs of adjustment.

Table 9.1
The Costs of Adjustment (*Imports/GDP*)

	1960	1970	1980	1992
Australia	15.8	13.6	15.1	18.3
Austria	31.5	24.5	31.8	48.6
Canada	15.1	16.8	23.6	33.7
Denmark	30.6	27.9	29.3	37.4
France	10.5	13.4	20.3	28.3
Germany	14.1	16.2	23.1	28.1
Italy	12.7	14.9	22.1	28.7
Japan	10.1	9.3	13.3	16.6
Netherlands	41.1	39.7	46.1	51.3
Norway	28.9	33.1	29.3	36.8
Sweden	20.8	21.0	26.9	37.8
Switzerland	25.8	30.7	35.8	45.0
United Kingdom	18.1	17.7	21.6	27.7
United States	3.2	4.2	9.6	12.4

Sources: OECD *Main Economic Indicators*, March, 1994; IMF *International Financial Statistics Supplement on Trade Statistics*, 1988.

deflationary fiscal policies to reduce their imports, incomes will fall, generally as trade decreases. This is partly what happened during the 1930s. In the post World War II period, the opposite happened; income growth in developed countries was accompanied by an expansion of world trade. These events are discussed in Part Three.

Balance of Payments Adjustment and the Exchange Rate

If the exchange rate is flexible, the demand and supply of foreign currency are equalized by exchange rate movements. Flexible exchange rates are a form of automatic adjustment in the sense that adjustment takes place without any explicit policy decision being made by the government. An excess demand for foreign exchange is removed by an increase in the exchange rate. An excess supply of foreign exchange is removed by a fall in the exchange rate. Therefore, because the exchange rate adjusts continuously to equate the demand and supply of foreign exchange, balance of payments deficits and surpluses do not occur under flexible exchange rates.

It is important to note that flexible exchange rates equate the total demand and total supply of foreign currency. This does not mean that the balance of trade, or the current account, will be zero.

Figure 9.5
Devaluation and the Balance of Payments

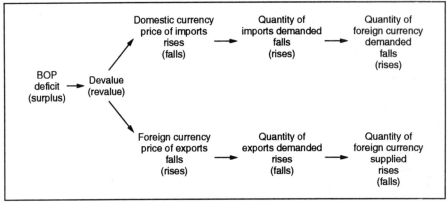

Devaluation

The process by which **devaluation** removes an excess demand for foreign exchange under fixed exchange rates resembles the process by which depreciation equates the demand and supply of foreign currency under flexible exchange rates. Devaluation increases the prices of imports in domestic currency and reduces the prices of exports in foreign currency. Domestic consumers are induced to switch from imports to domestic goods, and foreign consumers are induced to switch from foreign goods to buying the home country's exports. This is why devaluation is sometimes called an **expenditure switching** policy. The adjustment mechanism is summarized in the chart in Figure 9.5.

Elasticities and Devaluation

Under fixed exchange rates, the size of an exchange rate change is determined by the government. The size of the exchange rate change needed to remove an excess demand or excess supply of foreign exchange depends on the **elasticities** of demand and supply of foreign currency. The smaller the elasticities are, the greater the exchange rate change needed. However, a problem for policymakers is that elasticities are not constant. To be specific, the elasticities of demand for imports and exports will normally be greater in the long run than in the short run; therefore, the effects of a devaluation will be greater in the long run than the short run.

For simplicity, as in Chapter 6, let us assume that the elasticities of supply of traded goods are infinite, that is, that the prices of traded goods are

Figure 9.6
Devaluation and the Elasticity of the
Demand and Supply of Foreign Currency

At the initial exchange rate S_0 there is an excess demand for foreign currency ($QD_0 - QS_0$). In the short run, the excess demand for foreign currency can be removed by a devaluation which increases the exchange rate to S_{SR}. In the long run, demand and supply are equated at S_{LR}. The exchange rate needed to remove the excess demand for foreign currency is greater in the short run than the long run because the demand and supply of foreign currency are less elastic in the short run than in the long run.

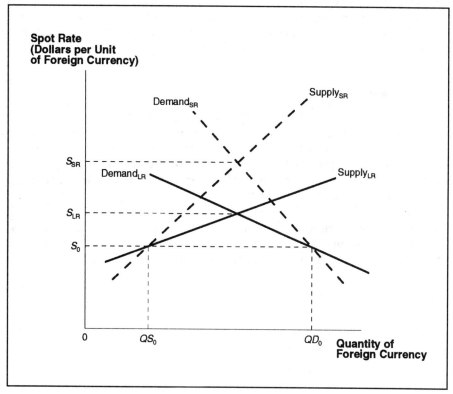

constant in the exporters' currency.[9] In this case, the elasticities of demand and supply of foreign exchange are determined by the elasticities of demand for imports and exports. Following an increase in the domestic prices of imports caused by devaluation, we would expect a fall in the quantity of

---

[9]Branson (1983) examines the importance of supply conditions for a successful devaluation.

imports demanded. However, it takes time for people to adjust to the price changes and switch from imported goods to domestically produced goods. The longer the time period, the more likely it is that consumers will find suitable domestic substitutes for imported goods. Therefore, the elasticity of demand for imports is likely to be greater in the long run than the short run. As a result, the effect of devaluation on the demand for foreign currency will be greater in the long run than the short run.

Similarly, following a fall in the foreign currency price of exports we would expect an increase in the quantity of exports demanded, and thus an increase in the quantity of foreign currency supplied. The longer the time period, the greater the increase in the quantity of exports demanded is likely to be, and the greater the increase in the quantity of foreign currency supplied will be.[10] This is shown in Figure 9.6.

The J Curve

In the short run it is possible that the balance of trade will decrease following a devaluation due to low demand elasticities.[11] As an extreme example assume that the demands for imports and exports are perfectly inelastic, and, for simplicity, assume that the prices of traded goods are constant in the exporter's currency. In this case, following a devaluation, the quantity of exports demanded does not increase. Since the foreign currency price of exports falls when a country devalues, the supply of foreign currency falls (given our assumption that the quantity of exports does not change). And, because the quantity of imports and the foreign currency price of imports are assumed constant, the demand for foreign exchange does not change.

---

[10]Assuming infinite supply elasticities, the condition for a devaluation to increase the balance of trade is that the absolute value of the sum of the elasticity of demand for imports (E_{dm}) and the elasticity of demand for exports (E_{dx}) exceeds 1, that is:

$$|E_{dm} + E_{dx}| > 1$$

This is called the **Marshall–Lerner condition**. It is a sufficient condition, not a necessary condition. If the supply elasticities are sufficiently small, the balance of trade may improve even if the Marshall–Lerner condition is not met. See Stern (1973).

[11]The possibility that low demand elasticities will lead to a fall in the balance of trade following a devaluation is also discussed in Chapter 6.

Figure 9.7
The _J_ Curve

When a country devalues, the demand and supply of traded goods do not change as much in the short run as in the long run. The balance of trade ($X - M$) may even decrease in the short run before increasing. If so, the time path of the balance of trade following a devaluation resembles a letter _J_.

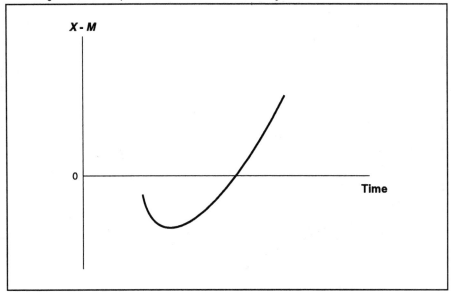

Therefore, in this case devaluation leads to a decrease in the balance of trade.[12]

As time passes, and the elasticities of demand for imports and exports increase, the balance of trade is more likely to increase. When we plot the time path of the balance of trade following a devaluation, as in Figure 9.7, it often seems to resemble a letter _J_. Hence, the delayed response of the balance of trade to a depreciation is known as the _J_–curve effect.

An example of the _J_–curve effect is shown in Figure 9.8. The American balance of trade decreased following the 1971 devaluation of the dollar, and then gradually the trade balance increased.

---

[12]Normally it is assumed that devaluation increases aggregate demand by increasing net exports. However, it has been shown that devaluation may reduce net exports, at least in the short run. Therefore, devaluation may initially reduce aggregate demand.

Figure 9.8
The American Balance of Trade 1971–73

The American dollar was devalued at the end of 1971 (as part of the Smithsonian Agreement under which exchange rates were realigned). This figure shows that the American balance of trade followed a *J* curve, that is, the trade balance decreased before increasing gradually.

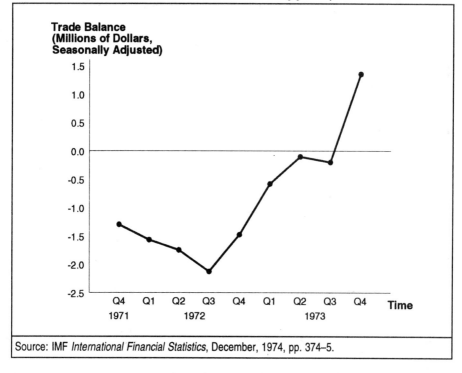

Source: IMF *International Financial Statistics*, December, 1974, pp. 374–5.

The general conclusion that emerges from the preceding discussion is that the response of the balance of trade to changes in the exchange rate is not immediate. Figure 9.9 shows the value of real net exports and the value of the dollar six quarters before. (The value of the dollar is shown on an inverted scale, that is, an increase in the value of the dollar is shown by a downward movement.) The correspondence between changes in the value of the dollar and changes in the real trade balance (six quarters later) is remarkable. For example, the value of the dollar rose from 1980 until the beginning of 1985, and real net exports decreased.

Figure 9.9
The Value of the Dollar and Real Net Exports

The figure shows the value of the of real net exports and the value of the dollar six quarters before. (The value of the dollar shown for the third quarter of 1986 is actually the value of the dollar in the first quarter of 1985.) The value of the dollar is shown on the vertical axis on the left using an inverted scale, thus an increase in the value of the dollar is shown by a downward movement. When presented in this form, the data strongly suggest that changes in the dollar's value lead to changes in the balance of trade (in the opposite direction). For example, an increase in the dollar's value from 1981–85 preceded a decrease in the balance of trade.

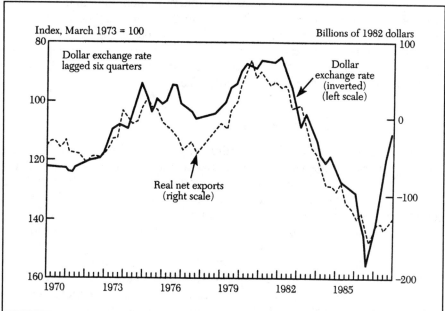

Note: The value of the dollar is the nominal trade–weighted value of the dollar against the other G–10 currencies plus the Swiss franc.

Source: *Economic Report of the President*, 1988, p.27.

Policy Responses to the J Curve

The preceding discussion has shown that when a country devalues, the balance of trade may not respond immediately, or may even decrease. The problem arises because the demand for traded goods is less elastic in the short run than the long run. One solution to the *J*-curve effect following a devaluation is for the government to adopt temporary policies to reduce the excess demand for foreign currency. For example, a temporary general tariff may be used to decrease the demand for imports and thus reduce the demand for foreign currency. Other policies such as deflationary monetary and fiscal policies may also be used. Alternatively, in the short run the government can use international reserves to increase the supply of foreign currency.

Arguments Against Devaluation

A common argument against devaluation is that the demand for exports is inelastic. By itself, this is not a valid argument against devaluation because the demand for exports may be inelastic in the short run and elastic in the long run. In this case other policies may be needed in the short run, but in the long run the devaluation will be effective. Moreover, even if the demand for exports is inelastic in the long run, the balance of trade will still increase if the demand for imports is sufficiently elastic.

Income, Prices, and Devaluation

In discussing the effects of devaluation, we have so far followed what has come to be called the **elasticities approach**, that is, we have assumed that income and prices remain unchanged and the change in the balance of payments has been described in terms of the elasticities of demand for traded goods. However, increases in income and prices following a devaluation may reduce the effectiveness of devaluation. Thus, a devaluation may need to be accompanied by other policies.

Devaluation increases the domestic prices of imports and thus contributes directly to inflationary pressure. Devaluation also increases the demand for domestic goods and services (because net exports increase following a devaluation). If the economy is operating at less than full employment, real income and employment increase. However, as real income increases, we would also expect the price level to increase (because the higher level of economic activity puts upward pressure on wages and prices). When an economy is already at full employment, output cannot increase, and the effect of increased aggregate demand will be inflation without any increase in real income. The exact combination of increased income and inflation which results depends on whether there are unemployed resources when the country devalues.

Increases in domestic income and prices tend to reduce the effects of a depreciation. One reason is that an income–induced increase in imports can be expected as part of the general increase in consumption that accompanies an increase in income. Also, an increase in domestic prices makes domestic goods relatively less attractive to domestic and foreign consumers; thus, imports increase and exports decrease. If devaluation takes place when the

Figure 9.10
Devaluation, Income, and Inflation

Devaluation shifts the $X - M$ line upward. As the level of income increases, prices increase and the $X - M$ line shifts downward to some extent. If the initial level of income (Y_f) is the full employment level, income cannot increase. The increase in aggregate demand (resulting from an increase in net exports) leads to an increase in the price level. As domestic prices rise, the $X - M$ line moves downward to its initial position, and the excess aggregate demand is eliminated. One way to increase the balance of trade at the initial income level is to devalue (shifting the $X - M$ line upward), and also reduce government spending or increase taxes (shifting the $S + T - I_p - G$ line upward).

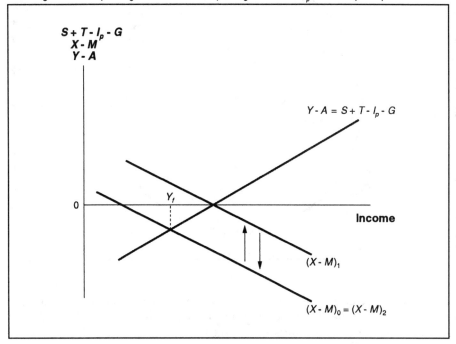

economy is already at full employment, the price level could rise until the effects of the devaluation are completely offset. The price and income effects of devaluation are shown in Figure 9.10.

The Vicious Circle

The inflationary effect of devaluation is particularly important for open economies where imported goods are a large percentage of consumption. In these countries, devaluation directly increases the prices of many goods. Wage demands are likely to rise as workers seek higher wages to offset increases in the cost of imported goods, and the prices of other goods will

Figure 9.11
The Vicious Circle

Devaluation increases the prices of imports and increases aggregate demand. The rate of inflation increases, and inflation results. Domestic inflation reduces competitiveness, and leads to a balance of payments deficit, another devaluation, and the cycle is repeated.

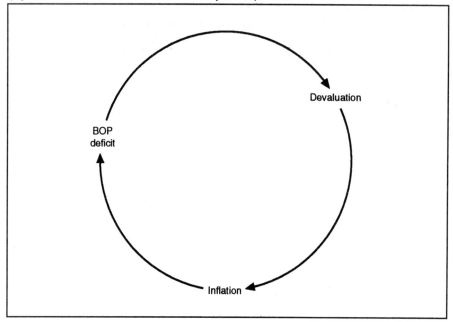

increase as wage costs rise. It is possible that a further devaluation could be used, and that further inflationary pressure would reduce its effects. Thus, a cycle of devaluation and inflation might even be established. The scenario of repeated inflation and devaluation is known as a **vicious circle** and is shown in Figure 9.11.

Increasing the Effectiveness of Devaluation

Clearly, if balance of payments adjustment is the major objective, it would be better if the inflationary effects of a devaluation could be offset by another policy. For example, a cut in government spending could be used to decrease aggregate demand. In a diagram such as Figure 9.10, devaluation shifts the $X - M$ line upward, and cutting government spending shifts the $S + T - I_p - G$ line upward. By an appropriate combination of deflationary fiscal policy and devaluation, an increase in the balance of trade can be achieved at the initial income level (and price level).

Alternatively, the government can prevent an increase in prices and incomes by reducing the rate of monetary growth. This policy would reduce the level of aggregate demand because an increase in the interest rate leads to a fall in interest–sensitive expenditures such as investment and purchases of consumer durables. Diagrammatically, a fall in consumption (a rise in saving) and a fall in planned investment lead to an upward movement of the $S + T - I_p - G$ line. In addition to removing the inflationary stimulus of the devaluation, lower monetary growth attracts foreign capital because the interest rate rises. Thus, monetary contraction removes the excess demand for foreign exchange by both current and capital account changes.

The Cost of Balance of Payments Adjustment by Devaluation

One cost of adjustment is that the prices of imports increase when a country devalues. If a country is already suffering from inflation, the inflationary stimulus of a devaluation may be undesirable. Unfortunately, even if deflationary policies are used to prevent inflation, there are still costs of adjustment because domestic absorption falls, the distribution of income changes, and there are costs of reallocating resources.

Recall that the balance of trade can be expressed as the difference between income and absorption:[13]

$$X - M = Y - A$$

Assuming that the demand for traded goods is sufficiently elastic, devaluation increases the balance of trade, that is, income rises relative to absorption. The reason income rises is that an increase in net exports increases aggregate demand and thereby increases income. As income increases, absorption increases, but the net effect is still an increase in net exports. Thus, devaluation may lead to export led growth.

The problem arises when income cannot increase, for example, because the economy is already at full employment. In this case, absorption must fall if the current account is to increase. Devaluation tends to reduce absorption

---

[13]In other words, the balance of trade is the difference between what a country produces (Y) and the goods purchased or absorbed by domestic residents. Goods are purchased for consumption (C), investment (I), and by the government (G). Thus, absorption (A) is defined as follows:

$$A = C + I + G$$

(It is not necessary to distinguish here between planned and actual investment because they are equal at the equilibrium level of income.)

by increasing the prices of imports and thus reducing consumption.[14] Absorption may also fall if deflationary policies accompany the devaluation (to increase the effectiveness of the devaluation). For example, a deflationary monetary policy increases interest rates and reduces investment. Deflationary fiscal policy may entail higher taxes leading to lower consumption or decreased government spending. The three components of absorption—consumption, investment, and government spending—add to welfare. Therefore, whichever policies are chosen, lower absorption from a given income implies lower welfare. The government can change the costs of adjustment, but the costs cannot be avoided.

Devaluation also redistributes income and alters the allocation of resources. People who consume above average quantities of imported goods suffer. On the other hand, exporters experience an increase in profits because their foreign currency earnings increase (as exports increase), and after a devaluation foreign currency is worth more relative to domestic currency. Also, there is an increase in the demand for import substitutes, and people in this sector may receive higher wages and profits. To the extent that production changes entail a reallocation of resources, devaluation inevitably leads to costs of adjustment because resources do not move freely from one sector to another.

Fixed and Flexible Exchange Rates

Historically, countries have usually intervened to influence the values of their currencies in the foreign exchange market. At the present time, although there is not a general agreement to fix exchange rates, countries continue to intervene in the foreign exchange market.[15] Some countries fix the values of their currencies formally in relation to the currency of a major trading partner; others fix against the average value of a group of currencies. Even when currencies are not linked formally to one or more other currencies, countries still intervene to influence the values of their currencies. If flexible exchange rates equate the demand and supply of foreign currency, why have governments traditionally limited exchange rate flexibility, and why do governments continue to intervene?

---

[14]Recall that imports are part of consumption.

[15]Table 6.2 shows countries' exchange rate arrangements.

The Argument for Flexible Exchange Rates

There are many arguments for and against flexible exchange rates. The basic argument in favor of flexible exchange rates is that the exchange rate, being the price of foreign currency, can and should be allowed to bring demand and supply into balance. An advantage claimed for such a system is that adjustment takes place continuously without the need for government intervention. Continuous adjustment, it is claimed, prevents the development of severe balance of payments problems and thus removes the need for policies to correct such problems. Put simply, domestic economic policies do not need to be sacrificed in order to maintain arbitrary exchange rate targets.[16] Flexible exchange rates also free countries from the need to hold stocks of international reserves for intervention in the foreign exchange market.

Exchange Risk as a Deterrent to Trade and Investment

Perhaps the most common and the most important argument used by proponents of fixed exchange rates is that exchange rate risk under flexible exchange rates deters trade and investment. One example is that of an exporter who has contracted for a certain price in foreign currency. As the value of foreign currency fluctuates, the value of the contract in domestic currency fluctuates. Expressing a contract in domestic currency merely shifts the exchange risk to the foreign importer. If the exchange rate changes, the foreign importer may seek to renegotiate the contract or simply not renew it. Therefore, regardless of the currency of invoice, exchange rate movements can cause losses of revenue or markets.

There are three replies to the exchange rate risk argument for fixed exchange rates. First, the argument presupposes that flexible exchange rates will be unstable rates. Proponents of flexible exchange rates argue that this supposition is false. Although flexible exchange rates may change in response to economic policies and conditions, proponents believe that flexible exchange rates are not inherently unstable. If policies were stable, exchange rates would be stable. Second, as shown in Chapter 6, traders can take forward cover against exchange rate risk. Although long–term cover is more expensive to obtain than short–term cover, or simply not available, the duration of most contracts is short enough for cover to be readily available. Third, experience suggests that exchange rate risk does not act as a barrier to trade and

---

[16]A related argument in favor of flexible exchange rates is that the effectiveness of monetary policy is greater under flexible than under fixed exchange rates. The effectiveness of monetary and fiscal policy under flexible exchange rates is discussed in Chapter 10.

investment: trade and investment grew rapidly during the 1970s and 80s even though the international fixed exchange rate system had been abandoned.

Long–Term Exchange Rate Movements

Intuitively it may seem that exchange risk must deter some firms from making long–term investments aimed at foreign markets. However, there are grounds for believing that exchange risk may not be a significant barrier even to long–term investment. If exchange rates are correlated with inflation rates through purchasing power parity, the fall in value of foreign revenue or assets that occurs when foreign currencies depreciate is accompanied by inflation–induced increases in the foreign currency values of foreign revenue or assets. Therefore, the rate of return in the long–run is determined independently of the exchange rate because increases in foreign currency prices offset losses from decreases in the value of foreign currency. Although exchange rate changes do not always conform to purchasing power parity exactly, we might expect that exchange rate changes that are not related to differences in inflation rates will tend to average out in the long–run. If firms take this into account, exchange risk will not be a barrier to long–term investments.

Even if long–term risk is a deterrent to trade and investment, this does not necessarily imply that fixed exchange rates are preferable to flexible exchange rates. In the long–run, if governments pursue different economic polices, we would expect inflation rates to differ, and ultimately exchange rates to change. This is true whatever the exchange rate system is. The argument that exchange risk will be lower under fixed exchange rates is based on the implicit assumption that governments will be constrained to pursue similar polices by the need to maintain the values of their currencies—in particular, that inflationary policies will not be adopted.

Exchange rate targets may have constrained government policies in the past, but it is unlikely that a return to fixed exchange rates would do so again. Governments now know that exchange rates can be changed without bringing the international financial system to an end. Indeed, international trade has survived and grown under flexible exchange rates. It is doubtful that governments would return to a system under which domestic polices are constrained by exchange rate targets.

Finally, the argument that exchange risk deters trade and investment is based on the implicit assumption that firms have significant assets or liabilities in particular currencies. In practice, multinational firms may face very little exchange risk in relation to turnover because their operations are spread out over many countries. What they gain on one currency they lose on another. The movement toward global manufacturing and marketing has reduced the significance of exchange risks associated with international trade.[17]

In conclusion, the exchange risk argument against flexible exchange rates is much weaker than it appears at first sight.

Elasticity Pessimism

Opponents of flexible exchange rates have suggested that the foreign exchange market is not stable. More specifically, they suggest that the supply of foreign exchange may be downward sloping due to an inelastic demand for exports; hence, the argument is referred to as **elasticity pessimism**. Although elasticity pessimism was once common among economists, the general opinion now seems to be that the elasticities argument is not an important objection to flexible exchange rates.[18]

Speculation

Opponents of flexible exchange rates argue that they encourage destabilizing speculation. However, advocates of flexible exchange rates argue that fixed exchange rates encourage destabilizing speculation. It is not clear which view is correct.

Generally, one would expect profitable speculation to be stabilizing. Profitable speculation entails buying a currency when its value is below average, and selling it when its value is above average. These actions tend to push the value of the currency toward the average (or trend); therefore, profitable speculation will be stabilizing.

Under flexible exchange rates, if the determination of the exchange rate is dominated by speculators who predict the exchange rate incorrectly, other market participants, such as importers and exporters, may suffer. Although destabilizing speculation may not be profitable, and is therefore unlikely to continue in the long run (because speculators will lose their money), periods of destabilizing speculation are possible in the short run. Destabilizing speculation is also possible under fixed exchange rates, because speculators may be encouraged to speculate against the official exchange rate if there is some doubt that the rate will be maintained.

Unfortunately, as is shown in Part Three, historical evidence does not clearly support either the view that speculation will usually be stabilizing or

---

[17]The same argument does not apply to political risk because the losses in one market are not necessarily matched by gains in another.

[18]The possibility that the foreign exchange market is unstable is examined in Chapter 6.

the view that it will be destabilizing. Speculators have behaved differently when faced by different systems, conditions, and policies. Therefore, although the role of speculation is an important issue, it is difficult to use speculative behavior to help determine which exchange rate system is preferable.

The Movement Toward Flexibility

The arguments for and against flexible exchange rates are inconclusive. Thus, it is not surprising that the abandonment of the Bretton Woods system in 1971 can be traced to specific attributes of that particular system.[19] Fixed exchange rates were definitely not abandoned because the flexible exchange rate proponents won.

The experience since the end of the international fixed exchange rate system does not clearly support the case for either fixed or flexible exchange rates. Trade and capital flows have increased, but exchange rate changes have seemed excessive at times. However, the worst fears of opponents of flexible exchange rates have not been realized, and now discussions are often concerned with how much intervention should take place and whether an exchange rate is a little too high or low, rather than whether a return to fixed exchange rates is needed. We return to this discussion in Chapter 14, which reviews the performance of the international monetary system in recent years.

Summary of Main Points

A balance of payments **deficit** may be defined as an excess demand for foreign exchange. When there is a balance of payments deficit under fixed exchange rates, the sale of foreign currency by the monetary authorities (to maintain the exchange rate) tends to reduce the money supply. Assuming that the monetary effects of intervention in the foreign exchange market are not offset (**sterilized**), a process of monetary adjustment begins that eventually removes the balance of payments deficit: domestic interest rates rise and the levels of prices and income fall.

A balance of payments deficit in one country is accompanied by a surplus in other countries. If the monetary effects of the surplus are not sterilized, adjustment in surplus countries takes place via falling interest rates and rising levels of income and prices.

Fiscal policy may be used to remove a balance of payments deficit because lower government spending reduces aggregate demand and hence

---

[19]The Bretton Woods system ended in August 1971 when the convertibility of the dollar into gold was suspended. An attempt to return to a fixed exchange rate system was made with the Smithsonian Agreement in December 1971, but the rates lasted only until the beginning of 1973.

the level of income. Import consumption falls with the income–induced fall in overall consumption. The size of the reduction in income needed to reduce imports by a given amount is determined by the **marginal propensity to import**. Domestic prices may also fall if lower government spending reduces inflationary pressure in the economy. A major cost of balance of payments adjustment via a fall in income is the that the overall level of consumption falls, not just the consumption of imports.

Under flexible exchange rates, the exchange rate adjusts to equate the demand and supply of foreign currency. Therefore, an excess demand for foreign exchange cannot exist under flexible exchange rates. Under fixed exchange rates, **devaluation** removes an excess demand for foreign exchange by increasing the price of foreign exchange.

The response of the balance of payments to devaluation is not immediate because the demand and supply of traded goods do not adjust instantly. If the demand for traded goods is inelastic, the balance of trade may even fall in the short run. In the long run, the balance of payments is more likely to increase because the demand for traded goods will be more elastic.

If the balance of trade is to increase, devaluation must reduce **absorption** relative to income; if income is fixed, absorption must fall. Devaluation increases the prices of imported goods, which tends to reduce consumption. If domestic wages are revised upward in response, the effectiveness of devaluation may be offset by inflation. To prevent domestic inflation from offsetting the effects of devaluation, the government may reduce government spending and the money supply.

Proponents of flexible exchange rates argue that the exchange rate should be allowed to adjust freely to equate the demand and supply of foreign currency. A flexible exchange rate frees economic policy from the constraints of maintaining a fixed exchange rate.

The traditional argument against flexible exchange rates is that exchange rate stability is needed if international trade and investment are to flourish. Proponents of flexibility argue that the assumption that flexible rates will be unstable is unwarranted. Also, they point out that forward cover can be taken to reduce exchange risk. The argument that exchange risk deters trade and investment does not seem strong in the light of the rapid growth of trade and investment under flexible exchange rates.

Although it seems that exchange risk must deter long–term trade and investment, it is doubtful that this is an argument for official exchange rate intervention. Long–term changes in exchange rates may reflect differences in inflation rates. In this case, a fall in the domestic value of a foreign good or asset, caused by foreign currency depreciating, will be offset by foreign inflation increasing the value. Fixed exchange rates would not prevent long–term exchange rate changes unless governments felt constrained to pursue similar policies.

Study Questions

1. Assume that a country has a balance of payments deficit. Show how monetary adjustment removes the deficit. What are the costs associated with monetary adjustment?
2. Show diagrammatically how an increase in taxes can lead to an increase in the balance of trade. Show that the same changes in the balance of trade could be produced by a devaluation. Why, in view of the other effects of these policies, might it be wise to use a combination of these policies rather than one?
3. Explain the adjustment process by which devaluation leads to the removal of a balance of payments deficit. (Assume that the demand for traded goods is elastic.)
4. Under what conditions will a devaluation lead to:
    a. an increase in the balance of payments deficit?
    b. domestic inflation with no change in the balance of trade?
5. The value of Luxembourg's imports is equal to over 80 percent of Luxembourg's national income. Why might Luxembourg be more willing to remove a balance of payments deficit by a deflationary (income–reducing) fiscal policy than the United States?
6. In an open economy where traded goods are a large percentage of consumption, why might other policies be needed to ensure that devaluation is effective?
7. In an open economy with full employment, whichever adjustment mechanism is chosen, an increase in the balance of trade can only be achieved if absorption falls relative to income. Show how a fall in absorption relative to income can be achieved by:
    a. monetary policy
    b. fiscal policy
    c. an exchange rate change
8. Assume that you are an economic adviser. You are asked to recommend fixed or flexible exchange rates. Taking into account the various arguments for and against each system, which would you choose and why?

Selected References

Alexander, S. S., "Effects of a Devaluation on a Trade Balance," *IMF Staff Papers*, 2, April 1952, pp. 263–78.

Artus, J. R. and J. H. Young, "Fixed and Flexible Exchange Rates: A Renewal of the Debate," *IMF Staff Papers*, 26, December 1979, pp. 654–98.

Branson, W. H., "Economic Structure and Policy for External Balance," *IMF Staff Papers*, 30, March 1983, pp. 39–66.

Frenkel, J. A. and H. G. Johnson, *The Monetary Approach to the Balance of Payments*, London: Allen and Unwin, 1975.

Friedman, M., "The Case for Flexible Exchange Rates," in M. Friedman, *Essays in Positive Economics*, Chicago: University of Chicago Press, 1953.

Hooper, P. and S. W. Kohlhagen, "The Effects of Exchange Rate Uncertainty on the Prices and Volumes of International Trade," *Journal of International Economics*, 8, November 1978, pp. 483–511.

Hume, D., "Of the Balance of Trade," first published in 1752 in *Essays, Moral, Political, and Literary*. Reprinted in C. Eichengreen, (ed.), *The Gold Standard in Theory and History*, New York: Methuen, 1985.

Johnson, H. G., "Towards a General Theory of the Balance of Payments," in H. G. Johnson, *International Trade and Economic Growth*, London: Allen and Unwin, 1958.

Johnson, H. G., "The Case for Flexible Exchange Rates, 1969," *Federal Reserve Bank of St. Louis Review*, 51, June 1969, pp. 12–24.

Kindelberger, C. P., "The Case for Fixed Exchange Rates, 1969," in *The International Adjustment Mechanism*, Federal Reserve Bank of Boston, Conference Series No. 12, 1970, pp. 93–108.

Magee, S. P., "Currency Contracts, Pass–through and Devaluation," *Brookings Papers in Economic Activity*, 1, 1973, pp. 303–23.

Mundell, R. A., *International Economics*, New York: Macmillan, 1968.

Stern, R. M., *The Balance of Payments: Theory and Economic Policy*, Chicago: Aldine, 1973.

Ten

Economic Policy in an Open Economy

Introduction

The previous chapter concentrated on balance of payments adjustment, that is, the attainment of external balance. This approach was useful for expository purposes, because it allowed us to examine the factors that influence international trade and investment. In this chapter we examine the effectiveness of monetary and fiscal policy in an open economy. We begin by assuming that the major concern of economic policy is the domestic economy (internal balance). Then the discussion is broadened to examine the policies that are appropriate for both internal and external balance. Finally, we consider how international economic fluctuations are transmitted between countries, and the effects of such fluctuations.

Monetary and Fiscal Policy Under Fixed Exchange Rates

Monetary Policy in a Closed Economy

Let us begin by summarizing the results of the basic macroeconomic model used in principles of economics courses. In a closed economy, we would expect an increase in the money supply to lead to an increase in aggregate demand. There are two reasons. First, monetary expansion leads to a lower interest rate, and interest sensitive expenditures (such as investment and purchases of consumer durables) increase. Second, monetary expansion leads to increased cash balances and higher consumption (as people increase expenditure to reduce their cash holdings to the desired level).

The effects of an increase in aggregate demand on income, employment, and inflation depend on the initial conditions in the economy. If the economy is already at full employment, an increase in aggregate demand leads only to inflation because real income and employment cannot increase. If the economy is at less than full employment, an increase in aggregate demand leads to a higher price level, but also to higher real income and employment. Therefore, if we consider the effects of monetary policy in an open economy, we can conclude that in some circumstances monetary policy may be a useful tool of macroeconomic policy.

The Effectiveness of Monetary Policy Under Fixed Exchange Rates

When a country fixes its exchange rate, the country loses some or all of its freedom to set domestic monetary policy. Capital flows help determine how much monetary policy independence the country has.

In the case of a small country, when the exchange rate is fixed, monetary policy ceases to be a useful policy instrument if there is a high degree of capital mobility. To illustrate the problem, assume that the country has unemployment, and that the monetary authorities attempt to stimulate the economy by increasing the money supply. Initially, the interest rate tends to fall (because at the initial interest rate the supply of money exceeds the demand for money). However, as the domestic interest rate falls relative to the interest rates of other countries, there is a decrease in capital inflows, and an increase in capital outflows, because foreign investments become more attractive relative to domestic investments. Thus, a balance of payments deficit (an excess demand for foreign exchange) develops.

In order to prevent a depreciation of domestic currency, the monetary authorities are obliged to sell foreign exchange (buy domestic currency), and the money supply falls as a result. As long as the interest rate is low relative to other countries, the balance of payments deficit continues, sales of foreign exchange continue, and the money supply keeps falling. The process ends when the money supply has fallen back to the initial level, and the domestic interest rate has risen to its original level.

When a country attempts to reduce the money supply, the adjustment process is the same, with the variables changing in the opposite directions. As the domestic interest rate rises relative to rates in other countries, capital inflows increase, outflows decrease, and there is a balance of payments surplus. To prevent an appreciation of domestic currency, the monetary authorities must buy foreign currency (sell domestic currency), and the money supply rises as a result. The process ends when the money supply has expanded enough to bring the interest rate down to its original level.

Therefore, monetary policy is ineffective under fixed exchange rates because the monetary effects of intervention in the foreign exchange market (to maintain the exchange rate) offset changes in the money supply. The monetary adjustment process under fixed exchange rates is shown in the chart in Figure 10.1.

In the case of perfect capital mobility, any slight tendency for the interest rate to change induces such a large change in capital flows that the change in the money supply is immediately offset. Capital flows keep the money supply at the level that is consistent with equality between the domestic rate

Figure 10.1
Monetary Policy Under Fixed Exchange Rates

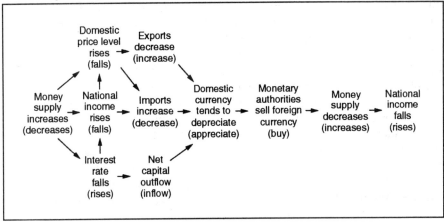

of interest and the world rate, and monetary policy is completely ineffective.[1] When there is a low degree of capital mobility, capital flows are not large enough to equalize interest rates immediately or completely, and monetary policy may have an effect. However, the effectiveness of monetary policy is less than in a closed economy because, to the extent that capital does flow, the monetary authorities must intervene to maintain the fixed exchange rate, intervention offsets the initial money supply change, and the interest rate tends to move to its initial level.

American Monetary Policy

The process is different for the United States than for most countries for two reasons. First, the American interest rate influences interest rates in other countries. Second, the value of the dollar has often been maintained by official intervention by the monetary authorities of other countries (rather than intervention by the American monetary authorities). Consider the effects of an increase in the American money supply. This leads to lower domestic interest rates and a tendency toward a net capital outflow from the United States. Other countries experience increased capital inflows and reduced

---

[1]To be more precise, capital mobility does not necessarily bring about absolute equality of interest rates because the disparity may reflect expectations that a currency will change in value, or differences between the riskiness of assets held in various countries. However, the basic conclusion that capital mobility reduces the effectiveness of monetary policy is still valid even if interest rates are not equated exactly.

capital outflows, and the result is they develop balance of payments surpluses. If foreign currencies are fixed in value relative to the dollar, foreign monetary authorities buy dollars to prevent their currencies appreciating. To buy dollars, they use their own currencies; thus, the money supplies of other countries rise and their interest rates fall. Therefore, American monetary expansion can lead to a similar monetary effect in other countries when other currencies are fixed relative to the dollar.

Let us briefly summarize the discussion to this point. We have seen that for a small country under a fixed exchange rate, the monetary effects of intervention in the foreign exchange market offset changes in monetary policy. However, monetary policy is a useful tool for the United States, if intervention to maintain the exchange rate is carried out by other countries. In this case, monetary changes in the United States can cause similar changes in other countries.

Although American monetary policy is effective, the capital outflow from the U.S. reduces the effectiveness to some extent. As a result of the capital outflow, some of the increase in the American money supply is held by foreign monetary authorities (in the form of international reserves). Some people have argued that this is what happened in the Bretton Woods system, that is, when other currencies were fixed against the dollar, the role of the dollar as an international reserve allowed the United States to finance capital outflows, the purchase of foreign assets, by printing dollars. This is discussed in Chapter 13.

It has been shown that monetary policy is less effective in an open economy than in a closed economy. This result is most relevant in the short run. In the long run, whether the economy is open or closed, the standard conclusion about the effects of monetary policy remains the same: attempts to raise the level of income above the full employment level merely lead to inflation.

The Effectiveness of Fiscal Policy Under Fixed Exchange Rates

When government spending increases under fixed exchange rates, the domestic price and income levels tend to rise in response to the increase in aggregate demand. (The effects of a cut in taxes are basically the same as an increase in government spending.) The demand for money rises with the price and income levels (as the value of expenditure increases). If we assume that the money supply is not changed, the interest rate increases as the demand for money increases. Also, in the case of an increase in government spending financed by borrowing, the interest rate rises because of the government borrowing.[2]

The balance of payments is subject to two influences. First, the balance of trade tends to decrease because imports increase and exports decrease as the domestic price and income levels rise. Second, the capital account tends to increase because of the increase in the interest rate. Thus, there is a net increase in the demand for foreign exchange from the balance of trade, and a net increase in the supply of foreign currency from the capital account. A major determinant of the relative importance of these two effects is the degree of capital mobility.

If capital is highly mobile, any slight increase in the rate of interest leads to a large net inflow of capital and a balance of payments surplus. Although the balance of trade falls, the capital inflow is much larger. Under fixed exchange rates, the monetary authorities must sell domestic currency to prevent its value from increasing, and the money supply increases as a result. Therefore, a monetary stimulus is induced to accompany the fiscal stimulus, that is, the effect of fiscal policy on aggregate demand is augmented by the induced change in the money supply. As a result, fiscal policy is an effective policy instrument under fixed exchange rates. Adjustment following a change in government spending is summarized in Figure 10.2.

The result is different if capital mobility is low. In this case, domestic currency tends to depreciate because the increased net capital inflow is not large enough to offset the decrease in the balance of trade. The monetary authorities are obliged to sell foreign currency, the money supply falls, and thus the overall effect of fiscal policy on aggregate demand is reduced. Clearly, the degree of capital mobility is important. For many developed countries, it is probably realistic to assume a high degree of capital mobility.[3] Therefore, for these countries we may conclude that fiscal policy will be effective under fixed exchange rates. However, this does not mean that a country can increase the level of real income in the long run by using government spending to increase aggregate demand. In the long run, government spending has other effects that tend to offset the effect on income, for example, government spending may reduce (crowd out) private sector investment.

---

[2]At the initial interest rate, there is an excess supply of bonds due to government borrowing (bond sales). Monetary equilibrium with a given money supply is achieved by a fall in the price of bonds (an increase in the interest rate).

[3]Capital flows have increased rapidly over the last few decades. The reasons are simple: communication links between countries have improved, computer technology has advanced (computers can now store and analyze vast amounts of data), and, perhaps most important of all, many countries have eased restrictions on capital flows.

Figure 10.2
Fiscal Policy Under Fixed Exchange Rates

In this figure we assume that capital mobility is high, thus domestic currency tends to appreciate when government spending increases (because the net capital inflow tends to be greater than the decrease in the balance of trade). As a result, the monetary authorities must intervene to prevent domestic currency from rising in value when government spending increases.

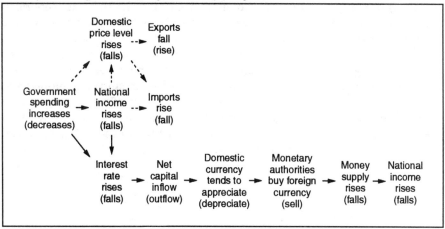

Monetary and Fiscal Policy Under Flexible Exchange Rates

Monetary Policy

Flexible exchange rates free monetary authorities from the obligation to intervene in the foreign exchange market. As a result, the money supply can be set independently of the exchange rate and the balance of payments. Let us consider the effects of monetary expansion in a small country that cannot affect the world interest rate.

For ease of exposition, let us initially assume that there are no capital flows. In this case, an increase in the money supply leads to an increase in aggregate demand as it would do in a closed economy. As the domestic price and income levels rise in response to the increase in aggregate demand, there is an increase in the demand for imports and a fall in the quantity of exports demanded by foreigners (as the foreign prices of exports rise). The increased demand and reduced supply of foreign currency lead to a rise in the exchange rate (the price of foreign currency), sufficient to keep the balance of trade equal to zero at the higher level of income. In other words, the tendency for net exports to decrease is offset by depreciation. Therefore, an increase in the supply of money is accompanied by a depreciation of domestic currency, and higher price and income levels.

Now let us make the analysis more realistic by introducing capital flows. In this case, as in the previous example, monetary policy leads to an increase in aggregate demand. In addition, the tendency for the interest rate to decline leads to a net capital outflow. This capital outflow pushes the value of the currency downward, and, even though domestic income and prices are rising, net exports increase.[4] An increase in net exports adds to the increase in aggregate demand resulting from the increased money supply, and the domestic price and income levels rise. The greater the degree of capital mobility, the greater the depreciation, the greater the increase in the balance of trade, and the greater the increase in aggregate demand. Therefore, under flexible exchange rates, monetary policy is an effective instrument for influencing aggregate demand, and the effectiveness increases with the degree of capital mobility. The monetary adjustment process under flexible exchange rates is shown in Figure 10.3.

Figure 10.3
Monetary Policy Under Flexible Exchange Rates

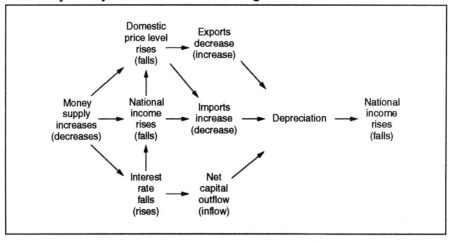

_____

[4]The currency depreciates by the amount needed to maintain equality between the overall demand and supply of foreign exchange. In this case, a trade surplus is accompanied by a capital outflow.

Monetary Equilibrium in the Long Run

How is equality between the domestic interest rate and the world rate restored following an increase in the money supply? We have seen that monetary expansion is followed by depreciation. The domestic price and income levels rise in response to the increase in aggregate demand (caused by the higher money supply and higher net exports).[5] The demand for money rises as the price and income levels rise, and the domestic interest rate rises in consequence. This process of depreciation and rising domestic income and prices continues until the demand for money has increased enough to push the domestic interest rate back up to the world level once more.

In the long run it is not possible to achieve higher real income by printing money. Assuming that purchasing power parity is established in the long run, the interest rate equals the world rate, and the price level and the exchange rate (the price of foreign currency) rise by the same amount. Therefore, the real exchange rate is unchanged, and net exports and real income return to their original levels. However, some economists have suggested that the benefit of being able to use monetary policy for short–run stabilization is an important argument in favor of flexible exchange rates.

Exchange Rate Overshooting

Although monetary policy affects price and income levels as well as interest rates, the price and income effects may take much longer than the interest rate effect. This can result in **exchange rate overshooting**. An example of exchange rate overshooting occurs when the long–run exchange rate rises following an increase in the money supply. (An increase in the money supply increases the domestic price level, and, assuming that purchasing power parity holds in the long–run, increases the long–run equilibrium exchange rate.) During the process of adjustment, the exchange rate rises to a point above the new equilibrium rate in the short run, before falling back to equal the new equilibrium rate in the long run. Overshooting is shown in Figure 10.4.

Overshooting may result from the effects of monetary expansion on relative rates of return between countries and the response of capital flows. In the short run, an increase in the money supply leads to a lower interest rate. Why would international investors be willing to hold investments in a country where the interest rate is lower than in other countries? They will do so if they expect an appreciation of the currency. For such an appreciation to take place, the value of domestic currency must fall below its new long–run

---

[5]The domestic price level also rises because import prices increase when domestic currency depreciates.

Figure 10.4
Overshooting Following Monetary Expansion

Following domestic monetary expansion, the long–run equilibrium exchange rate (domestic currency per unit of foreign currency) rises from S_0 to S_1. Overshooting takes place when the exchange rate rises above S_1 in the short–run before falling to S_1 in the long–run. In other words, the value of the currency falls below its long–run value and then appreciates to equal the long–run value.

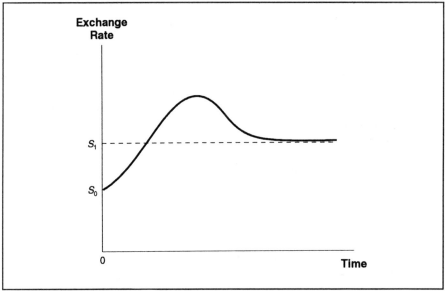

equilibrium value. In other words, the exchange rate must rise above the new long–run equilibrium value, that is, the exchange rate must overshoot. If the value of domestic currency is not below the new long–run equilibrium rate, investors refuse to hold assets in the currency, and the value of domestic currency falls until it is below the long–run rate.

Investors must expect an appreciation of the currency if they are to be willing holders of assets that bear an interest rate below the world rate. But this does not explain why the exchange rate should appreciate. One reason is that, in the long run, the volume of traded goods responds to the depreciation, that is, net exports increase. This causes an appreciation.

In the long run, the level of real income is not affected by the money supply, and the equality between the domestic interest rate and the world rate is restored as the rising domestic price level increases the demand for money, and the domestic interest rate rises.

A similar effect can be expected from monetary contraction. Initially, monetary contraction increases the interest rate and leads to a large fall in the exchange rate (appreciation of domestic currency). Higher interest rates attract investors and the currency appreciates until the currency is above its long–run value. At this stage the high interest rates on domestic investments are offset by an expected depreciation of domestic currency. In the long run, the price level falls, the interest rate falls to equal the world rate once more, and the exchange rate rises to its long–run equilibrium level (domestic currency depreciates). This scenario resembles what happened to the dollar in the early 1980s when many commentators suggested that a fall in the value of the dollar was imminent, but foreign investors were willing holders of dollar assets because the interest rates on dollar investments were high.

Fiscal Policy Under Flexible Exchange Rates

Under flexible exchange rates, an increase in government spending leads to two opposite effects on the exchange rate. First, government spending increases aggregate demand, and the levels of domestic prices and incomes rise. Net exports tend to fall because the domestic price level rises and because higher domestic income increases the demand for imports. Thus, there is a net increase in the demand for foreign currency from the trade effects of increased government spending. Second, government spending causes a net increase in capital inflows because increased government spending pushes up interest rates (either through the effects of government borrowing or because of the increase in the demand for money caused by higher income and prices). Thus, there is a net increase in the supply of foreign exchange from the effect of government spending on capital flows.

The effect on the exchange rate depends on the degree of capital mobility. If capital mobility is low, the net increase in the supply of foreign exchange (resulting from increased net capital inflows) is smaller than the net increase in the demand for foreign exchange (resulting from the trade effect). Thus, with low capital mobility, the currency depreciates to equate the demand and supply of foreign exchange. If capital mobility is high, the net increase in the supply of foreign exchange (from capital flows) is larger than the net increase in the demand for foreign exchange (from trade), and the currency appreciates.

From the chart in Figure 10.5 we assume that capital mobility is high enough for increased government spending to cause an appreciation of domestic currency. As a result of the appreciation and rising domestic income and prices, net exports decrease. Thus, the effect of increased government spending on aggregate demand is offset to some extent by a decrease in net exports. The higher the degree of capital mobility, the less effective fiscal policy will be. In the extreme case of perfect capital mobility, any tendency for income to increase leads to an increase in interest rates, currency appreciation, and a fall in net exports. The result is that government spending

Figure 10.5
Fiscal Policy Under Flexible Exchange Rates

In this figure we assume that capital mobility is high, thus when government spending increases, the exchange rate appreciates because the income induced decrease in the balance of trade is smaller than the interest rate induced increase in the net capital outflow.

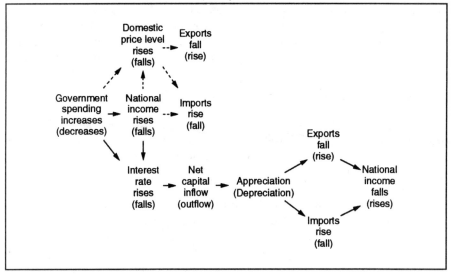

crowds out net exports and the level of income is unaffected. This extreme case is shown in Figure 10.6.

While the extreme case, where increased government spending is completely offset by lower net exports, may seem unrealistic, the basic proposition that increased government spending can crowd out net exports is strongly supported by American experience during the early 1980s: taxes were cut in the United States, government spending increased, the budget deficit exploded, and the American economy rapidly developed a massive trade deficit. Therefore, the expansionary effect from higher government spending and lower taxes was to some extent offset by lower net exports.[6]

German Reunification

The Berlin Wall came down in November 1989, and on October 3, 1990, East and West Germany formally became a single country again. Reunification led to a higher interest rate for two reasons. First, the East was in need of large

---

[6]See Chapter 7.

Figure 10.6
Government Spending Reduces Net Exports

An increase in government spending shifts the line showing $S + T - I_p - G$ downward, and the level of income tends to rise from Y_0 to Y_1. As the domestic price level and/or the level of income rises, the demand for money increases, the interest rate rises, and a capital inflow pushes up the value of domestic currency. In consequence, net exports decline from $(X - M)_0$ to $(X - M)_1$. In the case of perfect capital mobility shown here, the increase in government spending is completely offset by a fall in net exports.

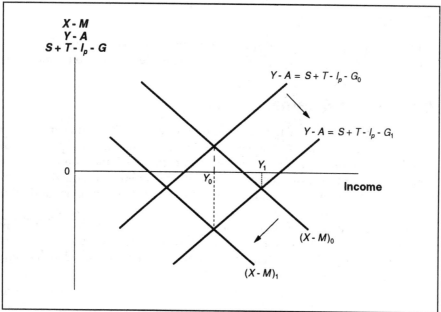

amounts of government aid, and as government spending increased, heavy government borrowing put upward pressure on interest rates. Second, aggregate demand increased as East Germans took advantage of their new freedom to buy West German consumer goods, and spent the deutsche marks they had received in exchange for their East German marks. Interest rates rose because the Bundesbank tried to keep inflationary pressures under control. Meanwhile, the interest rate in the United States was falling, and capital flowed into Germany in search of higher returns. In consequence, the deutsche mark increased in value and the German current account surplus was transformed into a deficit. Chapter 7 described how American government borrowing increased during the 1980s and net exports fell. Here again we see an example of increased government borrowing crowding out net exports.

Table 10.1
The Effectiveness of Monetary and Fiscal Policy

	Fiscal Policy	Monetary Policy
Fixed exchange rates	Effective	Ineffective
Flexible exchange rates	Ineffective	Effective

Summary

Table 10.1 summarizes the results of our discussion of the effectiveness of monetary and fiscal policy when there is a high degree of capital mobility.

Internal and External Balance

So far we have assumed that there is only one objective, either internal or external balance. In this section we examine the combinations of policies that should be pursued when both internal and external balance are targets. We consider two examples of internal imbalance: a combination of high inflation and low unemployment, and a combination of low inflation and high unemployment. We also consider two examples of external imbalance: a balance of payments deficit and a balance of payments surplus. We assume a fixed exchange rate because that is when external balance is an issue. Flexible exchange rates automatically adjust to equate the demand and supply of foreign exchange.

Case 1: Unemployment and a Balance of Payments Deficit

In this case, devaluation is the appropriate policy because it will increase the balance of trade and stimulate aggregate demand at the same time. Because there are unemployed resources and inflation is low, the inflationary impact of a devaluation (higher import prices and increased aggregate demand) is not a major concern. If aggregate demand is increased by an increase in the money supply, unemployment falls, but the balance of payments deficit increases. Therefore, expansionary monetary policy is not consistent with the objective of external balance.

Case 2: Unemployment and a Balance of Payments Surplus

In this case expansionary monetary policy is appropriate because an increase in aggregate demand leads to an increase in income and lower unemployment. Also, because the country initially has a balance of payments surplus, the outflow of capital caused by lower domestic interest rates and the fall in net exports caused by income growth are not problems. Devaluation would increase aggregate demand and increase employment, but the balance of payments surplus would increase. Thus, devaluation is not consistent with the objective of external balance.

Case 3: Inflation and a Balance of Payments Deficit

In this case, a reduction of aggregate demand by deflationary monetary policy is called for because a fall in aggregate demand helps reduce both the balance of payments deficit and the rate of inflation. A revaluation would reduce inflation by reducing import prices and lowering aggregate demand (through lower net exports), but revaluation would increase the balance of payments deficit. Thus, revaluation is not consistent with external balance.

Case 4: Inflation and a Balance of Payments Surplus

The appropriate policy in this case is a revaluation because it reduces both domestic inflation and the balance of payments surplus. Deflationary monetary policy is not appropriate because the balance of payments surplus would increase.

Fiscal Policy and the Problem of Internal and External Balance

The effect of increased government spending on the balance of payments depends on the degree of capital mobility. If capital mobility is low, an increase in government spending leads to a decrease in the balance of payments because net exports fall as the level of income rises (and the change in capital flows is relatively unimportant). Therefore, increased government spending could be used in Case 2 to increase aggregate demand and reduce the balance of payments surplus, and lower government spending could be used in Case 3 to decrease aggregate demand and reduce the balance of payments deficit.

When capital mobility is high, increased government spending leads to an increase in net capital inflows, as higher government spending pushes up interest rates. Although net exports fall, there is a net increase in the supply of foreign exchange because the effect of increased net capital inflows on the demand and supply of foreign exchange is stronger than the effect of lower net exports. Therefore, increased government spending can be used in Case 1 to increase aggregate demand and reduce the balance of payments deficit, and lower government spending can be used in Case 4 to reduce aggregate demand and reduce the balance of payments surplus.

In practice one policy alone is unlikely to solve internal and external balance exactly. A combination of policies will be needed. However, the preceding classification shows how domestic economic conditions and the balance of payments position can be used to select the primary adjustment policy.

Inflation and Unemployment

In the cases discussed previously, one policy helps solve two problems. A more difficult problem is the appropriate policy to adopt when a country has inflation and unemployment. The problem is that internal balance cannot be pursued by a policy that concentrates mainly on aggregate demand. To reduce unemployment, aggregate demand must be increased, whereas to reduce inflation, aggregate demand must be reduced. The "solution" adopted by many governments during the late 1970s was to concentrate on the problem of inflation. Unemployment was judged to be of secondary importance, in part because governments hoped that unemployment would return to normal levels after inflation had been reduced. Also, unemployment was seen as an unavoidable cost of reducing inflation. Balance of payments considerations were of secondary concern, and flexible exchange rates allowed governments to concentrate on domestic economic problems.

These policies had the desired result, and inflation was reduced. Unfortunately, as expected, unemployment increased. One way to remove unemployment and inflation would be for output (aggregate supply) to increase. In the United States, the Reagan administration claimed that tax cuts would achieve this by increasing the incentive to work. Whatever benefits this policy might have brought have probably been lost because spending was not kept under control. The budget deficit which emerged jeopardizes long–term growth because government borrowing absorbs the funds which might have been used to finance private investment. Also, government borrowing sucks in foreign capital. As a result, the United States is now a net debtor nation.

Unfortunately, there are no easy ways to increase output and reduce unemployment. Some economists favor policies that would improve education and increase investment incentives. Long–run policies such as these have not received sufficient political support in the United States, perhaps because politicians often do not look beyond the next election.

International Interdependence

The preceding discussion has shown the importance of trade and capital flows. As trade and capital flows have increased over the past few decades, interdependence between countries has increased. This interdependence is shown by the general increase in inflation throughout the world in the 1970s, and the general decline in inflation and growth in the 1980s. Also, clearly changes in the prices of traded goods, in particular the price of oil, can have significant effects. The following analysis will help us understand the history of the international monetary system, and analyze what is happening today.

We will examine how the economic policies of one country, the United States, may influence other countries. We refer to the effects of American policies because the United States probably has more influence than any other single country. However, the United States is not the only country that influences other countries. The economic policies of Germany in particular have often had great influence on other members of the European Monetary System.

Monetary Expansion

It has been shown that monetary expansion in the United States leads to a lower domestic interest rate and higher prices and income. The American balance of payments tends to move into deficit as a result of a net capital outflow and a balance of trade deficit. Assume that, as in the Bretton Woods system, other countries intervene in order to maintain the values of their currencies against the dollar. In this case, as the dollar tends to fall in value, other countries buy dollars with their own currencies and their money supplies expand. Thus, monetary expansion in the United States spills over to other countries, interest rates in other countries fall, and world prices rise. It is clear that monetary expansion in the United States could lead to world inflation.

This outcome is not inevitable. If other countries allow their currencies to rise against the dollar, American monetary expansion is not transmitted to other countries. With flexible exchange rates, foreign money supplies need not change because foreign monetary authorities do not intervene in the foreign exchange market. In the long run, under flexible exchange rates, the exchange rate (dollars per unit of foreign exchange) will rise by the same amount as the American price level if purchasing power parity holds.[7]

Monetary Contraction

American monetary contraction has the opposite effect. If other countries maintain fixed exchange rates, their money supplies fall, interest rates rise, and their price levels fall. Again, flexible exchange rates break the monetary

---

[7]The case of monetary expansion under flexible exchange rates was examined in more detail earlier in this chapter.

transmission mechanism by freeing foreign monetary authorities from the obligation to intervene in the foreign exchange market.

It has been shown that American monetary policy influences other countries' money supplies when other countries fix the values of the currencies against the dollar. Although many countries no longer have a formal fixed exchange rate, they continue to intervene in the foreign exchange market to stabilize their currencies against the dollar. Therefore, to some extent, other countries continue to be influenced by American monetary policy. Similarly, German monetary policy has had a strong effect on other members of the European monetary system (EMS) because currencies within the system are fixed against each other and Germany is the dominant economy.

Fiscal Expansion

An increase in government spending in the United States leads to an increase in the American interest rate, if the American money supply is not increased. Under fixed exchange rates, with a high degree of capital mobility, the effect is similar to that of monetary contraction: a net capital inflow into the United States leads to foreign balance of payments deficits and downward pressure on foreign money supplies. (Recall that when there is a balance of payments deficit, intervention to maintain a currency's value leads to a fall in the money supply and a higher interest rate.) If other countries choose flexible exchange rates, the dollar will rise in value relative to foreign currencies, and other countries will experience trade surpluses and capital outflows. However, the inflationary effects of depreciation, an increase in import prices and higher aggregate demand, may not be welcome in countries that already have inflation problems.[8]

An Increase in World Prices

Under fixed exchange rates, an increase in world prices can lead to domestic inflation. As world prices increase, net exports increase as the country's goods become more competitive. As a result, a balance of payments surplus develops, the money supply expands (as the monetary authorities buy foreign

---

[8]In the early 1980s, European governments were attempting to decrease inflation, and did not want their currencies to depreciate too much, because import prices would increase. They argued that the budget deficit and the low rate of monetary growth in the United States were forcing interest rates up. (Perhaps this argument should not be taken too seriously: European governments wanted to keep monetary growth down in order to reduce inflation, and were happy to put the blame on the United States.)

currency with domestic currency to stabilize the exchange rate), and aggregate demand increases. If the economy is already at or near full employment, an increase in aggregate demand leads to inflation. Again, flexible exchange rates can insulate an economy from world inflation. In this case, the difference between domestic and higher world inflation would be reflected in an appreciation of the country's currency.

An Increase in the Demand for a Country's Exports

An increase in the demand for exports raises the prices of exports relative to the prices of imports. The macroeconomic model we have used so far is not completely appropriate for the analysis of this case because it does not allow us to examine the effects of a change in relative prices. When the terms of trade improve, as in this case, trade theory and intuition lead us to expect that resources will move into the export sector from other sectors and that the level of real income will increase. The greater the ability of the country to increase export production, the greater the increase in real income will be. However, even without any increase in export production, real income increases because the value of a country's exports increases, that is, the revenue from a given amount of exports increases.

An Increase in the Supply of Exports

An increase in the supply of exports, resulting from an increase in a country's ability to produce, leads to an increase in real income.[9] Under fixed exchange rates, a balance of payments surplus develops as the balance of trade increases. This surplus increases the money supply (because the monetary authorities are forced to buy foreign currency). In this case, an increase in the money supply finances a higher level of economic activity, and does not necessarily cause inflation. Under flexible exchange rates the link between the money supply and the balance of payments is broken. Japan and Germany are obvious examples of countries which have enjoyed export success and increasing real incomes, but have also maintained low inflation rates by keeping control over their money supplies.

---

[9]We assume that the country is not large enough to influence the world prices of its exports significantly. In the case of a major exporter of a product, it is theoretically possible that a fall in the price of the export could outweigh the benefits of an increase in the quantity sold, and leave the country worse off after export growth. (This case is discussed in Chapter 2.)

Dutch Disease and Sectoral Adjustment

In recent years the experience of some countries has led economists to question the benefits of an expansion of exports under flexible exchange rates. We have seen that domestic currency tends to appreciate when the supply of exports increases. This appreciation reduces the net exports of sectors that are not growing, and possibly increases unemployment. Although overall real income increases when the supply of exports increases, not everybody gains from the increase. For example, some economists suggest that unemployment in the Netherlands and Britain resulted from Dutch exports of natural gas and British exports of oil. These exports tended to increase the values of the guilder and the pound, and led to unemployment in the manufacturing sectors of the Netherlands and Britain. In theory, if the growing sector employs a large number of people, and labor moves easily from one sector to another, unemployment may not be a problem. However, employment opportunities in the cases of natural gas and oil are minimal.

An Increase in the Price of Imports (An Oil Price Increase)

An increase in the prices of imports can also lead to inflation. As an example, consider an oil price increase. In this case, the domestic price level increases because consumers pay more for oil and oil products. However, the inflationary effects are much wider because production costs rise in sectors that use oil as an input, and because wage demands throughout the economy increase to reflect the increase in the cost of living. An oil price increase has other effects. The balance of trade decreases because imported oil costs more. Also, since more real income must be used to purchase oil, less is spent on other goods. Thus, the levels of real income and employment fall. Therefore, an oil price increase can cause unemployment and inflation.

As was shown at the end of the last section, there are no easy answers to the problem of unemployment and inflation. In deciding whether to take measures to influence the level of aggregate demand, the government in the short run must choose between lower inflation and lower unemployment. If the level of employment is maintained by increasing aggregate demand, inflation increases even more. If inflation is kept low, unemployment increases.

The good news is that a fall in the price of oil has the opposite effect: lower inflation and higher employment. This is why many economists welcomed the fall in the price of oil in the mid 1980s. Some economists doubted the benefits of the fall because they felt that the oil price would rebound and that instability was undesirable. Low oil prices may also be a long run problem in that they discourage conservation. Although a stable price might be better for oil importers and exporters, the problem is, of course, what that stable price should be.

Summary of Main Points

For small countries monetary policy is ineffective under fixed exchange rates. Following an increase in the money supply, the tendency for interest rates to fall and for income and prices to rise leads to a balance of payments deficit. The monetary authorities are obliged to sell foreign currency (buy domestic currency) to support the exchange rate, and the money supply tends to fall to its initial level. U.S. monetary policy may be effective because the U.S. is probably large enough to influence world monetary conditions.

If capital is mobile, fiscal policy is effective under fixed exchange rates because as income rises, interest rates rise and a balance of payments surplus results. Intervention to prevent domestic currency from rising in value leads to an increase in the money supply. Thus the effects of fiscal policy on aggregate demand are augmented by an induced increase in the supply of money. If capital mobility is low or capital flows are restricted, the effectiveness of fiscal policy is reduced under fixed exchange rates because a balance of payments deficit results from increased government spending and the money supply falls (the monetary authorities are forced to sell foreign exchange to support the exchange rate).

Under flexible exchange rates, monetary policy is effective because the tendency to develop a balance of payments deficit (following an increase in the money supply) leads to depreciation, which increases the expansionary effect on aggregate demand. In contrast, if capital mobility is high, fiscal policy is not effective because the tendency toward surplus leads to an appreciation of domestic currency, and falling net exports offset the expansionary effect of increased government spending.

One policy alone may move an economy toward internal and external balance. Devaluation increases net exports, aggregate demand, and import prices; thus, it is appropriate when an economy has unemployment, low inflation, and a balance of payments deficit. Revaluation reduces net exports, aggregate demand, and import prices; thus, it is appropriate when an economy has high inflation and a balance of payments surplus. Lower monetary growth is appropriate when the economy has inflation and a balance of payments deficit.

The effect of fiscal policy depends on the degree of capital mobility. Reduced government spending lowers aggregate demand and net exports increase as income falls. When capital mobility is low, lower government spending is appropriate for an economy with inflation and a balance of payments deficit. However, if capital mobility is high, reduced government spending lowers interest rates and leads to an outflow of capital, which increases the balance of payments deficit. Thus, when capital mobility is high, lower government spending is appropriate when an economy has inflation and a balance of payments surplus. In practice, one policy is unlikely to solve all problems, but the government may be able to achieve balance of payments equilibrium at full employment by combining exchange rate adjustment, monetary policy, and fiscal policy.

Countries are not independent; they feel the effects of international economic developments. For example, inflation can be transmitted from one country to another. A country may avoid inflationary developments in other countries by allowing its currency to rise in value. Increases in the prices of imported goods such as oil can lead to lower real income and inflation. Increases in the demand (and hence the price) of exported goods lead to higher real income. However, not all people benefit, since an increase in the foreign demand or domestic supply of exports may lead to appreciation that benefits one sector but hurts other sectors.

Study Questions

1. Why is monetary policy more useful under flexible exchange rates than under fixed exchange rates?
2. Why is fiscal policy more useful under fixed exchange rates than under flexible exchange rates?
3. Under what circumstances can an increase in government spending be expected to lead to:
   a. appreciation?
   b. depreciation?
4. Under flexible exchange rates, what is the effect of monetary expansion on the long–run exchange rate? During the process of adjustment following an increase in the money supply, why might the short–run exchange rate overshoot the long–run exchange rate?
5. Under fixed exchange rates, why does the expansionary effect of fiscal policy increase with capital mobility?
6. Why does the inflationary impact of monetary policy increase with the degree of capital mobility under flexible exchange rates?
7. "Capital controls are necessary under fixed exchange rates, otherwise governments cannot manage aggregate demand." Discuss with reference to the role of capital flows in determining the effectiveness of monetary and fiscal policy under fixed exchange rates.
8. Why might we expect a fall in the American money supply to lead to a world recession?
9. "If European countries do not like American monetary policy, they should stop intervening to influence the values of their currencies relative to the dollar." Discuss.
10. Why might an increase in German government spending (following German reunification) cause an increase in British interest rates?

Selected References

Branson, W. H., *Macroeconomic Theory and Policy*, 3e, New York: Harper & Row, 1989.

Corden, W. M., "Booming Sector and Dutch Disease Economics: Survey and Consolidation," *Oxford Economic Papers*, 35, 1984, pp. 359–80.

Dornbusch, R., *Open Economy Macroeconomics*, New York: Basic Books, 1980.

Dornbusch, R. and S. Fisher, *Macroeconomics*, 4e, New York: McGraw Hill, 1987.

Enders, K. and H. Herberg, "The Dutch Disease: Causes, Consequences, Cures and Calamatives," *Weltwirtschaftliches Archiv*, 69, 1983, pp. 473–97.

Fleming, J. M., "Domestic Financial Polices under Fixed and Floating Exchange Rates," *IMF Staff Papers*, 9, 1962, pp. 369–79.

Krause, L. B. and W. S. Salant, *Worldwide Inflation: Theory and Recent Experience*, Washington, D.C.: Brookings, 1977.

Kreinin, M. and L. Officer, *The Monetary Approach to the Balance of Payments*, Studies in International Finance No. 43, Princeton University Press, 1978.

Mundell, R. A., *International Economics*, New York: Macmillan, 1968.

Pippenger, J. E., *Fundamentals of International Finance*, Englewood Cliffs, NJ: Prentice Hall, 1984.

Rivera–Batiz, F. L. and L. Rivera–Batiz, *International Finance and Open Economy Macroeconomics*, New York: Macmillan, 1985.

Stern, R. M., *The Balance of Payments: Theory and Economic Policy*, Chicago: Aldine, 1973.

Part Three

Historical Experience

Eleven

The Gold Standard 1880–1914

Introduction

The gold standard was an international monetary system in which the relative values of currencies were determined by the values of the currencies relative to gold. The gold standard did not last long, 35 years at most, but it was an important period in international monetary history. A measure of the significance of the gold standard is that it continues to be the subject of debate, and recently the U.S. government set up a group to consider whether a return to the gold standard was desirable. The continued interest in the gold standard era arises from what many believe were certain characteristics of the period: incomes grew, free trade flourished, exchange rates were stable, and balance of payments crises did not occur. In this chapter we shall examine the nature and operation of the gold standard and attempt to assess the degree to which the gold standard was responsible for the economic success of the period. Such a study is an interesting exercise for its own sake, but it also helps us understand the present international monetary system.

The Evolution of the Gold Standard

The international gold standard was not created by collective decision; it emerged as different countries, for their own reasons, adopted gold as the basis of their currencies. In this section we shall examine the evolution of the system and how the system functioned. But first, let us consider how gold served as the basis of the system.

The Role of Gold

Under the gold standard, gold did not act as the sole common currency of countries in the system. Gold was not even particularly important as a currency; paper currency and coins circulated as they do now. Gold acted as a reserve backing for currencies. The amount of currency a government was allowed to issue was related to the quantity of gold it held; central banks were not allowed to print as much as they wished. The reason that countries linked their money supplies to their stocks of gold is that this reduced the danger of inflation arising from an increase in the money supply and fostered confidence in paper currencies. Countries also linked the values of their currencies to gold. Each country chose a price of gold expressed in its own currency, and bought and sold gold freely at the stated price, or **par value**. Thus, the value of a currency could be seen from the amount of gold a unit of currency was worth. (The regulations governing the relationship of each currency to gold were not international regulations—each country decided independently if, how, and when issues of its currency would be related to gold.)

Exchange Rates and the Gold Price

The system was a fixed exchange rate system because when two currencies were linked to gold, they were linked to each other through their relationship to gold. For example, if an ounce of gold is worth either X dollars or Y pounds, then it follows that X dollars are worth Y pounds, and the dollar sterling exchange rate equals X/Y. Actually, throughout the gold standard era, an ounce of gold was worth £4.248 in Britain and $20.67 in the United States. Therefore, the exchange rate was 4.866 dollars per pound sterling. As long as each currency was fixed in value relative to gold, the exchange rate remained fixed.[1]

Conditions for an International Gold Standard

If two currencies have established official gold prices, an international gold standard does not necessarily exist. People must also be allowed to convert currency into gold (by buying gold), or gold into currency (by selling gold), and imports and exports of gold must be free from control. If all these conditions are fulfilled, then the countries are on a gold standard. The beginnings of the gold standard can thus be traced to the decisions of various countries to fix the values of their currencies relative to gold, and to allow people to trade freely in gold at the fixed price.

The Early Years

The Coinage Act of 1816 authorizing the minting of gold sovereigns marks the beginning of Britain's movement toward a gold standard. By 1821, Britain permitted free trade in gold, and paper currency was convertible into gold at the official price. Other systems remained in use by other countries for many years after that. Some countries fixed the values of their currencies in

---

[1]If we think of gold prices as being rates of exchange of currencies against gold, the rate of exchange between two currencies is given by the cross rate, calculated in the way described in Chapter 6.

relation to silver, that is, they were on **silver standards**. Some countries fixed their currencies in relation to gold and silver, that is, they were on **bimetallic standards**, and some countries' currencies were not convertible. Currencies do not have to be convertible into precious metals to be useful; modern currencies are not convertible in this sense.

The movement toward an international gold standard began in the 1850s when the world price of gold fell as a result of discoveries of gold in California and Australia.[2] The United States was on a bimetallic standard at the time, which valued 1 unit of gold as the equivalent of 16 units of silver. As the supply of gold increased, gold tended to fall in value (to less than the 16:1 ratio). Gold therefore became overvalued in terms of silver at the official 16:1 ratio, and silver became undervalued in terms of gold. The result was that people were willing to sell gold to the monetary authorities, but not silver. Hence, increases in the money supplies of countries officially on bimetallic standards were determined by the supply of gold, that is, the countries were in effect on a gold standard. This experience illustrates a problem with bimetallic systems, namely, that both the official prices must be in line with market conditions or one of the metals will not function as a base for the system.

By 1870 the world was still not yet on a gold standard. Britain was still on gold; some countries that were officially on bimetallic standards were *de facto* on gold, for example, France; some countries, such as Germany, were still on silver standards; and some countries had currencies that were not convertible, for example, Russia, Austria–Hungary, Italy, and the United States. Wars and revolutions had forced the last group on to inconvertible currencies.[3]

The Beginning of the International Gold Standard

In the 1870s the movement toward an international gold standard accelerated. Germany led the movement when it switched from a silver standard to a gold standard following the end of the Franco–Prussian War and the receipt of gold from France as reparations. Germany took this action for a number of reasons. Some of its trading partners had been forced to abandon their link with silver and had inconvertible currencies. A large part of German trade was conducted through London, and since Britain was on a gold standard, it made sense for Germany to adopt the same policy. It was also felt that the

---

[2]People rushing to become gold miners in California were nicknamed Forty–Niners.

[3]Suspending convertibility allows a government to finance a war by printing money.

Table 11.1
Dates of Adopting Gold Standards

1816	Great Britain
1871	Germany
1873	Sweden, Norway, Denmark
1874	France, Belgium, Switzerland, Italy, Greece
1875	Holland
1876	Uruguay
1879	United States
1892	Austria
1895	Chile
1897	Japan
1898	Russia
1901	Dominican Republic
1904	Panama
1905	Mexico

Note: The dates are approximate only, for some countries made the change from bimetallism or silver monometallism to gold in several steps.

Source: Adapted from table on p. 472 of *The Economics of Money and Banking*, 4e, by Lester V. Chandler. Copyright 1948, 1953 by Harper & Row, Publishers, Inc. Copyright 1959, 1964 by Lester V. Chandler. Reprinted by permission of the publisher.

wealth and importance of Britain at the time was partly due to Britain's link with gold.[4]

When it changed to a gold standard, Germany began selling off its silver holdings. These sales added to an already existing world silver glut and led to a fall in the price of silver. Initially, countries on silver or bimetallic standards bought the silver, but they began to abandon silver because their money supplies were increasing (as they gave out currency and accumulated silver). The dates at which some countries adopted gold as the basis of their currencies are shown in Table 11.1. The international gold standard emerged as more and more countries adopted gold and relative currency values came to be determined by the values of currencies relative to gold (as shown by the gold prices).

The United States adopted a gold standard in 1879. However, silver mining interests opposed the change, which removed the guaranteed market for their output. The mining of silver coins had been suspended in 1873 while the country was using inconvertible "greenbacks," and over the next two decades there was pressure on the government to buy silver. This pressure

---

[4]It was said at the time: "Gold is the currency of rich countries, and silver is the currency of poor ones."

resulted in the passage of acts requiring the Treasury to buy specified amounts of silver: the Bland–Allison Act of 1878, and the Sherman Silver Purchase Act of 1890. The monetary role of silver was an issue in the 1896 election, but Bryan, who supported unlimited coinage of silver, was beaten by McKinley. It was not until 1900, when the Gold Standard Act was passed, that the system that already existed in the United States was embodied into law. This is one reason why some people date the gold standard from 1900. Another is that in 1900 there were more countries on the gold standard because some countries that had been on silver in 1880 had switched to gold.

The Gold Standard in Theory and Practice

Gold Flows and Exchange Rate Stability

It was thought that, under the gold standard, exchange rates were stabilized by gold flows. To see how this mechanism was supposed to have worked, we can use the dollar–sterling exchange rate as an illustration. From the previous discussion, we know that the exchange rate was 4.866, when calculated from the British and American gold prices. This was called the **mint parity** because it was calculated from the prices used by governments when they minted coins. Assume that the dollar–sterling exchange rate in the New York foreign exchange market tends to rise slightly above 4.866, because of an increase in the demand for sterling. People could get sterling by trading dollars for sterling in the normal way in the foreign exchange market, or they could buy gold with dollars, ship it to Britain, and sell the gold for pounds in London. This activity involves a cost: the cost of shipping and insuring the gold. However, if the exchange rate were to exceed the mint parity by more than the cost of shipping and insurance, it would be cheaper to obtain sterling by buying gold in New York and selling gold in London than from the foreign exchange market.

The Gold Points

The cost of transporting gold worth 1 pound was only 2 or 3 cents, so the exchange rate could not diverge very far from the mint parity of 4.866. As the dollar–sterling exchange rate rose toward 4.89, people wanting to buy pounds would do so by shipping gold from the United States to Britain; no one would be willing to buy pounds in the foreign exchange market at an exchange rate above 4.89. Similarly, there was a lower limit to the price of pounds. As the exchange rate fell, no one would be willing to sell pounds at less than 4.84 because at that price it was possible to covert pounds into dollars by buying gold with pounds in Britain and selling gold for dollars in the United States. The upper and lower limits within which the exchange rate

Figure 11.1
The Limits of the Dollar–Sterling Exchange Rate

The official prices of gold in dollars and sterling determined the mint parity of 4.866. The dollar–sterling exchange rate could not depart significantly from the mint parity. No one would pay more than 4.89 per pound because at that price it was possible to convert dollars into sterling by buying gold with dollars, shipping the gold to Britain, and selling it for pounds. Thus the demand for sterling becomes perfectly elastic at an exchange rate of 4.89. Similarly, no one would sell sterling for less than 4.84 because at that price sterling could be converted into dollars by shipping gold from Britain to the United States. Thus the supply of sterling becomes perfectly elastic at 4.84. The limits of the exchange rate, the gold points, were consequently determined by the cost of shipping and insurance.

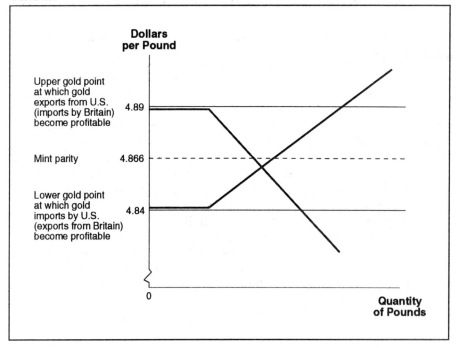

could fluctuate were known as the **gold points** and are shown in Figure 11.1.[5] The importance of convertibility at a guaranteed price and free trade in gold are obvious from this example.

---

[5]Speculators selling gold as the exchange rate approaches the upper gold point, and buying gold as the exchange rate approaches the lower gold point, could also make the supply and demand curves perfectly elastic (horizontal) at the upper and lower gold points, respectively. The actions of speculators are described presently.

Gold Flows and Adjustment

Gold flows were believed to have maintained fixed exchange rates. Gold flows were also credited with acting as part of an adjustment process that maintained balance of payments equilibrium at the fixed exchange rates. Gold fulfilled this role, it was suggested, because money supplies were linked to gold and gold flows led to money supply changes. To see how, assume that a country is becoming less competitive due to above average inflation. The country will tend to develop a balance of payments deficit. This will be reflected in the foreign exchange market by an upward movement of the exchange rate (the price of foreign currency) because at the initial exchange rate there is an excess demand for foreign currency. As the exchange rate rises and approaches the upper gold point, gold exports become profitable. Purchases of gold from the monetary authorities reduce official gold holdings, and because the money supply is linked to gold, the money supply is reduced. This causes domestic prices to fall, competitiveness to increase, and the balance of payments deficit to be removed. Similarly, in a surplus country where there is an excess supply of foreign exchange, as the exchange rate falls, gold begins to flow into the country, the money supply goes up, and the surplus is removed. This is the monetary adjustment process described in Chapter 9.

In theory, this adjustment mechanism would include a beneficial flow of resources to countries experiencing natural disasters. For example, if a very bad harvest reduces the supply of food, domestic prices rise, and imports of food increase. At the initial exchange rate there is an excess demand for foreign exchange equal to the cost of the extra imports. This puts upward pressure on the exchange rate, and a gold outflow takes place, as described earlier. Initially, the gold outflow pays for the excess imports. Gold outflows decrease the domestic money supply, and adjustment takes place as domestic prices fall relative to world prices. Although after adjustment the country consumes the value of what it produces, that is, exports equal imports, during the adjustment period the country consumes more than it produces.[6] When the harvest returns to normal, prices fall, there is an inflow of gold in exchange for exports, and for a period the country consumes less than it produces. Therefore, the gold standard included a mechanism whereby a country that had a poor harvest could consume more food than it produced, and consume less food later.

---

[6]Even if the adjustment process is fast, the country may consume more than it produces. It is the excess consumption that gives rise to the balance of payments deficit needed for the gold outflow and the fall in the money supply.

Gold Did Not Flow

What we have described so far in this section is how people believed the gold standard worked. This has been called the **myth of the gold standard**. But what we have described is not what appears to have actually happened. At the heart of the myth of the gold standard was the belief that gold flowed between countries. In practice, gold flows were not substantial, and economists were forced to try to explain how balance of payments adjustment took place without gold flows. We shall examine this question in a moment, but first we shall show how exchange rates remained constant without gold flows.

Stabilizing Capital Flows

During the period of the gold standard, people had confidence that the declared prices of gold would be maintained, and thus that exchange rates would not change.[7] This confidence gave rise to stabilizing capital flows. As a country moved toward a balance of payments deficit, the exchange rate moved toward the gold export point. Since this was the upper limit of the exchange rate (because gold flows would prevent the rate from rising further), it was believed that the rate would fall sooner or later. An exchange rate might not fall immediately, but the exchange rate could not rise above the upper gold point while the official gold prices remained unchanged (see Figure 11.2).

Recall that a fall in the exchange rate is an appreciation of domestic currency. Speculators holding domestic currency acquired at the upper limit of the exchange rate would be rewarded with a capital gain if the currency were sold after a fall in the exchange rate. For example, in the case of an American deficit, British speculators buying dollars at 4.9 to the pound might be able to sell the dollars at 4.866 dollars per pound and make a profit of 2.4 cents for each pound traded.[8] Therefore, as the dollar–sterling exchange rate moved toward the upper gold point, a capital inflow into the United States took place. Exchange risk was virtually zero. Governments were committed to maintaining the gold prices, and while they did so, exchange rates were fixed (within the limits set by the cost of shipping and insurance).

---

[7]In Britain in 1900, a person could have great confidence that some things never changed: sterling had been fixed against gold for about 80 years, Queen Victoria had been on the throne for over 60 years, the empire seemed reasonably safe . . .

[8]The gain may not seem large, but if it can be repeated a number of times a year, the return is more significant. In addition, investors received interest on the assets they invested their currency holdings in.

Figure 11.2
The Role of Capital Flows

The actions of speculators helped stabilize the exchange rate. At the upper gold point, the dollar was at its lowest possible value. Speculators bought dollars (sold pounds) knowing that the dollar could only rise in value. This tended to push the value of the dollar up, that is, the exchange rate tended to fall. At the lower gold point, the pound was at its lowest possible value. Speculators bought pounds knowing that the pound could only rise in value. This tended to push up the value of the pound. If speculators' actions were insufficient, the monetary authorities would use the interest rate to induce capital flows. Gold flows were not necessary to keep the exchange rate within the gold points.

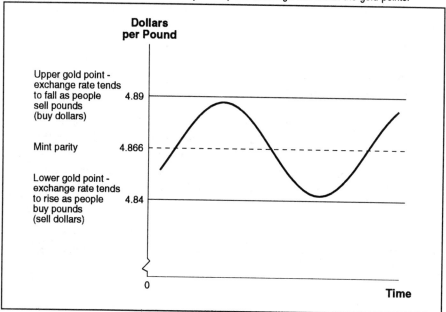

Bank Rate

In the discussion so far we have assumed that the central banks were passive, that is, that they allowed adjustment to take place through market forces. In fact, it was also possible for stabilizing capital flows to be encouraged by a central bank changing the interest rate that investors received. In Britain, the **bank rate** was a rate of interest set by the Bank of England, and it acted as the basis for other British interest rates: a rise in the bank rate led to a rise in other interest rates in Britain. (It was similar to the present day discount rate of the American Federal Reserve.) As the value of sterling began to depreciate, and the dollar–sterling exchange rate moved toward the lower gold point of 4.84 (the point at which gold exports from Britain were profitable), the Bank of England raised the bank rate. This attracted foreign capital and reduced pressure on the exchange rate. Even if a capital inflow did not occur, there was a reduction in the size of the capital outflow, which had a similar effect.

Belief in the effectiveness of the bank rate in attracting foreign currency or gold was reflected in the famous saying that if the bank rate were raised as high as 7 percent it would bring gold from the North Pole. Other central banks also manipulated interest rates. Clearly, the view that equilibrium was maintained automatically, in other words, without government intervention, is mistaken.

Movements in bank rate were believed to be more than just short–run palliatives. According to this view, higher interest rates reduced investment, lowered income and employment, and, as economic activity declined, caused prices to fall. An excess demand for foreign exchange was removed when the bank rate increased because a lower level of prices and incomes led to an improved current account balance. However, Lindert (1969) argues that:

> ". . . in the short run, bank rate increases worked on the balance of payments primarily through the capital account. Their impact on the trade balance via contractions in aggregate demand was probably too delayed to account for the speed and smoothness with which the Bank of England improved the exchanges and attracted gold." (p. 77.)

Britain was able to attract funds easily because it was at the center of the international monetary system. For other countries, the mechanism may not have been so smooth.

Fractional Reserve Banking

We have seen that, under a gold standard system, when there is a deficit the money supply goes down as people buy gold and send it abroad. Essentially, the government finances the deficit from gold reserves while downward adjustment of domestic prices is brought about by a falling money supply. Adjustment will be completed before the money supply reaches zero, and, therefore, if paper money is backed by gold holdings of an equal value, reserves will not be exhausted. However, in practice the backing for gold was less than 100 percent. This meant that gold reserves might fall by a large proportion before adjustment was completed. For example, if paper money is backed by gold equal to 10 percent of its value, a 10 percent fall in the money supply, brought about by people buying gold and exporting it, would exhaust the gold stock. Therefore, governments took action to speed the adjustment mechanism by ensuring that the money supply changed in proportion to the change in gold.

Fractional reserve banking may be part of the explanation of how exchange rates remained stable and adjustment took place when gold flows were not large: gold flows were of greater significance than they appear in retrospect because falling gold reserves prompted governments to adopt adjustment measures. This is another example of how, in contrast to the theoretical model, the system was not completely automatic.

Balance of Payments Adjustment

We have not considered how fundamental disequilibria in the balance of payments were removed. The reason is that fundamental disequilibria were not a problem for the important trading nations at the center of the system. During the period of the gold standard, prices and wages moved in harmony, so divergent trends in international competitiveness did not emerge. This harmony can be attributed to the absence of government restrictions on trade or capital flows that allowed disturbances to be transmitted between countries. Tariffs existed, but the prevailing philosophy was that of **laissez–faire capitalism**. In this environment, counties experienced similar inflationary/deflationary trends as their money supplies changed with the supply of gold.

Exchange rate stability was not universal. For countries at the center of the system (Britain, France, Germany, and the United States), exchange rates were stable, but Latin American countries frequently devalued. Downward revision of wages and prices was not necessary. Triffin (1968) states: "Wherever substantial inflation had been allowed to develop, international cost competitiveness was nearly invariably restored through devaluation rather than through downward price and wage adjustments." (pp. 6–7.) The monetary price adjustment mechanism described in Chapter 9, wherein deficits lead to monetary contraction, lower prices, and increased competitiveness, was not a significant feature of the gold standard.

Britain's Role

Finally, the position of Britain during the gold standard deserves special mention. Britain's commitment to free trade and a fixed gold value of sterling meant that sterling could act as an international money: it was as good as gold. The London money market led the world in the provision of banking and insurance services. Britain dominated international investment. Yeager (1976) reports: "British foreign investments shortly before World War I amounted to roughly twice the French, more than three times the German, and many times as large as the foreign investments of any other country." (p. 300.) Britain consistently ran a merchandize trade deficit, which was financed by interest earned on foreign investments; interest earnings were large enough to enable Britain to add to its foreign investments.

Nurkse (1954) reports that as much as 7 percent of British national income was devoted to foreign investment, this often taking the form of investment in public utilities. (Forty percent was in railways, 5 percent in other utilities, and 30 percent in loans to governments.) Nurkse states that roughly two–thirds "went to the so–called 'regions of recent settlement': the spacious fertile and virtually empty plains of Canada, the United States, Argentina, Australia, and other 'new' countries in the world's temperate latitudes." (p. 745.)

A Return to Gold?

Recently the gold standard became a topic for debate when the possibility of restoring a monetary role for gold was considered by the *Commission on the Role of Gold in the Domestic and International Monetary Systems*. The idea of returning to gold was rejected, but it is interesting to consider the types of arguments that have been put forward. This adds to our understanding of the gold standard and the way in which the international monetary system operates now.

The Myth of the Gold Standard

The arguments for a return to gold relate more to the myth of the gold standard than to what actually happened. It is said that during the gold standard the level of income rose in participating countries, and inflation was not a problem. A return to a gold standard would yield these desirable benefits, proponents suggest. Incomes did grow, but it does not seem appropriate to attribute the growth solely to the international monetary system because may factors could have influenced income, for example, the trend toward industrialization, or improvements in transport and communication. Moreover, even if we believe that the international monetary system helped, a gold standard is clearly not necessary because real incomes grew faster under the Bretton Woods system which existed after World War II (see Chapter 13).

As for price stability, prices in 1910 were about the same as they were in 1850. But Triffin (1968) shows that wholesale prices declined over the years 1872–1896 by 36 percent in Germany and 50 percent in the United States, and between the years 1896 and 1913 prices increased by 32 percent in the United Kingdom and 49 percent in the United States. Prices were not stable: they fell, then rose. This can be seen from the figures in Table 11.2.

Table 11.2
Wholesale Price Indexes, 1849–1913

	U.S.	U.K.	Germany	France	Italy
1849	80	90	71	96	—
1872	133	125	111	124	—
1896	67	76	71	71	74
1913	100	100	100	100	100

Source: *Our International Monetary System: Yesterday, Today and Tomorrow* by Robert Triffin, p. 18. Copyright 1968 by Random House, Inc. Reprinted by permission of the publisher.

Inflation and the Supply of Money

There is a striking similarity between the movements in price levels of the major countries, suggesting that they were affected in similar ways by changes in the supply of money. The explanation of the general fall and rise in prices is that the supply of gold, and thus money supplies (because they were linked to gold holdings), did not increase as fast as real incomes in the earlier period, and in the later period the supply of gold increased more rapidly than real incomes.[9]

An argument used in favor of returning to gold is that linking money to gold would take the control of money out of the hands of the government. It is said that governments have used their control over money to achieve political objectives at the expense of economic stability. However, under a gold standard the stability of the money supply is determined by the stability of the supply of gold, and it is unlikely that the supply of gold will grow in line with real incomes. Therefore, a return to a gold standard is not a guarantee of price stability.

Government Intervention

A gold standard is attractive to economists who favor minimal government intervention. The theoretical model does not require discretionary government action: the system adjusts automatically. Deficits are removed by

---

[9]The average annual growth in monetary gold stocks was 6.2 percent between 1849 and 1872, 1.4 percent between 1873 and 1892, and 3.6 percent between 1893 and 1914. Over the same periods, the total money supply increased by 4.2 percent, 3.3 percent, and 4.3 percent, while uncovered money, that is, money in excess of gold and silver reserves, increased by 6.5 percent, 4.0 percent, and 5.4 percent, respectively. (Triffin, 1968, p. 28.)

a falling money supply and surpluses by a rising money supply. In practice, governments did intervene during the gold standard as we have seen (for example, interest rates were used to influence gold/capital flows). However, at the turn of the century government intervention in domestic affairs was less than now because during the gold standard period governments had limited economic objectives. It is unrealistic to suppose that modern governments would sacrifice domestic economic objectives if they conflicted with maintaining a fixed gold price. A more likely scenario is that direct controls would be introduced, or the fixed price of gold abandoned.

Fixing the Gold Price

The initial problem that would be faced if a gold standard were to be restored is: What would the price of gold be? At $100 per ounce, people would rush to buy gold and official gold reserves would be depleted quickly. At $3,000 per ounce, people would sell gold for paper currency. Assuming that the United States could choose a price so that demand and supply would be in approximate balance, changes in the demand and supply might make it difficult to maintain the price, especially if speculators expected a change in the gold price.

Is an International Gold Standard Likely?

An international gold standard would only exist if other countries linked their currencies to gold, and why should they? One reason other countries might be reluctant to adopt a gold standard is that the working of the last fixed exchange rate system, the Bretton Woods system, was not entirely satisfactory (see Chapter 13). The Bretton Woods system collapsed largely because governments were unwilling to pursue domestic economic policies that were consistent with exchange rate stability. Governments now know that exchange rates can be changed; they are not set by God. This means that they can, if they wish, allow domestic economic objectives to take precedence over the need to maintain balance of payments equilibrium. They are unlikely to give up this right and agree to have domestic economic polices determined by international forces. Even if they say they will, they could always change their minds later and abandon convertibility at a fixed gold price. As Hawtrey (1927) said:

> "The gold standard can only be established in a country by legislation. In an emergency it can be swept away at a moment's notice by new legislation." (p. 88.)

Therefore, even in the unlikely event of a gold standard being reestablished, people would not have the confidence in the system that they had before, and stabilizing capital flows would be less likely. The world has changed since the gold standard period, and duplication of the gold standard is impossible.

Conclusion

The gold standard shows how an international monetary system can work when there is confidence. The gold standard worked in large part because people expected it to continue. Some people favor a return to a gold standard, but it is unlikely that a return is feasible in the foreseeable future. Even if official gold prices were established, it would be virtually impossible to create confidence that the system would be maintained. Without confidence, any system is probably doomed to failure. We shall see in the next chapter that the interwar gold standard failed in part because of a lack of confidence in the system.

Summary of Main Points

An international gold standard exists when countries fix gold prices, the monetary authorities buy and sell gold in order to maintain the prices, and free trade in gold is permitted. The gold standard emerged in the last quarter of the nineteenth century as countries adopted these requirements.

A gold standard is a fixed exchange rate system because the relative values of two currencies (the **mint parity**) can be calculated from the official gold prices of the currencies. At the time, more importance was given to the role of gold flows than appears to be warranted. In particular, the role of gold in maintaining fixed exchange rates and balance of payments equilibrium was overemphasized. This misplaced emphasis has come to be called the **myth of the gold standard**.

It was thought that gold flows maintained fixed exchange rates. As the demand for foreign currency increased, the price of foreign currency increased. However, under the gold standard, it was possible to buy gold, ship it abroad, and sell it for foreign currency. Thus, the price of foreign currency could not exceed the mint parity by more than the cost of shipping and insurance. Similarly, the price of foreign currency could not fall far below the mint parity because people with foreign currency could buy gold abroad, ship it home, and sell it for domestic currency.

Gold flows were credited with maintaining balance of payments equilibrium through their influence on money supplies. Gold flows from deficit to surplus countries led to monetary contraction in deficit countries and monetary expansion in surplus countries (because money supplies were linked to gold). In deficit countries, balance of payments adjustment took place by an increase in interest rates, and downward pressure on the price and income levels. Surplus countries experienced changes in the opposite direction.

Later observers pointed out that gold flows were too small to have maintained fixed exchange rates and balance of payments equilibrium. They looked for other explanations. In the short run, capital flows played an important role. Speculators believed that gold prices would be maintained. An exchange rate might depart from the mint parity, but the size of the departure was limited by the cost of shipping and insurance. Therefore, currencies bought at the lower limit of their value could be sold again later if they had risen in value. Although governments were not supposed to manipulate monetary conditions, in fact they often used interest rates to induce stabilizing capital flows.

In the long run, balance of payments crises did not occur; countries were subject to similar influences because their money supplies were linked to gold and their inflation rates moved together. Also, countries were closely linked by trade and governments did not attempt to exert a major influence on economic conditions.

Some people advocate a return to a gold standard, claiming that prices and exchange rates would be stable, and government intervention would be constrained. Such a view is often based on a misrepresentation of the experience of the gold standard period: some proponents of a new gold standard claim that prices were stable during the gold standard when in fact they were not. Also, proponents of the gold standard appear to confuse characteristics of the period with the results of the gold standard.

It is almost certain that the proposal to return to gold will not succeed in the near future. Even if the United States were to favor such a return, other countries would not follow. However, the debate over a possible return to gold is interesting in that it helps us focus on particular aspects of the international adjustment process that are still relevant today.

Study Questions

1. What were the gold points? Describe why gold flows would take place, and in what direction, for the case of a country with a payments surplus, and for the case of a country with a payments deficit.
2. Automatic adjustment takes place without government intervention being needed to bring it about. Describe the automatic adjustment mechanism by which adjustment was believed to take place during the gold standard.
3. How were exchange rates fixed under the gold standard? Why were convertibility and the absence of restriction on trade in gold important?

4. How and why did stabilizing capital flows take place? What actions could the monetary authorities take to encourage them?
5. Explain why, under the myth of the gold standard, we would expect prices in deficit and surplus countries to move in opposite directions. In fact, countries' prices followed similar long–run trends. Why?
6. Using demand and supply curves for foreign currency, show how an American balance of payments deficit might be removed by a gold outflow. Now show how the corresponding British surplus is removed. What factors are likely to influence the speed of adjustment?
7. Write a report arguing for a return to a fixed exchange rate system based on gold. What are the weakest points in the argument?

Selected References

Bloomfield, A. I., *Monetary Policy under the International Gold Standard: 1880–1914*, New York: Federal Reserve Bank of New York, 1959.

Bordo, M. D., "The Gold Standard, Bretton Woods and Other Monetary Regimes: A Historical Appraisal," *Federal Reserve Bank of St. Louis Review*, 75, March/April 1993, pp. 123–191.

Eichengreen, B., *The Gold Standard in Theory and History*, New York: Methuen, 1985.

Gold Commission, *Report to the Congress of the Commission on the Role of Gold in the Domestic and International Monetary Systems*, Washington, DC: U.S. Government Printing Office, 1982.

Hawtrey, R. G., *The Gold Standard in Theory and Practice*, London: Longmans Green, 1927.

Lindert, P. H., *Key Currencies and Gold 1900–1913*, Princeton Studies in International Finance No. 24, Princeton, NJ: International Finance Section, Princeton University, 1969.

Nurkse, R., "International Investment Today in the Light of Nineteenth Century Experience," *Economic Journal*, 64, 1954, pp. 134–50.

Triffin, R., *Our International Monetary System*, New York: Random House, 1968.

Yeager, L. B., *International Monetary Relations*, 2e, New York: Harper & Row, 1976.

Twelve

The Interwar Years: The Road to Bretton Woods

Introduction

The interwar years represent an important part of international monetary history. The lessons of this period had a strong influence on the international economic and monetary system that was adopted after World War II, and they continue to influence international economic policy even now. References to these years are common, and analogies are often drawn between current events and the experience of that period. In this chapter we do not attempt to give a detailed description of the events of these years. Our objective is to identify the major trends, policies, and lessons of the period.

After World War I, the reestablishment of a gold standard was part of the process of postwar recovery, and by the mid–1920s a gold standard had been reestablished. The success was short–lived; by 1932 the interwar gold standard had collapsed. We shall examine the return to a gold standard and the reasons for its collapse. This study is interesting for its own sake, and because it illustrates the general problems of establishing and maintaining fixed exchange rates.

The collapse of the interwar gold standard was followed by a period of economic nationalism during which countries took little account of the effects of their policies on other countries. For example, there were many devaluations, and protectionist policies were adopted with little concern for international monetary stability or international trade. Countries soon realized that such policies were harmful, and economic nationalism began to give way to policies that acknowledged the interdependence between countries. World War II stopped this process, but also gave the world the chance to design a new international monetary system, the Bretton Woods system. As is shown in the next chapter, the Bretton Woods system was an attempt to avoid the problems of the interwar period: exchange rate instability and economic nationalism.

The Effects of the War

World War I led to the breakup of the gold standard. The first signs of the end of the system began to show as war became more likely toward the end of July 1914.[1] London was the major center of the international monetary system at that time. A strong demand for sterling developed as British investments were repatriated, British banks stopped lending abroad, and other countries repatriated their investments through London. As a result, the value of sterling began to increase.

Under the prewar gold standard the value of a currency could not rise significantly above the mint parity because the currency could be obtained by shipping gold.[2] However, at this time shipping was not safe, so the option of obtaining sterling by buying gold in the U.S. with dollars, and shipping the gold to London, was removed. Thus, outside of Britain the value of sterling could rise substantially above the mint parity. For example, the pound rose to $6.35 in New York in the last week of July 1914. (Recall that the mint parity was $4.866.) The exchange rate diverged from mint parity as the gold points widened because of an increase in the cost of shipping and insurance. On August 12, the Bank of England agreed to accept gold in Canada in exchange for sterling, and the price of sterling fell. Faced with the prospect of a loss of gold, American bankers reached an agreement to limit their gold shipments. However, gold shipments were small because the excess demand for sterling was quickly reduced by the effects of the war. By December 1914, the British demand for imported materials had pushed the value of the pound below the mint parity.[3]

Inflation and Government Policy During the War

In the warring countries, the need to finance the war naturally took precedence over the desire for monetary stability and concern for the gold standard. Financing the war effort led to inflation: taxes were not sufficient to finance the increase in government spending, and budget deficits were met by borrowing or creating new money. Even neutral countries experienced inflation as the war increased the prices of traded goods and balance of payments surpluses led to monetary growth.[4]

The conditions for a gold standard to exist include the freedom to buy gold from the central bank, or sell gold to the central bank, at the official price (convertibility between currency and gold), and the right to import or

---

[1]Britain declared war on August 4 following the German invasion of Belgium.

[2]The mint parity and the role of gold are discussed in Chapter 11.

[3]These events are described in more detail in the first chapter of Brown (1940).

[4]This experience is an example of the effects of an increase in world prices on domestic prices. The theory is described in Chapter 10.

Table 12.1
Postwar Wholesale Prices

	1913 = 100		
	1918	**1919**	**1920**
Canada	199	209	244
France	344	356	506
Germany	217	415	1,486
Italy	409	366	624
Netherlands	373	304	292
United Kingdom	225	235	283
United States	194	206	226

Source: League of Nations, *Memorandum on Currency and Central Banks: 1913–1924*, Geneva, 1925, pp. 206–16.

export gold. Convertibility and trade in gold were suspended by most countries, central banks took measures to acquire all the gold they could, and capital exports were restricted.[5]

These measures allowed countries to maintain their prewar exchange rates during the war. Even though rates of inflation varied from country to country, exchange rates did not reflect these differences because trade and financial links between countries were disrupted. Recall that one of the reasons why divergent price trends did not develop in the prewar gold standard was that economies were closely linked by trade and capital flows. An indication of wartime inflation is given in Table 12.1, which shows the postwar value of the wholesale price index relative to its 1913 value.

Economic Conditions After the War

When the war ended, wartime restrictions began to be relaxed. Trade and foreign investment began to return to normal, and it became impossible for countries to continue with the pretense of prewar exchange rates. The divergences between the purchasing powers of currencies were too great. As a result, most currencies were floated. Inflation did not end when the war ended. In some countries, such as Britain, Canada, and the United States, inflation was brought under control by 1920. In others, such as France and Germany, budget deficits financed by monetary expansion caused inflation to continue longer.

---

[5]Some neutral countries restricted gold imports in an attempt to avoid the inflationary effects of payments surpluses.

The changes that had taken place in the purchasing powers of currencies were not the only reason why an immediate return to the prewar gold standard was impossible. The war had changed countries' international economic and financial positions. For example, European countries found that their dominance of international trade had diminished. Trade with Russia virtually ceased after the revolution in 1917. In the postwar climate of increasing protectionism, it was difficult for countries to redevelop trading relationships. The war had disrupted international trade and encouraged the spread of industrialization. After the war, protectionist policies were often used to support the industries that had developed, and international competition was more intense.

The war also changed the structure of international indebtedness. The United States was transformed from being a net debtor to a net creditor by loans made during the war and later to finance postwar reconstruction. (However, many loans made in the war were never collected.) Britain's dominant prewar position as an international creditor was eroded by the sale of foreign assets to pay for materials for the war. Germany was transformed from being an important creditor to a debtor: like Britain, it had depleted its foreign assets, and after the war Germany was faced with demands for reparations payments from the Allies. Also, Britain, France, and Germany lost assets in Russia when, following the revolution, the government refused to acknowledge debts incurred under the czar. Belgium, France, and Italy owed money to each other and to Britain, and they all owed money to the United States.

The Return to a Gold Standard

The United States left the gold standard in 1917 (when licenses were introduced for the export of gold), and returned to it in June 1919 at the prewar price of $20.67 per ounce. This was possible because U.S. inflation had been lower than that of other countries, it had great export capacity, and it had become a net creditor during the war. When the war ended, the United States held almost 40 percent of the world's official gold reserves.

In other countries, a return to the gold standard was seen as part of the necessary overall rebuilding. The prewar gold standard appeared to have worked well, and the sooner it was restored, the better. The link of the dollar to gold, and the importance of the American economy, meant that the purchasing power of the dollar set the pace for other countries wanting to return to gold. Wholesale prices in the United States rose until 1920 and then fell. In 1924, American prices were equal to 150 percent of their 1913 level. Thus, in 1924 an ounce of gold could buy two thirds of the goods that could have been bought in 1913. Countries that had experienced higher inflation than the United States could either devalue their currencies by adopting high gold prices or deflate their economies in order to bring their price levels down to American levels.

Germany After the War

Germany experienced the worst postwar inflation, due to the economic policy of the government. It spent more than it received in taxes and financed the difference by printing money. The German wholesale price index rose to well over 100 trillion, from a base of 100 in 1913. As German inflation soared above inflation in other countries, the value of the mark fell, as Table 12.2 shows. This period in German history is a classic example of hyperinflation and the working of purchasing power parity.

Inflation reached its climax at the end of 1923 when the government replaced the old mark with a new one worth 1 trillion old marks. The old currency had virtually ceased to be useful as money and the new currency was welcomed by the public. The government brought spending under control, increased taxes, and monetary stability was restored. In 1924, with the help of foreign loans, Germany linked the new mark to gold. The new mark was worth about 24 cents. The monetary reform was a success: inflation did not return and the gold price was maintained. The lessons of this period continue to influence German policy. Germany has avoided inflationary monetary policy more diligently than most countries.

The Reparations Issue

Germany was forced to agree to pay reparations to the allies by the terms of the peace treaty signed at Versailles in 1919. Early demand for reparations

Table 12.2
The Decline in the Value of the Mark

Average Number of Cents per Mark		
December	1914	22.32
December	1918	12.09
December	1919	2.0
December	1920	1.37
December	1921	0.53
December	1922	0.01
June	1923	0.001
December	1923	0.000 000 000 022 7

Source: Young (1925), pp. 531–32.

were unrealistic, and Germany responded by claiming that it was unable to meet the payments. In 1921, the Reparations Commission assessed the damage at over $30 billion.

In order to meet reparations payments, large amounts of German currency would have had to have been converted into foreign currency. Germany was incapable of earning enough foreign currency to make the reparations payments. German production had not recovered from the war, the economy was experiencing massive inflation in the early 1920s, and Germany did not have the necessary export capacity. In any case, other countries would have been unable or unwilling to absorb enough goods for Germany to earn the foreign currency needed by exporting. In 1924, Germany received foreign loans under the Dawes Plan. These loans helped Germany return to the gold standard and meet reduced demands for reparations. For the first time since the war, reparations payments began to proceed smoothly. In fact, German borrowing from other countries after 1924 was greater than reparations repayments; thus, Germany did not have to run a trade surplus. When these loans ceased, German payments ceased.[6]

British Economic Policy After the War

After the war the objective of the British government was to return to the prewar parity as soon as economic conditions allowed. The return was seen as a matter of national pride and honor. For example, it was argued that holders of sterling assets acquired before the war should be able to sell the assets for the same amount of gold as when they were acquired. Also, it was felt that a link between sterling and gold was needed to prevent monetary expansion, to remove uncertainty, and to maintain and strengthen London's position as an international financial center.

In order to return to the prewar parity, Britain had to restore its competitive position that wartime inflation had eroded. One of the first steps was to bring government spending under control. During the war, a budget deficit had been financed by printing new money. After the war, it was felt that a budget deficit was no longer justifiable, and certainly should not be financed by money creation if Britain was to return to gold. A large budget deficit in 1918–19 was turned into a budget surplus in 1920–21 by cuts in government spending and increased taxes. The money supply was brought under control and reduced, and prices began to fall. While the battle to

---

[6]German payments ended in 1931 when, as part of the breakdown of the interwar gold standard, there was a flight of capital from Germany and payments on war debts were suspended. See Yeager (1976), p. 340.

Figure 12.1
The Dollar–Sterling Exchange Rate, 1919–1926

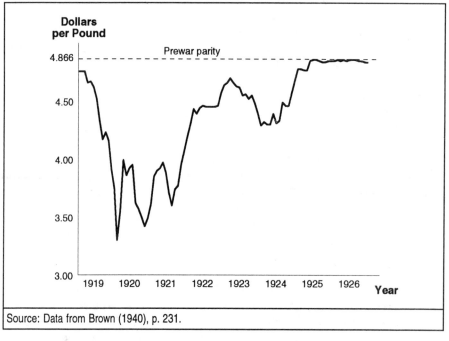

Source: Data from Brown (1940), p. 231.

reduce prices was taking place, the pound was allowed to float.[7] This was seen as a temporary measure pending the return to an official gold price and fixed exchange rates.

The pound gradually rose in value over the following years, as Figure 12.1 shows. The deflationary policy, and the rise in the pound, meant that British exports were less competitive and some traditional markets were lost (which added to unemployment problems). Britain also lost markets because other countries were growing. For example, cotton textile exports by Britain suffered as Japan entered the export market and domestic production in India displaced imports from Britain.

In April 1925, Britain returned to the prewar gold price after negotiating loans to help support sterling and raising the bank rate to attract short–term capital to Britain. Even at the time, the logic of restoring the prewar gold price was questioned by some people, notably the economist John Maynard

---

[7]Britain abandoned the gold standard officially after the war; wartime measures and conditions made it irrelevant during the war.

Keynes. He argued that the gold standard was a "barbarous relic" and that the world had moved to a paper system:

> Advocates of the ancient standard do not observe how remote it now is from the spirit and the requirements of the age. A regulated non–metallic standard has slipped in unnoticed. **It exists.** (Keynes, 1942, p. 187.)

Unfortunately for the British, Keynes' argument against the restoration of the prewar gold price was not heeded, and the economy suffered as a result.[8] The suffering continued after the restoration of the prewar gold price because the task of reducing the British price level had not been fully completed. The prewar parity is thought to have overvalued sterling by about 10 percent. Thus, the government had to maintain a high interest rate and continue with a deflationary policy. Unemployment during the 1920s (and 1930s) was always above 10 percent; before the war, unemployment of 5 percent or less had been common.[9] The British balance of payments problem is illustrated in Figure 12.2.

Yeager (1976) concludes his discussion of the era as follows:

> In short, British monetary experience in the 1920s consisted of several years of deflationary struggle back to the prewar parity; temporary success in this questionable effort; and then continued business stagnation and chronic unemployment, the need for relatively high interest rates, and a precarious accumulation of mobile short–term foreign funds—all under the influence of an inappropriate exchange rate. (p. 324.)

French Economic Policy After the War

France had problems similar to Germany's, but not on quite the same scale. The franc was allowed to float following the war, and as so often happens when a currency is floated, it sank. The government was committed to reconstruction, and although government spending exceeded taxes, it was felt there was no need for concern because reparation payments from Germany would finance reconstruction. The French government financed its excessive

---

[8]In the 1960s, British economic growth was again sacrificed to maintain an exchange rate that overvalued the pound. Many economists believe that the British devaluation of 1967 was too little too late.

[9]The experience of these years helps explain the British preference for low unemployment in the Bretton Woods period.

Figure 12.2
The Overvaluation of Sterling

Britain's policy of deflation was supposed to increase the value of sterling by increasing the demand for sterling and reducing the supply of sterling. This is shown by the shift of the supply curve to the left (S_0S_0 to S_1S_1) and the shift of the demand curve to the right (D_0D_0 to D_1D_1). When Britain returned to gold at the prewar parity of \$4.866, the policy had not been completed, and the supply (S_1S_1) was still greater than the demand for sterling (D_1D_1). The value of sterling was maintained by a capital inflow (which increased the demand for sterling to D_2D_2).

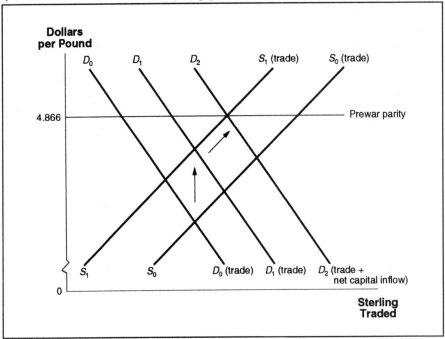

spending by printing money, which led to inflation, and the franc fell further.

The value of the franc was also influenced by speculation. Speculators feared that the franc might collapse as the mark had. They saw the franc fall, anticipated further decreases, and sold francs. This flight of capital pushed the value of the franc lower. Thus, speculators' actions were self–fulfilling. The monetary authorities did not attempt to support the franc at this time, and French gold reserves were not affected. The flight of capital, shown by a capital account deficit, was financed by a current account surplus.

French Stabilization

The stabilization of the French economy began in 1926. After a succession of governments, a new government (headed by Poincaré) raised taxes and removed the budget deficit. The franc, which had been weakened by speculation, began to recover: from just over 2 cents in July, it rose to over 3.9 cents in December. The government stabilized the rate in December 1926 and France was back on a fixed rate. The return to a gold standard was made official in 1928.

Postwar inflation in France had lasted long enough to make the prewar parity of 19.3 cents irrelevant, and the new rate of 3.9 cents undervalued the

Figure 12.3
The Undervaluation of the French Franc

When France returned to gold, a current account surplus financed a capital account deficit. The current account surplus is shown by the difference between the demand and supply of francs resulting from international trade, DD and $S_0 S_0$, respectively. The overall demand and supply of francs, DD and $S_1 S_1$, were equal because the excess demand for francs from trade was met by a supply of francs from the French capital outflow. When the capital outflow ceased, the French monetary authorities had to sell francs (purchase foreign currency) to prevent the franc from rising in value.

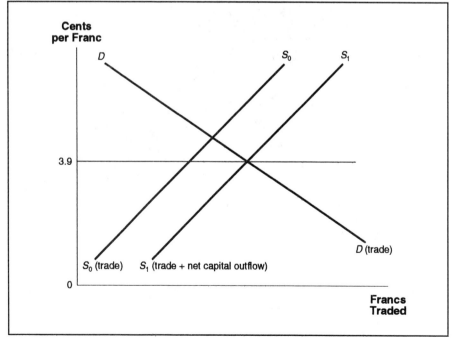

franc slightly. As a result, from 1926 onward France ran balance of payments surpluses (which added to Britain's problems of maintaining an exchange rate which overvalued sterling). Another factor adding to France's surpluses was the repatriation of capital that had fled France prior to stabilization. As the French monetary authorities intervened to maintain the value of the franc, they accumulated international reserves.[10] The domestic monetary effects of the balance of payments surpluses were sterilized to prevent inflation. The undervaluation of the franc is illustrated in Figure 12.3.

Figure 12.4
The Rise and Fall of the Interwar Gold Standard

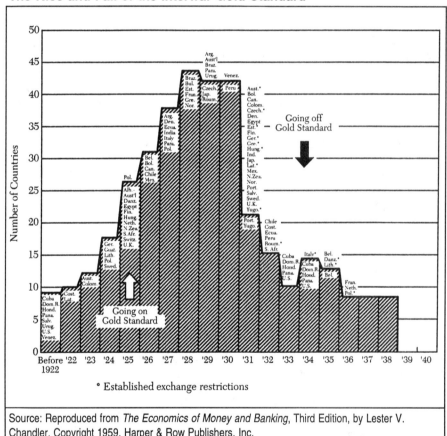

Source: Reproduced from *The Economics of Money and Banking*, Third Edition, by Lester V. Chandler. Copyright 1959, Harper & Row Publishers, Inc.

---

[10]French international reserves increased from less than $1 billion to about $2.5 billion from the end of 1925 to the end of 1928.

The movement toward a gold standard was not confined to Europe. Over the period 1924–28, a large number of countries moved back to gold (see Figure 12.4). Many people expected that the restoration of a gold standard would lead to the restoration of prewar economic conditions. However, the interwar gold standard was different from the prewar gold standard.

Comparing the Prewar and Interwar Gold Standards

Before the war, London had been the undisputed center of international finance. Britain was the most important investing and trading nation, and there was confidence in sterling and the British banking system. Imbalances between other countries could be settled by transferring the ownership of sterling balances. Small imbalances between Britain and the rest of the world were reflected in changes in the bank rate, which increased or reduced British lending abroad without disrupting international markets to any great extent. This system worked because people had confidence that exchange rates would remain unchanged, because money supplies were linked to gold, and because countries in general (Britain in particular) did not pursue independent monetary policies.

Economic Policies

After the war, New York rivalled London as the most important financial center. However, the United States is large and trade was relatively unimportant to it. Thus, American monetary policy was not sensitive to the balance of payments. For example, during the early 1920s, the American balance of payments surplus was sterilized to prevent inflation resulting from a rising money supply. In fact, American prices fell during the interwar gold standard. This added to the adjustment problems of other countries, notably Britain. Without sterilization, the American money supply and price level would have risen, and the amount of British deflation needed would have been smaller.

During this period, governments began to accept that they bore some of the responsibility for domestic economic problems such as inflation and unemployment. They became reluctant to allow balance of payments considerations to dictate economic policy. Although declining reserves forced deficit countries to adjust or devalue, surplus countries, such as the United States and France, faced no such pressure. Lack of adjustment by surplus countries increased the adjustment problems of deficit countries. This problem plagued the Bretton Woods system, and continues to be a problem even now.

Capital Flows and Protectionism

When there is more than one international monetary center, people can shift funds between the centers. If there is confidence in the stability of exchange rates, this possibility may not be important. But, as confidence in the parities of the interwar gold standard declined (at the beginning of the 1930s), large capital flows made the maintenance of fixed exchange rates impossible. Countries responded by abandoning fixed exchange rates and introducing capital controls.

Another difference between the interwar and prewar periods is that protectionist policies were more common during the interwar period. Protectionism began to take hold before World War I, but after the war protectionist pressures increased as countries concentrated on national economic interests. This issue is examined in Chapter 15.

Exchange Rates

Exchange rates were not chosen to ensure international consistency: each country fixed its gold price independently at what was thought to be appropriate for its own economic conditions and interests. This meant that some countries had payments surpluses and others had deficits. Adjustment might have taken place eventually (if countries had maintained gold prices and allowed their money supplies to be determined by their balances of payments), but domestic economic problems were often of greater concern than the external balance, so automatic adjustment was not permitted.

The Role of Gold

Gold played a smaller role in the interwar gold standard than it had before the war. Wartime measures had reduced the value of gold in private hands, gold coin had been replaced by paper currency, and people had become accustomed to paper currency. The role of gold as a base for the monetary system also changed. Official gold stocks had not increased in line with real income.[11] In order to economize on limited amounts of gold, countries

---

[11]When nominal gold prices are fixed, as under a gold standard, inflation reduces the real gold price (because the amount of goods that can be purchased with an ounce of gold declines). As the real price of gold declined during and after World War I, the supply of newly mined gold declined.

adopted **gold exchange standards**.[12] Under a gold exchange standard, countries count as part of their gold reserves currencies of other countries that are convertible into gold. This meant, for example, that gold held in the Bank of England supported issues of sterling, and some of the sterling supported paper currency issued by other countries. Therefore, two or more countries could increase "gold reserves" simply by holding each other's paper currency.

Confidence in the System

The interwar system only worked as long as people had confidence that the currencies were as good as gold. If lack of confidence caused people to demand the limited gold on which the pyramid of paper money was built, the system could collapse. Two currencies that were particularly vulnerable were sterling and the dollar. Both currencies were held in significant amounts by foreign central banks as international reserves. Thus, Britain and the United States could be faced with demands for conversion of large amounts of their currencies into gold. As the interwar system moved toward collapse, this is exactly what happened.[13]

The Collapse of the Interwar Gold Standard

Background

When France legally returned to gold in 1928, the central bank was prevented from accepting convertible currencies. The French monetary authorities demanded gold for the foreign exchange obtained from foreign exchange market intervention. (Recall that the French balance of payments was in surplus.) This put pressure on the gold reserves of Britain and the United States, and undermined confidence in the link of sterling and the dollar to gold. French gold reserves increased from $1.3 billion at the end of 1928 to $3.3 billion at the end of 1932. According to Nurkse: "The fate of the gold exchange standard was sealed when France decided to take nothing but gold

---

[12]The gold exchange standard was recommended by the Genoa Conference of 1922, and central bank statutes were amended to allow them to hold foreign exchange rather than gold as a backing for issues of money.

[13]See League of Nations (1944), pp. 39–41.

in settlement of the enormous surplus accruing to her from the repatriation of capital and the current balance of payments."[14]

The collapse of the international monetary system can also be traced to the Wall Street Crash of 1929 and the beginnings of the Great Depression (1930–33). The Wall Street Crash followed a period of record investment in the United States and the bubble burst when opportunities for profitable investment were exhausted. As investment fell, the American economy moved into recession. Another very important factor contributing to the depression in the United States was a decline in the money supply. Lack of confidence led to runs on banks, the Federal Reserve failed to fulfill its duty to act as lender of last resort, banks failed, and the money supply declined.

Some countries moved into recession before the United States. During the 1920s, the supply of primary products and agricultural products increased more rapidly than the demand for these products (because of technological progress and the development of new sources of supply). The consequent collapse in prices led to lower export earnings for the less–developed countries which relied on exports of these commodities. The collapse of American foreign investment at this time added to the international recession.

A decline in the American demand for imports, partly because of the recession and partly because of protectionism, was another factor contributing to the spread of the recession. The Smoot–Hawley tariff of 1930 drastically curtailed American imports, and other countries responded with their own protectionist policies. World trade fell dramatically, and this added to recessionary forces. This is an example of the foreign trade multiplier at work. The imports of one country are the exports of other countries. Protectionist policies that reduce imports reduce other countries exports and, hence, the income of other countries.[15]

The Collapse

The interwar gold standard was inherently weak and could not survive major financial crises. The collapse of the interwar gold standard began in Austria. In May 1931, a revaluation of the assets of the Austrian Credit–Anstalt revealed that it was insolvent and a run began on it and other Austrian banks. Austria was forced to abandon convertibility. Attention then began to focus on Germany. The German Danat (Damstadter und National Bank) faced a run when the fall of a major textile company it had made loans to was announced. The German government responded to the ensuing flight of

---

[14]League of Nations, p. 39. (Most of this report was written by Ragnar Nurkse). Chapter 11 of Eichengreen (1985) is an extract of this publication.

[15]Commercial policy during this period is described in more detail in Chapter 15.

capital by raising the discount rate and introducing exchange controls in August 1931. In effect, this marked the departure of Germany from the gold standard because free trade in gold was severely curtailed.[16]

Britain Abandons Gold

Against this background of bank failures and flights of capital, the weak British balance of payments position did not help maintain confidence in the value of sterling. Confidence was further undermined by the report of the Macmillan Committee in July 1931, which showed that London's short–term claims on foreigners were far smaller than London's liabilities to foreigners: London had a net short–term liability of over $1 billion. Britain used reserves, borrowed, and raised the bank rate in an attempt to maintain sterling's value. However, when some Royal Navy sailors protested against their pay on September 15, it was reported as a mutiny, and a serious run began on sterling. The new coalition government was not in the mood for further deflation because there was already massive unemployment, so Britain abandoned the gold standard on September 21, 1931.[17]

Incidentally, other countries suffered losses when Britain devalued and the value of sterling assets fell. In view of these losses, it is not surprising that some countries showed a preference for holding their international reserves in the form of gold rather than foreign exchange during the years preceding the collapse of the Bretton Woods system. It is also interesting to note in passing that by April 1934 the pound had rise to a value of over $5, that is, its value was more than the $4.866 value that Britain had been unable to maintain in 1931.

Other Countries Follow Britain's Departure

Other countries followed Britain's abandonment of the gold standard, in part because they wanted to avoid being put at a competitive disadvantage by a rise in the value of their currencies relative to other currencies. Also, speculators believed that countries would be unable to maintain gold prices and their activities made the maintenance of gold prices difficult. The desire of international investors to avoid loss was probably as strong a motive for capital flows as the desire for profit.

---

[16]Devaluation was rejected because, as a result of the German experience of the early 1920s, devaluation was associated with inflation.

[17]Following Britain's break with gold, a group of countries with close trade and financial links with Britain pegged their currencies to sterling and held sterling reserves. This group made up the **sterling area**.

Meanwhile, in the United States, the domestic monetary system was under strain. Over one third of American banks collapsed in the years from 1930 to 1933. People increased their holdings of currency and gold as they lost confidence in the American monetary system, and gold left the United States. Following a rush of gold and currency hoarding, President Roosevelt declared a "bank holiday" on March 6, 1933, to prevent further gold losses. Gold exports were outlawed, and the right of Americans to hold gold was suspended.[18]

The United States abandoned the gold standard officially on April 20, 1933. Devaluations of other currencies had weakened the American competitive position, but this was not the primary reason for the break of the link with gold. The recently elected Roosevelt administration felt that a rise in prices was needed to stop the recession, and it was thought that by some mysterious mechanism commodity prices would rise with the gold price. The dollar was devalued by raising the gold price. A price of $35 an ounce was fixed in January 1934.

1934–39

The American departure from gold effectively marks the end of the interwar gold standard, although some currencies clung to gold for a while longer. For example, Belgium did not devalue until March 1935, and France and Switzerland devalued in September 1936. The collapse of the interwar gold standard in 1933 was the beginning of a period in which there were many devaluations.[19] Although exchange rates fluctuated as the interwar gold standard collapsed, Table 12.3 shows that by the end of 1936 exchange rates were roughly what they had been in 1930. This suggests that weaknesses in the system and speculation played a large role in determining the size of devaluations. The devaluations do not appear to have been an attempt to realign currencies with underlying competitive forces.

---

[18]Americans were required to sell their gold to the Treasury. The ban on private gold holding remained in effect until 1974.

[19]Some economists describe the ensuing muddle as "a period of competitive devaluations" during which countries sought to reduce the relative value of their currencies in order to gain a competitive advantage over other countries. Rolfe and Burtle (1973) argue that this is not an accurate description of the polices of the most important trading nations, although some small primary producing countries may have behaved in this way.

Table 12.3
Exchange Rates in the 1930s

	(December 1930 = 100) December Values of Currencies Against the U.S. Dollar		
	1934	1935	1936
Argentina	76	99	98
Brazil	80	86	91
Australia	59	88	87
Sweden	67	95	94
India	68	102	101
United Kingdom	67	102	101
Canada	87	101	100
Czechoslovakia	100	141	119
Italy	100	162	100
Belgium	100	168	121
France	100	168	119

Source: League of Nations (1944), p. 129.

One characteristic of this period was the adoption of exchange controls by countries in Central Europe and Latin America.[20] These were often designed to reduce capital flows. Earnings of foreign exchange had to be sold to the monetary authorities, who either rationed the availability of foreign exchange or charged different prices for foreign exchange, according to how it was to be used. Germany controlled the availability of foreign exchange for virtually all purposes, including imports of goods. Bilateral trade agreements, such as barter, were used to maintain trade. As a result, countries became concerned with bilateral trade balances, and the gains from specialization and trade were undermined. Countries without exchange controls, such as Britain, were induced to take part because they had frozen assets in the countries with exchange controls and they wanted some form of service payment on loans they had made.[21]

The value of the French franc, established in 1936, lasted only nine months. Following speculation, the franc was floated in July 1937, then

---

[20]See Chapter 7 in League of Nations (1944).

[21]As a result of 170 clearing agreements, barter accounted for 70–75 percent of European trade in 1937. Bilateral clearing was less important for other countries, and accounted for at most 12 percent of world trade, (Pollard, 1982, pp. 303–4.)

pegged against sterling in April 1938. This arrangement lasted into World War II. Meanwhile, under Hitler, Germany continued to exercise controls over international transactions.

The dollar sterling exchange rate was reasonably stable around 4.95 until the summer of 1938. Then a British currency account deficit and rising international tensions led to speculation and a slight fall in the rate. In 1939, the dollar–sterling rate was stable at 4.68 until August, when transfers of funds increased as war seemed inevitable. Britain declared war on September 3, 1939. As in World War I, international trade and financial links were broken or tightly controlled.

Conclusion

The collapse of the interwar gold standard is not surprising in view of the inherent weaknesses in the system. It is difficult to summarize the events of the interwar period, but the lesson of the period is clear: if counties pursue their own interests without taking into account the effects of their policies on other countries, all countries suffer. This lesson was to have a major influence on the postwar economic system, and remains relevant today.

Summary of Main Points

After World War I, countries wanted to return to a gold standard. Differences between countries' inflation rates had altered the purchasing powers of currencies and made an immediate return to prewar gold prices and exchange rates impossible. Also, the trade and financial position of countries had changed.

The United States was able to return to gold soon after the war, and it did so at the prewar gold price. This meant that other countries wishing to return to gold had to bring their price levels down to the American level, or devalue their currencies in terms of gold. Germany and France experienced inflation well above that of the Untied States. When monetary stability was eventually restored in these countries, gold prices were fixed that set the value of their currencies below the prewar levels.

Britain chose to return to gold at the prewar gold price. To bring the British price level down to the American price level, the government pursued a deflationary policy that resulted in low growth and high unemployment. When the gold price was reestablished, the deflationary policy and high interest rates had to be maintained because the British price level had not fully fallen to the American level.

Britain's difficulty in returning to gold was made worse by the decision of the Federal Reserve to sterilize the monetary effects of the American surplus. In the absence of sterilization, American prices would have been higher, and Britain's deflation need not have been to severe. Also, the French franc was undervalued and France ran balance of payments surpluses.

It was clear that the exchange rates that had been established were not equilibrium rates: some currencies were overvalued and others were undervalued. Also, the willingness of governments to sacrifice domestic economic objectives to maintain fixed exchange rates was in doubt. The interwar gold standard began to come under strain with bank failures in Europe and America, the Wall Street Crash, and the onset of the Great Depression. These events led to a collapse of confidence, and, amid increasing speculation, countries were forced to abandon their links with gold.

During the period following the collapse, currencies were often devalued and countries used protectionist policies in an attempt to increase domestic employment. Trade and financial links between countries were disrupted. The 1930s are often quoted as an example of the dangers of pursuing national policies without regard for their effects on other countries.

Study Questions

1.   Explain what is meant by purchasing power parity with reference to the problems of restoring a fixed exchange rates system after World War I.
2.   Using the demand and supply of the currency, show how the value of a currency can be increased by deflation. (Use dollars per unit of currency as the exchange rate.) Why did Britain pursue a deflationary policy after World War I?
3.   Show that if the demand and supply of a currency are equal when there is a large capital outflow, the currency will be undervalued if the capital outflow ceases. (Use dollars per unit of currency as the exchange rate.)
4.   Why was there a capital outflow from France in 1925? Why did it cease after 1926?
5.   Why did the gold standard end during World War I? Why did most countries adopt flexible exchange rates after World War I?
6.   Why did the decision of the Federal Reserve to sterilize the monetary effects of American balance of payments surpluses make it difficult for Britain to return to and maintain the prewar value of sterling?
7.   Using the concept of purchasing power parity, describe how Britain returned to gold. What were the costs of Britain's return to gold?
8.   Why might capital flows have been stabilizing under the prewar gold standard and destabilizing under the interwar gold standard?

Selected References

Ashworth, W. A. A., *A Short History of the International Economy Since 1850*, 4e, New York: Longman, 1987.

Brown, W. A., Jr., *The International Gold Standard Reinterpreted: 1913–1934*, New York: National Bureau of Economic Research, 1940.

Chandler, L. V., *The Economics of Money and Banking*, revised edition, New York: Harper and Row, 1953.

Clarke, S. V. O., *The Reconstruction of the International Monetary System: The Attempts of 1922 and 1933*, Princeton Studies in International Finance No. 33, Princeton NJ: Princeton University Press, 1973.

Eichengreen, B., (ed.), *The Gold Standard in Theory and History*, New York: Methuen, 1985.

Ellsworth, P. T., *The International Economy*, 4e, Toronto: Macmillan, 1969.

Kenwood, A. G. and A. L. Lougheed, *The Growth of the International Economy: 1820–1980*, Boston: George Allen and Unwin, 1983.

Keynes, J. M., *Monetary Reform*, New York: Harcourt Brace and Co., 1924.

League of Nations, *International Currency Experience: Lessons of the Interwar Period*, Geneva, 1944.

Pollard, S., *Peaceful Conquest: The Industrialization of Europe 1760–1970*, revised edition, New York: Oxford University Press, 1982.

Rolfe, S. E. and J. Burtle, *The Great Wheel: The World Monetary System*, New York: Quadrangle/New York Times Book Co., 1973.

Schuker, S. A., *American Reparations to Germany, 1919–1933: Implications for the Third World Debt Crisis*, Princeton Studies in International Finance No. 61, Princeton NJ: Princeton University Press, 1988.

Yeager, L. B., *International Monetary Relations*, 2e, New York: Harper & Row, 1976.

Young, J. P., *European Currency and Finance*, Commission of Gold and Silver Inquiry, United States Senate, Washington DC: Government Printing Office, 1925.

Thirteen

The Bretton Woods System

Introduction

In July 1944, while World War II was still in progress, 44 countries met in Bretton Woods, New Hampshire, to discuss the structure of the international monetary system that would be created when peace returned. The experience of the interwar years had shown that when countries pursue their own national interests without regard for the interests of others, all countries suffer. In particular, the participants felt that frequent changes in exchange rates, the use of exchange controls, and protectionist policies should be avoided.

At the conference it was agreed to establish an international monetary system incorporating fixed exchange rates. A new organization, the **International Monetary Fund (IMF)**, was created to oversee the functioning of the system. It was also agreed to establish the **International Bank for Reconstruction and Development**, now usually referred to as the **World Bank**. The World Bank was to be concerned with postwar reconstruction and later with international development.[1]

The IMF and the Bretton Woods System

Objectives

The objective of the IMF as described in Article 1 of the Articles of Agreement is to facilitate the pursuit of full employment and growth. This is to be done by creating a stable international monetary system for trade and investment, and by promoting international monetary cooperation and consultation. Members are to be assisted in reducing balance of payments disequilibria, and exchange rate stability is to be increased, without members needing to resort to "measures destructive of national or international prosperity." This was a reference to the intention to avoid the problems that had plagued the 1930s.

---

[1]Although the IMF and the World Bank often work closely together, their major concerns are different. Criticisms of the IMF often reflect a lack of understanding of the roles of the World Bank and the IMF. See Nowzad (1981).

Fixed Exchange Rates

The Bretton Woods system was based on **fixed but adjustable** exchange rates. The value of the dollar was defined relative to gold, there being $35 per ounce. The United States agreed to sell gold to the monetary authorities of other countries at this price. There was no commitment to sell gold in the private market. Thus, limited convertibility of the dollar was established. The values of other currencies were defined relative to the dollar. The chosen values were called **par values**. Members agreed to maintain the values of their currencies within 1 percent of their par value. Thus, currencies were fixed in value relative to each other through their links with the dollar (the exchange rate between two currencies being equal to their cross rate).

The IMF agreement is significant because it recognized that the value of a currency was of common concern. A member country could only change the value of its currency after consultation with the IMF, and only in cases of **fundamental disequilibrium**.[2] The term "fundamental disequilibrium" was not defined in the agreement, but refers to payments imbalances that reflect a country's long–term relative competitive position (rather than imbalances that are inherently short–term, such as seasonal fluctuations in trade). For example, a fundamental disequilibrium might develop from one country having an inflation rate above the world rate.

The Fund of Reserves

A fund of international reserves was established. Counties could draw on these reserves for the purpose of maintaining declared parities during temporary payments difficulties. This fund of reserves is still in use. Each country was allocated a **quota**, which was based on a country's trade, national income, and international reserves. Countries paid this quota to the IMF, 25 percent in gold or dollars and 75 percent in their own currencies. Thus, a stock of international reserves was created from which countries could borrow. The initial allocation of quotas in 1945 was 8.8 billion, which represented less than 20 percent of total reserves at the time. The other types of international reserve are gold, foreign exchange, and, after 1970, special drawing rights (SDRs).

IMF quotas are reviewed and increased regularly, and have also increased as more countries have become members of the IMF. In October 1993, the total value stood at SDR 145 billion (about $205 billion), which was equal to about 20 percent of non–gold international reserves. The countries with the largest quotas are shown in Table 13.1.

---

[2]The IMF could not object if the proposed change and previous changes amounted to less than 10 percent of the initial par value.

Table 13.1
IMF Quotas

	Millions of SDRs	Percentage of Total
Canada	4,320.3	2.98
China	3,385.2	2.34
France	7,414.6	5.12
Germany	8,241.5	5.69
India	3,055.5	2.11
Italy	4,590.7	3.17
Japan	8,241.5	5.69
Netherlands	3,444.2	2.37
Russian Federation	4,313.1	2.98
Saudi Arabia	5,130.6	3.54
United Kingdom	7,414.6	5.12
United States	26,526.8	18.32

Source: *IMF Survey*, October 1993, p. 2.

Voting in the IMF

In passing we may note that the quotas are used to determine voting rights in the IMF. Major changes in IMF policy need a majority of 85 percent; thus, the larger, richer nations, which have the biggest quotas, dominate the voting. The United States is in a unique position because its quota exceeds 15 percent; thus it holds the right of veto. This characteristic of the system has been criticized by smaller, poorer countries. If IMF quotas are revised to reflect the growing economic importance of other countries, the United States will eventually lose the power of veto.[3]

Borrowing from the Fund

A country borrows by depositing its own currency or SDRs with the IMF and then withdrawing foreign currency.[4] The amount that a country can borrow

---

[3]Because of the relationship between quotas and voting rights and because quotas are seen as a symbol of national power, political considerations have prevented quota revisions reflecting the relative economic importance of countries, e.g., the quota for the United Kingdom is unjustifiably large.

[4]IMF financing under the structural adjustment facility and extended structural adjustment facility is in the form of loans.

is determined by its quota. A country can borrow 25 percent of its quota by right without restriction. This 25 percent is called the **reserve tranche** and is counted as part of a country's international reserves. Further drawings can usually be made up to an additional 100 percent of the quota, the 100 percent being divided into four **credit tranches**. Countries may borrow additional amounts under other IMF financial facilities described later.

The IMF lays down conditions for the loans it makes. The conditions become more stringent as the amount that a country wishes to borrow increases. The conditions are intended to ensure that the loans are part of a program "aimed at establishing or maintaining the enduring stability of the member's currency at a realistic rate of exchange." The IMF charges interest on the credit advanced, and a member is expected to repay IMF loans when it has brought its balance of payments under control. The repayment is made by the member repurchasing its own currency. Although many countries have moved toward more flexible exchange rates, IMF loans continue to be an important part of the international monetary system.

The financial facilities of the fund and the conditions attached to them are as follows:

First Credit Tranche. Member must demonstrate reasonable efforts to overcome balance of payments difficulties during the program period. Purchases are not phased and are not subject to performance criteria. Repurchases are made in 3¼–5 years.

Upper Credit Tranches. Member must have a substantial and viable program to overcome its balance of payments difficulties. Resources normally provided in the form of stand–by arrangements that provide purchases in installments linked to the observance of previously specified performance criteria. Repurchases are made in 3¼–5 years.

Extended Fund Facility. Medium–term program aims at overcoming structural balance of payments maladjustments. A program generally lasts for three years, although it may be lengthened to four years . . . performance criteria and drawings in installments. Repurchases are made in 4½–10 years.

Structural Adjustment Facility. Resources are provided on concessional terms to low–income developing countries facing protracted balance of payments problems, in support of medium–term macroeconomic and structural adjustment programs. . . . Detailed annual programs are formulated prior to disbursement of loans under annual arrangements that include quarterly benchmarks to assess performance. Interest is 0.5 percent annually, and repayments are made in 5½–10 years.

Enhanced Structural Adjustment Facility. Objectives, eligibility, terms, and basic program features of this facility parallel those of the structural adjustment facility (SAF); differences relate to provisions for access, monitoring, and funding. . . . Adjustment measures are expected to be particularly strong, aiming to foster growth and to achieve a substantial strengthening of the member's balance of payments position. Loans are made semiannually, and repayments are made in 5½–10 years.

Compensatory and Contingency Financing Facility. The compensatory elements provide resources to a member to help compensate for a shortfall in export earnings or an excess in cereal import costs that is temporary and is owing to factors largely beyond the member's control. The contingency element helps members with IMF–supported adjustment programs to maintain the momentum of adjustment efforts in the face of a broad range of unanticipated, adverse external shocks. Repurchases are made in 3¼–5 years.

Buffer Stock Financing Facility. Resources help finance a member's contribution to an approved international buffer stock scheme. Repurchases are made in 3¼–5 years.

Systematic Transformation Facility. This temporary facility provided resources to member countries facing balance of payments difficulties arising from severe disruptions of their traditional trade and payments arrangements owing to a shift from significant reliance on trading at non–market prices to multilateral, market based trade. . . . Repurchases are made in 4½–10 years.[5]

Special Drawing Rights

In response to fears that the supply of international reserves was not keeping pace with the need for reserves, the IMF created a new international reserve asset in 1967, the **Special Drawing Right** (SDR). SDRs are bookkeeping entries that members agree to accept as they would other reserve assets. They were allocated for the first time in 1970, the allocation being made in relation to countries' IMF quotas.[6] Further allocations have brought the total to SDR 21.4 billion. In 1993 this represented approximately 2 percent of non–gold international reserves. Thus, SDRs are not significant in relation to total international reserves. The SDR is sometimes used as a unit of account. The value of the SDR is determined by the values of a "basket" of five currencies as shown in Table 13.2.[7]

---

[5]Abridged from *IMF Survey*, Supplement on the IMF, October, 1993, p. 2.

[6]The method of allocating SDRs has been the subject of much debate. The proposal to use the allocation of SDRs as a form of international aid is discussed in Chapter 18.

[7]Table 13.2 is taken from *IMF Survey*, October 1993, p. 11.

Table 13.2
SDR Valuation on October 11, 1993

Currency	1 Currency Amount	2 Exchange Rate on October 11	3 U.S. Dollar Equivalent
Deutsche mark	0.4530	1.60120	0.282913
French franc	0.8000	5.61850	0.142387
Japanese yen	31.8000	106.10000	0.299717
Pound sterling	0.0812	1.53670	0.124780
U.S. dollar	0.5720	1.00000	0.572000
		Total	1.421797

SDR 1 = U.S. $1.42180
U.S. $1 = SDR 0.703335

Column 1: The currency component of the SDR basket.
Column 2: Exchange rate in terms of currency units per U.S. dollar except for the pound sterling which is expressed in U.S. dollars per pound.
Column 3: The U.S. dollar equivalents of the currency amounts in Column 1 at the exchange rates shown in Column 2, that is, Column 1 divided by Column 2.

The Scarce Currency Clause

The IMF was designed to provide resources to countries while measures were being taken to remove their balance of payments deficits. It was recognized that surplus countries would not need to borrow from the IMF and would face little pressure to adjust. The **scarce currency clause** provided for measures (such as discriminatory exchange controls for current account transactions) to be taken against a country that continually had a surplus. Given that the participants at Bretton Woods expected American post–war surpluses to continue, the inclusion of the scarce currency clause was seen by other countries as a significant concession by the United States. Things did not turn out as expected; the United States soon began running deficits. The clause was never used against the countries that did have surpluses.

Exchange Controls

The Bretton Woods agreement prohibited the use of exchange controls on current account transactions. In other words, transactions in foreign currency arising from trade in goods and services were not to be restricted. Members were permitted to retain controls for a transitional period. It was not until

1958 that most European countries restored convertibility to nonresidents for current account transactions. Members were permitted to use exchange controls to limit capital flows, and many countries retained capital flows throughout the Bretton Woods period. However, the effectiveness of such controls is never complete because there is an incentive to evade controls by using foreign currency earned through trade or purchased for trade to finance capital transfers.[8]

The General Agreement on Tariffs and Trade

The Bretton Woods agreement showed that participants recognized that there are gains from trade. The agreement was mainly concerned with financial stability, but international trade cannot flourish if countries maintain trade barriers. The problem of barriers to trade was addressed in 1947 by the **General Agreement on Tariffs and Trade (GATT)**. GATT is an international organization that attempts to regulate commercial policies and reduce trade barriers. During the Bretton Woods period, GATT helped countries negotiate substantial reductions in trade barriers. GATT is examined in more detail in Chapter 15.

The Bretton Woods System 1945–60

Reconstruction and the Implementation of the Bretton Woods System

The physical destruction caused by World War II was greater than that of World War I, and this severely reduced the productive capability of the belligerents. The war affected all stages of the production process. To begin with, the war reduced the supply of factors of production. Millions of people were killed. Also, capital was depleted by the war. The major belligerents ran down their foreign assets, used up their inventories, and borrowed from other countries to finance their war efforts. Maintenance was not a priority during the war, and obsolete machines were not replaced, so the quality of the capital stock fell. Many factories were destroyed or converted to military production. The remaining resources had to be reallocated, from production for the war to peacetime production. People as well as machines had to change activities. Finally, the distribution network of harbors, roads, and railways which had been military targets was badly in need of repair. Not surprisingly, the first priority when peace was restored was reconstruction.

---

[8]The use of capital controls and other policies restricting international transactions is summarized each year in the IMF *Annual Report on Exchange Arrangements and Exchange Restrictions*, Washington, D.C.

Post–War Financial Conditions

As had happened during World War I, economic policy was geared to the war effort. The rate of inflation varied between different countries, but exchange rates did not reflect inflation differentials because of wartime controls and disrupted trade. Even neutral countries experienced a measure of inflation because the prices of traded goods increased in response to wartime demand, and balance of payments surpluses led to monetary expansion.

Differential rates of inflation and varying degrees of destruction of productive capacity meant that exchange rates at the end of the war were unrealistic. European countries ran balance of trade deficits because their currencies were overvalued relative to the dollar and their consumption was higher than their production. In 1947, Europe was consuming about 5–6 percent more than it was producing, the difference being reflected in a current account deficit of about \$7 billion. Over two thirds of this deficit resulted from Europe's trade deficit with the United States.[9] The dominance of the United States is further shown by the fact that, at the time, the United States accounted for a third of world exports but only a tenth of world imports. This trade imbalance gave rise to the **dollar shortage**: the demand for dollars to pay for imports of American goods was greater than the supply of dollars earned from exports to the United States (at the maintained exchange rates).

Why Not Devalue?

Devaluation of the European currencies relative to the dollar could have removed the dollar shortage, but, in the early postwar years, European countries were reluctant to rely on this strategy. Imports were needed to help postwar reconstruction. Also, even though the trade balances of European countries were small in relation to GNP, it was felt that the costs of adjustment were unacceptable in economies that had been weakened by the war. The weakness of European countries was seen as a temporary phenomenon that would disappear as reconstruction progressed. The experience of the 1930s may also have added to the generally accepted view that devaluations were not the answer.

---

[9]Triffin (1957) contains useful data relating to this period.

The Need for Aid

In the absence of devaluations, aid from the United States was needed to finance the balance of payments deficits. Initially, postwar reconstruction was financed partly through direct American loans and partly through the United Nations Relief and Rehabilitation Administration (UNRRA). However, it became clear by 1947 that this approach was not working. Europe remained weak and there were fears in the United States that economic weakness might lead to political instability. Also, Americans felt sympathy for their European friends.

The Marshall Plan

American support for reconstruction was organized through the Marshall Plan, which came into effect in 1948. Under this plan American grants and loans were made to Europe and Japan to help finance postwar recovery. By the end of 1951, Europe had received almost $11.5 billion, 90 percent in grants and 10 percent in loans.[10] However, there was far more to Marshall aid than American handouts. European countries were encouraged to restrict their imports from the United States, increase their trade with each other, and increase their exports to the United States. Even though many currencies had fallen in value since the end of the war, the United States insisted that recipients of aid devalue their currencies (because it did not want the aid to be exhausted in attempts to defend unrealistic exchange rates).[11] These policies reflected the view that the American trade surplus and strength in world markets in the immediate postwar period was likely to continue.

European Recovery

The pace of European recovery was spectacular. In 1947, production was 9 percent lower than before the war. By 1948, this gap had been closed, and for the following three years production increased by about 7 percent each year. This growth cannot be attributed solely to Marshall aid, which was not large

---

[10]Yeager (1976), p. 385.

[11]Some countries followed Britain's lead and devalued by 30.5 percent. For some other countries, the 1949 devaluations were only part of a process of exchange rate adjustment. The French franc fell in value by over 60 percent from the end of the war until 1949. The replacement of the reichsmark by the deutsche mark in 1948 entailed a depreciation of over 90 percent. In 1949, the deutsche mark was devalued by 20.7 percent. The postwar value of the yen (371 to the dollar) represented a devaluation of over 98 percent relative to the prewar value (of 4 to the dollar).

in relation to the economies of the recipients. During the years 1947–50, Marshall aid accounted for between 5 and 10 percent of European GNP, or a quarter of Europe's imports of goods and services.[12] However, Marshall aid helped Europe maintain a reasonable level of consumption while undertaking high levels of investment. Also, the devaluations of 1949 were of great importance. They helped make European countries competitive even before full recovery had been completed.

The American Balance of Payments

Postwar reconstruction, the 1949 devaluations, and the outbreak of the Korean War reduced the American trade surplus from $5.5 billion in 1949 to $1.5 billion in 1950. The overall balance of payments, as measured by the liquidity balance, was +4567 in 1947, +1005 in 1948, +175 in 1949, and –3580 in 1950.[13] The deficit in 1950 was the beginning of a phenomenon that was to continue throughout most of the Bretton Woods period and that would lead ultimately to the collapse of the system. However, at the time it was thought that, because of the strength of the American economy, an American deficit could only be temporary.

Although the trade balance declined after 1949, a deficit was not recorded on America's balance of trade until 1971. Thus, we must look for other explanations of the American deficits. Military expenditure is one part of the story: typically this accounted for a debit entry of $2–3.5 billion in the Bretton Woods years. After 1950, U.S. government grants usually added another $2 billion to the deficits. Finally, private American foreign investment, particularly long–term investment, was a major part of the deficits. For example, between 1950 and 1960, there was a net long–term private capital outflow from the United States of $19 billion.[14] This capital outflow continued and grew in the 1960s.

Deficits and Dollars

The method by which American balance of payments deficits were financed must be understood if we are to appreciate how the Bretton Woods system worked and why it collapsed. American deficits meant that more dollars were being supplied than were demanded (there was an excess demand for foreign exchange by Americans). Foreign central banks were obliged to

---

[12]Yeager (1976), p. 385.

[13]*Economic Report of the President*, 1967, p. 301.

[14]*Economic Report of the President*, 1967, p. 301.

Table 13.3
The Balance of Payments of the United States, 1947–60
(millions of dollars)

	Current Account Balance	Official Settlements Balance	Net Changes in Liabilities to Foreign Official Holders	Reserves (−increase)
1947	8922	—	—	−3315
1948	1993	—	—	−1736
1949	580	—	—	−266
1950	−2125	−3312	1554	1758
1951	302	538	−505	−33
1952	−175	−822	1237	−415
1953	−1949	−2104	848	1256
1954	−321	−1523	1043	480
1955	−345	−741	559	182
1956	1722	−261	1130	−869
1957	3556	1145	20	−1165
1958	−5	−3027	735	2292
1959	−2138	−2283	1248	1035
1960	1794	−3592[a]	1449	2143

[a]Slight differences in the definition of liabilities to official agencies are responsible for the difference between the 1960 official settlements balances shown in Tables 2.2 and 2.4.

Sources: *Economic Report of the President*, 1966, p. 301; 1975, p. 351.

intervene in the foreign exchange market to maintain the values of their currencies against the dollar. Given the excess supply of dollars, this meant that foreign central banks bought dollars and added them to their reserves. Between the beginning of 1950 and the end of 1960, an official settlements balance of $16 billion was financed by an increase in U.S. official liquid liabilities of $9.3 billion and a decline in international reserves (gold) of $6.7 billion. (See Table 13.3.)

The United States was able to finance balance of payments deficits with its own currency because the dollar was an international reserve currency. The ability of the United States to buy foreign goods or assets and pay for them with dollars (or American debt) was criticized by some countries (notably France), which charged that the United States was able to accumulate "debts without tears." Charles de Gaulle called this the "exorbitant privilege" of the United States. However, American deficits provided the world with international reserves.

Although some observers were aware of the underlying weaknesses of the Bretton Woods system, the forces for change were not great in the period up to 1960. Countries recovered from the war, trade barriers and currency restrictions were gradually removed, and trade grew quickly. The forces for change were stronger after 1960 because the underlying disequilibrium became more obvious as American deficits increased.

The Problems of the Bretton Woods System

From Dollar Shortage to Dollar Glut

The first signs of weakness in the Bretton Woods system began to show in 1958 when the first of a series of large American deficits was recorded. It became clear that there was no longer a dollar shortage but a **dollar glut**. This led to speculation in 1960 that there would be a devaluation of the dollar. Because the value of the dollar was defined in terms of gold, a devaluation would have increased the gold price. People began selling dollars and buying gold, pushing the price to $40 in October 1960. The price was forced down by official American gold sales. Also, speculation slackened in response to statements made by John F. Kennedy at the end of October 1960, in the presidential campaign, that he was committed to maintaining the dollar price of gold.

In November of the following year, the Gold Pool was formed to maintain the gold price in private markets at $35 an ounce by official intervention.[15] The members, and the United States in particular, were afraid that, if the private price was allowed to rise above the official price, then this might undermine confidence in the value of the dollar. For example, private investors might sell their dollar assets and official holders of dollars might be tempted to convert dollars into gold in anticipation of an American devaluation. The Gold Pool succeeded in maintaining the gold price until 1968.

The deficit of the United States continued, as Table 13.4 shows. American capital controls failed to halt the flow of American foreign investment as the private sector found ways to evade them. American deficits were reflected in surpluses in other countries. Germany in particular had a very strong position in 1960: the economy was booming and there was a trade surplus. The payments surplus led to inflationary pressure, so the Bundesbank pursued a restrictive monetary policy. This raised interest rates and attracted foreign capital. In response to market pressure, the deutsche mark was

---

[15]The members were Belgium, Britain, Germany, the Netherlands, Switzerland, and the United States. France declined to join.

Table 13.4
The Balance of Payments of the United States, 1960–73
(millions of dollars)

	Current Account Balance	Current Account Plus Long–term Capital	Official Settlements Balance	Liabilities to Foreign Official Agencies	Reserves (–increase)
1960	1794	−1191	−3403	1258	2145
1961	3070	2	−1348	742	606
1962	2460	−1028	−2650	1117	1533
1963	3199	−1328	−1934	1557	377
1964	5788	−75	−1534	1363	171
1965	4287	−1829	−1290	67	1222
1966	1943	−2110	219	−787	568
1967	1544	−3723	−3418	3366	52
1968	−962	−1935	1641	−761	−880
1969	−1633	−3637	2739	−1552	−1187
1970	−324	−3778	−9839	7362	2477
1971	−3817	−10559	−29753	27405	2348
1972	−9807	−11235	−10354	10322	32
1973	450	−1026	−5304	5095	209

Source: *Economic Report of the President*, 1975, p. 351.

revalued on March 6, 1961, by 5 percent. The Netherlands revalued the guilder by the same amount the following day. The German revaluation was needed but it was not sufficient to remove the German trade surplus, which although slightly lower in 1962, rebounded in 1963 and continued throughout the 1960s.

The Adjustment Problem

The continuing surpluses of Germany and the Netherlands are examples of the **adjustment problem** in the Bretton Woods system. Surpluses came to be associated with success. Surplus countries that were experiencing export–led growth had little or no incentive to reduce balance of payments surpluses. They argued that deficit countries should take measures to live within their means.[16] Surplus countries could accumulate reserves and avoid adjustment

---

[16]In recent years, similar arguments have sometimes been used to counter criticisms of Japanese trade surpluses.

by sterilizing the monetary impact of the balance of payments. (The scarce currency clause was never used.)

In contrast, deficit countries were under pressure to adjust. Deficit countries must sell foreign currency (buy domestic currency) if they are to maintain the value of their currencies. However, in cases of fundamental disequilibrium, exchange market intervention by itself is not a long–run policy option for deficit countries because they eventually run out of reserves. Countries can borrow additional funds from the IMF, but resources are limited, conditions are attached to the loans, and the IMF charges interest.

In the long run, a deficit country must take measures to remove the deficit. The choice is between devaluation and domestic deflation of prices and income. Recall that, in the absence of real growth, an increase in the balance of trade implies a fall in domestic absorption. This is true whether devaluation or deflation is used. Naturally, adjustment was not an attractive prospect to a deficit country. Also, under the Bretton Woods system, devaluation came to be regarded as a sign of failure. Misleading analogies were drawn and, unfortunately, continue to be drawn, between the strength of a country, the strength of an economy, and the value of its currency. However, although devaluations were delayed, some countries did devalue during the Bretton Woods years.[17]

A second dimension of the adjustment problem was lack of adjustment between sterling, the dollar, and other currencies. Britain and the United States felt that they could not devalue their currencies because a devaluation of either would have resulted in capital losses for central banks that held stocks of the currencies as reserves. Also, it was felt that such action would have undermined confidence in the international monetary system. It is true that sterling was forced to devalue in November 1967 (from $2.8 to $2.4), but not until strong efforts had been made to avoid this course of action.[18]

The Liquidity Problem

Trade grew rapidly during the Bretton Woods period, and there was an increase in the demand for international reserves to offset fluctuations in the balance of payments. The **liquidity problem** arose because the Bretton Woods system lacked a mechanism whereby the level of reserves might increase in

---

[17]For example, France devalued in 1957, 1958, and 1969. Yeager (1976) discusses the French franc during the Bretton Woods period (see his Chapter 23).

[18]The slow response of the British balance of payments to the devaluation is an example of the J–curve effect.

line with the need for reserves.[19] The creation of the *special drawing right* (SDR) was an attempt to overcome this problem, but the first allocation of SDRs was not until 1970. Before SDRs, there were three types of international reserve assets: gold, foreign exchange, and a country's reserve position at the IMF.

At the officially maintained price of $35 dollars per ounce of gold, the private market absorbed the supply of new gold; thus, the stock of gold held as international reserves did not increase.[20] IMF quotas were increased, but they did not grow as fast as trade, and they have never been a significant form of international reserves. International stocks of foreign exchange (mainly dollars) accounted for over 50 percent of the increase in reserves from 1950 to 1960, and for over 80 percent of the increase in reserves from 1960 to 1970 (see Table 13.5). Apart from availability, there were other reasons to hold dollars. Central banks could convert their dollars into gold, and dollars could be held in the form of short–term interest–bearing assets. However, relying on dollars for increased reserves meant that the growth of international reserves was determined by the size of American deficits rather than by need.

The distribution of new international reserves was also a source of concern. Foreign exchange was accumulated by surplus countries rather than deficit countries, thus the countries that claimed to "need" reserves did not receive them. We must be skeptical of the claims made by deficit countries that they were deprived of reserves. It is true that inadequate reserves may force countries to take adjustment measures to offset temporary balance of payments deficits, when it might be better to finance such deficits from reserves and avoid disrupting economic policies. However, deficit countries may be tempted to use reserves in cases of fundamental disequilibria rather than incur adjustment costs. If deficit countries delay adjustment to fundamental disequilibria until reserves are exhausted, any level of reserves will be inadequate.[21]

---

[19]To offset a 10 percent fluctuation in $100 billion requires more reserves than offsetting a 10 percent fluctuation in $50 billion.

[20]An increase in the price of gold would have increased the value of reserves and increased the quantity of new gold supplied to the monetary authorities. This method of increasing reserves was rejected because countries with the largest gold reserves would have received the largest capital gains. Thus, the plan would have benefitted the countries (notably France) that had "undermined" the system by demanding gold in exchange for dollar reserves.

[21]Flanders, J., "International Liquidity Is Always Inadequate," *Kyklos*, 22, 1969, pp. 519–29.

Table 13.5
The Growth and Composition of International Reserves
1950–73
(billions of dollars)

	Gold[a]	Foreign Exchange	IMF Position	SDRs	Total
1950	35.3	13.3	1.7	—	50.3
1960	37.9	18.5	3.6	—	60.0
1970	37.2	44.8	7.7	3.1	92.8
1971	35.9	75.0	6.4	5.9	123.1
1972	35.6	95.9	6.3	8.7	146.7
1973	35.6	101.8	6.2	8.8	152.4

[a]Valued at $35 per ounce.
Source: IMF *International Financial Statistics*.

Confidence

The nature of the confidence problem was that people did not have confidence that official exchange rates would be maintained. As a result, speculators shifted funds between currencies. This lack of confidence is not surprising in view of the clear imbalances that existed and the reluctance of countries to adjust. The rules of the system were partly to blame. A country could only change the value of its currency in a case of fundamental disequilibrium, not to prevent such a disequilibrium from developing. However, once a clear disequilibrium had developed, speculators knew which way the currency was likely to change. Deficit countries might devalue, they would not revalue. Therefore, allowing disequilibria to develop encouraged speculation because speculators could not lose.

One factor contributing to the lack of confidence in the value of the dollar was the change in official American assets and liabilities over the Bretton Woods period. At the beginning of the postwar period, the value of American gold reserves was greater than the value of dollars held abroad. But, as foreign official holdings of dollars increased, the ratio fell. The ratio of gold to official short–term liabilities was 7:1 in 1946, 1:2 in 1970, and 1:5 in 1971 (see Table 13.6). This change in the gold backing for dollars undermined confidence in the system, because there was clearly not enough gold to allow all central banks to exercise their right to sell dollars for gold should they have chosen to do so.

Table 13.6
The Gold and Liabilities of the United States
(billions of dollars)

	Gold	Liabilities to Foreign Official Agencies[a]
1946	20.7	3.0
1950	22.8	3.1
1960	17.8	11.9
1970	11.1	24.4
1971	10.2	51.2
1972	10.5	61.6
1973	11.7	66.8

[a]Before 1960, data refer to long–term and short–term U.S. government obligations.
Sources: U.S. Department of Commerce, *Historical Statistics of the United States: Colonial Times to 1970*, Part 2, p. 869; and *Economic Report of the President*, 1976, p. 281.

The Collapse of the Bretton Woods System

Speculation and Underlying Weakness in the System

At the time of the devaluation of sterling in 1967, there was also speculation that the dollar would be devalued. Between September 1967 and March 1968 the Gold Pool sold about $3.5 billion of gold to meet the demand of people selling dollars for gold in anticipation of a rise in its price. Of these sales, the United States accounted for about $2.4 billion, which was nearly 20 percent of its gold reserves.[22] Faced with a substantial decline in gold stocks, the Gold Pool stopped maintaining the private gold price in March 1968. Official transactions continued between central banks at $35 per ounce, but the private market price was allowed to fluctuate; that is, there was a **two–tier** gold market.

This arrangement did not end speculation. The weaknesses in the Bretton Woods system were clear. In May 1968, shortly after the collapse of the Gold Pool, political unrest and a general strike in France led to fears that the franc would be devalued. German surpluses continued, and there was also speculation that the deutsche mark would be revalued again. Speculation carried little risk: even if France did not devalue or Germany revalue, there was little danger of losing by selling francs and buying marks. In three days

[22]Solomon (1982), p. 119.

in November 1968, the Bundesbank acquired almost $1.8 billion in an effort to prevent the mark from rising further.[23] Speculative sales of French francs for marks accounted for much of these purchases. (Foreign exchange market intervention is usually carried out in dollars; thus, the Bundesbank acquired mainly dollars.) The pressure was resisted in 1968 (France adopted exchange controls), but eventually speculators were rewarded when France was forced to devalue (by 11.1 percent in August 1969) and Germany revalued (by 9.5 percent in October 1969).

German Intervention

Germany's experience is a good example of how lack of adjustment led to speculation that exchange rates would change. German balance of payments surpluses were shown by an excess demand for marks. The excess demand for marks can also be described as an excess supply of foreign currency (dollars). The Bundesbank sold marks (bought dollars) to prevent the mark from rising in value. The sales of domestic currency were sterilized to prevent inflation, thus the German surplus remained. However, as speculators bought marks in anticipation of a revaluation, their sales of foreign currency increased the intervention needed to prevent the mark from rising. International reserves increased, and offsetting the inflationary effects of the surplus by sterilization became more difficult. Eventually, the Bundesbank revalued the mark and speculators were rewarded with a capital gain (see Figure 13.1).

Balance of Payments Imbalances in the Final Years

The American official settlements balance was actually in surplus in 1968 and 1969, although trade fell substantially. This fall in trade can be partly explained by the effects of the Vietnam War, which increased aggregate demand and the demand for imports. The official settlements surplus was largely the result of surpluses in the short–term capital account. A tight monetary policy combined with increasing income led to an increase in interest rates in 1968 and 1969, and induced an inflow of capital. In 1970, American monetary policy was relaxed and interest rates fell. The capital that had flowed into the United States began to flow out, and the United States recorded a record official settlements balance deficit of $9.8 billion, by far the largest deficit the world had seen. In 1971, capital outflows continued, and a new record was set with a deficit of $29.8 billion. As part of the 1971 deficit, the United States recorded its first trade deficit of the post–war period.

---

[23]Yeager (1976), p. 507.

Figure 13.1
Germany's Balance of Payments Position in 1968–69

The balance of payments surplus of Germany is shown by the excess demand for marks ($QD_0 - QS_0$) at the official exchange rate of 25 cents. The Bundesbank sold marks (bought dollars) to prevent the mark from rising. Speculators realized that the mark was undervalued and bought marks (sold dollars) on a large scale. Their purchases increased the demand for marks from D_0D_0 to D_1D_1. When the mark was revalued to 27.3 cents, speculators were rewarded with a capital gain.

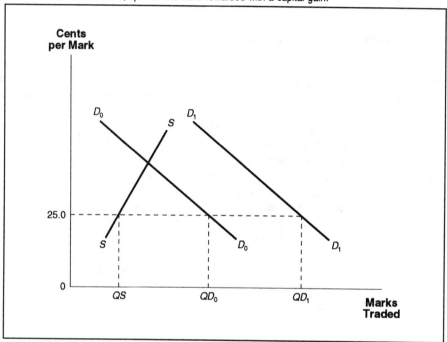

The American deficit was reflected in surpluses in other countries, which experienced increasing reserves and inflationary pressure. President Nixon adopted the policy of **benign neglect**: since the United States could not devalue (because of the reserve currency role of the dollar), American deficits were allowed to take their course in 1970 and 1971. The large capital flows from Europe to the United States in 1968 and 1969, followed by flows from the United States to Europe in 1970, led to complaints that European monetary policy was being destabilized by the American balance of payments.[24]

Meanwhile, the strength of the German economy and its balance of payments continued, and in May 1971 there was speculation that the mark would be revalued again. The Bundesbank bought $1 billion during trading on May 3 and May 4. It bought the same amount in 40 minutes on Wednesday May 5, before the market was closed.[25] When the market reopened on May 10, the mark was floated.

The Collapse of the Bretton Woods System

During mid–1971, attention again turned to the dollar. When American balance of payments figures for the second quarter were announced showing a balance of trade deficit, pressure became stronger. The report by the Reuss Committee (August 6) that the dollar was overvalued intensified speculation. The dollar reserves of other countries were increasing rapidly as they intervened to prevent their currencies from rising in value. The United States was faced with requests from foreign central banks for some of these dollars to be converted into gold. The conversion of dollars into gold could quickly have exhausted American gold reserves. Therefore, on August 15, 1971, President Nixon announced the suspension of convertibility of the dollar into gold. This action marked the end of the Bretton Woods system.

The problem of the American balance of payments remained. A 10 percent import surcharge was imposed by the United States, and a domestic price and income freeze was adopted. Surplus countries were faced with the choice of accumulating inconvertible dollars (if they maintained the value of their currencies against the dollar) or revaluing against the dollar. Negotiations began on a realignment of currencies and, in the meantime, currencies were floated.

---

[24]Dissatisfaction with the performance of the international monetary system was one of the factors that led to pressure for European monetary integration. This topic is discussed in Chapter 17.

[25]Yeager (1976), p. 512.

The Smithsonian Agreement

In December 1971, the Group of Ten met at the Smithsonian Institution in Washington and agreed on a series of exchange rate changes.[26] Under the Smithsonian agreement the dollar was devalued (7.9 percent) against gold by raising the price of gold from $35 to $38 an ounce. The yen was revalued (7.7 percent), as were the German mark (4.6 percent) and the Benelux currencies (2.6 percent).[27] The French franc and sterling remained unchanged, and the lira was devalued (1 percent).[28] In addition, exchange rates were made more flexible by increasing the permitted range of variation from ±1 percent to ±2.5 percent. As part of the package, the United States agreed to remove its import surcharge.

The Smithsonian agreement was an attempt to return to fixed exchange rates. However, the parities chosen were influenced by historical and political forces. There was no attempt to make an objective assessment of how currencies might be realigned to reflect underlying competitiveness. Stability was restored temporarily, but, with the benefit of hindsight, it is not surprising that the Smithsonian parities were not sustainable.

During 1972 the American deficit fell, but it was still the second largest ever. Speculative sentiments fluctuated, and intervention was sufficient to maintain exchange rates.[29] However, at the beginning of 1973, a number of factors combined to cause a crisis that led to the end of the fixed exchange rate system.

The Final Collapse

In the United States, lack of progress in ending the Vietnam War, a large budget deficit, and the relaxation of price controls led to fears that inflation would increase. The announcement that the trade deficit for 1972 ($6.4 billion) was substantially greater than the deficit for 1971 ($2.3 billion) weakened confidence in the value of the dollar. Meanwhile, German and Japanese trade surpluses continued.

---

[26]The Group of Ten was made up of Belgium, Britain, Canada, France, Germany, Italy, Japan, the Netherlands, Sweden, and the United States. Switzerland was an associate member.

[27]The Benelux is made up of Belgium, the Netherlands, and Luxembourg.

[28]These exchange rate changes refer to changes in a currency's value against gold.

[29]Britain was forced to abandon its Smithsonian parity in June 1972 following reports of poor economic performance.

Switzerland led the move to abandon fixed exchange rates, following strong speculation that the Swiss franc would rise in value. Growing uncertainty was increased further by inopportune statements from American officials that the dollar was probably overvalued again. Speculators again turned to the German mark: the Bundesbank bought about $6 billion during the first seven trading days of February 1973.[30] The dollar was devalued for the second time on Monday, February 12, when the gold price was raised from $38 to $42.22 per ounce (an 11 percent devaluation). Some countries floated immediately following the devaluation and many more followed in early March when it became clear that the devaluation of the dollar had failed to restore confidence.

Discussions about restoring the system continued for some time afterward, but essentially the Bretton Woods system had collapsed in August 1971 when the convertibility of the dollar was suspended. The Smithsonian agreement merely papered over the cracks.

Conclusion: Success or Failure?

Was the Bretton Woods system a success? To some extent it clearly was. Trade and incomes grew rapidly and there were no major recessions during this period. Also, countries recognized their mutual interdependence and cooperated in the planning and implementation of an international monetary system.

As with the gold standard, we may question whether the international monetary system played a major part in promoting trade and growth. Trade and incomes continued to grow in the 1970s following the collapse of the Bretton Woods system. This suggests that fixed exchange rates were not necessary for growth. Also, there are many other explanations of post–war growth, for example, technological progress, faster and cheaper international transport, and improved communications.

Summary of Main Points

International monetary instability in the 1930s induced countries to cooperate in establishing the Bretton Woods system. Currencies were fixed in value relative to the dollar, and thus were fixed in value relative to each other. It was hoped that fixed exchange rates would encourage trade and economic growth.

---

[30]Yeager (1976), p. 515. Given that the American official settlements balance deficit for the whole of 1973 was only about $10 billion, the importance of speculation is obvious.

The **International Monetary Fund (IMF)** was created to oversee the system and promote international consultation and cooperation. Each member of the IMF has a **quota** that represents its subscription to the IMF. These quotas established a fund of resources available to countries with balance of payments difficulties. The amount a country may borrow is determined by the country's quota. The IMF attaches conditions to the loans it makes, and the conditions become more stringent as the amount borrowed increases.

The major concern after World War II was reconstruction. As this progressed, controls on trade were gradually relaxed and international trade grew. At first, the United States ran large surpluses, and it was assumed that this would continue. However, the United States gradually developed an overall balance of payments deficit. This deficit was reflected in surpluses in other countries, which were forced to buy dollars in order to prevent their currencies from appreciating. Thus, American balance of payments deficits provided the world with dollars that were added to the stocks of international reserves.

The Bretton Woods system was characterized by lack of adjustment. Surplus countries had no incentive to adjust, and deficit countries avoided adjustment. Devaluation was seen as a sign of failure and downward adjustment of the domestic price and income levels was resisted because it entailed a cut in welfare. At times, it became clear that existing exchange rates were not sustainable. This encouraged speculators to gamble that an official exchange rate would be changed. The direction of change was obvious from the country's balance of payments problems, thus there was little risk of loss.

The weaknesses of the Bretton Woods system became clear toward the end of the 1960s. Sterling was devalued in 1967, the agreement to maintain the dollar price of gold in private markets was abandoned in 1968, and in 1969 the French franc was devalued and the German mark revalued. Speculators played a major role in these events and in the collapse of the Bretton Woods system.

In 1971, the United States' deficit reached record levels. Foreign monetary authorities were accumulating large amounts of dollars, partly because of the deficit, but mainly because speculators were selling dollars in anticipation of a devaluation of the dollar. Foreign monetary authorities had the right to convert dollars into gold at $35 per ounce. Faced with the prospect of a depletion of American gold stocks, President Nixon suspended the convertibility of the dollar on August 15, 1971. This marked the end of the Bretton Woods system.

In December 1971, the Smithsonian agreement was signed under which exchange rates were realigned. This agreement lasted a little over a year before it collapsed amid renewed speculation.

Study Questions

1. How were the lessons of the 1930s reflected in the Bretton Woods agreement?
2. What was the adjustment problem in relation to:
   a. deficit and surplus countries?
   b. the dollar relative to other countries?
3. Why did confidence in the gold value of the dollar diminish?
4. What were the adjustment, confidence, and liquidity problems? How were they related?
5. How were American deficits financed during the Bretton Woods system?
6. Why did capital flows reduce divergences from official exchange rates during the pre–1914 gold standard, but sometimes force countries to abandon official exchange rates under the Bretton Woods system?
7. Under the Bretton Woods system, the world moved from a period of dollar shortage to dollar glut. Discuss the role of this development in the collapse of the system.
8. Keynes said that the Bretton Woods system was the opposite of a gold standard: "For instead of maintaining the principle that the internal value of a national currency should conform to a prescribed **de jure** external value, it provides that its external value should be altered if necessary so as to conform to whatever **de facto** international value results from domestic policies."[31] Discuss with reference to the system in theory and practice.

Selected References

Adams, J., *The Contemporary International Economy*, 2e, New York: St. Martins, 1985.

Ashworth, W. A., *A Short History of the International Economy Since 1850*, 4e, New York: Longman, 1987.

Bordo, M. D., "The Gold Standard, Bretton Woods and Other Monetary Regimes: A Historical Appraisal," *Federal Reserve Bank of St. Louis Review*, 75, March/April 1993, pp. 123–191.

Machlup, F., et al., *International Monetary Arrangements: The Problem of Choice*, Report on the Deliberations of an International Study Group of 32 Economists, Princeton, NJ: Princeton University Press, 1964.

Meier, G. M., *Problems of a World Monetary Order*, 2e, New York: Oxford University Press, 1982.

---

[31]From Keynes' speech to the House of Lords recommending acceptance of the Bretton Woods agreement. Cited in Meier (1982), p. 49.

Mikesell, R. F., "The Bretton Woods Debates: A Memoir," *Essays in International Finance*, 192, Princeton, NJ: Princeton University Press, 1994.

Nowzad, B., "*The IMF and its Critics*," Essays in International Finance, No. 146, Princeton, NJ: Princeton University Press, December 1981.

Rolfe, S. E. and Burtle, J. B., *The Great Wheel: The World Monetary System*, New York: Quadrangle/New York Times Book Co., 1973.

Solomon, R., *The International Monetary System: 1945–1981*, New York: Harper & Row, 1982.

Southard, F. A., "*The Evolution of the International Monetary Fund*," Essays in International Finance, No. 135, Princeton, NJ: Princeton University Press, December 1979.

Triffin, R., *Europe and the Money Muddle*, New Haven: Yale University Press, 1957.

Yeager, L. B., *International Monetary Relations*, 2e, New York: Harper & Row, 1976.

Fourteen

The International Monetary System After Bretton Woods

Introduction

The international monetary system that has existed since 1973 is often described as one of floating or flexible exchange rates. It is true that the majority of countries have fixed exchange rates, but it has been estimated that, because the major trading nations have floating exchange rates, between two–thirds and four–fifths of trade is covered by floating exchange rates. Exchange rate policies differ widely, and the rules governing the international system are, to put it charitably, rather loose. Thus, some people question whether it is appropriate to refer to the present arrangements as a system. We do so for want of a better term.

After examining the rules governing exchange rate policy under the present system, we look at how the system works. Dissatisfaction with the performance of the international monetary system has led to numerous reform proposals. We examine the major characteristics of these proposals, and then end the chapter by investigating the effects of oil price fluctuations.

Legal Changes in the System

Following the collapse of the Smithsonian agreement in 1973, countries discussed possible reforms of the international monetary system. For a while, floating exchange rates were seen as a temporary measure until the shock waves from the collapse of the Bretton Woods system died down. Attempts to establish a reformed international monetary system failed for two main reasons. First, international economic conditions were not conducive to the launching of a new system. For example, during 1973–74 the world experienced the first oil crisis, rising inflation, and a dramatic fall in economic growth. Second, many countries had been unhappy with their experience under the Bretton Woods system, especially in the last few years of the system, and they were reluctant to commit themselves to a new international monetary system.

The Jamaica Agreement

The rules governing the present system, such as they are, result from a meeting of the members of the IMF in Jamaica in 1976. At this meeting, the members acknowledged that the Bretton Woods system was no more by amending Article IV of the IMF charter to allow floating exchange rates.[1] Until then, floating exchange rates had been illegal. Following the Jamaica agreement, countries were free to choose their exchange rate system.

The IMF is required to exercise "surveillance" over members' exchange rate policies, and has adopted three principles to guide these policies:

A. A member shall avoid manipulating exchange rates or the international monetary system in order to prevent effective balance of payments adjustment or to gain an unfair advantage over other members.

B. A member should intervene in the exchange market if necessary to counter disorderly conditions which may be characterized **inter alia** by disruptive short–term movements of the exchange value of its currency.

C. Members should take into account in their intervention policies the interests of other members, including those of the countries in whose currencies they intervene.[2]

Developments that might indicate a need for a discussion between the IMF and a member include "protracted large–scale intervention in exchange markets in one direction; an unsustainable level of . . . borrowing or lending for balance of payments purposes; restrictions or incentives affecting current transactions, payments, or capital flows; the pursuit, for balance of payments purposes, of monetary and other domestic financial policies that provide abnormal encouragement or discouragement to capital flows; and behavior of the exchange rate that appears unrelated to underlying economic and financial conditions."[3]

The loose set of guidelines governing the present system leaves much to be desired. The adjustment mechanism is virtually ignored: members are not supposed to prevent balance of payments adjustment, but no mention is

---

[1] Article IV had required members to declare par values for their currencies.

[2] *IMF Survey*, Supplement on the Fund, September 1986, p. 7.

[3] *IMF Survey*, Supplement on the Fund, September 1988, p. 8.

made of when or how adjustment should take place. This lack of attention to adjustment issues is not surprising. Under the present system, countries do not have to maintain fixed exchange rates; therefore, the balance of payments is not as important as it was under the Bretton Woods system. Indeed, there is very little consensus about what significance should be attached to balance of payments statistics.

The agreement reflects an important change in attitude: exchange rate stability is to result from economic stability, not vice versa. However, the IMF does not have the power to make countries pursue policies that will lead to exchange rate stability. The statement that a member should use its policies to foster "orderly economic growth with reasonable price stability" is merely a statement of the objectives that would be pursued for domestic economic reasons. It is significant that the IMF was required to exercise "surveillance," not control, over members' policies.

The agreement to promote exchange rate stability is not very significant. Why would countries want to promote instability? With respect to intervention, the guidelines do not specify the exact conditions under which countries should intervene, how central banks should coordinate their intervention, or how appropriate exchange rate targets might be determined. In practical terms, the Jamaica agreement did little more than legalize the status quo.[4]

Exchange Rates

Many observers feel that the changes in exchange rates since 1973 have been excessive, in the sense that variability has been far greater than seems warranted by changes in economic conditions. In particular, attention has focused on the lack of relationship between inflation rates and exchange rates. Purchasing power parity theory leads us to expect that exchange rate changes will reflect the difference between inflation rates. This has not been the case. For example, the inflation rate of the United Kingdom was consistently higher than the rate in the United States, and this cannot explain the behavior of the dollar–sterling exchange rate shown in Figure 14.1.

The increase in the value of the yen from 205 yen per dollar at the beginning of 1981 to over 277 yen per dollar in 1982, and the dramatic decline in the value of the dollar beginning in the fall of 1985, is another example (see Figure 14.2). Japan had an inflation rate below that of the United States throughout the 1980s. The lack of relationship between inflation and exchange rates illustrates our discussion of purchasing power parity in

---

[4]One minor change was that the agreement reduced the role of gold in the international monetary system. Currencies and the SDR were no longer to be defined in terms of gold, and gold sales from official reserves were allowed.

Figure 14.1
The Dollar–Sterling Exchange Rate, 1980–94

Chapter 6, in that the theory is not particularly useful for predicting short–term exchange rate changes.

Significance of Exchange Rate Behavior

In assessing the potential effects of exchange rate changes, a useful distinction can be made between the effects of exchange rate variability on trade and investment, and the effects of exchange rate misalignments. The effects of exchange rate variability were discussed in Chapter 8. While it seems possible that exchange rate changes lead to uncertainty, which may deter some trade and investment, empirical studies of the effects of exchange rate variability on trade have produced mixed results. Perhaps part of the explanation is the widespread availability of instruments that firms can use to reduce exchange risk (for example, forward, futures, and options markets). The failure of many studies to find a significant adverse effect of exchange rate variability on trade, and the substantial increase in trade that has occurred since 1973,

Figure 14.2
The Yen–Dollar Exchange Rate, 1980–94

suggest that it is appropriate to conclude that exchange rate variability does not have a significant adverse effect on trade.[5]

Williamson (1985) argues that currency misalignments are potentially more important than volatility and until recently have often been ignored. A currency is misaligned when it is overvalued or undervalued relative to the long–term equilibrium exchange rate. For present purposes, we may think of the long–term equilibrium exchange rate as the long–term trend of the exchange rate. It is clear from the preceding discussion that exchange rates have fluctuated above and below their long–term trends. These divergences can have significant welfare effects.

If a currency is overvalued for a long period, perhaps a year or more, employment and income tend to fall because of the effects of overvaluation on net exports. When the overvaluation ends, the economy cannot return to "normal" as though nothing had happened. There are four effects of

---

[5]The trade effects of exchange rate variability are considered in "Exchange Rate Volatility and World Trade," *IMF Occasional Paper* No. 28, 1984. The study failed to find significant effects of exchange rate variability.

overvaluation. First, markets for traded goods are disrupted. For example, an overvalued exchange rate gives foreign producers of imports the time and resources needed to establish a distribution network. Also, export markets are lost and must be redeveloped when the currency eventually falls in value. Second, overvaluation is likely to increase protectionist pressures from producers who must compete with imported goods. (A lower level of real income may be the result if protection does increase.) Third, changes in the allocation of resources lead to adjustment costs. For example, people suffer from unemployment, loss of income, and career disruptions, and when firms have closed and employment has fallen, it takes time and resources to restart production. Finally, future incomes are lower because a current account deficit accompanied by a capital account surplus (net capital inflow) erodes a country's net investment position. The country will receive less interest on foreign assets relative to the interest it pays to foreign holders of domestic assets.

The effects of undervaluation may not be so bad because a current account surplus increases the country's income, and the accompanying capital account deficit (capital outflow) adds to net assets. However, when export industries are established on the basis of an undervalued domestic currency, adjustment costs are born if these industries subsequently have to contract when the currency appreciates. (If an error is to be made, it is probably better to have an undervalued currency rather than an overvalued currency. In fact some countries seem to have pursued policies designed to maintain "low" values for their currencies in the face of continuing current account surpluses.)

There is reason to believe that exchange rate misalignments, and to a lesser extent exchange rate volatility, are damaging to welfare. Let us now review the possible causes of exchange rate misalignments and exchange rate variability.

Explanations of Exchange Rate Behavior

There are two broad explanations of exchange rate misalignments and variability: (1) exchange market inefficiency, such as exchange rate overshooting or instability resulting from capital flows, and (2) unstable or different macroeconomic policies.[6] In practice, it may be difficult to

---

[6]Williamson (1985) adds a third explanation of exchange rate behavior: misguided official intervention. Although intervention may not always have been stabilizing, it seems unlikely that large swings in exchange rates can be attributed to misguided official intervention. However, it is certainly possible, and perhaps even likely, that official intervention and statements made by officials have not always been stabilizing.

distinguish between these two explanations because capital flows are often related to economic policies.

Overshooting

The theory of **exchange rate overshooting** developed as an explanation of the behavior of exchange rates. Overshooting is one reason why exchange rates do not always reflect contemporaneous economic conditions. For example, one model suggests that when the money supply increases, the interest rate tends to fall, and the long–term equilibrium value of the currency falls (because a higher money supply leads to a higher price level). For investors to be willing holders of low interest assets in the currency, they must expect an appreciation; thus, the currency depreciates by a large amount and then appreciates. In other words, overshooting implies a period in which the currency increases in value following an increase in monetary growth. (See the discussion of Figure 10.4.)

Exchange rate overshooting seems plausible to many observers. However, knowing that exchange rates may behave in this fashion does not really help policymakers or market participants. The problem is to define and measure the long–run equilibrium exchange rate. For example, many observers felt that the dollar was overvalued in 1984 and 1985, but there was little agreement on how much it was overvalued. Furthermore, even if one could define the long–run equilibrium rate, and thereby measure overvaluation, whether the market rate could actually be pushed toward the long–run equilibrium rate is another question.

Exchange Market Instability

Whether markets are inherently stable in the absence of official intervention is impossible to say. Economists often argue that speculative flows of capital can play a stabilizing role, but press and television reports often suggest less desirable behavior. Two effects are bandwagon effects and bubbles. A **bandwagon effect** is self–propelling once it has begun. Essentially, people hope to profit by the continuation of the effect. Quite often this behavior pays off. For example, some people profited by joining the gold bandwagon that increased the price of gold from $520 in December 1980 to $850 in January 1981. Others, those who joined the bandwagon too late and did not get off in time, lost when gold fell by over $200 in the week from January 21 to January 28.

A second effect is the **bubble**. In this case, people may expect a fall in a currency's value, but they are willing to buy and hold the currency because they do not expect the fall to occur just yet. For example, as mentioned above, many people felt that the dollar was overvalued in 1984–85, but there was a large net capital inflow into the United States, which shows that foreigners were willing buyers and holders of dollar assets.

Attempts to test whether these types of behavior are common have been inconclusive. One obvious explanation is that people behave differently at different times. For example, bandwagon effects may have occurred, but whether any particular bandwagon is likely to keep rolling is a very different problem.

The Problem of Capital Mobility

Greater capital mobility allows a more efficient allocation of capital. However, fluctuations in capital flows can lead to substantial exchange rate changes over short periods of time. Capital flows may be influenced by expectations of possible future events as much as by current events. Since expectations cannot be observed, it is often difficult to explain or predict the behavior of capital flows. This in turn makes predicting the exchange rate difficult.[7]

The amount of capital which can potentially move from one country to another, and the speed with which it can move, have sometimes led to problems for countries trying to maintain fixed exchange rates. If investors believe an official exchange rate will not be maintained, their actions may make it very difficult for the rate to be maintained.[8] Capital flows played an important role in bringing about the end of the Bretton Woods system, as shown in the last chapter, and capital flows were largely responsible for the effective breakdown of the European Monetary System in 1993 (described in Chapter 17).

One "answer" is to tax or prohibit capital flows. This approach can be likened to throwing the baby out with the bath water. The benefits of an international capital market would be lost because "there is no reliable (**ex ante**) method of separating "productive" from "nonproductive" capital flows by reference to such factors as maturity (short–term versus long–term) or ownership (portfolio versus direct investment)."[9] Also, capital controls are notoriously ineffective, and it would be difficult to make them effective

---

[7]Although some observers verge on claiming that capital flows are random disturbances, there are often (*ex post*) plausible explanations of capital flows. For example, expectations that real growth would lead to capital gains from higher share prices were probably partly responsible for the capital inflow into the United States in the early 1980s.

[8]See Figure 6.6.

[9]IMF (1984), p. 52.

without considerable invasion of privacy and restrictions on liberty.[10] Exchange rate variability may be the price we have to pay for an international capital market.

Economic Policy

Before examining the effect of domestic policies on exchange rates, let us briefly consider the effect of the exchange rate system on economic policy. One common argument used against floating exchange rates was that floating rates allow countries to pursue inflationary policies without worrying too much about the exchange rate. This freedom allegedly contributed to the problem of international inflation during the 1970s. In contrast, fixed exchange rates supposedly entail a beneficial monetary discipline. High inflation countries tend to develop balance of payments deficits, and deficit countries face more pressure to adjust than surplus countries. The removal

Table 14.1
Inflation and Growth in Industrial Countries, 1973–87

	Inflation	Growth
1973	7.7	6.1
1974	13.1	0.5
1975	11.1	−0.6
1976	8.3	5.0
1977	8.4	4.0
1978	7.2	4.1
1979	9.0	3.4
1980	11.8	1.4
1981	10.0	1.5
1982	7.4	−0.3
1983	4.9	2.8
1984	4.7	5.0
1985	4.1	3.3
1986	2.3	2.7
1987	3.0	3.3

Note: Inflation is measured by the change of consumer prices, growth by the change of real GNP.

Sources: IMF *World Economic Outlook*, 1983, p. 170, and p. 175; and October 1988, p. 60 and p. 67.

[10]For example, all international communications would have to be monitored (to prevent people from making private arrangements to avoid the controls).

of a deficit inevitably entails adjustment costs. Thus, fixed exchange rates penalize countries that pursue inflationary policies.

It is clearly not true that floating exchange rates necessarily lead to inflation, because inflation has been brought down under floating rates, as Table 14.1 shows. Also, the diversity of countries' inflationary experiences suggests that countries do have a measure of control over their own destinies.[11] We return to this topic in the next section where we discuss the effects of oil price increases.

Exchange Rates and Domestic Policies

It is often implicitly assumed that governments favor stable exchange rates. However, it seems that some countries have used exchange rate changes to complement their domestic economic policies. For example, the increase in the value of sterling from over $2.0 at the beginning of 1979 to over $2.4 in October 1980 was welcomed, if not deliberately encouraged, by the British government, because the decline in the prices of imported goods helped reduce inflation. In retrospect, it is clear that sterling was overvalued in 1980; the pound fell to $1.8 in September 1981.

Similarly, the value of the dollar increased as the United States began to reduce its rate of monetary growth (in October 1979). Again, appreciation over the following years helped reduce inflation by lowering the cost of imported goods. More recently, in an attempt to stimulate the economy, American short–term interest rates were halved: the rate on 3–month Treasury bills fell from 6 percent in early 1991 to under 3 percent in early 1993. The resulting fall in the value of the dollar was welcomed by the Clinton Administration because it helped stimulate the economy. The fall in the value of the dollar relative to the yen was particularly welcomed, due to the large trade imbalance between the United States and Japan.[12]

Policy Instability and Diversity

If governments pursue different economic policies, and these policies are constantly changing, exchange rates will probably change too. The response

---

[11]Chapter 10 showed that flexible exchange rates allow countries to pursue independent monetary policies. This does not imply that inflation is more likely under flexible exchange rates. For example, Germany and Switzerland, which experienced difficulty sterilizing the monetary effects of payments surpluses, probably found it easier to pursue low inflation policies when they abandoned fixed exchange rates.

[12]In early 1994, the Clinton administration even threatened to push the yen higher if Japan did not agree to import more from the United States.

of exchange rates to changes in macroeconomic policy is not simple. For example, trade responds with a lag, and capital flows may be influenced by expectations as much as by current events. The question of how much we can attribute exchange rate changes to the pursuit of different policies, or unstable policies, is constantly debated. Sometimes it is clear that the exchange rate change was the result of a change in domestic economic policy; for example, the dramatic fall in the American interest rate in 1991 and 1992 was a major reason for the fall in the dollar's value. The upward pressure on the German mark in 1991–92 was clearly the result of high German interest rates following reunification (and falling American interest rates). However, not all exchange rate changes are so easily explained, even with the benefit of hindsight.

The Role of Policy Coordination

Some of the arguments in favor of fixed exchange rates suggest that exchange rate instability is a cause of domestic economic instability. The preceding discussion suggests that the reverse is also true, that is, exchange rate instability can be the result of domestic economic instability or differences in economic policies. Although governments often claim to be in favor of exchange rate stability, they do not show many signs of being willing to adopt similar policies to achieve this goal. But if countries retain independent policies, exchange rate changes are inevitable.

Reform Proposals

Given the lack of agreement on the need for reform, we shall not give a detailed description of the myriad reform proposals, but rather concentrate on the main issues.

Open or Secret Exchange Rate Targets

Assuming that some degree of intervention is to take place, the first issue is whether the monetary authorities should announce their exchange rate target. If they do so, they may invite speculation against the target. But if speculators believe that the target will be successfully pursued, stabilizing speculation may result. The degree of confidence in the likelihood of the target exchange rate being maintained plays a crucial role in determining how speculators are likely to behave.

Proponents of flexible exchange rates argue that market participants would predict the long–run exchange rate and stabilizing speculation would push the market rate toward the long–run rate. Proponents of open targets argue that experience under floating exchange rates shows that this does not happen. Exchange rate forecasts differ widely, and without the announcement of official targets, there is little to guide market participants. It is feared that secret targets will be ineffective because foreign exchange reserves are small in relation to the volume of transactions in the foreign exchange market. Also, open official targets would place some pressure on authorities to achieve the announced rate. If targets are secret, the authorities can describe any rate as the "right" rate.

The Degree of Flexibility

A second issue is the degree of flexibility that should be allowed. Governments are probably unwilling to return to a system in which domestic policy is of secondary importance to balance of payments considerations. But in the absence of common domestic policies, exchange rates must change. If exchange rate changes are infrequent, imbalances build up, and the direction

Figure 14.3
Intervention Rules and the Profits from Speculation

In both diagrams, there is the same underlying upward trend in the exchange rate. The target rates of exchange are shown by e_0 and e_1. In the figure on the left (a), the exchange rate is held within the narrow band by official intervention. When the authorities revise the target from e_0 to e_1, speculators profit because the market exchange rate changes by a large amount. In the right–hand figure (b), the band is wide. As the currency approaches the upper limit, the band is moved upward. The market exchange rate does not jump when the target is revised, it merely continues along its trend. The revision of the band does not generate large profits for speculators.

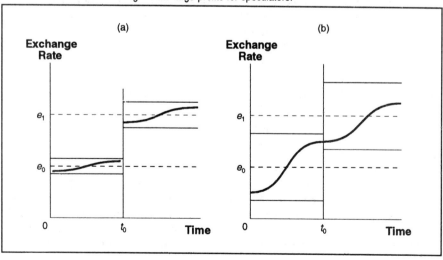

of change is likely to be predictable. Large flows of capital may take place in anticipation of exchange rate changes.

One solution is to combine wider bands with regular parity revisions. If the band around the target rate is narrow, and the market exchange rate is held down by intervention, a change in the target rate can lead to a large jump in the market exchange rate, and large profits for speculators. This is shown in Figure 14.3(a). If the band is wide, as shown in Figure 14.3(b), and the target is revised regularly, the currency may continue rising gradually in value without large jumps occurring each time the target is revised. This reduces the profits from speculation.[13] However, if exchange rate targets are revised too often, or the band width is too great, little extra stability might be gained.

The European Monetary System

The success of the European Monetary System in its early years with regular reviews of targets led some economists to advocate the adoption of a similar system by other countries. However, the EMS virtually collapsed in 1993, as a result of intense speculation. The Bank for International Settlements attributed part of the blame to increased capital mobility, and part to lack of flexibility:

> "The gradual transformation of this mechanism from a regime of fixed but adjustable exchange rates into a system of frozen parities bears much of the responsibility for the severity and spread of the crisis. It stood in the way of preventative parity adjustments that would have been warranted by the gradual emergence of fundamental exchange rate misalignments and other major imbalances. The adjustments ultimately had to be made in conditions of crisis, precipitately, triggering speculative attacks even in cases where the fundamentals were sound." (BIS, 1993, p. 6.)

Analogies between the international monetary system and the EMS are misleading. The EMS survived for so long because there was a strong political will that it should succeed. It became a symbol of European unity, and members showed a willingness to sacrifice a degree of independence in

---

[13]In 1993, the band width for exchange rates of currencies in the European Monetary system had to be increased to ±15 percent, because the narrow band of ±2¼ could not be sustained. Only a few months later, at the beginning of December 1993, most currencies were within or very near to the narrow band. (Perhaps speculative pressure diminished when speculators were no longer able to bet against narrow bands.)

policy making in order to make the system work. Also, stable exchange rates are probably more important for the members of the EMS than for other countries because the members are so closely linked through trade. For members of the EMS, economic stability may be increased by exchange rate stability. Finally, because the European Union is much more than an exchange rate system, compromise packages are possible: a member may agree to an exchange rate change in the expectation of gaining from another policy of the European Union.

How Much Should an Exchange Rate Change?

A third issue relates to the criteria by which exchange rate changes are decided. A number of **objective indicators** have been proposed to indicate the appropriate size of changes in exchange rates, but a consensus has yet to be reached. Such a consensus is unlikely to emerge because different factors may be important to different countries at different times. Also, an "equilibrium" exchange rate may reflect expectations of future developments as well as current conditions. Therefore, no measure of current conditions will be sufficient. Finally, even if an appropriate indicator could be identified, speculation in advance of exchange rate changes based on the indicator could become a problem. Unfortunately, in the absence of such an indicator, disagreements between countries over the "correct" values of currencies are inevitable.

Lack of Agreement on the Need for Reform

There are two main reasons for the lack of consensus on the need for reform. First, although many people argue that the present system is imperfect, assessments of the importance of these imperfections differ greatly. If trade and investment flourish, does it matter if exchange rates bounce around a little? Second, some people recognize that imperfections in the present system do not justify a return to fixed exchange rates. Nor do imperfections necessarily justify adopting perfectly flexible exchange rates (which would entail the complete abandonment of exchange market intervention). No system will ever be perfect. The real question is whether there is a better alternative to the present system. So far, countries have not been able to agree on one.

It is difficult to imagine a fixed exchange rate system that could have survived the economic and political disturbances the world experienced after 1973. For example, in the first ten years of floating exchange rates there were a number of regional conflicts, two oil crises that were accompanied by financial disruptions, discoveries of natural resources, two global recessions, a period of international inflation, a debt crisis, and large differences between countries' policies and economic conditions. These were "accommodated without either suspending the operation of exchange markets or implementing wide–scale restrictions on trade or capital flows."[14] Viewed in this way, the performance of the present system has been rather impressive.

Oil Prices

The use of floating exchange rates since 1973 is partly due to their ability to accommodate major disruptions, such as oil price increases. In October 1973 the "Yom Kippur" war broke out when Egypt and Syria invaded Israel. Arab oil exporters declared an oil embargo against the Netherlands and the United States because of their ties with Israel. As oil companies bid for the limited supply, the price of oil rose dramatically.

The embargo was a failure in the sense that it did not stop the flow of oil to the United States or the Netherlands, which bought oil from other producers and obtained OPEC oil by having it shipped through other countries. However, in a few months the price of oil quadrupled (to $11–$12 a barrel) and OPEC discovered that it made sense to restrict output. Because the demand for oil is inelastic in the short–run, oil revenue increases when output is cut and the price increases.[15]

Effects of an Increase in the Price of Oil

The increase in the price of oil had two effects on the economies of oil importers. First, the oil price increase added to the inflation that industrial countries were already experiencing. Oil is used in the production and distribution of many goods, so the oil price increase led directly to higher prices for these goods. Inflation spread throughout the economies of the oil importers, as workers in other sectors sought higher wages to compensate for the higher prices. Second, the oil price increase tended to reduce real income because more real income was devoted to paying for oil. (In this respect, oil price increases are similar to increases in taxes.) The effect on world inflation and growth is shown in Table 14.1: prices rose and real income stagnated in 1974 and 1975.

---

[14]IMF (1984), p. 45.

[15]This experience is the mirror image of the immiserizing growth case described in Chapter 2. Recall that growth can lead to a fall in welfare if the growth of exports leads to a large fall in the price of exports relative to the price of imports. In this case, OPEC found that a fall in the supply of exports led to a large increase in the price of exports (oil) relative to the price of imports, so OPEC's welfare increased.

Table 14.2
Current Account Balances, 1973–82ᵃ
(billions of dollars)

	Industrial Countries	Non–oil Developing Countries	Oil Exporting Countries
1973	20.3	−11.3	6.7
1974	−10.8	−37.0	68.3
1975	19.8	−46.3	35.4
1976	0.5	−32.6	40.3
1977	−2.2	−28.9	30.2
1978	32.7	−41.3	2.2
1979	−5.6	−61.0	68.6
1980	−40.1	−89.0	114.3
1981	0.6	−107.7	65.0
1982	−1.2	−86.8	−2.2

ᵃThe current account balances in this table do not sum to zero because of errors and omissions, for example, non–market economies are excluded.

Source: IMF *World Economic Outlook*, 1983, p. 185.

The effect on current accounts was also dramatic, as Table 14.2 shows. The current account surplus of the industrial countries of $20.3 billion in 1973 was transformed into a current account deficit of $10.8 billion in 1974. Developing counties were also affected. The current account deficit of non–oil developing countries rose from $11.3 billion in 1973 to $37 billion in 1974.

Financing of Oil Deficits

Current account deficits were largely financed through capital flows. The Eurocurrency market played an important role in recycling funds from oil exporters to oil importers: oil revenue was deposited in the Eurocurrency market and loaned to oil importers.[16] Part of the debt problem of developing countries can be traced to debts incurred at this time.[17] These events demonstrated the resilience of flexible exchange rates, since trade and

---

[16]The success of the Eurocurrency market in recycling funds is discussed in Chapter 16.

[17]The debt problems of developing countries are discussed in Chapter 18.

international investment were able to continue against this background. It is doubtful whether fixed exchange rates could have survived.

Commodity Prices and Inflation

We have seen that the effects of an increase in the price of oil can be dramatic. Other commodity prices were also increasing in 1972–73. This observation seems naturally to lead to the proposition that increasing commodity prices were a cause of world inflation. This proposition cannot be accepted without qualification. An increase in the domestic price level may result from an increase in aggregate demand. Similarly, the prices of commodities may increase in response to an increase in demand. This is exactly what happened in 1971–73. When an increase in demand pushes up prices in general, the increase in commodity prices should be viewed as being part of inflation, not an independent cause of it.

To a large extent the causes of the 1973–74 oil price increase were political, not economic. Therefore, in this case it may be appropriate to think of oil prices as an independent cause of the increase in the world price level. However, a single increase in the price level is not inflation. By definition, inflation is a continuing increase in the general price level. In the long run, this will not happen unless the monetary authorities increase the money supply.

Commodity price increases represent short–run inflationary stimuli that can be neutralized by a tight monetary policy. This course of action would lead to unemployment in the short run (until real incomes are revised downward), but inflation is not a necessary result. An alternative policy is to "accommodate" the oil price increase by increasing the money supply. In this case real incomes fall as the price level rises.[18] The increase in prices and the fall in growth in 1974–75 suggest that countries pursued a policy that partly accommodated and partly offset the inflationary effect of the increase in oil prices.

The Second Oil Price Increase

A second oil price increase occurred in 1978–79, following the disruption of oil exports as a result of the Iranian revolution. The overall supply was almost unaffected because other producers increased output, but speculative/precautionary inventory accumulation pushed prices upward. The spot price rose from $16.80 in June 1978 to $44.24 on February 21, 1979,

---

[18]In either case, real incomes fall because an increase in the amount paid for oil reduces the amount remaining as income.

and led to higher contract prices. The average price of oil was $29 in 1980 compared to $13 in 1978.[19]

Inflation had moderated slightly in the mid–1970s, but it was still a problem in 1978–79 at the time of the second oil price increase. There was a general move underway to reduce inflation at the end of the 1970s. This, combined with the income effects of the oil price increase, led to a recession in 1980. The recession lasted longer than that of 1974, but inflation did not rise as much as in 1974–75 and was quickly brought under control (see Table 14.1).

Developments in the 1980s and 1990s

Developments in the oil market over the last decade show the difficulty of maintaining a successful cartel. OPEC's earlier success sowed the seeds that undermined OPEC's market power. High oil prices encouraged the use of other forms of energy, and led to a slowing in the growth of the demand for oil. Also, high oil prices encouraged other non–OPEC suppliers to enter the market. In an effort to maintain prices, OPEC cut back on production, and its share of the world oil market fell. With demand remaining sluggish, and oil exporters in need of export revenue, OPEC has had difficulty in reaching agreements on production quotas, and agreements have not lasted.

Supplies from Iraq were disrupted by the Gulf War. Oil from Iraq began to re–enter the market at the end of 1993, and producers argued over which countries should cut output. The price of oil fell by 25 percent in 1993, and in early 1994, it was only $12–15 per barrel. In other words, the price of oil was not much different in nominal terms from the price 20 years earlier. In real terms, it was much lower. Clearly, the forecasts made in the 1970s of sky–rocketing prices and the depletion of oil reserves were very wrong.

Summary of Main Points

Following the collapse of the Smithsonian Agreement in 1973, countries have allowed exchange rates to fluctuate in response to market forces. However, exchange rates have not been perfectly free; official intervention in the foreign exchange market is common. The loose guidelines for monitoring the present system, which the IMF adopted in 1976, did little more than legalize the status quo. The IMF is supposed to exercise surveillance over developments, but the questions of when and how adjustment should take place have not been addressed.

---

[19]These figures are taken from Danielson (1982).

Many people have argued that exchange rate changes have been excessive. Exchange rate changes have not been closely related to inflation differentials, and **real exchange rates** have fluctuated widely. Explanations of exchange rate volatility include overshooting, destabilizing capital flows, and unstable/different macroeconomic policies. These explanations of past behavior do little to help us predict future behavior because past behavior need not be repeated. Lacking a consensus on how to define and measure the long–term exchange rate, measurements of departures from the long–term exchange rate, and predictions of future behavior, inevitably differ.

Exchange rate **volatility** has traditionally been used as an argument for intervention, and the behavior of exchange rates has led to calls for reform of the present system. Also, swings in exchange rates (taking place over a few years) have focused attention on the effects of **misaligned** exchange rates. Reform proposals include fixed exchange rates with a wider band of permitted fluctuation and regular parity revisions. The objective of these proposals is to stabilize the foreign exchange market and to avoid large changes in official parities which can encourage speculation and reward speculators.

There are no signs of agreement on the costs of floating exchange rates or on the type of reform (if any) that is needed. The present (non–) system has allowed international trade and investment to continue and flourish despite major international disruptions which would have led to the collapse of a fixed exchange rate system.

The first oil price increase in 1973–74 had a significant effect on international economic relationships and helped prevent a return to a fixed exchange rate system. An increase in the price of oil tends to reduce real income and increase prices in oil–importing countries. The first oil price increase was followed by lower economic growth and higher inflation.

When oil prices increased again in 1978–79, inflation was already a serious problem, and many countries chose to prevent inflation and accept a (short–term) fall in economic growth. The sequence of events was reversed in the mid–1980s as lower oil prices helped non–inflationary growth in oil–importing countries. The fall in oil prices illustrates the problem of maintaining a successful cartel: the quantity demanded tends to fall as higher prices induce consumers to conserve and non–cartel producers to enter the market.

Study Questions

1. Why might the rules governing the present international monetary system be insufficient to guide policies?
2. What arguments might be used in favor of reform of the present international monetary system?

3. What arguments might be used against reform of the present international monetary system?
4. Why are exchange rate changes inevitable if countries do not pursue similar economic polices?
5. What are the causes of exchange rate variability?
6. What are the effects of:
   a. overvaluation?
   b. undervaluation?
7. Critically evaluate the proposals for reform of the international monetary system.
8. In 1985, many people agreed that the dollar was overvalued, but there was little agreement about the extent of the overvaluation. How might one assess whether a currency is overvalued, and why might differences of opinion arise?
9. What are the effects of an increase in the price of oil on:
   a. the value of the dollar?
   b. the level of real income in the United States?
10. What are the effects of a fall in the price of oil on:
   a. real incomes of oil importers?
   b. price levels of oil importing countries?

Selected References

Adams, J., (ed.), *The Contemporary International Economy*, 2e, New York: St. Martin's, 1985.

Aliber, R. Z., (ed.), *The Reconstruction of International Monetary Arrangements*, New York: St. Martin's, 1987.

Baldwin, R. E. and J. D. Richardson, (eds.), *International Trade and Finance: Readings*, 3e, Boston: Little Brown, 1986.

BIS, 63rd *Annual Report*, June 1993.

Bordo, M. D., "The Gold Standard, Bretton Woods and Other Monetary Regimes: A Historical Appraisal," *Federal Reserve Bank of St. Louis*, 75, March/April 1993, pp. 123–187.

Danielson, A. L., *The Evolution of OPEC*, New York: Harcourt Brace Jovanovich, 1982.

Dornbusch, R., "Exchange Rate Economics: 1986," *Economic Journal*, 97, 1987, pp. 1–18.

Federal Reserve Bank of Boston, *The International Monetary System: Forty Years after Bretton Woods*, Proceedings of a conference held in May 1984 at Bretton Woods, New Hampshire.

Goldstein, M., et al., "Policy Issues in the Evolving International Monetary System," *IMF Occasional Paper* No. 96, Washington DC: IMF, June 1992.

IMF, "The Exchange Rate System: Lessons of the Past and Options for the Future," *IMF Occasional Paper* No. 30, 1984.

Koromzay, V., J. Llewellyn, and S. Potter, "The Rise and Fall of the Dollar: Some Explanations, Consequences and Lessons," *Economic Journal*, 97, 1987, pp. 23–43.

Meier, G. M., *Problems of a World Monetary Order*, New York: Oxford University Press, 1982.

Solomon, R., *The International Monetary System: 1945–1981*, 2e, New York: Harper & Row, 1982.

Williamson, J., *The International Monetary System*, Washington DC: Institute of International Economics, revised edition, 1985.

Fifteen

Commercial Policy in Practice

Introduction

This chapter examines the history of U.S. commercial policy against the background of international commercial policy trends, and illustrates how the arguments for protection have changed over the last two centuries. It is interesting that many of the same arguments for protection used today were made many years ago.

Europe and America followed different courses during the nineteenth century, and for this reason their experiences during this time are examined in different sections. Then we look at the interwar years when their experiences were more alike: protection increased and the collapse of world trade contributed to the depression of the early 1930s. The General Agreement on Tariffs and Trade (GATT), signed in 1947, reflected a consensus that barriers to trade were detrimental. We examine how GATT has performed and the commercial policy issues which exist today.

Commercial Policy Before World War I

Mercantilism

The mercantilist era lasted from about 1500 to 1750. The objective of countries during this period was to achieve and maintain an export surplus in order to acquire precious metals, in particular gold. There were many reasons why countries sought to accumulate gold. One was that gold reserves could be used to finance wars, thus additions to the stock of gold reserves added to the power of the state. Another was that thrift and the accumulation of wealth were thought of as good habits, and what was good for individuals was good for countries. Finally, it was thought that general economic activity could be increased by encouraging exports and discouraging imports.

The mercantilist objective of accumulating precious metals was pursued with the use of tariffs on imports and subsidies on exports. Mercantilists recognized that countries had to import raw materials, but laws ensured that the materials were carried on domestically owned ships so that the profits from transportation were earned by domestic firms. A strong navy was needed to protect domestic shipping (and could also harass foreign vessels).

The British Free Trade Movement

The classical economists, Adam Smith, David Ricardo, and John Stuart Mill, rebelled against the mercantilist doctrine. They argued that specialization increases output and free trade increases welfare. Exports and imports are neither good nor bad in themselves, but are part of the process of specialization and trade.

The free trade movement was strongest in Britain, the most important trading nation of the time. One barrier to the success of the free trade lobby was that the British government depended on tariff revenue. (Tariffs levied for the purpose of raising revenue are called **revenue tariffs**.) Thus, although a free trade movement was under way at the time in Britain, tariffs were increased when Britain went to war with France at the beginning of the nineteenth century. After the war, Napoleon was defeated at Waterloo in 1815, and British tariffs were reduced as the need for tariff revenue decreased. With the introduction of income taxes in 1842, it became possible to make significant progress toward free trade.

The Corn Laws

However, opposition to free trade continued in Britain. British agriculture was protected by the Corn Laws under which tariffs were levied on imported wheat. Farmers opposed the abolition of the Corn Laws: Farmers benefitted because protection raised the price of domestic wheat. The argument used by the agricultural lobby was that English rents were so high that tariffs were needed to help domestic farmers compete with imported grain.

David Ricardo argued that tariff supporters did not understand the determination of land prices. In his view, the high rents were the result of protection. Ricardo assumed that agricultural land had no other uses and was fixed in supply. The Corn Laws raised the price of wheat and increased the revenue from farming. As a result, the demand for land increased. Because the quantity of land was fixed, the increase in the demand for land was reflected in higher rents and land prices. Figure 15.1 illustrates Ricardo's argument.

Ricardo argued that agricultural protection is not necessary to ensure domestic supply. In his view, land would not disappear or be left idle if agricultural support were eliminated; it would always be better for the owner to earn as much as possible from the land. Thus, Ricardo was able to argue for the removal of the Corn Laws without worrying about the effect on the

Figure 15.1
Ricardo's Argument Against the Corn Laws

The domestic supply of grain is determined by the amount of land and is therefore perfectly elastic, as shown by the vertical line at QS. The world supply of grain is shown by the horizontal line because Britain is a small country and cannot affect the world price. Under these conditions, a tariff (t) that raises the domestic price from P_0 to P_1 does not increase the domestic quantity supplied but does reduce the quantity demanded from QD_0 to QD_1. Consumer surplus falls by P_0P_1ef, farm revenue increases by P_0P_1ba, and government revenue increases by $abed$. Thus, there is a net loss of welfare of def. Farmers gain temporarily from an increase in revenue, but as the demand for land increases, higher revenue is offset by higher rents and land prices.

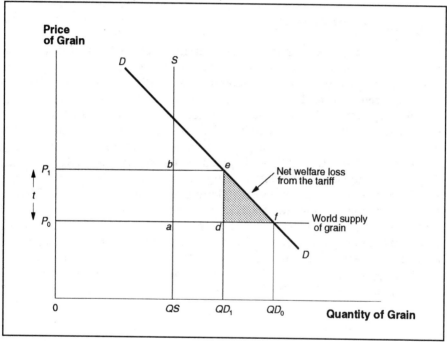

domestic supply of agricultural produce.[1] The problem for the free trade movement in the nineteenth century was that the landowners resisted the threat to the value of the land they owned. A similar debate continues today.

---

[1]Perhaps the assumption that the domestic supply of agricultural products is unaffected by changes in tariffs (because domestic supply is perfectly inelastic) is unrealistic. However, the assumption sometimes used by modern supporters of protection, that domestic supply will disappear completely without protection, is equally unrealistic.

High land prices are still frequently used as a justification for agricultural support.

The Corn Laws were repealed in 1846. Their repeal was not the result of a general acceptance of Ricardo's analysis, but because restricting imports of grain while many thousands of people were starving to death during the Irish famines of 1845–46 led to the widespread condemnation of the Corn Laws. The Crimean War (1854–56) increased the need for revenue and halted Britain's free trade movement temporarily. After the war, the movement was able to resume. The budget of 1860 removed most of the tariffs that remained and Britain became a free trade nation.

The Spread of Free Trade

Britain negotiated commercial treaties with many countries. One of the most important was the Cobden–Chevalier Act of 1860 between Britain and France. An interesting feature of Britain's commercial treaties was the inclusion of a **most favored nation** clause, that is, when a country signed a treaty with Britain it automatically received any concessions made by Britain to other countries. In other words, a signatory was accorded tariff concessions equal to those given to the most favored nation.[2] This type of clause prevents trade discrimination and turns bilateral agreements into multilateral agreements.

Britain and France negotiated treaties with other European countries. The 1862 treaty between France and the German customs union, the Zollverein, was a high point in the free trade movement. Other countries also moved toward free trade, and conventions studied ways of improving communications (canals, railways, postal services, and the like). This free trade movement contributed to a rapid increase in world trade. Over the whole period 1800–1913, trade grew by 33 percent per decade; during the shorter period 1840–1870, trade grew by 53 percent per decade.[3]

---

[2]One result of Britain's free trade policy was that colonies began to lose the preferential access to the British market that they had enjoyed. Canada turned to trade with the United States and signed a trade treaty in 1854. Although this treaty did not last, it helped develop a close relationship between the two counties that continues to this day. The Canada–United States trade agreement and the North American Free Trade Agreement, discussed later, are the most recent attempts to reduce barriers between the two countries.

[3]Kenwood and Lougheed (1983), pp. 79–80.

The Protectionist Trends of 1880 Onward

Toward the end of the nineteenth century, broad trends were leading toward protection. International competition, and hence demands for protection, increased as specialization spread and communications improved. This was the era when railroads and steamships revolutionized transport. Growing nationalism added to demands for protection to help domestic industries, and tariffs provided revenue to finance new government programs and armaments expenditures. European nationalism also led to a competition for colonies. The division of Africa occurred at this time.

Against this background, two events helped slow the European free trade movement: the world depression of 1873–79, and a flow of cheap grain from the United States and Russia to Europe. Demands for protection came from both industry and agriculture. The result was that after about 1880, trade restrictions began to grow again. However, in general, trade was not seriously impaired. The countries that remained most committed to free trade until 1913 were Britain, Denmark, and Holland.

U.S. Commercial Policy Before 1913

In contrast to the European experience, the United States followed a protectionist policy throughout most of the nineteenth century. Tariffs were first used in the United States as a way of raising government revenue. In the decade after independence, states levied their own tariffs. The Constitution of 1787 ended state tariffs and gave the right to levy tariffs to the federal government. When Congress met in 1789, the first national tariff act was passed. At that time, customs duties were generally low and changes in tariffs usually reflected the need for more revenue or the collection of too much revenue.

Revenue remained the main justification for tariffs until after the Civil War when the infant industry and cheap labor arguments began to influence policy. During the first decade of the twentieth century, tariff revenue still accounted for about 50 percent of government revenue. After that, tariffs declined in importance as government expenditure increased and other forms of taxation, notably the income tax, were developed (see Table 15.1).[4]

---

[4]The Sixteenth Amendment to the Constitution in 1913 made possible the introduction of the income tax (in the Underwood Tariff Act of 1913) to replace lost revenue from tariffs.

Table 15.1
Percentage of Federal Revenue from Customs Duties

1789–91	99.6
1850	91.0
1910	49.4
1920	4.9
1970	1.3

Source: U.S. Department of Commerce, *Historical Statistics of the United States: Colonial Times to 1970*, pp. 1105–106, Washington DC, 1975.

Early Tariff Arguments

The **infant industry argument** was put to Congress by Alexander Hamilton in 1791, but because American manufacturing was in its infancy and was not a powerful lobby, the argument did not have an impact on legislation at that time. As manufacturing grew in importance, the power of the protectionist lobby grew. Manufacturing benefitted from the disruption of trade caused by blockades during the Napoleonic Wars and the War of 1812. Following the end of hostilities and the resumption of trade, the young American industries faced competition, and protectionist pressure helped shape the Tariff Act of 1816. The pressure continued, and further protectionist policies were adopted. The trend culminated in the Tariff Act of 1828, sometimes known as the Tariff of Abominations. This act increased tariffs to over 45 percent. For some goods, the new tariff rates were prohibitive.

The early tariff debate in the United States evolved into a conflict between the interests of Northern manufacturers and Southern cotton producers. The manufacturers wanted protection from imports. The Southern cotton producers opposed tariffs: they did not want to pay higher prices for manufactured goods to support domestic manufacturers, free trade was seen as part of the slavery system that the South wanted to maintain, and they did not want to risk foreign retaliation that might jeopardize the export market for their cotton.

The Tariff Act of 1828 was the result of a political maneuver that backfired. Southern members in Congress hoped to ensure that no tariff legislation would be passed. To do this, they tried to make the bill unacceptable to both North and South. The bill included high tariffs on manufactured goods that would lead to opposition from Southerners and high tariffs on raw materials used by Northern manufacturers. To the surprise of the Southerners, the bill was passed. Opposition to the high tariffs was strong, especially in the South, and there was even talk of secession. The tariff issue was seen as a question of states' rights. South Carolina passed an act saying that the tariff would not be effective in that state. This prompted

Figure 15.2
U.S. Tariffs, 1821–1992

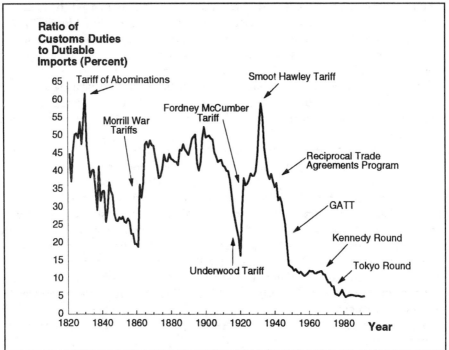

Note: The ratio of tariff revenue to the value of dutiable imports is an imperfect measure of the level of protection. One problem is that goods that are free from duty are not shown by the ratio. Also, prohibitive tariffs are not shown by the ratio because there is no tariff revenue when there are no imports.

Sources: U.S. Department of Commerce, *Historical Statistics of the United States from Colonial Times to 1970*, Washington D.C., 1975, and *Statistical Abstract of the United States*, 1975 and 1993.

President Andrew Jackson to announce that he was prepared to use the military to enforce national laws. The dispute was resolved by the Compromise Tariff Act of 1833, which provided for a gradual reduction of tariff rates.

Over the following years tariffs drifted down, in part because tariff revenue was too high. The downward trend was checked briefly by the Tariff Act of 1842, but the Acts of 1846 and 1857 continued the reduction of tariffs. By 1860, the United States was as close to free trade as it was to become in the nineteenth century. An indication of the evolution of tariff rates is given by Figure 15.2.

American Tariffs 1860–1914

The trend toward free trade ended when the Civil War increased the need for revenue. Tariff rates were increased with the passage of the Morrill Tariffs during 1861–63. At the end of the Civil War, the anti–protectionist lobby failed to bring tariffs down. Industries had been established or expanded behind the high tariffs introduced during the war, and the people associated with these industries argued that they would be ruined by tariff reductions. It was also argued that American industries could not compete with industries in other countries that had access to cheap labor (the **cheap labor argument**).

The protection of American industries from the Civil War until 1913 shows the difficulty of removing tariff protection once it has been granted. American industries grew, but they came to depend on tariffs and the pressure for protection continued. It is interesting to note that the Republican party, which drew support from industrial areas in the East and agricultural areas in the Midwest, was the party of protectionism. Manufacturers and workers favored protection to support domestic industries, whereas farmers were persuaded that tariffs maintained higher incomes in industrial areas and meant better markets for them. The Democratic party was split on the issue, but was more in favor of free trade than the Republican party. For example, Southern farmers favored free trade, but there was strong support for protection from Democrats representing manufacturing interests in Pennsylvania.

The split in the Democratic party resulted in the failure of an attempt to reduce tariffs in 1886. This prompted President Grover Cleveland (a Democrat) to devote the whole of his annual message in December 1887 to the issue of tariffs. He argued that high tariffs were generating too much revenue and pointed to the inequity of taxing consumers to support manufacturers.[5] The tariff issue figured prominently in the 1888 presidential election, but although Cleveland won more votes, Harrison (a Republican) received a majority of the electoral college. The Republican party's success was followed by higher tariffs with the passage of the McKinley Tariff Act in 1890. President Cleveland was returned to office in 1892 with Democratic control over both houses of Congress, and slightly lower tariffs were achieved with the passage of the Wilson–Gorman Tariff Act of 1894.

The Republican party led by William Mckinley was returned to power in 1896, and the following year tariffs were increased by the Dingley Tariff Act. Tariffs remained high until 1913 when the Underwood Tariff Act was passed. Again, the tariff reduction was carried out by the Democrats.

---

[5]Ratner (1972) contains many important historical readings, including the text of Cleveland's message.

However, although tariffs were eventually reduced, the American market effectively remained closed to international competition because World War I disrupted international trade and provided greater protection than tariffs.

Commercial Policy from 1914–1945

Protectionism began to take hold before World War I, but after the war protectionist pressures increased internationally as countries concentrated on national economic interests. The international trend toward protectionism led the League of Nations to convene a conference in 1927 to address the issue. After temporary success in reducing protectionism, the problem increased significantly in the early 1930s.

U.S. Policy in the Early Twentieth Century

When World War I ended, the United States adopted protection before international trade had recovered. In part, postwar protection reflected desires for self–sufficiency and security that had grown during the war. Also, industries that had prospered while trade had been disrupted now demanded protection. The victory of the Republican party, still the party of protection at this time, paved the way for an increase in tariffs. Agricultural prices were declining and representatives of agricultural states were willing to support any measure they thought would strengthen domestic markets.

The Fordney–McCumber Tariff of 1922 raised tariff levels to 38 percent.[6] This act made use of the principle of the **scientific tariff** by giving the president the authority to increase or decrease tariffs by up to 50 percent to compensate for differences between foreign and domestic costs. The term "scientific tariff" might lead one to suppose that such tariffs are desirable. This would be a mistake. Tariffs determined in this way could virtually eliminate trade by removing one of the reasons for trade: differences in production costs. Only products that the domestic country cannot produce at all would continue to be imported. For example, imports of natural resources that are not available domestically would not be affected, and imports of agricultural products requiring special climates could continue (unless the goods could be produced domestically by duplicating the climate artificially).

---

[6]This act, and the Smoot–Hawley Tariff of 1930, made it difficult for countries to repay money they had borrowed from the United States. Some present policies, such as the Multifiber Agreement, have a similar effect.

The Smoot–Hawley Tariff of 1930

The protectionist climax was reached with the passing of the Smoot–Hawley Act in 1930, which drastically curtailed American imports. Originally designed to provide moderate support to farmers, the proposed tariff levels were increased during the passage of the act in response to the stock market crash of 1929 and the onset of the Great Depression. The proposed tariffs escalated as votes were traded in Congress; members supported tariffs to help other members' regions in return for tariffs to help their own regions. In particular, Western support of tariffs for manufactured goods was conceded in return for Eastern support of agricultural tariffs. The act raised the level of tariffs to over 53 percent, the highest level in U.S. history. Over one thousand American economists signed a petition asking President Herbert Hoover to veto the bill, and other countries made strong protests against it. The strength of these protests reflected the importance of the American economy in the world. American commercial policy was no longer purely a domestic issue.

The Spread of Protectionism

The combined effect on imports of the U.S. depression and the Smoot–Hawley Tariff was devastating: merchandise imports declined from $4.3 billion in 1929 to $1.3 billion in 1932. Although tariff rates increased, duties collected declined from $580 million to $260 million because of the fall in the value of imports. Other countries retaliated against American protectionism with their own tariffs; over 60 countries increased their tariffs within two years. (The policies adopted by foreign countries were also a response to their own unemployment problems.) For example, Britain passed the Import Duties Act in 1932, establishing a 10 percent **ad valorem** tariff on all imports except for food, raw materials, and goods from countries in the Empire. Some countries, in particular France, resorted to import quotas. By 1937, 58 percent of French imports were subject to quotas.[7] Another problem was a proliferation of exchange controls, which have similar effects to barriers to trade. Exchange controls were widely used by Germany.

Rolling Back Protectionism

The dangers of protectionism were eventually recognized, and a movement away from tariffs began. The first step to bring down tariffs was taken in

---

[7]Pollard, S., *Peaceful Conquest: The Industrialization of Europe 1760–1970*, revised edition, New York: Oxford University Press, 1982, p. 302.

1934 when the first Reciprocal Trade Agreements Act was passed by the United States. The act gave the president the power to negotiate tariff reductions of up to 50 percent. This action was supposed to take tariff policy out of the political arena. It was hoped that protectionism would not be used to support special interests, as had happened when Congress passed the Smoot–Hawley Tariff. In requesting the authority from Congress, President Franklin Roosevelt emphasized the gain from increased exports and said that American producers would not be hurt. (Although an overall gain from trade was to be expected, it was inevitable that opening up the American market to more competition from imports would hurt some producers.)

Under the Reciprocal Trade Agreements Act, the United States negotiated bilaterally with the chief supplier of a product. Agreements reached under the act included the most–favored–nation clause whereby a tariff reduction negotiated with the chief supplier of a product was extended to imports of the product from other countries that signed commercial treaties with the United States. Between 1934 and 1945, the United States negotiated treaties with 27 countries. These treaties covered almost two–thirds of American dutiable imports and reduced tariffs by an average of 44 percent.[8] The success of the reciprocal Trade Agreements Act may be partly explained by the high tariff levels that were in place after Smoot–Hawley.

For the United States, the mid–1930s marked the beginning of a new era. The dangers of protectionism were recognized and the United States began to pursue a policy of free trade for the first time in her history. The experience of the 1930s still influences economic policy. For example, the 1988 *Economic Report of the President* used this period as an example of the dangers of protectionism:

> "The lesson from Smoot–Hawley is that the passage of protectionist legislation by the United States will increase protectionist activities in the rest of the world, poison the international climate for trade diplomacy in general, and slow the process of trade liberalization for years to come. Since the United States is a major trading nation, it could suffer major economic losses in the event of increased global protectionism." (p. 149.)

---

[8]Evans (1971), p. 7.

The General Agreement on Tariffs and Trade

The First GATT Agreement

The experience of the 1930s convinced most countries that trade was mutually beneficial. In 1944, the Bretton Woods agreement was signed establishing a fixed exchange rate system. It was hoped that exchange rate stability would encourage international trade. However, the Bretton Woods agreement would have been insufficient by itself: international trade could not have flourished if countries had maintained trade barriers. The problem of barriers to trade was addressed by the **General Agreement on Tariffs and Trade (GATT)**.

GATT is an international organization based in Geneva, Switzerland. The two main functions of GATT are settling trade disputes and the surveillance of trade policies. GATT began in 1947 with a meeting of a group of countries that wanted to reduce trade barriers.[9] The agreement went beyond tariff concessions and included a code of conduct and procedures for the resolution of trade barriers by negotiation. Subsequent agreements have reduced trade barriers further and included codes of conduct relating to non–tariff barriers to trade. GATT has helped developed countries reduce tariffs on manufactured goods from around 40 percent in the late 1940s to under 5 percent today. Over 120 countries are now GATT members and more than 80 percent of international trade is covered by GATT agreements.

Principles

One of the most important principles of the GATT is that of **nondiscrimination**. This principle is reflected by the incorporation of the **most–favored–nation** clause, that is, if the tariff on imports from one country is reduced, the tariff on all imports of the same good from other GATT members must be reduced. The tariff concessions resulting from bilateral negotiations at the 1947 conference automatically became multilateral as a result of the application of this principle. There are two exceptions to the principle of nondiscrimination. First, when a free trade area or customs union is formed, countries may apply lower tariffs on trade with members than on

---

[9]The original GATT treaty was to have been a step toward creating an International Trade Organization (ITO), which would have monitored international trade as the International Monetary Fund monitors international monetary developments. The ITO charter was never ratified because of fears that the charter would interfere with the independence of domestic policies.

imports from nonmembers. Second, lower tariffs may be applied to imports from less developed countries.

A second important GATT principle is that, in general, quotas are not permitted. One reason is that they violate the principle of nondiscrimination: it is difficult to allocate a quota without discriminating between alternative sources of supply. Which producers get the quota? Also, the degree of protection given by quotas is often difficult to judge. The GATT signatories were anxious that international trade disputes should be avoided by making barriers to trade "transparent," that is, ensuring that the nature and degree of protection be clear. Quotas are allowed when countries are experiencing balance of payments difficulties or when quotas are part of an economic development program. At the request of the United States, another exception was made for quotas that are needed as part of a domestic agricultural program.

GATT in Practice

The 1947 negotiations achieved an average reduction in tariffs of 35 percent covering 54 percent of dutiable imports (giving a weighted average reduction of 18.9 percent).[10] The following four rounds of tariff reductions were not so successful, and it seemed that there was little prospect of significant benefits from further bilateral bargaining for tariff cuts on particular products.

The Kennedy Round

The creation of the European Economic Community and development of its policies led to fears that access to the European market would be lost; this prompted further efforts to control trade barriers. At the request of the Kennedy administration, the Trade Expansion Act of 1962 gave the president the power to negotiate multilaterally for across–the–board tariff reductions of up to 50 percent.[11] After lengthy negotiations, agreement was reached in 1967 on tariff cuts of 35 percent on manufactured goods.[12] These tariff negotiations affected 64 percent of American dutiable imports and came to

---

[10]Evans (1971), p. 12.

[11]The common external tariffs of the European Economic Community reflected compromises among members. Across–the–board tariff reductions were less likely to upset the balance of national interest than tariff reductions that varied from one good to another.

[12]Evans (1971), pp. 281–3.

be called the **Kennedy round**. This round succeeded in reducing average tariff rates for the major industrial countries to less than 10 percent.

Trade Adjustment Assistance

An interesting aspect of the legislation authorizing the U.S. administration to negotiate on tariff issues was the allocation of funds to compensate workers who became unemployed as a result of trade and to help them retrain for other activities. The logic was that **trade adjustment assistance (TAA)** would help people accept changes caused by trade and allow society to enjoy the gains from trade. However, TAA did not have an important impact because few workers qualified for the programs, and where they did qualify, the funds were usually used for income support rather than retraining.

The logic of TAA was dubious. Why should workers who become unemployed through international trade be treated any differently from workers who become unemployed for other reasons (such as technological advance)? Also, in practice it is often difficult to tell what was the cause of an industry's decline. For example, imports may be increasing because the competitive position of domestic firms is being weakened by lack of investment or by compensation increasing faster than productivity.[13] Which came first, the industry's poor performance or the imports? TAA expired in 1985 and was not renewed. The Reagan administration felt that the benefits paid to unemployed workers provided an incentive to delay their search for new positions.[14] Also, it was said that TAA was not needed because there were already programs to help retrain and relocate unemployed workers.[15]

The Tokyo Round

Another successful round of negotiations, the **Tokyo round**, began in 1973 and was completed in 1979. The Tokyo round was a surprising achievement in view of the uncertainty and instability in the international monetary system at the time. In this round, a formula was adopted that ensured that the higher the tariff, the greater the tariff cut would be. This approach was

---

[13]Some economists have argued that the reason the automobile and steel industries face strong competition from imports is because of lack of investment and excessive wage settlements.

[14]This logic would seem to justify the elimination of all benefits for the unemployed.

[15]The administration's views are summarized in the 1986 *Economic Report of the President*, pp. 126–8.

Table 15.2
Tokyo Round Tariff Cuts by Stage of Processing, Selected Countries
(percent)

Country and Period	All Industrial Products	Raw Materials	Semi– Manu– facturers	Finished Manu– facturers
United States				
Rates before Tokyo	6.5	0.9	4.5	8.0
Rates after Tokyo	4.4	0.2	3.0	5.7
Percent cut	31	77	33	29
European Community				
Rates before Tokyo	6.6	0.2	5.1	9.7
Rates after Tokyo	4.7	0.2	4.2	6.9
Percent cut	29	15	27	29
Japan				
Rates before Tokyo	5.5	1.5	6.6	12.5
Rates after Tokyo	2.8	0.5	4.6	6.0
Percent cut	49	67	30	52
Canada				
Rates before Tokyo	13.6	1.0	14.8	13.8
Rates after Tokyo	7.9	0.5	8.3	8.3
Percent cut	42	48	44	40

Note: Observe that the tariffs are higher on manufactured goods than on raw materials. This results in higher rates of effective protection for manufacturers in developed countries than the rates that would result from a uniform tariff structure.

Source: Reproduced from the 1989 *Economic Report of the President*, p. 156.

intended to achieve more uniformity of tariff rates. The negotiations covered about 90 percent of industrial trade among developed countries, and, for the United States, resulted in an average tariff cut of 31 percent on manufactured goods. Tariff rates before and after the Tokyo round are shown in Table 15.2.

Since many tariffs had already been reduced to low levels by earlier agreements, one of the most significant aspects of the Tokyo round was that the problem of non–tariff barriers was tackled. Agreements were reached in six areas: subsidies and countervailing duties, anti–dumping procedures, government procurement, technical barriers to trade, customs valuation, and import licensing. The codes that were negotiated were general agreements that it was hoped would be replaced by more specific regulations.

Table 15.3
Uruguay Round Tariff Reductions on Industrial Products[1]

Imports from	Import value	Weighted Average		
		Pre	Post	Percentage reduction
Developed economies	736.9	6.3	3.9	38
Developing economies				
(other than least developed countries)	167.6	6.8	4.3	37
Least developed countries	3.9	6.8	5.1	25

[1]Excluding petroleum.

Source: GATT, *Increases in Market Access Resulting from the Uruguay Round*, Geneva, 1994.

The Uruguay Round

The Uruguay round of GATT negotiations was launched in Punta del Este, Uruguay, in 1986. An agreement was signed in April 1994 by 121 countries. Under the Uruguay agreement, countries will eliminate or reduce tariffs reductions on a broad range of goods (developed countries' tariffs falling by 38 percent). Table 15.3 shows the effects of the Uruguay round on tariffs. Furthermore, commitments not to increase tariffs (**tariff bindings**) were agreed on, and these commitments cover 99 percent of the trade of developed countries. This is seen as an important guarantee of market access. Other important aspects of the Uruguay round relate to actions to counter unfair trade practices, textiles, services, intellectual property rights, and agriculture.

It was also agreed to set up a **World Trade Organization (WTO)** which will replace GATT and oversee the implementation of the Uruguay round. The objectives of the WTO include those of the GATT, namely, ensuring full employment and rising living standards by encouraging production and trade. But the WTO objectives go beyond the GATT objectives and include references to "sustainable development," the need to protect the environment, and the need for positive efforts to help developing countries. The creation of the WTO may turn out to be one of the most significant parts of the Uruguay agreement. The WTO will provide an international forum for the settlement of disputes. Also, it will coordinate policies with the IMF and the World Bank to achieve consistent international policies.

Although the Tokyo round and the Uruguay round made some progress toward tackling non–tariff barriers, these barriers remain one of the main obstacles to trade. One reason there are now more non–tariff barriers is that GATT has been a victim of its own success: countries have turned to non–tariff barriers because GATT agreements prevented them from using tariffs. This trend has been dubbed the "new protectionism" and is examined in the next section.

Recent Issues in Commercial Policy and the Uruguay Round

Escape Clauses or Safeguards

Escape clauses or **safeguard measures** in GATT agreements allow countries to restrict trade if increased imports have caused or threaten to cause serious injury to a domestic industry.[16] Significant tariff concessions are bound to hurt some sectors, so why have escape clauses? Escape clauses may reflect the desire of governments to secure markets for exporters without accepting that some domestic industries will suffer because freer trade will lead to more imports. Since serious injury was not defined adequately in GATT agreements, and potential injury rather than actual injury can be used for grounds for protection, there has been wide scope for abuse of this provision.

Voluntary Export Restraints

Voluntary export restraints (VERs) are often used as a safeguard measure, and they have become one of the most common forms of non–tariff barrier. VERs, like other forms of non–tariff barrier, violate the basic principles of GATT—they inevitably discriminate between alternative sources of supply, and the level of protection given to domestic producers is not transparent. The cost of VERs falls mainly on consumers in the importing country; foreign exporters are able to charge a higher price because of the artificial scarcity that is created. For example, the costs to American consumers of restricting imports of Japanese automobiles from 1981 to 1985 have been estimated at over $4 billion, and the costs per job protected in the automobile sector are put at over $200,000 per year.[17] Two other sectors where VERs have had a significant impact are steel and textiles.

The Uruguay agreement tried to address the problem of "safeguard measures" (actions that are taken when imports are causing or are expected to cause serious injury to an industry, for example, voluntary export

---

[16]A similar provision is the U.S. national security clause under which protection can be given to industries that are necessary for national security.

[17]These figures in 1983 dollars are taken from Tarr and Morke (1984). See also, Organization for Economic Cooperation and Development, *The Costs of Restricting Imports: The Automobile Industry* (OECD, Paris, 1987).

restraints). Measures were adopted relating to the initiation and conduct of investigations, and the criteria for assessing serious injury. New rules limit the duration of safeguard measures to four years (with a possible four year extension), they require the measures to be gradually relaxed while in operation, and the rules say that the measures should not be reintroduced.

Dumping and Countervailing Duties

Under GATT rules, countries may use anti–dumping tariffs in cases of **dumping**. Dumping is deemed to have occurred if a firm sells a product abroad for less than its production cost or price in the exporter's domestic market. In cases where the low price results from foreign government subsidies to exporters, **countervailing duties** may be levied to offset the effects of the subsidies. Anti–dumping and countervailing duties are responses to what is seen as unfair trade. It is worth considering the unfair trade argument carefully, because it is often used as an excuse for protection.

The Effects of Dumping

There are two main problems caused by dumping and by foreign subsidies on goods. First, cheap imports may reduce competition by driving some domestic firms out of business. Second, if cheap imports are only available for a short period, unnecessary adjustment costs are incurred (domestic firms close then reopen when the price returns to normal). Tariffs may protect firms from the temporary price fall and allow them to maintain production.

Although many economists believe that there is a valid argument for protection from temporarily low prices, the validity of the case rests on the low prices being temporary. The argument against cheap imports simply because they are cheap is not economically valid. If foreigners are kind enough to subsidize our consumption, why should we refuse? To illustrate the problem more dramatically, if the Japanese government wanted to give us one thousand free Honda cars each year, and the supply would be permanent, should we refuse them?

U.S. Trade Policy

The basic problem that arises in assessing allegations of unfair trade is the assessment of what is a fair market price. The problem is made more difficult when a good is produced solely for export. In the case of countries that do not have market–determined prices, i.e., non–market economies (NMEs), it is very difficult to assess whether a price is fair. The 1994 *Economic Report of the President* describes the approach taken in these cases as follows:

"U.S. law instructs the Commerce Department to construct cost estimates based on costs in a 'surrogate' country at a similar stage of development. In practice, the surrogates are often at quite **dissimilar** stages of development, thus potentially tilting the calculation toward finding large dumping margins. For example, the Department of Commerce has used Swiss, Canadian, Dutch, French, German, and Japanese producers as surrogates for Chinese firms in antidumping petitions." (p. 224.)

The report goes on to describe the Polish golf cart example:

"In the mid–1970s an antidumping petition was filed against Polish electric golf carts. Because Poland was an NME that had no golf courses and therefore little domestic demand for golf carts, the U.S. authorities rightly concluded that it was impossible to compare the prices at which the carts were sold in the United States with the prices in Poland. Instead, the authorities employed a surrogate–country approach: they attempted to estimate what golf carts cost in a country similar to Poland. Canada was chosen. Unfortunately, Canada didn't produce golf carts either, so the final determination was based on what golf carts would have cost in Canada—if Canada had actually produced them." (p. 224.)

In this case, dumping was not proved, but the decision could easily have gone the other way.

The United States makes more extensive use than other countries of investigations and actions against (what it sees as) unfair trade.[18] This has led to charges that the United States interprets GATT rules unilaterally, and has not acted in the spirit or letter of GATT agreements. The passage of the Omnibus Trade and Competitiveness Act in 1988 heightened international concern because the legislation requires the U.S. government to respond to what American law defines to be unfair foreign trade practices. The Act became dubbed as "super 301" because it built on provision 301 of the Trade Act of 1974.

The threat of action is often by itself enough to influence countries. In 1984, the president rejected a recommendation from the International Trade Commission for escape clause action to protect the steel industry, but VERs were negotiated with 16 countries. In reporting these events, the 1986 *Economic Report of the President* commented that: "Several countries have requested agreements to ensure themselves a share of the U.S. market and to obtain immunity from unfair trade actions." (p. 116.) So much for free trade!

---

[18]See Kelly et al. (1988).

One of the reasons Canada wanted to reach a free trade agreement with the United States was to avoid the costs associated with defending against investigations of unfair trade practices.[19]

The Uruguay Round on Dumping and Subsidies

Controls of government subsidies to industry were agreed on in the Uruguay round. "The new agreement established three categories of subsidies: 'prohibited' (based on export performance or favoring domestic inputs); 'actionable' (harms the trade interests of another signatory); and 'non–actionable' (e.g. research, assistance to disadvantaged regions and some dealing with environmental concerns)."[20] For cases of alleged unfair subsidies or dumping, the rules for initiating and investigating cases were tightened, as were the criteria for determining injury, and the rules governing the imposition and duration of duties.

Textiles

The Multifiber Agreement (MFA) is an important example of a non–tariff barrier that adversely affects developing countries. The original agreement was supposed to be a temporary arrangement to provide for the orderly expansion of the world textile market. In practice, it has been used by developed countries to restrict the access of developing countries to their markets and until recently seemed to have become a permanent policy. Exporters are assigned quotas representing shares of developed countries' markets. Through time the restrictions have been gradually extended as new fibers and new exports have entered the market. This agreement is particularly odious because the countries that suffer the most are some of the poorest countries in the world. The textile sector is not the only sector that suffers from the MFA—growth of the textile sectors in poor countries would provide income and employment that would spill over to other sectors. When

---

[19]The European Union now produces an interesting annual report giving its view of U.S. trade policy. For example, see the European Community *Report on United States Trade and Investment Barriers 1994*, distributed in the United States by the European Community Office of Press and Public Affairs, Washington D.C. This report is fascinating reading for people living in the United States: the American media air many complaints about unfair foreign competition but seldom provide the other side's viewpoint.

[20]GATT, *News of the Uruguay Round*, "The Uruguay Round Deal: An Outline of the New Multilateral Trading System," Geneva, 1994.

poor countries claim that developed countries are not really serious about free trade, they have only to point to the MFA to prove the point.

Perhaps one of the most important parts of the Uruguay agreement for developing countries is the agreement to phase out the multifiber agreement over a period of 10 years. If trade in textiles and clothing is actually freed (and who knows what restrictions will emerge to replace it), many poor countries will benefit.

Services and Intellectual Property Rights

An omission from GATT that has begun to attract attention is that of trade in services. The service sectors of developed countries have grown rapidly in recent years. For example, services have grown from 31 percent of U.S. output in 1950 to over 50 percent at the beginning of the 1990s. International trade in services accounts for more than 20 percent of world trade. Although the importance of the sector is clear, removing obstacles to trade in services raises problems that freeing trade in goods does not.[21]

Goods can be allowed to enter a country without the producer operating within the country. In contrast, some services, such as construction, require labor and capital to be located where the service is provided. Other services, such as banking and insurance, may be provided from a distance, but local companies often have a competitive advantage over foreign companies (for example, because they have lower communication costs and can be more responsive to the needs of their customers). Increasing trade and competition in services implies relaxing rules that prevent foreigners from establishing companies or that restrict labor and capital mobility between countries. Countries adopt rules governing foreign access for cultural, economic, and political reasons, and it will be difficult to achieve widespread agreement to relax these rules.

Developed countries are likely to have a comparative advantage in capital–intensive services using modern technology, for example, communications and financial services. Agreement to allow greater trade in this type of service is possible between some countries. Developing countries do not feel that they will gain from these changes because many of their service industries are in their infancy and would not be able to compete. Also, the comparative advantage of developing countries probably lies in labor–intensive services where the barriers are related to immigration issues. It may be difficult to reach agreement allowing trade in labor–intensive services. For example, is the United States ready to accept Korean or Indian construction teams?

---

[21]The following comments draw on World Bank (1987).

In the Uruguay round, services were brought within the GATT framework for the first time, albeit to a limited degree, with some commitments to improve access. (Most offers related to travel and tourism.) But agreement could not be reached on free trade in major areas such as banking and insurance. Intellectual property rights (such as designs, trade secrets, patents, copyrights, and trademarks) received some protection: rules were created for enforcement of rights and for settling disputes.

Agriculture

Gatt agreements have done little to promote free trade in agriculture. Protection has helped Europe and the United States become self–sufficient in most of the products that do not require tropical climates. Not only have these markets been denied to other countries, but Europe and the United States dispose of their surplus produce by dumping it on world markets or donating the surpluses as food aid. The result is that world prices of agricultural products are unstable and artificially low. Also, export markets have been lost for other countries. The recent resurgence of interest in agricultural issues might arise from a genuine desire to enjoy the benefits of freer trade. A plausible alternative explanation is that the agricultural polices of Europe and the United States have become so expensive that reform can no longer be avoided.

Agriculture was addressed by GATT for the first time in the Uruguay round. Agreement was reached to replace non–tariff barriers by tariffs, which will then be reduced. Limits on government subsidies to exports were introduced, and limits were agreed on to reduce subsidies to farmers that lead to overproduction. Whether much actually comes from the agreement remains to be seen. The agreement in agriculture was certainly the subject of very hard bargaining between the United States and the European Union. In fact, the problem of agriculture almost led to the failure of the whole Uruguay round.

The Cultural Exception

The United States and the European Union failed to reach agreement on trade in audio–visual products, such as films. The entertainment industry is a very important export earner for the United States. Foreign countries, with smaller domestic markets, find it very difficult to compete, and have resorted to protection. For example, some European countries have introduced laws requiring television and radio broadcasting to have a specified minimum domestic content.

Apart from the desire to protect domestic industry, there is an important cultural argument which is made in Europe, particularly by France. European countries object to what they see as the undermining of European culture and societal values by American lifestyle/values. Examples include the threat to the French language from the continual encroachment of American words and expressions, or the ambivalence toward guns and violence contained in American movies. It is difficult to be precise, because the criticisms are usually vague. During the GATT negotiations in 1993, the slogan in France was that commerce and culture are different. This promises to be an interesting area of discussion and conflict in the future.

Regional Alliances

Although restrictions affecting particular sectors are a problem, another more general problem facing developing countries is the formation of customs unions between rich countries. Customs unions and free trade areas are permissible exceptions to the GATT principle of non discrimination. When a group of countries forms a free trade area or a customs union, member countries may levy tariffs on imports from nonmembers even though they do not impose tariffs on imports from other member countries.

Two major developments are worth noting. First is the creation of a North American free trade area including Canada, Mexico, and the United States. Second, in recent years European integration has been taking place: the European Union has been adding members and expanding its policies.

The North American Free Trade Agreement

The free trade agreement between the United States and Canada came into effect in 1989. The North American Free Trade Agreement (NAFTA), which added Mexico to the free trade area, came into effect in 1994 and created a free trade area of 370 million people. The agreement was a recognition of the importance of the strong trade links among the three countries. The United States is the most important trading partner for Canada and Mexico. For exports from the United States, Canada is the most important destination and Mexico is the third most important destination.

Under NAFTA, most tariffs will be removed or eliminated gradually over a period of five to ten years (15 years for some agricultural products). Approximately 65 percent of U.S. agricultural and industrial exports to Mexico will be duty-free within five years. The agreement gave people from other member countries the same rights as nationals to establish, acquire, and operate firms. Also, the agreement protects against restrictions on the repatriation of capital, profits, and royalties, and against expropriation. "Side agreements" were negotiated to ensure that competition is not based on the exploitation of low environmental standards or adverse labor conditions.

Also, there is a safeguard mechanism which can be used to protect sectors which are harmed by rapid trade growth.

NAFTA has been the subject of intense debate in the United States where there are fears that American jobs will be lost to cheap Mexican labor. In Canada the fear is that jobs will be lost to the United States (costs being higher in Canada because of the taxes needed to pay for Canada's health and welfare systems). The view of the Clinton administration and most economists is that low–skilled jobs will be lost in the United States (and Canada), but that increased exports of high technology products will create other better paying jobs. Also, the overall expansion of trade among the three countries will increase the overall level of income and employment.

The Expansion and Development of the European Union

The European Union is the world's most successful free trade area. In 1993 the twelve members of the European Union had a combined population of about 350 million with an income of $6¼ trillion.[22] The 12 members were Belgium, Denmark, France, Germany, Greece, Ireland, Italy, Luxembourg, the Netherlands, Portugal, Spain, and the United Kingdom. Moreover, in 1994 the Union agreed to the membership of Austria, Finland, Norway, and Sweden. Norway rejected EU membership in a referendum in November 1994; the other three countries became EU members on January 1, 1995.

The European Union goes beyond free trade. There are also agreements to ensure freedom of movement for services, capital, and even for people. There is also a gradual tendency for European law and European policies to replace national laws and policies. European integration is leading to a single European market. While this will undoubtedly benefit Europeans, it may be more difficult for firms outside the area to sell to the European Union. Therefore, it is not surprising that many foreign companies, particularly Japanese companies, have opened manufacturing plants within the Union to guarantee access to this important market. Also, it seems that most of the countries bordering the Union have applied or will apply for membership. No one wants to be left outside. For those countries that are left outside, the European Union may look more like "fortress Europe" than a step toward free trade.

---

[22]At current prices and exchange rates, the EU and the United States had roughly the same national incomes in 1993.

Developing Countries and GATT

Developing countries have not been active in GATT until recently. At first they rejected the principle of reciprocity: they had little to offer in return for tariff concessions, and they felt that the disparity between rich and poor countries justified concessions without reciprocity. Also, they wanted to be able to use tariffs to help development of their industries.[23] During the Kennedy round they succeeded in obtaining a modification of the most–favored–nation clause to allow developed countries to levy **preferential** (lower) tariff rates on imports from developing countries than on imports generally. However, the preferential tariffs that were granted did not cover all goods, and the concessions included escape clauses that allowed the concessions to be removed if there was serious injury to domestic producers. (In other words, the concessions only last as long as developing countries are not too successful!) As a result, the system of preferences appears to have done little to help developing countries.

The experience of developing countries in sectors such as textiles has contributed to widespread pessimism. It is felt that developed countries are not sincere in their declared support for free trade and that developing counties have little to gain from attempts to increase exports. It is not hard to imagine the feelings of poor countries with large foreign debts when they are told by rich countries that the way to get richer and to pay off their debts is to export more, but they cannot do so because of trade restrictions.

Developing countries participated in the Uruguay round, but they were not completely happy with the results. If the Uruguay round has its intended effect in the agricultural sector, world prices will be slightly higher and they will be more stable. Some poor food–importing countries have expressed concern that they will lose as a result of this aspect of the Uruguay agreement. A second aspect of the Uruguay round that concerns developing countries is the reduction in trade preferences (entailed in the tariff reductions). Given that trade preferences do not seem to have helped developing countries, the reduction probably has little significance. Developing countries stand to gain in two areas: from the elimination of the multifiber agreement, and from agreements to improve market access and security (the conversion of non–tariff barriers into tariffs, a reduction in tariff escalation, and the binding of tariffs).

---

[23]The misguided notion that restricting competition can lead to competitive industries probably did great damage, as we see in Chapter 18.

Threats to Future Trade

A new danger to world trade emerged recently when France and the United States cooperated to place workers' rights and cheap labor on the agenda of the World Trade Organization.[24] If trade barriers are erected to stop imports from countries with low wages, or poor working conditions, trade will cease, and all countries will lose. Moreover, the argument that poor countries are "cheating" looks a little silly when examined more closely. The argument often seems to be that poor people deliberately pay themselves less to gain an unfair competitive advantage. This is ludicrous. Poor countries are simply those that have low output, and thus low income per head. They are not poor by choice. Trade is one of the few ways by which they can improve their standard of living.

Environmental issues also threaten future trade. Some countries have introduced barriers to trade in products from natural areas, such as imports of wood from rain forests. It is in everyone's interests that the environment be protected, but the issue is how. As rich countries developed economically, they destroyed most of their own natural areas; for example, they chopped down forests and drained wet areas. Now, because there are few natural areas left, they seek to protect natural areas in poor countries. Poor countries sometimes view the interest taken in the natural areas of their countries as a threat to their sovereignty, and they see excessive concern for the environment as a barrier to their economic development.

Finally, there is the continual pressure for protection from those who stand to gain. Governments recognize the benefits of exports, but still often respond to pressure from producers for protection. The interests of consumers are largely forgotten. This threat to trade never seems to go away.[25]

Summary of Main Points

During the nineteenth century, tariffs in Europe and the United States were often **revenue tariffs**. The benefits of free trade were recognized by European countries and the development of other forms of taxation (such as the income

---

[24]The cheap labor argument was discussed in Chapter 5.

[25]In an attempt to press governments to reach an agreement in the Uruguay round, the GATT Secretariat issued a short report, the subtitle of which sums up the problem beautifully: "Trade, the Uruguay Round, and the Consumer: The sting—how governments buy votes on trade with the consumer's money." GATT, *Focus* (GATT Newsletter), August–September 1993, pp. 4–7. The report includes interesting examples of studies of the cost of protection to consumers.

tax) allowed governments to reduce tariffs. Growing competition and nationalism checked the European free trade movement at the end of the nineteenth century.

The United States did not participate in the nineteenth century free trade movement. Moderate revenue tariffs were replaced by high tariffs in 1828 when a plan by supporters of free trade backfired. They had hoped that the inclusion of high tariffs on a wide range of inputs and final products would lead to general opposition and prevent the Tariff Act of 1828 from being passed. However, the act was passed and became known as the Tariff of Abominations. Strong opposition to the high tariff rates and excess tariff revenue led to tariff reductions. Tariffs were increased to raise revenue during the Civil War. The **cheap labor** and the **infant industry argument** were used to justify protection after the Civil War.

After World War I protection grew and culminated in the **Smoot–Hawley Tariff** of 1930. This act led to protectionist policies in other countries and a decline in world trade. The Reciprocal Trade Agreements Act of 1934 allowed the president of the United States to negotiate tariff reductions with the major supplier of a product. The incorporation of the **most–favored–nation** clause helped reduce barriers by ensuring that tariff concessions were extended to other countries.

The experience of the interwar years led to the formation of the General Agreement on Tariffs and Trade (GATT). This organization coordinated negotiations to reduce trade barriers, interpreted rules governing the conduct of trade policy, and administered procedures for negotiated settlement of trade disputes. GATT was based on the principles of nondiscrimination, the resolution of disputes through negotiation, and the avoidance of quotas. GATT helped reduce developed countries' tariffs for manufactured goods to insignificant levels.

The last GATT agreement, the Uruguay round, was completed in 1994. Under the agreement there are to be lower tariffs, less support for agriculture and lower agricultural subsidies, tighter controls of policies to counter unfair trade, and a phasing out of the multifiber agreement. Also, a World Trade Organization will replace GATT. Non–tariff barriers remain a serious problem, and trade in services is still highly controlled. Other threats to trade include regional free trade agreements and concerns about low wages, differences in working conditions, and environmental issues.

Study Questions

1. Ricardo was not concerned about the effects of the repeal of the Corn Laws on the supply of domestic agricultural products. Consider the role of the domestic elasticity of supply of import substitutes in assessing the effects of protection.

2. What are the major reasons for the use of tariffs by the United States during the nineteenth century? When and why did the United States begin pursuing a free trade policy?
3. What are the economic principles on which the GATT and the WTO are based? What is the economic rationale for these principles?
4. Why did non–tariff barriers increase in the early 1980s? Give three examples of non–tariff barriers to trade.
5. Why might infant industries that have grown into efficient industries continue to argue for protection?
6. What are the most important international commercial policy problems today? Which problems were addressed by the Uruguay round?
7. What are voluntary export restraints? Give an example. Why are VERs inconsistent with GATT principles?
8. What legally constitutes a case of dumping? What is the economic rationale for protection against dumping? What are the difficulties that may be encountered in assessing whether a product is being dumped?
9. "If foreign countries have tariffs, we should impose them." Comment on this view with reference to the experience following the Smoot–Hawley Act.

Selected References

Coughlin, C. C. and G. E. Wood, "An Introduction to Non–Tariff Barriers to Trade," *Federal Reserve Bank of St. Louis Review*, 71, January/February 1989, pp. 32–46.

Dam, K., *The GATT: Law and International Organization*, Chicago: University of Chicago Press, 1970.

DeVault, J. M., "The Impact of U.S. Unfair Trade Laws—A Preliminary Assessment," *Weltwirtschaftliches Archiv*, 1993, pp. 735–51.

Dobson, J. M., *Two Centuries of Tariffs: The Background and Emergence of the International Trade Commission*, Washington, DC: U.S. Government Printing Office, 1976.

Evans, J. W., *The Kennedy Round in American Trade Policy: The Twilight of the Gatt?* Cambridge, MA: Harvard University Press, 1971.

GATT, *Focus* (GATT Newsletter), GATT, Geneva, Switzerland.

GATT, *News of the Uruguay Round*, various issues as follows:
"The Final Act of the Uruguay Round"
"The Uruguay Round Deal: An Outline of the New Multilateral Trading System"
"The World Trade Organization"
"Increases in Market Access Resulting from the Uruguay Round"
Published in April 1994, by GATT, Geneva, Switzerland.

Kelly, M., et al., *Issues and Developments in International Trade Policy*, International Monetary Fund Occasional Paper No. 63, Washington DC: IMF, December 1988.

Kenwood, A. G. and A. L. Lougheed, *The Growth of the International Economy: 1820–1980*, Boston: George Allen and Unwin, 1983.

Ratner, S., *The Tariff in American History*, New York: Van Nostrand Company, 1972.

Tarr, D. G. and M. E. Morke, *Aggregate Costs to the United States of Tariffs and Quotas on Imports: General Tariff Cuts and Removal of Quotas on Automobiles, Steel, Sugar, and Textiles*, Washington, DC: Federal Trade Commission, December 1984.

Taussig, F. W., *The Tariff History of the United States*, 8e, New York: G. P. Putnam's Sons, Capricorn Books Edition, 1964.

Tussie, D., *The Less Developed Countries and the World Trading System: A Challenge to the GATT*, London: Francis Pinter, 1987.

U.S. Department of Commerce, *Business America* (special NAFTA issue), October 18, 1993.

World Bank, *World Development Report 1987*, New York: Oxford University Press, 1987.

Part Four

Topics in International Economics

Sixteen

International Banking and the Eurocurrency Market

Introduction

The rise of the Eurocurrency market is one of the most significant developments in international finance since World War II. The market's rate of growth has been spectacular. During the 1960s and 1970s the market grew by more than 20 percent per year. The Eurocurrency market is the major part of an international banking market with a value of $3,720 billion in 1993. This market is now a far more important source of international loans than official institutions such as the IMF. Some argue that the market is beneficial because it increases the efficiency of the world capital market and thereby increases world income. Others have blamed the market for causing inflation and exchange rate instability. In this chapter we shall describe the nature and functions of the market and critically evaluate the major arguments used by those who argue that the market should be regulated.

The Nature of the Market

The **Eurocurrency market** is an international banking market. London is the largest center and accounts for between 20 and 25 percent of the market. Eurocurrency banking centers also include other European countries, the Bahamas, Bahrain, Canada, the Cayman Islands, Japan, Hong Kong, Singapore, and the United States.[1] The "Euro" part of the term Eurocurrency reflects the European origins of the market, not its current location.

Loans and deposits are made in many currencies, but the U.S. dollar is the most popular currency for transactions. Hence, the market is sometimes referred to as the **Eurodollar market**. A **Eurodollar** is a dollar deposit held by a bank outside the United States. More generally, a **Eurocurrency deposit** is a deposit with a bank located outside the country from which the deposited currency originates. For example, a **Euromark** is a mark–denominated deposit held with a bank outside Germany, and a

---

[1]See the discussion of IBFs (to come) for comments relating to the U.S. share of the market.

371

Eurofranc is a franc–denominated deposit held with a bank outside France. Because the banks in one country deal in the currencies of other countries, the market is sometimes known as an **offshore banking market**. We shall refer to Eurocurrencies and the Eurocurrency market unless specifically referring to deposits in a particular currency.

The Size of the Market

International lending can be thought of as being divided into three types of activity: first, lending to foreigners (cross–border lending) of domestic currency; second, cross–border lending of foreign currency; and third, lending in foreign currency to domestic residents. (Eurocurrency lending can be defined as foreign currency lending to residents and nonresidents.) Foreign currency lending to nonresidents is by far the largest of the three sectors of international banking.

Table 16.1 shows the size of these three sectors and the overall size of the international banking market. Lending to foreigners is shown in the table as "cross–border claims" and lending of foreign currency in the domestic market is shown as "local claims in foreign currency." The gross figures represent total loans and are an overestimate of the credit provided by the market because a deposit in one bank may be loaned to another bank before being loaned to a final user. The net figure of $3,720 billion for the international banking market represents the size of the market after adjustment for interbank transactions, and is a more accurate indication of credit provision.

Table 16.1
International Lending

Cross–border claims	6227.9
in domestic currency	1640.9
in foreign currency	4587
Local claims in foreign currency	1097.5
Total international bank claims	7325.4
minus interbank double counting	3605.4
A) Net international bank credit	3720
B) Net Euronote placement	209.5
C) Net international bond financing	1774.9
Total international financing (A + B + C)	5704.4
minus double counting[a]	604.4
Total net international financing	5100

[a]International bonds purchased or issued by banks included above in bank credit.

Source: BIS, *International Banking and Financial Market Developments*, Basle, November, 1993.

Table 16.2
Currency Breakdown of Bank Liabilities

	Cross Border		Foreign Currency to Residents
	Domestic Currency	Foreign Currency	
Dollar	609.0	1609.8	571.3
Other	766.3	1745.6	396.1
Of which,			
Deutsche mark	145.1	570.7	136.5
French franc	120.5	135.6	28.5
Japanese yen	179.0	154.3	35.8
Sterling	131.4	120.1	24.6
Swiss franc	55.1	148.7	34.1
ECU	—	172.6	50.3

Source: BIS, *International Banking and Financial Market Developments*, Basle, November, 1993.

Even after adjusting for interbank deposits, the market is large. By way of illustration, the American money supply (M1) in 1994 was about $1,300 billion, approximately one third of the net size of the international banking market.

Table 16.2 shows the currency composition of bank liabilities (deposits). The table shows clearly the importance of the U.S. dollar in the Eurocurrency market: Eurodollars account for about half of Eurocurrency liabilities.

The Eurodollar market allows nonresidents to trade ownership of dollar deposits held in banks in the United States. For example, when a dollar deposit is made with Barclays Bank International in London, Barclays may deposit the dollars in its account with a bank in the United States. In this case, Barclays has an asset, a claim on an American bank, and a liability to the depositor. The dollar deposit in London is a Eurodollar deposit. When Barclays makes a loan, it transfers ownership of the deposit with the American bank. Therefore, a necessary condition for the operation of the Eurodollar market is that the United States does not restrict holdings or transfers of dollar deposits, that is, nonresident convertibility must not be restricted. A second condition is that foreign countries must not restrict their citizens from holding or transferring foreign currency deposits.

Why Dollars?

These two conditions allowed the Eurodollar market to grow, but why were dollars chosen? The use of the dollar in the Eurocurrency market is a reflection of the role of the dollar in the international monetary system. The dollar is used as the currency of denomination for most international contracts. Why are international contracts between residents of other countries usually expressed in dollars and not in the currency of one of the contracting parties? The reason is that by using one currency, people reduce the amount of information they need. When contracts are negotiated in dollars, traders only need to know the value of their currencies relative to the dollar. (During the Bretton Woods period, the dollar was a natural currency for people to choose because countries fixed the values of their currencies against the dollar.) Also, some contracts tend to take place in dollars because the United States is the world's most important trading nation.

The Availability of Loans in Other Currencies

Although half of Eurocurrency loans are made in dollars, loans in other currencies are easily obtained. There are two ways of obtaining a loan in another currency. The first is to borrow the currency directly from a Eurobank. The second is to borrow dollars from a Eurobank, convert the dollars into the required currency in the foreign exchange market, and cover the price of dollars needed to repay the loan in the forward exchange market. Because people can borrow other currencies directly or obtain the currencies via dollar loans, arbitrage ensures that the costs of these loans are virtually identical. For example, arbitrage ensures that the forward premium between dollars and marks is almost identical to the difference between the interest rates charged on Eurodollars and Euromarks.

The International Bond Market

The international bond market is much smaller than the Eurocurrency market. Governments, international institutions, and large companies are the major borrowers in the bond market. There are many types of international bonds. For example, a Eurobond is a bond sold outside the country that issues the currency in which the bond is denominated. International bonds are sometimes used as a way of avoiding the regulatory restrictions that apply to issues of bonds within national capital markets. From the investors' perspective, the bond market differs from the Eurocurrency market because Eurocurrency deposits are nonmarketable claims against financial intermediaries (banks), whereas bonds are marketable claims against borrowers (governments or corporations) that are held directly by lenders. From the borrowers' perspective, Eurocurrency loans are usually made for short periods at flexible interest rates, whereas bonds are for long periods and usually have fixed interest rates.[2]

Functions of the Eurocurrency Market

The Functions of the Market

In order to understand the reasons for the growth of the Eurocurrency market, we must appreciate the services it performs. Essentially, the Eurobanks perform the same services as banks in the domestic money market, that is, they act as financial intermediaries and engage in maturity transformation.

Financial Intermediation

Banks act as financial intermediaries by taking funds from people who want to lend and making loans to people who want to borrow. Banks reduce the transaction costs of loans because borrowers and lenders do not have to "find each other." Another aspect of the service is that a bank substitutes its creditworthiness for that of its borrowers. For example, a customer holding a deposit with Barclays has a claim on Barclays, not on the person who borrows the money from Barclays. Banks can do this because they have experience and information that allow them to assess risk more accurately than individuals. Also, the scale of their operations means that losses on some loans are expected and accepted because they are offset by profits on other loans. It is less likely that the number of transactions undertaken by an individual would be large enough to average out risk in this way.[3]

It is clear from Table 16.1 that interbank transactions are an important part of the market. Interbank transactions are partly a reflection of the role of banks as financial intermediaries. When a bank takes a deposit, it does not need to have a borrower waiting because it can lend the funds to other banks who are in need of funds. But interbank transactions have other important functions. For example, they allow banks to alter the composition of their balance sheets to take account of factors such as currency composition and loan maturity. Also, interbank trading provides banks with information about the market and maintains contacts with other banks.

---

[2]Euronotes are short–term securities. Floating rate notes, bonds with flexible interest rates, are also available, but they are less common than fixed rate issues.

[3]Some loans are even too large for individual banks. A group of banks may form a syndicate to provide a large loan and spread the risk.

Maturity Transformation

Eurocurrency deposits are time deposits, that is, depositors cannot withdraw their funds at will. The deposit period may be as short as one day, or six months, or more. The majority of deposits are for less than six months. These funds are often loaned out for much longer periods, sometimes for years. When banks borrow for short periods and lend for longer periods it is known as **maturity transformation**. Banks can do this because many deposits that are made for short periods are reinvested at the end of the deposit period, and funds that are not reinvested are replaced by new funds. Thus, banks can behave as though the funds had been invested for a much longer period.

National Banking and the "Need" for Eurocurrency Banks

National banks dealing in the currency of the country in which they are located can and do provide these services to the international community, as Table 16.2 shows. Thus, in a sense, the Eurocurrency market is not strictly necessary. Why, then, do people bother with Eurobanks? Why not use an American bank for dollar banking services and a British bank for sterling banking services? One simple reason is that multinational companies need to be able to make deposits and obtain loans in a wide range of currencies.

Eurobanks can compete with national banks because they are able to pay higher interest rates on deposits and charge lower interest rates on loans. The difference or **spread** between the deposit and loan rates is one way in which banks make money.[4] Figure 16.1 shows the normal relationship between the spread on dollars for a Eurobank and an American Bank.[5]

The main reason why Eurobanks can operate with a narrower spread than national banks is that Eurobanks are not subject to regulations; in particular, there are no reserve requirements in the Eurocurrency market. The larger the percentage of deposits that a bank is able to loan out, the larger the revenue of the bank. American banks are required to maintain minimum ratios of reserves to deposits, which prevents them from lending out all the money deposited with them. Therefore, Eurobanks can operate with a narrower spread than American banks because a higher percentage of their deposits are loaned out. Reserve requirements foster confidence in the national banking system and ensure that there are adequate funds to meet day–to–day withdrawals. Eurobanks only handle time deposits and do not

---

[4]A bank may also charge a fee when a loan is made.

[5]Dufey and Giddy (1978, pp. 52–54) discuss the comparability of interest rates in the Eurocurrency market and the American money market.

Figure 16.1
Spreads in the Eurodollar and American Markets

The difference between the rate paid to depositors and the rate charged to borrowers is called the spread. Banks earn money from the size of the spread. Because Eurobanks are not regulated and do not pay deposit insurance, they are able to operate with a smaller spread than American banks.

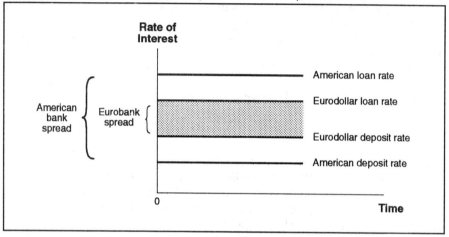

need to maintain reserves to meet withdrawal requests. A second reason why Eurobanks have a smaller spread than American banks is that Eurobanks are not subject to the deposit insurance charges levied by the Federal Deposit Insurance Corporation on national banks.

Another reason for the narrow spread, which is often quoted, is that Eurobanks only deal in large sums of money ($5 million or more). The paperwork is similar for transactions of $1 thousand or $5 million. Thus, the percentage change needed to cover the costs of the transaction declines as the size of the transaction increases. However, this explanation of the narrow spread offered by Eurobanks is not convincing because there is nothing to prevent national banks from reducing spreads by dealing in large sums.

Political Risk

The Eurocurrency market would be able to attract funds even if there were no financial incentive to use it. The reason is that it allows customers to reduce **political risk**. When a person invests in a country, the investment lies within the political jurisdiction of that country. Taxes may be imposed, the assets may be seized, or controls may be introduced by the government to deprive the investor of the right to withdraw the funds. For example, in 1979 Iranian assets in the United States were frozen following the siege of the

American embassy in Tehran and the taking of the American hostages. Iranian dollar deposits with banks outside the United States were outside the political jurisdiction of the United States and were not affected. This incident contributed to the growth of Arab banking in centers such as Bahrain.

The risk that a government will seize the assets of a Eurobank is small. Eurobanks do not maintain reserves, and their assets (loans) and liabilities (deposits) are usually with nonresidents. Thus, there is virtually nothing to seize in a Eurobank. Also, since only one branch of an international bank is likely to be affected, the bank would merely have to announce that its bookkeeping had moved to another branch.

The Growth of the Eurocurrency Market

Soviet Gold

Many people suggest that the origins of the modern Eurocurrency market can be traced to the early 1950s, when the proceeds from Soviet gold sales were deposited by the Moscow Narodny bank with European banks. It would have been somewhat strange for the leader of the communist world to invest its funds in the largest and richest capitalist nation.[6] Also, the funds would have been within the political jurisdiction of the American government, which, during the Cold War, would not have been a sensible investment. In other words, the Soviet Union sought to avoid political risk by investing dollars outside the political jurisdiction of the United States.

The Importance of Regulations

Although Soviet deposits of revenue from gold sales are an interesting explanation of the origins of the Eurocurrency market, two regulatory changes at the end of the 1950s were more important. The first concerned the international role of sterling. After World War II, London resumed its role as a center of international finance, and British banks provided sterling finance for trade between third countries. When the Bank of England restricted the provision of sterling credit to nonresidents (during a period of speculative capital flows in 1957), people turned to the use of dollars, and British banks tried to maintain their international business by dealing in dollars. The second change occurred in 1958 when European countries reduced restrictions on their citizens holding dollars (as part of the return of their

---

[6]Eurobanks often loaned the funds to the United States; therefore, the Soviet Union was lending indirectly to the United States.

currencies to convertibility). These two regulatory changes set the stage for the growth of international dollar banking.

American banks might have provided dollar banking services to the world, had American regulations not prevented them from doing so. The explosion of the Eurodollar market that began in the mid–1960s was largely the result of regulations imposed by the United States. One famous regulation, Regulation Q, limited the interest rates that could be paid to depositors in the United States. Eurobanks were not subject to this regulation and were able to offer higher rates of interest to attract dollar deposits. Eurodollar deposits taken from American customers were sometimes even loaned back to American banks or American customers because the interest rate ceiling resulted in a shortage of funds in the American money market.[7] American banks were also restrained from providing loans for investment abroad (voluntary restraint in 1965 was followed by mandatory controls in 1968). Note, however, that the United States did not restrict nonresident convertibility, thus offshore dollar banking was feasible.

The growth of international dollar banking by American banks was constrained by regulation, but the British government took steps to separate domestic and international banking. British banks were allowed to provide foreign currency banking services to nonresidents, and restrictions were imposed to prevent British residents from using these facilities to transfer funds into or out of Britain. In this way, Britain was able to provide international banking while retaining protection from what was thought to be the danger of destabilizing capital flows. It was feared that capital flows would undermine the stability of sterling's exchange rate and disrupt the British monetary system.[8]

More recently, American regulations have been relaxed in the hope of attracting international banking business. In 1981, the Federal Reserve allowed American banks to establish **international banking facilities (IBFs)**. IBFs are exempt from domestic American reserve requirements, although they are subject to (lower) Eurocurrency reserve requirements. They can only take deposits from foreigners, and deposits and withdrawals cannot be for less than $100,000. The purpose of these regulations is to allow American banks to compete in the international banking market while allowing the Federal

---

[7]Borrowing by American banks from the Eurodollar market fell as a result of restrictions imposed by the Federal Reserve in 1969 and the easing of Regulation Q in 1973.

[8]Britain abolished capital controls in October 1979.

Reserve to retain control over banks providing funds to the domestic market.[9]

The Eurocurrency Market and the American Balance of Payments

One early explanation of the growth of the Eurodollar market was that American balance of payments deficits increased the amount of dollars held by foreigners.[10] In fact, the growth of the Eurodollar market is not directly related to American balance of payments deficits. American deficits are neither necessary nor sufficient for the Eurodollar market to grow. Two facts are enough to illustrate this: (1) the Eurodollar market has grown continuously, in years of large deficits and small deficits; and (2) Euromark and Euroyen deposits increased even though Germany and Japan did not have balance of payments deficits. It is easy to show how the Eurodollar market can grow without an American deficit. When an American makes a deposit in the Eurodollar market that finances a loan to another American, a capital outflow is matched by a capital inflow, the balance of payments is not affected, but the Eurodollar market increases by the amount of the deposit.

American balance of payments deficits did help the growth of the Eurodollar market in one way. In the early 1970s, countries were trying to maintain fixed exchange rates. Faced with large American deficits, foreign central banks bought dollars to prevent their currencies from rising against the dollar. Some of these dollars were deposited in the Eurodollar market, and the market expanded. Depositing international reserves in the Eurodollar market is still a common practice.

OPEC Recycling

The Eurocurrency market received a boost when OPEC oil revenue was deposited in the market following the oil price increase of 1973–74. The oil price increase had led to fears that oil importing countries would be short of funds to finance their deficits. The Eurocurrency market played its role as a financial intermediary by quickly and efficiently recycling funds from oil exporters to oil importers, and a crisis was avoided. The size of Eurocurrency

---

[9]The regulations governing IBFs are described in the Federal Reserve Bulletin, October 1982. IBFs accounted for under 6 percent of the market in June 1993, measured as a percentage of the stock of liabilities resulting from external positions. (BIS, *International Banking and Financial Market Developments*, Basle, November, 1993).

[10]In this context, the term *balance of payments* refers to a measure such as the basic balance or official settlements balance.

market activity in these years was unprecedented. The flow of funds from oil exporters into the market was about $24 billion in 1974.[11] This recycling was achieved without massive disruption, and is often used as an example of the efficiency of the Eurocurrency market.

Other Explanations of the Growth of the Eurocurrency Market

Finally, the Eurocurrency market may have grown because traders and investors who use foreign currencies continuously find the proximity of Eurobanks useful. Communications between countries were not as efficient in the mid–1960s as they are today, and it understandable that Europeans would have preferred European banks to American banks. Even now, although dollar banking with American banks may be technically feasible for Europeans, local banks may be more familiar with and responsive to their customers' needs.[12] In addition, European banks keep the same hours as European investors; the minimum time difference between the United States and Europe is five hours.[13]

Although many factors contributed to the growth of the Eurocurrency market, the basic justification for Eurobanks is probably economic. When Eurobanks offer higher deposit rates and charge lower loan rates than national banks, why look any further? However, the growth of Eurobanking should not be seen in isolation. It took place against a background of increasing trade and improved communication between countries. When viewed against this background, the Eurocurrency market's growth can be seen as a response to the desire of investors and borrowers to increase the international diversity of their assets and liabilities.[14]

---

[11]Bank for International Settlements, *45th Annual Report*, 1975, p. 139.

[12]Given that Luxembourg is bordered by Belgium, France, and Germany, it is not surprising that Luxembourg has become a major banking center. (Luxembourg has strict banking secrecy laws, and customers from neighboring countries have been able to avoid regulations and taxes by banking in Luxembourg.)

[13]This suggests that banks are more likely to compete with other banks in the same time zone than with banks in different time zones. Thus, IBFs in New York are more likely to compete with Eurocurrency centers in the Caribbean, such as the Bahamas or the Cayman Islands, than with European centers.

[14]One of the reasons for the lack of growth in 1991 was that Japanese banks decided to invest less abroad (after experiencing losses from a decline in the value of the dollar relative to the yen).

Criticisms and Proposals for Reform

The Eurocurrency market increases the efficiency of the international market by reducing the cost of capital transfers. Therefore, we would expect the world level of income to increase as a result of a more efficient allocation of capital. Regulation of the market would increase the costs of capital transfers and reduce capital mobility, but some people have argued that regulation is needed.

Confidence in the Banking System

One of the most common arguments in favor of regulation is that the Eurocurrency market is inherently unstable. It is argued that because the participants are closely linked through interbank deposits, the collapse of one bank could lead to the collapse of other banks, and therefore to international monetary chaos. This argument is plausible in the sense that the banks are closely linked by interbank deposits. However, the scenario is less convincing when we consider how a bank might collapse.

The classic scenario of a loss of confidence leading to a run on the bank, as happened in the 1930s in the United States, is not possible because Eurocurrency deposits are time deposits. They cannot be withdrawn at will. Deposits might be withdrawn gradually, but the answer to falling deposits is simple: raising interest rates will attract new deposits or persuade customers not to withdraw their funds. The banks are able to increase interest rates because they do not give fixed interest rate loans. Long–term loans include provisions to revise the interest rate at regular intervals to reflect changes in market interest rates. The loan rate is usually defined as a margin above the U.S. prime rate or the London interbank offer rate (LIBOR), the rate at which one bank can obtain funds from another bank.

Default Risk

A default by one or more major borrowers that leads to a loss of assets is a more serious potential source of instability. This danger seems important to observers who compare traditional national banking and Eurobanking because domestic banks are protected by the monetary authorities from bankruptcy. For example, the Federal Deposit Insurance Corporation guarantees deposits up to $100,000, and ultimately the stability of the American monetary system is protected by the Federal Reserve. There is no guarantee or protection for depositors in the Eurocurrency market. This problem has received some attention as a result of defaults by developing countries that are significant borrowers from the market. One answer has been to set aside reserves to offset possible defaults. However, these reserves may not be enough to offset a default by a major borrower.[15]

Although there is a possibility that defaults will lead to the collapse of Eurobanks, the problem is not confined to the Eurocurrency market; the problem exists whether national or international banks have made such loans. Put simply, the danger of collapse is not a justification for regulation, because regulation of Eurobanks cannot prevent defaults by debtor countries. Also, experience in the United States (in the savings and loan sector) shows that when banks are protected from collapse, they have less of an incentive to make prudent loans.

There is little reason to be concerned about the risk that Eurocurrency deposits will be lost if a Eurobank collapses. That is a risk depositors accept when they make a deposit (in a bank which does not have deposit insurance).[16] The significance of the possibility of collapse is that domestic money supplies may be disrupted. Eurobanks are overseas offices of large domestic banks. If a domestic bank is at risk, the domestic monetary authorities should intervene to ensure that the collapse of one or more banks does not lead to a collapse of the domestic money supply. This can be achieved by the Federal Reserve guaranteeing deposits held with domestic banks. To some extent, Eurocurrency deposits may be protected indirectly by support for the parent banks from the domestic monetary authorities in their home countries.

Increased Capital Mobility

It has been suggested that the Eurocurrency market reduces welfare by encouraging destabilizing short–term capital flows. Capital flows can be financed by loans from traditional national banks, but it may be that the Eurocurrency market encourages capital transfers by reducing their cost. The alleged problems caused by short–term capital mobility include a reduction of national monetary autonomy and increased exchange rate instability.

---

[15]Setting aside reserves has stopped the downward trend in the ratio of bank equity to total assets, and reduced the ratio of developing countries' debt to total assets.

[16]Perhaps there is an argument for regulation to prevent depositors losing from mismanagement or even fraud. The collapse of the Bank of Credit and Commerce International (BCCI) illustrates this danger. The bank was able to avoid supervision because BCCI had headquarters in London, Luxembourg, and the Cayman Islands. However, is there a problem if depositors lose money when they knew they were investing in a bank which was not subject to national regulations and not part of a national deposit insurance scheme?

Lack of Monetary Autonomy

Assume that a country attempts to reduce aggregate demand by reducing its money supply. Domestic interest rates tend to rise relative to world rates and the value of domestic currency tends to increase (because capital inflows increase relative to capital outflows). Recall that under fixed exchange rates, as the value of domestic currency tends to rise, the monetary authorities must intervene in the foreign exchange market and sell domestic currency for foreign currency. In this case, the initial reduction in the money supply tends to be offset by an expansion of the money supply caused by foreign exchange market intervention. Thus, under fixed exchange rates, the effectiveness of monetary policy is reduced by capital flows.

There is less reason to be concerned about monetary autonomy being undermined by capital flows when a country does not have a fixed exchange rate, because the monetary authorities do not have to intervene to stabilize the value of domestic currency. Thus, changes in the money supply are not offset by the effects of intervention in the foreign exchange market. On the contrary, when a country has a floating exchange rate, the effectiveness of monetary policy may be increased by capital flows. For example, if the cut in the money supply is part of a counter–inflation package, an appreciation of domestic currency may be welcomed because it will help keep prices down: appreciation reduces import prices and reduces aggregate demand by reducing net exports.

Exchange Rate Stability

While most major countries have abandoned rigidly fixed exchange rates, most countries still attempt to maintain stable exchange rates in one way or another. Under the present exchange rate system, one of the main issues is the effect of capital flows on exchange rate stability.[17] There seems to be some evidence that capital flows may have increased exchange rate variability, but there is little agreement on the size of the costs of exchange rate variability. Also, some people have argued that unstable capital flows reflect unstable economic policies, that is, they are not an independent source of instability. It may be that restricting capital flows would have little effect on economic stability. Although the benefits of reduced capital mobility are disputed, the costs of reduced capital mobility are clearer. Restricting capital flows would prevent some productive investments from being undertaken, and would reduce real income. This result is inevitable because it is

---

[17]See Chapter 14.

impossible to distinguish between short–term speculative capital flows and flows of capital that finance productive investments.[18]

International Inflation

The view that the growth of the Eurocurrency market leads to world inflation is usually based on the idea that the market creates money in the same way as the domestic banking system. It is true that the Eurocurrency market can lead to an increase in total bank deposits. For example, when a person withdraws dollars from an American domestic bank and deposits them with a Eurobank, the Eurobank may then deposit the dollars with an American bank. In this case, American bank deposits remain unchanged and the Eurocurrency market has grown, thus total world bank deposits have increased. A broad measure of money (such as M3, which includes long–term time deposits) would show an increase in the world money supply.[19]

However, if a narrow definition of money is adopted (such as M1, which focuses on the role of money as a medium of exchange), the Eurocurrency market does not lead to an expansion of the money supply. This is because Eurocurrency deposits cannot be spent. They are time deposits, and Eurocurrency checking accounts do not exist. In other words, Eurocurrency deposits are a store of value, not a medium of exchange. Therefore, it is more appropriate to think of Eurocurrency deposits as investments rather than as money. Returning to the example of the creation of a Eurodollar deposit, there is only one sum of dollars to be spent. When the Eurobank makes a loan, it transfers ownership of these dollars; it does not create money.[20] Therefore, monetary policy can still be used to control inflation by controlling the supply of dollars.

Two qualifications must be added. First, companies may hold their working balances in the form of short–term Eurocurrency deposits rather than demand deposits. If so, funds that would otherwise have been left idle are loaned out through the Eurocurrency market. Therefore, the velocity of

---

[18]It is disconcerting to find politicians stating that stable exchange rates are necessary to encourage international trade and investment, and that in order to maintain stable exchange rates, controls on capital flows (investment) are needed.

[19]The overall American money supply would stay the same because American money supply figures include dollar deposits with American banks even if they are held by nonresidents. The figures would merely show a transfer of ownership of an American deposit (from the individual to the Eurobank).

[20]In contrast, when a domestic bank makes a loan, it creates a new deposit, which is a form of money because checks can be drawn against the deposit.

circulation of money is increased, and this may have a small inflationary effect. Second, future financial developments in the market may lead to easier access to deposits and blur the distinction between investment funds and narrowly defined money. To the extent that such developments make it easier to conduct transactions with Eurocurrency deposits, there is a potential inflationary effect.

One simple argument against the view that the Eurocurrency market causes inflation is that the rate of inflation has not been related to the growth of the market. It is true that during the 1970s inflation accelerated while the Eurocurrency market was growing, but inflation fell during the 1980s as the Eurocurrency market continued to grow. Therefore, the argument that the growth of the market necessarily causes international inflation is unacceptable. However, the Eurocurrency market may have had an inflationary effect in some countries.

The Eurocurrency Market and International Adjustment

During the 1970s, countries in balance of payments difficulties were able to avoid IMF conditions on loans by borrowing from the Eurocurrency market. This may have contributed to international inflation by allowing some countries to pursue inflationary policies. For example, international loans allowed governments to finance budget deficits and maintain overvalued exchange rates. Opponents of regulation point to the ease with which petro–dollars were recycled. Loans made to finance oil imports added to the debts of developing countries, but at the time there was probably no other way to pay for imported oil. Oil imports could not be cut quickly, and it would have been difficult for a country to pay for imported oil by reducing its consumption of other imported goods. Moreover, if all oil–importing countries had attempted to pay for oil imports by cutting back their consumption of other imports, there would have been a collapse of world trade and a severe world recession. Therefore, it was desirable that oil imports be financed to some extent by debt.

The international debt problem, rather than international inflation, led to the recognition that Eurocurrency loans may have been too easily obtained. As a result, banks now often require that countries secure IMF loans and agree to IMF conditions before new bank loans are made. This procedure is sometimes criticized, in part because there is substantial controversy over the appropriate conditions (if any) that the IMF should attach to international loans.

Will Regulation Happen?

The most important argument against regulation is the most simple: it is unlikely to happen. The major reason is that there are wide differences of opinion over whether there is a need for regulation. Even if countries agreed on the need for reform, and the nature that the reform should take, there would always be an incentive for one country to refrain from joining in the hope that it would increase its share of the Eurocurrency market. Regulation by one country is not feasible. If one country attempted to regulate the banks, the banks would simply find a more hospitable place from which to work.

It is conceivable that a group of countries might try to act together. For example, the European Union is moving toward unified regulations and standards for goods and services as part of an effort to create a single European market.[21] While some control may be possible, regulation of European Eurocurrency banking would encourage competition from banks outside Europe. Within the European Union, a move toward more similar regulations might have an adverse effect on countries that have been able to succeed in banking because they have had appropriate national laws, for example, the United Kingdom.

Summary of Main Points

A **Eurocurrency deposit** is a deposit held by a bank outside the country that issues the currency in which the deposit is denominated. For this reason, Eurocurrency banking is sometimes known as **offshore banking**. Eurocurrencies are time deposits with maturities from one day to six months or more.

The banks that provide Eurocurrency banking provide basically the same services as domestic banks: **financial intermediation** and **maturity transformation**. Because Eurobanks do not have to pay deposit insurance or comply with regulations such as reserve requirements, they can usually offer higher deposit rates and charge lower loan rates than national banks offering the same services to foreigners. Also, Eurocurrency deposits allow investors to reduce **political risk** because the deposits are held outside the political jurisdiction of the country that issues the currency in which the deposits are denominated.

The modern Eurodollar market is often traced to Soviet deposits of dollar revenue from gold sales. Tight American regulation of banking activities

---

[21]For example, the Commission of the European Union has introduced a banking directive which will require that all deposits in the European Union are protected by the same minimum level of deposit insurance.

combined with relatively unregulated dollar banking in Europe was a major factor contributing to the growth of the market in the early 1960s. The market continued to grow as central banks deposited international reserves and OPEC deposited revenue from oil sales. The recycling of oil revenue as loans to oil importers is an important example of the Eurocurrency market acting as a financial intermediary.

The growth of the Eurocurrency market can be viewed as part of the overall trend toward greater international trade and investment. The market provides international banking services to governments and multinational corporations. Because the market is highly efficient, it reduces the cost of transactions, leads to increased capital mobility, and contributes to higher global income.

The Eurocurrency market has been criticized for contributing to exchange rate instability (by increasing capital mobility). Although there may be some truth in this criticism, restricting capital flows would tend to reduce welfare by reducing productive investments. Lack of regulation has led to fears that the Eurobanks could collapse and to proposals for regulation. However, there is little danger of a run on Eurobanks because they offer time deposits. Also, the Eurobanks make variable interest rate loans; thus, a gradual reduction in deposits could be halted by increasing deposit and loan rates.

To some extent, the banks are also protected because they are overseas offices of large domestic banks. Thus, the obligation of the monetary authorities to prevent domestic banks from collapsing implicitly provides some protection to the Eurobanks. The main danger to Eurobanks is that defaults by major debtor nations could lead to a loss of assets. This danger is not a justification for regulation of Eurocurrency banking, because national banks face the same problem, and regulation of the Eurocurrency market would do nothing to prevent defaults.

The market has been criticized for contributing to world inflation. However, there is little evidence to support this criticism. The market did grow during the 1970s as inflation increased, but it continued to grow in the 1980s as inflation fell. Also, although the Eurocurrency market leads to an increase in global bank deposits, the Eurobanks do not create money in the same way as domestic banks: Eurobanks do not offer checking accounts because Eurodeposits are time deposits. However, perhaps the access to loans without conditions may have allowed some countries to pursue inflationary policies.

The major argument against regulation is that an international agreement to regulate the market is unlikely and regulation by one country would be ineffective because the banks could move their operations to non–regulated markets.

Study Questions

1. What is a Eurodollar? What is a Euromark? Use the regulatory changes of 1957–58 mentioned in the text to illustrate the conditions for a currency to be used in the Eurocurrency market.
2. Explain why the growth of the Eurocurrency market has been described as a response to regulation.
3. Why can Eurobanks offer higher deposit rates and lower loan rates than American banks?
4. How can Eurobanks operate without reserve ratios?
5. Domestic banks are regulated in order to maintain confidence in the system and to prevent collapse. How can the Eurocurrency market survive without regulation?
6. Why can't Eurobanks give long–term, fixed interest rate loans to developing countries?
7. In evaluating the argument that the Eurocurrency market causes inflation, why is it important to note that deposits in the Eurocurrency market are time deposits and that Eurocurrency loans are made by transferring ownership of bank deposits?
8. Critically evaluate the argument that the Eurocurrency market should be regulated with reference to the effects of the market on:
   a. exchange rates
   b. monetary autonomy
   c. inflation

Selected References

Bank for International Settlements, *63rd Annual Report*, BIS, Basle, Switzerland, 1993.

Bank for International Settlements, *International Banking and Financial Market Developments*, BIS, Basle, Switzerland, November 1993.

Davies, A. and A. Ball, "International Banking Markets," *Barclays Review*, 59, May 1984, pp. 37–41.

Dufey, G. and I. H. Giddy, *The International Money Market*, Englewood Cliffs, NJ: Prentice Hall, 1978.

Dufey, G. and I. H. Giddy, *The International Money Market*, 2e, Englewood Cliffs, NJ: Prentice Hall, 1994.

Frydl, E. J., "The Debate Over Regulating the Eurocurrency Markets," *Federal Reserve Bank of New York Quarterly Review*, Winter 1979–80, pp. 11–19.

Johnston, G. and A. Ball, "The Euromarkets and Monetary Expansion," *Barclays Review*, 55, February 1980, pp. 9–12.

Karlick, J. R., "Some Questions and Brief Answers About the Eurodollar Market," in R. E. Baldwin and J. D. Richardson, (eds.), *International Trade and Finance*, 2e, pp. 516–33, Boston: Little Brown, 1981.

Lewis, M. K. and K. T. Davis, *Domestic and International Banking*, Cambridge, MA: MIT Press, 1987.

McKinnon, R. I., *Money in International Exchange: The Convertible Currency System*, New York: Oxford University Press, 1979.

Park, Y. S. and J. Zwick, *International Banking in Theory and Practice*, Reading, MA: Addison Wesley, 1985.

Savona, P. and G. Sutija, (eds.), *Eurodollars and International Banking*, New York: St Martin's Press, 1985.

Throop, A. W., "Eurobanking and World Inflation," *Voice*, Federal Reserve Bank of Dallas, August 1979, pp. 8–23.

Watson, M., et al., *International Capital Markets: Developments and Prospects*, IMF Occasional Paper No. 43, Washington DC: International Monetary Fund, 1986.

Seventeen

The European Union[1]

Introduction

Exciting developments are taking place in Europe. Economic integration is being accompanied by social and political changes. Some countries have agreed to abolish passport requirements, and people can usually travel from one member country to another without being stopped at the border. People can and do live in one country and work in another. Language differences are still a barrier, and there are cultural differences. But a large part of Europe is gradually beginning to resemble a single country.

At the heart of these changes is the European Union (EU), the most important example of economic integration. Its twelve members are: Belgium, Denmark, France, Germany, Greece, Ireland, Italy, Luxembourg, the Netherlands, Portugal, Spain, and the United Kingdom.[2] In 1993, the group of twelve had a population of 346 million, and the income of the EU and the United States were about equal (at $6¼ trillion). Clearly, the union is an important market. The EU is also the world's largest trading block. If exports from one member to another are excluded, in 1992 the EU accounted for 13.6 percent of world exports, the United States accounted for 12.2 percent, and Japan 9.8 percent.

At present the three most important EU policies are a customs union, an agricultural policy, and an exchange rate policy. In this chapter we shall examine each of these polices. Proposals for European integration in other areas have been made, but progress has sometimes been difficult. We shall examine the prospects for further integration. In particular, we shall consider the proposal for European monetary union (a single European currency). Let us begin by considering the forms that economic integration may take.

---

[1]On November 1, 1993, the European Community became the European Union, as a result of the Maastricht agreement.

[2]Austria, Finland, and Sweden became members on January 1, 1995.

Degrees of Economic Integration

A **free trade area** is an area in which members remove barriers to trade between themselves, but retain separate barriers with nonmembers. To prevent goods moving into the area over the lowest national barrier, goods are taxed according to their origin. For example, an imported good may enter the area through a low–tariff country, but additional taxes are payable if the good then moves to a high–tariff country. The European Free Trade Area (EFTA) is an example of such an arrangement.[3]

A **customs union** goes beyond a free trade area with the addition of a common external tariff. A **common market** adds free mobility of factors of production to the requirements for a customs union. In other words, a common market embodies the freedom of movement of goods, services, people, and capital. The EU is rapidly approaching a common market, often referred to as the "single European market."

A **monetary union** is an area in which there is a single currency and capital flows are unrestricted. Economic policy need not necessarily be unified; for example, Belgium and Luxembourg have a single currency but separate economic policies.[4] However, it is normally assumed that economic and monetary union go together. In an **economic union**, government spending and taxation are carried out at a supranational level, although some taxes and spending may be under the control of national governments, in the same way that states have fiscal powers in the United States. The EU adopted monetary union as a target when the Treaty on EU (the Maastricht Treaty) was signed in February 1992.

---

[3]In 1992, the members of EFTA were: Austria, Finland, Iceland, Norway, Sweden, and Switzerland.

[4]An important example of a monetary union is the CFA (Communauté Financière Africaine), a group of 14 African countries which use the CFA franc (linked to the French franc) as their currency. The CFA is described in *IMF Survey*, January 24, 1994, p. 18.

History of the European Union

Early Cooperation

Proposals for European integration have been made for centuries.[5] The main driving force behind early proposals was usually the maintenance of peace, and it was for this reason that the proposals began to receive serious consideration following the experience of World War II. There was an element of idealism in the postwar era. People thought about the type of world they would like to create. European integration was seen as the way forward; for example, Winston Churchill referred to the development of a "United States of Europe." The United States helped the cause of integration by encouraging European countries to cooperate in their postwar recovery effort. It was felt that this was the only way Europe might eventually be able to compete with the United States. Also, European cooperation was encouraged for political reasons: a strong united Europe was seen as a deterrent to Soviet expansionism.

The European Coal and Steel Community

The movement that eventually led to the creation of the EU began with a proposal by Robert Schuman in 1950 to establish a body, the European Coal and Steel Community (ECSC), to plan the production and consumption of coal, iron, and steel in Europe. It was hoped that the ECSC would make war impossible by controlling the materials needed to wage war and establishing a common market in those materials. A revolutionary aspect of the proposal was that the body would be administered by a supranational authority with powers delegated to it by national governments. The ECSC came into existence in 1951. The six founding members were France, Germany, Italy, and the Benelux countries (Belgium, Luxembourg, and the Netherlands). Attempts to extend economic cooperation into political integration, by developing a common defense policy and forming a European army, failed because these measures would have reduced national sovereignty. Despite these setbacks, proposals for European cooperation and integration continued

---

[5]William Penn, after whom Pennsylvania is named, proposed in 1693 that central government in Europe was a way of achieving peace.

and resulted in the members of the ECSC signing the Treaty of Rome in 1957, which established the European Economic Community (EEC).[6]

The Treaty of Rome

The objective of the Treaty of Rome was to encourage economic growth and political harmony. Free trade between the members was seen as playing a crucial role in achieving this objective, but the founding members had more ambitious plans than the mere creation of a customs union. The treaty included policies to increase factor mobility with the objective of establishing a common market. The treaty also included provisions for common policies in the areas of agriculture and transport, and envisaged the development of policies to tackle regional and social problems. However, the only policy that was clearly outlined in the treaty was the common agricultural policy (CAP). National economic policy remained under the control of national governments, but members agreed to cooperate and coordinate policies.

The Progress of Integration

European economic integration proceeded well during the 1960s. The customs union was established and the agricultural policy adopted. In international monetary policy, progress was made beyond the Treaty of Rome with the development of a community exchange rate policy. After an initial failure in the early 1970s, the community successfully established the European Monetary System in 1979. Another development was the expansion of community membership. The membership of the European Economic Community increased to nine in 1973 when Denmark, Ireland, and the United Kingdom joined. In 1981, Greece became a member, and in 1985, Spain and Portugal joined. In 1994, membership terms were agreed on between the EU and the governments of Austria, Finland, Norway, and Sweden. Referenda were held in these four countries and all except Norway approved the terms of membership. Austria, Finland, and Sweden are scheduled to become members on January 1, 1995. The EU's membership will

---

[6]The United Kingdom was invited to join the ECSC but refused, in part because the government was unwilling to give up power to a European body. The United Kingdom did not join the EEC in 1957, partly for the same reason, and also because of concerns that its links would be weakened with former colonies that were members of the British Commonwealth.

probably expand again in the future because many of the countries that were part of the Soviet bloc want to join.[7]

A recent policy development is the attempt to remove the remaining barriers to trade in goods and services, and the remaining barriers preventing free movement of factors of production, thereby creating what is truly a single European market. This topic is discussed in the next section. Another interesting recent development is the serious interest in the possibility of creating a European monetary union. We discuss this topic later.

Commercial Policy

The EU is a customs union, that is, there is free internal trade and a common external tariff.[8] Also, because there is a common external tariff, the EU bargains as a group with other countries in international organizations such as GATT. To promote fair and free trade within the customs union, the EU's industrial policy promotes competition and regulates state support for industries. (The EU is not strictly a common market yet, because some barriers to factor mobility still exist. However, these barriers have been greatly reduced.)

The Effects of the Customs Union

The economic effects of a customs union were discussed in Chapter 5. The reader may recall that one of the difficulties in assessing the impact of a customs union is that a customs union promotes trade by lowering trade barriers between members, but trade between members may grow at the expense of trade with nonmembers. In practice, it is virtually impossible to say whether this is so because we cannot be sure how trade would have

---

[7]The people of Norway rejected EU membership partly because they were worried that their fishing would be destroyed. The EU's fishing policy is a disaster—the coastal waters around Europe are virtually dead as a result of over-fishing. There was also concern that the highly subsidized Norwegian farmers might lose from the EU's agricultural policy. Another issue was the financial cost of EU membership.

[8]The European Economic Area (EEA), which came into being at the beginning of 1994, joined Austria, Sweden, Finland, Norway, and Iceland with the EU in a free trade area of 372 million consumers with a combined gross domestic product approaching $7 trillion. This EEA effectively merged the European Free Trade Area with the EU. Switzerland, a member of EFTA, voted not to join the EEA because of concerns about possible immigration and because the Swiss feared that traffic crossing the alps by road would destroy the environment. The Swiss have voted to divert traffic crossing the Alps from roads to rail. While many people applaud the policy, it is opposed by the EU.

Table 17.1
The Changing Nature of EU Trade[a]

	As % of EU Trade		As % of EU Income	
	Intra–union Imports	Intra–union Exports	Intra–union Imports	Extra–union Imports
1980	49.2	55.7	12.1	12.4
1985	53.4	54.9	13.7	12.2
1990	58.8	61.0	13.5	9.7
1992	59.3	61.3	13.1	9.0

[a]The figures relate to the twelve members of the EU (excluding East Germany), even though Greece, Portugal, and Spain were not EU members for the whole period.

Source: *European Economy*, No. 55, 1993.

grown in the absence of the customs union. Table 17.1 shows the growth of trade of the twelve members of the EU. Imports from other members (intra–union imports) have increased as a percentage of total imports. Similarly, a larger share of exports now goes to other members. While the nominal value of trade with nonmembers has increased, trade with nonmember countries has declined as a percentage of union income.

The Welfare Effects of Customs Unions

In order to assess the effects of customs unions, it is necessary to predict what trade would have been if the customs union had not happened. The problem of what might have been plagues empirical studies of the effects of tariffs. Therefore, estimates of the welfare effects of the formation of the customs union cannot be perfect. Given this qualification, estimates of the static welfare effects of the formation of the customs union have generally suggested small welfare gains (less than 1 percent of the combined national incomes of the members). Why have studies suggested only small welfare gains?[9]

One reason is that the formation of a customs union only affects traded goods. For example, the output of the construction industry and a large part of the output of the service sector are not traded and are not directly affected by the removal of trade barriers. Another reason may be that tariffs are usually small to begin with (because countries avoid costly forms of protection), so the creation of a customs union entails the removal of small

---

[9]The following reasons are given by Swann (1988), p. 111.

barriers. Perhaps the most important explanation is that many of the benefits of a customs union are long–term benefits (such as economies of scale) resulting from an increase in the size of the market and increased competition. Studies of the short–term welfare effects of customs unions miss these long–term gains. The long–term benefits of a single market were used as part of the rationale for the union's attempt to progress beyond a customs union toward a full common market, the single European market. We shall return to this topic in a moment.

The Common External Tariff and EU Revenue

Tariffs paid for about one fifth of the budget of the EU in 1992. It may seem strange that we should find a revenue tariff used by a group of developed countries, since there are more efficient revenue raising methods of taxation than tariffs. The use of tariffs to fund the EU's activities is partly because agreement cannot be reached on establishing a union tax. Members of the EU have agreed to use value added taxes, part of the revenue of which is used to help finance the EU. However, the rates and the goods covered vary among member countries. Indeed, differences between taxes are one reason why goods still cannot move completely freely between countries. For example, as of late 1994, taxes on alcohol were higher in the United Kingdom than in other member states. While people returning there from holiday in another member country can import alcohol for personal consumption, they cannot import large amounts and resell it in the United Kingdom.

Establishing a Single European Market[10]

The objective of a single market was embodied in the Single European Act of 1987, which was the first amendment of the Treaty of Rome. The EU has not yet achieved its objective of removing all barriers to trade. An obvious sign that the European market is not free from restriction is that there are still customs posts between member countries. Although people travelling between countries within continental Europe usually face little inconvenience, goods cannot be moved without restriction. Apart from the direct costs arising from fees and taxes, customs posts act as barriers to trade because delays at borders and paperwork add to the costs of shipping goods across borders.

Before customs posts can be completely removed, ways to tackle non–economic issues such as public security and drug control must be found. For example, attempts are being made to develop a union immigration

---

[10]The following draws on Commission of the European Community, (1985).

policy—Germany faces particularly strong immigration pressure from poorer countries to the east. Economically, customs posts are necessary because of differences between members' technical standards and fiscal systems. Also, customs posts enforce bilateral agreements which members of the union have negotiated with nonmember countries, such as voluntary export restraints for cars and textiles. (Attempts are being made to replace these national agreements with union agreements.)

Differences Between Taxes and Technical Standards

People have an incentive to engage in cross–border shopping if indirect taxes differ significantly. For example, in the United States it is sometimes worthwhile to shop in a nearby state to avoid sales tax. Consumers living along the Canadian or Mexican borders often find a shopping trip over the border worthwhile. Taxes levied at borders can prevent this, but do so by weakening the unity of the market. Asking national governments to give up their rights to determine national tax rates seems unrealistic, but if customs posts are to be removed, fiscal systems must at least be approximated. This is one of the main challenges that the union faces in the next few years. For some people, approximation of fiscal systems is seen as a step on the road to full economic and monetary union.

Another barrier to trade is that technical standards differ between member countries. In order to promote market integration, the Commission attempts to replace national regulations, such as safety standards or packaging rules, by regulations applying to the whole union. This often creates controversy, such as when Germany was instructed to permit the sale of foreign beers that do not conform to the historical German definition of beer.[11] Writing and revising regulations is a continuous process because regulations must be updated and amended to take account of technical progress.

Factor Mobility and the Common Market

The Treaty of Rome obliged members to reduce restrictions on capital flows "to the extent necessary to ensure the proper functioning of the common market." In practice, member states retained restrictions on capital flows and regulated their capital markets in different ways. Most members have removed capital controls as part of the process toward the creation of a single European market. Fortunately, the costs of barriers to capital mobility were

---

[11]The sixteenth century *Reinheitsgebot* required that beer be made only from barley, hops, yeast, and water.

reduced by the development of a private international capital market, the Eurocurrency market.

Labor mobility is permitted in theory, but in practice labor mobility is not significant. Migrant workers from other member countries make up less than 2 percent of the union workforce. Unskilled labor faces few official obstacles, but skilled labor and professionals sometimes face problems because the qualifications earned in one member state are not always automatically accepted in other countries. The greatest progress has been made in the health sector. Doctors, nurses, dentists, veterinarians, midwives, and pharmacists now follow harmonized basic training, and have the right to practice in all member states. The major barriers to labor mobility are probably differences between cultures and languages. (Nine different languages are used in the twelve member countries of the EU.)

The Customs Union and Regional Policy

Lack of labor mobility contributes to regional differences between per capita incomes. The Treaty of Rome states that the objectives of the community are to be attained by reducing disparities between regions, but does not outline a policy. Some people feel that an effective regional policy should accompany a free trade policy because some regions may suffer as a result of free trade. For example, funds could be used to retrain workers. When Britain and Ireland joined the community, they pressed for the development of a regional fund. Although such a fund was established, in terms of resources, regional policy at the union level is virtually nonexistent. With the entry of Greece, Spain, and Portugal, pressure for a meaningful regional policy increased. However, the union does not have sufficient resources to fund a regional policy, and there is resistance to a large increase in the union's budget. The governments of member states have their own budget difficulties, and there is concern that the union budget is not always spent wisely. (The amount of funds spent on supporting, rather than reforming, inefficient agriculture is often cited as an example.)

The Single Market and Nonmember Countries

As barriers are brought down inside the union, there is a possibility that trade between members will take the place of trade with nonmembers. Nonmember countries have expressed concern that the union has embarked on a policy that will close the European market to foreign firms.[12] Critics of the single market policy have dubbed it "Fortress Europe."

---

[12]In other words, the fear is that trade diversion will be stronger than trade creation.

The Commission has argued that an expanding European market offers an excellent opportunity for foreign firms. Also, the Commission points out that European countries favor and must maintain an open world trading system: a large percentage of union output is exported and the union will continue to depend on foreign markets. Not everybody shares this optimistic view; some companies have decided to shift plants to Europe to ensure that they have a foothold within the single market. Only time will tell whether the attempt to create a single market has led to a more or less open world trading system.

The Common Agricultural Policy

The objectives of the **Common Agricultural Policy (CAP)** as outlined in Article 39 of the Treaty of Rome are:
1) to increase agricultural productivity
2) to ensure a fair standard of living for the agricultural community
3) to stabilize markets
4) to ensure the availability of supplies
5) to ensure that supplies reach consumers at reasonable prices

In practice, the operation of the CAP is dominated by the objective of producer support—over 90 percent of agricultural spending is devoted to producer support. In this respect, the CAP is similar to the agricultural policies of most other countries. Farm support is the usual objective. The primary method by which farmers are supported in Europe is by the maintenance of high market prices for agricultural products. Two policy instruments are used: a tariff and intervention buying.

The Variable Levy

Agricultural production in the EU is protected by a tariff wall, called the **variable levy**, which raises the price of imported products to a chosen European price. As the world price rises or falls, the variable levy is reduced or increased to ensure that the post–tariff price of imported agricultural products remains the same.

The effects of the variable levy are an excellent example of the inefficiency of tariffs. Figure 17.1 shows the effects of the variable levy. The levy raises the price of the imported food from P_0 to P_1. EU producers benefit because the tariff raises the prices they receive. The benefit to producers is shown by the increase in producer surplus (P_0P_1ba). Consumers suffer because they must pay a higher price for the food. The loss to consumers is shown by the decline in consumer surplus (P_0P_1ef). In addition, the Commission receives tariff revenue, shown by the rectangle ($cbed$). There is

Figure 17.1
The Effects of the Variable Levy

EU demand and supply are shown by *DD* and *SS*, respectively. At the world price of imports P_0, QD_0 is demanded, QS_0 is supplied domestically, and imports equal $QD_0 - QS_0$. A tariff (t) raises the EU price of imports to P_1. The quantity demanded falls to QD_1, the quantity supplied by the union rises to QS_1, and imports fall to $QD_1 - QS_1$. Consumer surplus falls by P_0P_1ef, producer surplus rises by P_0P_1ba, and tariff revenue of *cbed* is collected. The net loss from the tariff equals *abc* + *def*. If the world price were to fall, say to P_2, the tariff would be increased to ensure that the EU entry price (P_1) remains the same.

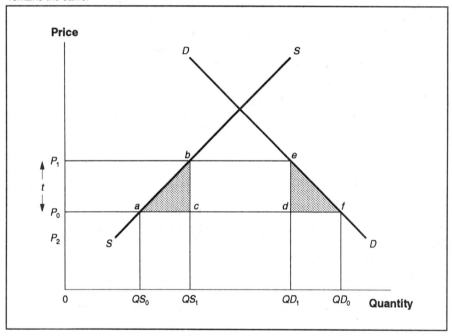

a net welfare loss (*abc* + *def*) from the tariff because the loss to consumers is greater than the sum of the tariff revenue and the welfare gain to producers.

The discussion in Chapter 4 shows that a tariff can be thought of as the equivalent of a consumption tax and a producer subsidy. Because of the tariff, consumers pay a higher price for food, just as they would if food were taxed. The higher price is received by producers, who gain just as they would from a subsidy. The tax consumers pay is shown by the difference between world prices and union prices. An indication of the effect of the CAP is given by the difference between the price producers receive in the EU and the lowest price in another rich country—producer prices in the EU are two to three times as high.[13] In effect, taxes on food finance producer subsidies and help finance the activities of the EU. High food prices have a particularly severe impact on poor people who normally spend a higher proportion of their incomes on food than rich people.

Intervention Buying

Union prices are stabilized by **intervention buying**. Ideally, produce purchased when the market price is below the intervention price is sold when the price rises above the intervention price, thus the market price is stabilized around the intervention price. In practice, lobbying by producers has often succeeded in pushing intervention prices up so high that the authorities buy more than they sell. Surplus stocks are sometimes sold on world markets, but, because union prices exceed world prices, exports must be subsidized. For example, the EU has often sold subsidized butter and grain to Eastern European countries. In effect, price supports lead to overproduction and high prices for consumers, and taxpayers are faced with the cost of storing or disposing of the surplus output. Some people find this aspect of the CAP rather strange.

The Cost of the CAP

One view popular with economists is that if the true costs of the CAP were publicized, the CAP would not be acceptable to the electorate. To put it more bluntly, the CAP allows governments to give in to the agricultural lobby, and buy votes in agricultural regions, by a method which is accepted only because the true costs of the policy are hidden. How many people would vote for farm income subsidies financed by taxes on food?

Estimates of the effects of the CAP typically lead to the result that transfers from consumers and taxpayers to producers are around 3 percent of GDP.[14] The net welfare loss (after deducting the tariff revenue generated and the gain to producers) may be around 1 percent of GDP. However, these estimates assume that the alternative to the CAP is no agricultural support

---

[13]See OECD, *Agricultural Policies, Markets and Trade*, Paris: OECD, 1993.

[14]The OECD estimates the cost of the CAP to EU consumers in 1992 to have been $450 per head. In comparison, agricultural support in the United States cost American consumers $360. (OECD, 1993.)

at all. As the Commission has pointed out, this is probably a "politically implausible" scenario.[15]

Ricardo and the Farm Problem

In Britain at the beginning of the 1800s, it was generally thought that high land prices caused high grain prices, and tariffs were necessary to protect domestic farmers from cheap imported food. Ricardo pointed out that tariffs on imported grain pushed up domestic grain prices, high domestic prices increased the demand for land, and thus tariffs led to high land prices. Often when agricultural policy is discussed it appears that Ricardo's analysis has been forgotten.[16]

There is strong reason to believe that the present CAP will never achieve the objective of significantly raising farm incomes. Price support does little to increase agricultural incomes in the long run because high prices eventually lead to higher prices for inputs. For example, price support encourages people to pay more for land, thus the effects of price support are eroded by higher land costs. This view is supported by the fact that farm incomes have remained low relative to incomes in other sectors despite decades of farm support.

The Effects of the CAP on Nonmembers

The CAP has an adverse effects on the welfare of countries outside the EU that export agricultural products. There are three reasons. First, these countries lose sales because the CAP encourages overproduction and discourages EU imports of agricultural products. Second, they receive lower prices for their exports because world prices are depressed by subsidized EU exports, and because world prices would be higher if the EU imported more. Third, the CAP contributes to an unstable world market for agricultural products. The larger the size of the market for agricultural goods, the more stable prices are likely to be (because low output in one area will sometimes be offset by higher output somewhere else). The CAP closes off a major section of the world; thus, price fluctuations are greater than they would be

---

[15]See Commission of the European Community, *European Economy*, No. 35, March 1988, p. 80.

[16]Ricardo's argument is examined in Chapter 15.

otherwise. Also, the practice of occasionally selling union surpluses on world markets further disrupts the world market.[17]

Reform of the CAP

The CAP is clearly in need of reform. Chapter 4 showed that subsidies are preferable to tariffs. That conclusion is appropriate in the case of agricultural support. Some farmers' incomes are low, and direct income subsidies could address this problem. At present tariffs lead to high prices, which reward all farmers regardless of need and encourage overproduction. Consumers and taxpayers are the losers.

International Monetary Policy

The Treaty of Rome was not directly concerned with international monetary issues. However, because trade between members of the union was a major objective, the treaty recognized that national economic polices and currency values were matters of common interest. The members soon realized that exchange rates were a potentially important influence on trade, but little action was taken because the international monetary system of the early 1960s was reasonably stable.

The Development of a Union Exchange Rate System

Serious interest in monetary union can be traced to the foreign exchange crises of the late 1960s and the collapse of the Bretton Woods system in the early 1970s. Against a background of international instability, a fixed exchange rate system providing a zone of monetary stability in Europe seemed attractive. Then as now, fixed exchange rates were seen by some as a first step on the path to monetary union, and by others as a desirable policy in their own right. A second element, perhaps more important at the time than now, was the feeling that European countries had been hurt by the powerful role played by the dollar in the Bretton Woods system.[18]

---

[17]The Uruguay round led to an agreement to cut export subsidies and agricultural subsidies which encourage overproduction. See Chapter 15.

[18]There was also concern that currency fluctuations made the operation of the CAP difficult because the CAP is based on the principal of common and stable agricultural prices. To maintain equality between domestic and foreign agricultural support prices, support prices in domestic currency must fall if domestic currency becomes more valuable relative to other currencies, and rise if domestic currency becomes less valuable.

The Snake

The first attempt to limit exchange rate fluctuations started in 1972. The founding members were France, Italy, Germany, and the Benelux. Members limited the divergence of their currencies from the agreed target exchange rates (or parities) to 2.25 percent. The parities used were those of the Smithsonian agreement and were defined in terms of the dollar. Against the dollar, members maintained the Smithsonian parity band of ±2.25 percent. The agreement was called **the snake** because the pattern traced by a group of currencies rising or falling together through time might resemble the movement of a snake.[19] The snake operated as well as might be expected given the uncertainty that surrounded the international monetary system at that time. Speculative attacks were a continuous problem. Realignments were needed because the parities on which the system was based were not sustainable. These realignments allowed the snake to struggle on, but the snake ceased to be a community system because some members of the community found it impossible to maintain fixed exchange rates against other members.

Reasons for the Death of the Snake

One reason for the failure of the snake may have been a lack of commitment. The independence of monetary policy allowed when exchange rates were not fixed was just being discovered in the post–Bretton Woods period, and countries were reluctant to sacrifice domestic policies to maintain exchange rates. Another fundamental problem was that the exchange rates which were chosen were the Smithsonian parities. As a result of lack of exchange rate flexibility or adjustment during the Bretton Woods period, some currencies were overvalued and others were undervalued. It was only a matter of time before this became obvious. (Members did not try to identify new equilibrium exchange rates. It would have been difficult to determine an equilibrium set of exchange rates, and probably impossible to reach agreement on such a set.) Finally, the international monetary system was in a state of flux, and the international monetary instability which created the desire for fixed exchange rates paradoxically made a European policy difficult to implement.

---

[19]Member currencies could change by ±2.25 percent against the dollar. Therefore, the width of the band of permitted exchange rate fluctuation against the dollar (4.5 percent) was twice the width of the band of a member currency against another member currency. The dollar band was called the "tunnel," and the two bands together were called the "snake in the tunnel" because the narrow snake could wiggle within the wider tunnel.

The European Monetary System

A European exchange rate system remained an objective both of those favoring fixed exchange rates and those favoring European monetary integration. The **European Monetary System (EMS)** was created in 1979 in response to dissatisfaction with the performance of flexible exchange rates, and to a continued preference for fixed exchange rates. The basic characteristic of the EMS is that a member agrees to intervene in the foreign exchange market to stabilize the value of its currency against other member currencies.

The value of a currency is expressed in **European Currency Units (ECUs)** and converted into a set of bilateral parities using the declared parities of other currencies. For example, if there are 40 Belgian francs per ECU, and 2 marks per ECU, there are 20 Belgian francs per mark. At first most currencies were maintained within 2.25 percent of their declared parities against other currencies. In our example, intervention would be required to maintain the franc–mark exchange rate between 20.45 and 19.55. Intervention is only required at the limits, but central banks have often tried to keep exchange rates well within the permitted band. This helps foster confidence in the exchange rate and avoids the buildup of speculation in favor of a parity change that may occur when a currency is at its limit. Flexible arrangements provide for a member to borrow funds for intervention from other members.

The ECU

As shown, the ECU serves as the **numeraire** of the EMS, but it may be worth emphasizing that the ECU is not actually a currency but rather a basket made up of national currencies. The use of the ECU as a unit of account by private banks has grown. The reason is that the ECU tends to be more stable than a single national currency because its value is determined by the average value of the currencies of the members of the union, and the values of most of the currencies are stabilized by official intervention in the foreign exchange market.

The Performance of the EMS

The EMS proved remarkably resilient. In part, the durability of the EMS is attributable to the fact that it became a symbol of European integration:

countries wanted to stay within it and be "full" members of the EC.[20] Also, at first the EMS was much more flexible than earlier fixed exchange rate systems. In its early years, frequent parity changes were needed because the economic performance and inflation rates of the members differed.[21] Later, as inflation rates were brought down and became more alike, parities had to be changed less often. As exchange rate changes became less frequent, and less acceptable politically, exchange rate disequilibria developed.

The Case of the United Kingdom

The United Kingdom did not join the EMS at first. One stated reason was that influences on the value of sterling are sometimes different from the influences on other currencies' values. For example, the United Kingdom is a net exporter of oil whereas other union members are oil importers. Also, trade with other members is not quite as important for the United Kingdom as it is for other members; thus, stable exchange rates with other union members are less important. Another reason for not joining was the fear that domestic economic policy would be dominated by the need to maintain the value of sterling. However, the main reason for Britain remaining outside the EMS for so long was ideological: the British government, and in particular Britain's prime minister at the time, Margaret Thatcher, felt that exchange rates should be determined by market forces and not maintained by official intervention.

The experience of the United Kingdom is an interesting example of the difficulty of maintaining a fixed exchange rate. The United Kingdom joined the EMS in 1990. The main driving force behind membership was political: it was felt that membership was necessary if the United Kingdom was to be seen to be playing its full role in Europe. The rate chosen for entry (DM2.95 = £1) was simply the rate that existed in the market at the time of entry. As a result, it rapidly became apparent that sterling was in fact overvalued, prompting speculators to sell sterling. Rather than devalue, the British government made statements about its commitment to defend the value of sterling.

---

[20]The United Kingdom was not a member until 1990, and its failure to join the system was frequently described as a lack of commitment to the European ideal. One of the reasons given by the government for joining and staying in the EMS was that the United Kingdom wanted to play its full role in Europe.

[21]There were two parity changes in each of the following years, 1979, 1981, and 1982, and one change in 1983. In total, there were twelve parity changes during the first decade of the EMS (March 1979 to March 1989).

In general, the more often such statements are made, the more pressure a currency is under, and the more likely it is that the currency will be devalued. In this case, the exchange rate was described as the "cornerstone of British economic policy," and the commitment of the government was repeatedly stressed. Speculators did not believe the rhetoric—they sold sterling and bought marks. The similarity to the collapse of the Bretton Woods system is very strong.

Sterling's Departure from the EMS

The British government used international reserves and increased interest rates in an attempt to defend sterling's value by attracting foreign investment. However, the potential gain from an increase in the value of other currencies relative to sterling dominated the market, and pressure on sterling continued.[22] On September 16, 1992, two interest rate increases were announced, and there was massive intervention to support sterling. However, later that same day the government was forced to pull sterling out of the EMS. The Bank of England spent over $160 billion during four months in its attempt to support sterling. Most of this spending took the form of sales of marks. To put the U.K. intervention into perspective, it is interesting to note that the 1992 budget for the European Community as a whole was about 66 billion ECUs, or about $90 billion, i.e., the U.K. spent more on intervention than the value of the whole EC budget.

Other Problems[23]

The Bank of Italy spent about $200 billion defending the lira between June and December 1992, about half in September alone. The lira was forced to leave the EMS at the same time as sterling. Sweden's experience was also dramatic. Although not a member of the European Community, Sweden tried to keep the krone stable relative to EMS currencies. Speculation that Sweden would devalue mounted, and on September 16 the government raised the overnight interest rate to 1.25 percent, i.e., about 500 percent on an annual basis. Following the failure of the government to win approval for a tough fiscal package, people sold krone and the Swedish government was forced to

---

[22]German reunification increased German government borrowing, the Bundesbank maintained a tight monetary policy because of fears of inflation, and German interest rates increased. The German mark came under upward pressure, which added to speculation by raising the possibility that the deutsche mark would be revalued.

[23]The following paragraph draws heavily on Bank for International Settlements (1993), p. 188.

let the krone float in mid–November. Sweden had spent $26 billion defending the krone, i.e., about 11 percent of Sweden's GNP.

The European monetary system came under speculative attack again in 1993, and the permitted band of fluctuation had to be raised to ±15 percent. This meant that exchange rates could fluctuate so much that the system became almost meaningless. Speculation decreased because speculators could no longer win by betting that an official exchange rate within a narrow band would be abandoned.

Reasons for the Collapse of the System

The basic reason for the failure of the EMS is that the system became too rigid—parity changes were avoided even when they were necessary. The lesson which stands out from the EMS experience is that countries cannot have independent policies, free capital mobility, and fixed exchange rates. (This is the same lesson which can be learned from the collapse of the Bretton Woods system.) The lesson for Europe is clear: Policy independence must be sacrificed if exchange rates are to be stabilized. In the next section we examine a proposal to remove monetary policy independence, in other words, the proposal for European monetary union.

European Monetary Union

A few years ago monetary union seemed a dream. In December 1991 the members of the EC agreed at the Maastricht summit meeting to a process which could eventually lead to European monetary union. The timetable in the Maastricht agreement envisaged monetary union taking place by January 1, 1999. This almost certainly cannot happen due to the virtual collapse of the European Monetary System (EMS) in 1992–93. But although the creation of a monetary union may be delayed, the principle of monetary union has not been abandoned.

The Maastricht agreement laid down four conditions which each country must meet to become a member of the economic and monetary union:

1) A country's inflation rate must not exceed the average of the lowest three members' rates by more than 1.5 percentage points.
2) The interest rate on long–term government bonds must not exceed the average of the rates of the three lowest inflation countries by more than 2 percentage points.
3) The budget deficit must not exceed 3 percent of GDP, and outstanding debt must not exceed 60 percent of GDP.
4) The country's currency must have been within the narrow EMS band without realignment for at least two years.

As late of 1994, no country meets all four conditions.

The Definition of Monetary Union

Monetary union may be defined as an area in which there is a single currency and capital flows are unrestricted. The EU has attempted to reduce exchange rate fluctuations since the early 1970s, claiming that reducing exchange rate fluctuations is a step toward monetary union. But fixed exchange rates are not really the same as monetary union.[24] An area in which exchange rates are fixed is an **exchange rate union**. In theory, exchange rate union and monetary union are equivalent in a world of certainty, no restrictions on capital flows or convertibility, and zero transactions costs. However, in practice, even if governments commit themselves to irrevocable parities, convertibility, and unrestricted capital flows, exchange rate union and monetary union are not equivalent. Why, if exchange rates are **irrevocably** linked, would national currencies and national central banks with the power to print money be maintained?

Exchange Risk and Conversion Costs

One of the basic arguments in favor of monetary union is that exchange risk is completely removed. Also, the cost of converting one currency into another is removed by monetary union (although it must be acknowledged that conversion costs are minute as a percentage when large sums are being converted). While the effects on trade of removing exchange risk and conversion costs may be small, clearly there will be a gain from a single currency. A related argument for monetary union is that the system of flexible exchange rates has led to periods of exchange rate misalignment: overvaluation or undervaluation.[25] Temporary artificial swings in competitiveness are clearly undesirable when countries are closely linked by trade.[26]

---

[24]Attempting to maintain fixed exchange rates may even lead countries to adopt policies that reduce the degree of monetary integration between members. For example, national monetary authorities may use capital controls to defend fixed exchange rates.

[25]The effects of misalignment were discussed in Chapter 14.

[26]Fixed exchange rates may be a way to reduce volatility: there is some evidence that currencies within the EMS were less volatile than non–EMS currencies over some periods. However, the danger of large swings resulting from the collapse of a fixed exchange rate agreement, is clearly demonstrated by the exchange rate changes which marked the collapse of the EMS.

Inflation and the Transition to Monetary Union

One of the traditional arguments made against monetary union is based on the idea that there is a trade–off between inflation and unemployment. It has been argued that low inflation countries would have to accept more inflation and high inflation countries would have to accept more unemployment. This view is not so common now because many people believe that there is not a long–run trade–off between inflation and unemployment. A related argument is that countries have different inflation rates, thus movement toward a single currency and a single inflation rate entails adjustment costs. At least in the short run, unemployment will increase as the inflation rate is brought down in the high inflation areas. While adjustment does entail costs, these costs would only be born once. Also, there is considerable doubt about how large they would be. If the new central bank is committed to a stable monetary policy, adjustment may be rapid.

Monetary union entails members giving up their rights to independent monetary policies. But if monetary policy is not effective in the long run, nothing significant is being sacrificed. With respect to macroeconomic policy, it may be that economic thinking and objectives have changed. Some members of the EU appear to have recognized that:

1) domestic monetary policy is not fully independent,
2) monetary policy is ineffective not only in the long run but even over a period which is short enough to be relevant for politicians,
3) membership of a monetary union may be needed to allow some nations to enjoy the fruits of low inflation policies.

Inflation and the Effectiveness of Monetary Policy

Within a monetary union, it may be easier to pursue a credible low inflation policy than within the member states individually. The reason is that the central monetary authority may be less susceptible to political/public pressure to increase the money supply to reduce unemployment. One critical issue is whether the central monetary authority can act independently and pursue a low inflation policy without political interference. This issue was recognized in the Maastricht agreement which calls for an independent European central bank.[27]

---

[27]The European Monetary Institute was created on January 1, 1994. It is based in Frankfurt and is the forerunner of a future European central bank.

The Inflation Tax

The right to print money yields revenue to the government which has the right to spend the new money, i.e., the government gains from seignorage. New money adds to inflation, thus the use of new money to finance government spending is known as an **inflation tax**. In the transition to monetary union, national governments lose this source of revenue and the central European government gains. However, other resource transfers will no doubt be occurring, and seignorage from printing a European currency could in principle be shared; therefore, seignorage should not be a significant issue.[28]

Regional Adjustment

A problem arising from monetary union is that prices and wages are easily compared across the whole union.[29] If workers bargain for equal wages, and their productivity differs, unemployment will increase in low productivity regions. Nations have this problem already, but within a monetary union the problem may be much worse. The unemployment in Eastern Germany following reunification is a dramatic example of the possible effects of monetary union. Perhaps market forces will work, wage adjustment will take place, and wage differences will reflect productivity differences, although this will take time, and market forces have not prevented regional unemployment problems within nations.

Capital Mobility

Freedom from capital controls is a vital part of a common market. While the benefits of trade are clear, there seems to be little belief in the benefits of capital flows. But equal competition requires that firms with the same risks/opportunities throughout the market face the same interest rates and availability of capital. Therefore, if Europe is to proceed toward a true single market, capital flows must be free.

Since expectations of exchange rate changes have generated massive short–term speculative flows, one can be reasonably certain that capital flows

---

[28]A single European currency would no doubt be held as an international reserve by other countries. To the extent that future holdings of the single currency exceed present holdings of union members' currencies, the union would benefit from international seignorage.

[29]One can easily imagine the response of a worker: "Why should I be paid less than . . ."

within a monetary union will be more stable than at present. Capital flows are also motivated by political risk: investors seek to avoid capital controls and taxes which reduce the value of their capital. Monetary union entails unrestricted capital mobility in an area controlled by a single monetary authority. Thus, political risk in a monetary union is probably lower than between separate countries with different monetary authorities, and investors have less reason to fear making long–term investments in a monetary union. Therefore, one might expect long–term capital mobility to increase.

Perhaps long–term capital mobility will ease the regional problem, but it is difficult to see why this should happen. Capital mobility has not prevented large regional disparities within nations. Indeed, there is a danger that capital mobility may even increase regional disparities, as the high productivity regions with the best infrastructure attract more investment. There is already some concern that regional income levels are much higher in the center of the union than around the periphery.

The Role of Fiscal Policy

One of the main ways in which income is redistributed within countries is via income related taxes and income related government spending. Existing EU policies are inadequate for this purpose. One option is to move toward a federal system. Countries would retain the right to tax and spend, but there would be a union tax system as well. If a negative income tax were adopted, this would avoid some of the problems we see with tax–benefit systems at the national level.[30] While the EU may not be ready yet for a union tax–benefit system, such a development may be necessary if regional problems within a future monetary union are to be reduced. Also, as the powers of the European Parliament increase, no doubt there will soon be calls for the right to tax and spend.

Some Problems Related to the Path to EMU

There are basically three ways to approach monetary union. None of them is without cost. The first method we shall discuss is a gradual narrowing of exchange rate bands. The other two methods are the immediate adoption of a single currency (the big bang), and the parallel currency approach.

If there is one clear message from our experience with fixed exchange rates, it is that fixed exchange rates are not compatible with independent monetary policies. Stable exchange rates may emerge as a result of policy

---

[30]For example, the EU could establish a desired EU minimum family income, say 20,000 ECUs. With a tax rate of 5 percent, a family with an income of 40,000 ECUs would pay 1,000 ECUs, while a family with zero income would receive 1,000 ECUs.

harmonization and cooperation, but they are not sufficient to force policy convergence. The very fact that national currencies are maintained and policies are not harmonized should be enough to make one skeptical of the durability of any fixed exchange rate system.

Exchange rates should probably be thought of as indicators, not as targets. If appropriate policies are pursued, exchange rates will be stable. If inappropriate policies are pursued, exchange rate changes are inevitable. In fulfilling its role of guiding the EU toward monetary union, instead of trying to limit exchange rate differences, the European Monetary Institute should perhaps try to set limits around policy differences. For example, countries should be expected to adopt growth rates for their money supplies within a target range.

The second method of approaching monetary union is the "big bang." The main issue here is that there has to be a very strong political will for the policy to be adopted. Given the uncertainty surrounding the effects of monetary union, the step can be described as a "leap of faith" or a "leap in the dark." If countries are committed to a single currency, the issue becomes the rates at which national currencies are to be exchanged for the union currency. If a currency is overvalued, the country can expect inadequate aggregate demand and unemployment (because its high wages and prices will make it uncompetitive). Undervaluation is likely to lead to inflation. If a stable monetary policy is pursued in the union, and policies encourage labor market flexibility, eventually one might expect adjustment. However, the process entails a fall in welfare at least for the short run. It is difficult to imagine countries committing themselves to an irrevocable process unless fiscal policy safeguards are already in place.

Germany had the political will and was able to adopt the big bang approach; Germany's economic policy is now dominated by the effects of reunification. Germany had policies in place, and added to them, yet there were still problems. There is nothing at the European level even remotely approaching the complex systems of taxes and benefits that exist at national levels. As the Bank for International Settlements has put it: "Though some conditions would be very different, the experience of German currency union suggests possible problems with European monetary union to which little thought has so far been given."[31]

The third method is to adopt a parallel currency which would circulate alongside national currencies. In order to maintain monetary control, the parallel currency would have to substitute for national currencies, it could not merely be added to the money supply. Gradually, national currencies could be phased out and the parallel currency would gain in usage. This

---

[31]Bank for International Settlements, *62nd Annual Report*, (1st April 1991–31st March 1992), Basle: June 1992, p. 126.

proposal is very attractive because it avoids the high political commitment needed for the big bang; a country could always back out. However, speculative attacks would be possible, and in order to maintain control of the money supply within the system, countries would have to sacrifice a degree of monetary autonomy at the outset.

The Future of the European Union

The membership of the EU is expanding and may continue to expand because almost every independent European country would like to join. For example, the pressure is increasing to allow former communist countries to join. Where will the line be drawn? Indeed, should a line be drawn? Does the success of the union depend on its being selective? If countries are willing to agree to present EU policies, it will be difficult to keep them out.[32] However, while they would like to join the present union, whether new members would share the dream of creating a much closer economic and political union is much more questionable.

The future development of the EU is uncertain. The Commission is fond of suggesting that the option facing the EU is whether to go forward or to go back, but it is also possible that the union will attempt to consolidate and improve existing policies.

One of the main barriers to further significant new policies is political: the EU has probably reached the point where further economic integration cannot take place unless national governments hand over more power to European bodies. While some people look forward to European government, others want to maintain national power (and traditions). Another problem is that there are few policies that benefit all members (free trade is a possible exception), and present EU policies are not sufficient to guarantee that gains are shared (because there are no policies capable of significantly redistributing income within the union). As a result, members often block policies that are not in their national interests, even when the policies might benefit the group as a whole. The most notorious example is probably the repeated failure of the Commission to secure agreement on reform of the CAP.

Even without any new policies, a financial problem will develop for the union as existing policies (in particular the CAP and the regional policy) are extended to cover new members. Further expansion of the union can only add to the financial problems. This will make new polices difficult to achieve. Perhaps the union must soon choose between new members and new policies.

---

[32]The basic requirements for a country to be a member are that it is a European country, respects human rights, and a democracy.

One way to progress may be for some members to go ahead with new policies without the others. This idea is alien to many pro–Europeans, but it was explicitly recognized as a possibility in the Maastricht agreement which envisaged a single currency being adopted by some members and not others. Monetary union for a small group of countries bordering Germany is a very strong possibility.

Finally, perhaps further significant economic integration cannot, or at least should not, take place without major changes in the institutional structure of the EU. The decision–making process in the EU is not designed to wield power democratically at a union level. New policies are proposed and adopted, but at present there is nothing resembling a national government at the European level to control economic policy and be held accountable.[33] This has been dubbed the "democratic deficit" of the EU. But, returning to the first point, it is difficult to imagine member countries sacrificing national sovereignty and establishing a true European government.

Conclusion

Has European integration been a success or a failure? Probably the customs union and the EMS may be counted as successes of the EU, but it is difficult to view the CAP favorably. However, in assessing the EU we must keep in mind that the primary objective of the founders was to make a European war impossible. No one now considers a European war likely. To the extent that the EU has contributed to this achievement, for the founders of the EU this alone would be sufficient to justify its existence.

While it is difficult to be objective, it seems that there is a growing European feeling and identity which goes beyond national boundaries. This may be because of increased communication between countries; perhaps the EU is a reflection of increased European feeling as much as a cause of it. But if it is true that the people of Europe are begining to feel that they are Europeans, further economic and political integration is inevitable.

---

[33]The European Parliament is elected, but it is not a European government. For example, the parliament does not set taxes, most community spending is outside of its control, it does not initiate legislation, and in most areas legislation does not even need parliament's approval. Legislation is proposed by the Commission, the civil service of the community, and it is representatives of member governments who decide whether proposals will be adopted. In most areas the parliament's duties are merely advisory. However, the parliament is slowly gaining more powers.

Summary of Main Points

The EU grew out of postwar economic cooperation and was established by the Treaty of Rome in 1957. There are three main policies: a free trade agreement, an agricultural policy, and an exchange rate system. In addition, there is an increasing body of European law which takes precedence over national law.

In a **customs union**, trade between members is free of tariffs or quotas, and a common tariff wall surrounds the union. Although tariff barriers and quotas between members have been removed, trade between members of the EU is not completly free of restriction. Tax rates differ between countries and there are differences between regulations and standards in member countries. These differences act as barriers to the free mobility of goods. The mere existence of customs posts acts as a barrier to trade because they lead to higher costs from paperwork and delays at borders. Plans have been put forward and progress has been made to reduce these barriers to trade.

The **common agricultural policy** of the union is a classic example of an agricultural policy designed to benefit farmers with little attention to consumers' interests. A tariff is used to increase the price of imported food and maintain high prices in the union. Farmers have responded to high prices by increasing production; surpluses are purchased by intervention agencies to prevent the union price from falling. These surpluses are often sold on world markets.

The members of the union are closely linked through trade and have an incentive to maintain stable exchange rates. The first attempts to establish a European exchange rate system in the 1970s, the **snake**, failed. The **European Monetary System (EMS)** was established in 1979 and survived remarkably well until 1992–93. The EMS is an agreement to stabilize exchange rates within bands around target rates. At first, these target rates were revised when needed, and with sufficient regularity to ensure that major realignments of exchange rates were not needed. As parity adjustments became less frequent, disequilibria built up, and the system virtually collapsed in 1993.

The **European Currency Unit (ECU)** is an accounting unit based on the values of European currencies. Because it is made up of a basket of currencies, and many of the currencies are members of the EMS, the ECU tends to be reasonably stable. This has led to its use as an international unit of account, although it is not actually a currency.

A **monetary union** is an area in which there is a single currency and capital flows are unrestricted. Plans for a single European currency have been discussed, and broad outline proposals adopted. The main benefit of a single currency would be that trade and investment could take place without worrying about exchange rates or monetary controls. The problem is that national governments would have to give up their control of monetary policy to a European monetary authority. Lack of national monetary policy might mean higher unemployment in some areas, and unemployment is certainly likely during the adjustment process.

Prospects for the adoption of significant new policies by the union do not seem strong because the budget of the EU is already under pressure, members have different interests, and few policies benefit all countries. Further expansion of the membership is likely to make agreement on new policies more difficult. Also, further integration can only occur if national governments surrender power to authorities at the union level.

Study Questions

1. In what ways is the EU customs union incomplete?
2. What are the economic and non–economic reasons for customs posts between countries?
3. What are the possible benefits from the creation of a single European market (with virtually no barriers to trade) on members of the EU?
4. What are the possible effects on countries outside the EU of the creation of a single European market?
5. What are trade diversion and trade creation? Explain why attempts to measure these are difficult, and usually fail to capture the full effects of customs unions.
6. Using the CAP as an example, discuss the effects of tariffs on food.
7. What are the effects of the CAP on members and nonmembers of the EU?
8. What are the main features of the EMS? In what ways does it resemble the Bretton Woods system, and in what ways is it different?
9. Can and should the world attempt to establish a system like the EMS?
10. What are the costs and benefits of a single European currency?
11. In what ways are fixed exchange rates and monetary union similar? How do they differ?
12. What difficulties have arisen when the EU has attempted to move toward monetary union by fixing exchange rates?

Selected References

Bank for International Settlements, *62nd Annual Report*, (1st April 1991–31st March 1992), Basle: June 1992, p. 126.
Bank for International Settlements, *63rd Annual Report*, (1st April 1992–31st March 1993), Basle: BIS, June 1993, p. 188.

Bofinger, P., "The German Monetary Unification (Gmu): Converting Marks to D–Marks," *The Federal Reserve Bank of St. Louis Review*, 72:4, July/August 1990, pp. 17–36.

Boltho, A., (ed.), *The European Economy*, New York: Oxford University Press, 1982.

Cecchini, P., et al., *The European Challenge, 1992, The Benefits of a Single Market*, Brookfield, Vermont: Gower Publishing Co., 1988.

Commission of the European Communities, *Completing the Internal Market: White Paper from the Commission to the European Council*, Luxembourg: Office for Official Publications of the European Communities, 1985.

Commission of the European Communities, *Opening up the Internal Market*, Office for Official Publications of the European Communities, Luxembourg, 1991.

de Grauwe, P., *The Economics of Monetary Integration*, Oxford: Oxford University Press, 1992.

Fleming, J. M., "On Exchange Rate Unification," *Economic Journal*, 81, 1971, pp. 467–90.

Fratianni, M. and T. Peeters, *One Money for Europe*, London: Macmillan, 1978.

Grayboyes, Robert F., "The EMU: Forerunners and Durability," *Federal Reserve Bank of Richmond Economic Review*, 76:4, July/August 1990, pp. 8–17.

Habermeier, K. and H. Ungerer, "A Single Currency for the European Community," *Finance and Development*, September 1992, pp. 26–29.

Hildebrandt, P., "The Path to European Monetary Union," *Federal Reserve Bank of Kansas City Economic Review*, March/April 1991, pp. 35–48.

Hitiris, T., *European Community Economics*, 2e, New York: St. Martin's Press, 1991.

Masson, P. R. and Taylor, M. P., "Issues in the Operation of Monetary Unions and Common Currency Areas," in Goldstein, M., et al., "Policy Issues in the Evolving International Monetary System," *IMF Occasional Paper* No. 96, Washington DC: IMF, June 1992.

Robson, P., *The Economics of Integration*, 2e, Boston: George Allen and Unwin, 1984.

Rosenblatt, J., et al., *The Common Agricultural Policy of the European Community: Principles and Consequences*, International Monetary Fund Occasional Paper No. 62, Washington: 1988.

Sinn, H. W., "How Much Europe? Subsidiarity, Centralization and Fiscal Competition," *Scottish Journal of Political Economy*, 41, February 1994, pp. 85–107.

Swann, D., *The Economics of the Common Market*, 6e, London: Penguin, 1988.

Ungerer, H., et al., "The European Monetary System: Developments and Perspectives," International Monetary Fund Occasional Paper No. 73, November 1990.

Ypersele, J. van, *The European Monetary System*, Brussels: Commission of the European Communities, 1985.

Eighteen

Developing Countries

Introduction

The theory of comparative advantage suggests that countries gain from specialization and trade. Developing countries have participated in international trade, but many have remained poor. This has led some people to question the idea that countries gain from trade. In this chapter we examine the relationship between trade and economic growth.

We begin by considering the characteristics of developing countries and the importance of international trade for these economies. The long–term trend in the terms of trade of developing countries has attracted a great deal of attention. We describe the issues involved and comment on their significance. Then, we consider the role of international trade in international economic development. Finally, we examine international capital flows and the debt problems faced by poor countries.

The Characteristics of Developing Countries

The basic characteristic of a developing country is the obvious one—its people are poor. Although there is not a clear dividing line between rich and poor, for simplicity in most of this chapter countries are classified as either **advanced countries (ACs)** or **developing countries (DCs)**. Developing countries are also sometimes known as less developed countries. The term "less developed" is probably more appropriate than "developing" because, unfortunately, many of these poor countries are not developing economically, or are developing very slowly.[1] ACs include the industrial market economies of North America, Western Europe, Australia, New Zealand, and Japan. DCs make up the rest of the world and include most of the countries in Africa, Asia, the Middle East, South America, and Oceania (excluding Australia and New Zealand).

Table 18.1 shows the income levels of some of the larger countries in the world. The difference between the income levels of rich and poor is dramatic: incomes in the richest countries are between one and two hundred times the

---

[1]We use the term *developing country* because this term is common in official publications, and the term *less developed country* is now unfashionable.

Table 18.1
Per Capita Incomes in Large Countries

Country	Population (millions 1991)	GNP per Capita (dollars 1991)
Ethiopia	52.8	120
Bangladesh	110.6	220
India	866.5	330
Nigeria	99.0	340
China	1149.5	370
Pakistan	115.8	400
Indonesia	181.3	610
Egypt	53.6	610
Philippines	62.9	730
Columbia	32.8	1,260
Thailand	57.2	1,570
Turkey	57.3	1,780
South Africa	38.9	2,560
Argentina	32.7	2,790
Brazil	151.4	2,940
Mexico	83.3	3,030
Korea	43.3	6,330
United Kingdom	57.6	16,550
France	57.0	20,380
United States	252.7	22,240
Germany (West)	80.1	23,650
Japan	123.9	26,930

Source: World Bank, *World Development Report, 1993.*

size of incomes in the poorest countries.[2] Table 18.2 gives average income levels for some classifications of countries used by the World Bank. Sixty percent of the world's population lives in "low income" countries, that is, on an annual per capital income of $635 or less.

---

[2]Although the qualitative conclusion that DCs are relatively and absolutely poor is correct, too much weight should not be given to the figures. DCs do not have the resources needed to collect accurate data. Also, non–market transactions are more important in DCs.

Table 18.2
Per Capita Income and Population (1991)

	Income Range (Dollars)	Population (Millions)	Average Income (Dollars)
Low Income	635 and below	3,127.3	350
Lower Middle Income	636–2,555	773.8	1,590
Upper Middle Income	2,556–7,910	627.0	3,530
High Income	7,911 and above	822.3	21,050
World		5,351.0	4,010

Source: World Bank, *World Development Report, 1993.*

Problems Associated with Poverty

Poverty is associated with problems such as lack of education, poor health, and malnutrition. These problems exist in all DCs, but are worst in the poorest countries. The level of education in low income economies is reflected in an adult illiteracy rate of 40 percent compared to 4 percent in ACs. (The illiteracy rate for low income economies is 48 percent if China is excluded because China has an unusually low level of illiteracy.) Malnutrition is common in DCs; they often do not have enough food even to meet the average daily calorie requirements of their people. Poverty, disease, and malnutrition lead to short life expectancies in DCs. Life expectancy is 57 years in low income economies (excluding China), 68 years in middle income economies, and 77 years in high income countries. Table 18.3 compares values of these indicators of health and welfare for some DCs with the average figures for ACs.

Incomes and Growth

Some countries have grown rapidly over the last two or three decades. One group of countries which achieved high rates of growth was the **newly industrialized countries** (**NICs**). This group included Brazil, Mexico, Hong Kong, Singapore, South Korea, and Taiwan. Spectacular rates of growth have also been achieved by China, Indonesia, Malaysia, and Thailand. However, growth has been slowest in the low income economies. As a result, the share of world income received by the world's poorest countries fell over the three decades 1960–90. One reason that the poorest countries have not grown is that they are trapped with low output, low savings, and low investment: low output per head implies low income per head; if people do not earn much,

Table 18.3
Life Expectancy and Adult Illiteracy

	Life Expectancy at Birth (1991)	Adult Illiteracy–% (1990)
Ethiopia	48	—
Bangladesh	51	65
India	60	52
Nigeria	52	49
China	69	27
Pakistan	59	65
Indonesia	60	23
Egypt	61	52
Philippines	65	10
Columbia	69	13
Thailand	69	7
Turkey	67	19
South Africa	63	—
Argentina	71	5
Brazil	66	19
Mexico	70	13
High Income	77	4

Source: World Bank, *World Development Report, 1993.*

they cannot save much, and without savings there are no funds available for investment, so output is low. . . . (Inflows of foreign investment may be a way out of this cycle.) Malnutrition aggravates the problem of low productivity.

Inequality and the International Economic System

The share of world income going to each income group is shown in Table 18.4. For example, the poorest 20 percent of the world's population is the first quintile. Over the period 1960–90, the income going to the first quintile fell from 5.0 to 3.4 percent. There was an increase in the income of the third quintile, which increased from 7.0 in 1979 to 11.5 percent in 1990. However, the Bank for International Settlements, in reporting these results, points out that: "This gain is entirely due to the exceptional performance of China, which accounts for almost 20 percent of the world's population and occupies the whole of the third quintile. China's per capita income growth has averaged almost 7 percent per year since the start of the economic reforms in 1977–78, compared with only 1½ percent previously. If China is excluded (column (b) of the table) there is a clear increase in inequality, with the

Table 18.4
The Widening Gap?

Population grouped by quintile	Percentage of World Income Received (Column a including China, Column b excluding China)										Change 1960–90	
	1960		1969		1979		1987		1990			
	a	b	a	b	a	b	a	b	a	b	a	b
1st	5.0	3.9	4.2	3.3	3.3	2.6	3.4	2.9	3.4	2.9	−1.6	−1.0
2nd	6.2	4.9	5.2	4.0	5.9	3.7	6.1	3.6	6.0	3.7	−0.2	−1.2
3rd	7.3	9.6	6.0	8.8	7.0	9.3	10.6	8.8	11.5	8.4	4.2	−1.2
4th	17.9	23.3	18.5	24.8	18.9	25.8	17.1	22.0	16.3	20.4	−1.6	−2.9
5th	63.7	58.3	66.1	59.1	64.9	58.6	62.7	62.7	62.8	64.6	−0.9	6.3

Source: Bank for International Settlements, *63rd Annual Report*, Basle, Switzerland, June 1993.

richest countries gaining relative to all other groups, especially the poorest 20 percent."[3]

The income disparity between rich and poor countries does seem large. For example, per capita income in the United States is about 60 times higher than per capita income in India. This disparity of incomes is often used as an indictment of ACs and the world economic system as a whole. For example, the United Nations Declaration on the Establishment of a New International Economic Order states:

> The greatest and most significant achievement during the last decades has been independence from colonial and alien domination of a large number of peoples and nations which has enabled them to become members of the community of free peoples. Technological progress has been made in all spheres of economic activities in the last three decades, thus providing a solid potential for improving the well–being of all peoples. However, the remaining vestiges of alien and colonial domination, foreign occupation, racial discrimination, apartheid and neocolonialism in all its forms continue to be among the greatest obstacles to the full emancipation and progress of the developing countries and all the peoples involved. The benefits of technological progress are not shared equitably by all members of the international community. The developing countries which constitute 70 percent of the world's population, account for only 30 percent of the world's income. It has

---

[3]Bank for International Settlements, *63rd Annual Report*, Basle, Switzerland: 1993, p. 61.

proved impossible to achieve an even balanced development of the international economic community under the existing international economic order. The gap between developed and developing countries continues to widen in a system which was established when most of the developing countries did not even exist as independent states and which perpetuates inequality.[4]

Although the disparity between countries' per capita incomes is a source of concern, especially in view of the limited attempts made by ACs to foster international economic development, we must be careful when attempting to blame ACs for causing lower per capita incomes in DCs. The growth of DCs has often been very rapid, sometimes far greater than growth in ACs. But, as Table 18.5 shows, income growth can be offset by population growth. The population growth rate in poor countries is three or four times the rate of growth in high–income countries. It is difficult to see how ACs are responsible for this problem. Differences between the performance of DCs also cast doubt on the view that there is an inherent bias in the international economic system. (If the system is so biased, how is it that some poor countries grow? For example, how did the East Asian economies succeed?) We must look for other explanations of both growth and stagnation. A useful starting point is to consider the structure and composition of DC trade.

Table 18.5
The Growth of Population and Income 1980–91

	Growth of Population	GNP	Growth of per Capita
India	2.1	5.4	3.2
China	1.5	9.4	7.8
Other	2.6	3.7	1.0
Middle Income	1.8	2.3	0.3
High Income	0.6	2.9	2.3

Source: World Bank, *World Development Report, 1993.*

---

[4]The text of this declaration and a summary of the discussion that accompanied its adoption is contained in the *Yearbook of the United Nations, 1974*, New York: United Nations. Extracts of the declaration are reprinted in Adams (1985), pp. 468–77.

Table 18.6
The Structure of World Trade (1992)

	Percentage of Exports from		
	Developed Economies	**Developing Economies**	**Eastern Europe and Former USSR**
Going to			
Developed economies	75.0	58.1	61.6
Developing economies	22.4	38.9	17.6
Eastern Europe and former USSR	2.5	2.3	19.1

Note: Totals may not sum to 100 percent because of rounding errors and omissions.
Source: Calculated using data from United Nations *Monthly Bulletin of Statistics*, June 1993.

The Trade and Production of DCs

Table 18.6 shows that DCs trade mainly with ACs. This is not surprising because they export mainly **primary products**. (Primary products include agricultural products, metals, minerals, and fuels.)[5] There is limited scope for trade between countries that only produce a few primary products. Exports of manufactured products by DCs have increased over the last two decades, but the gains have largely been recorded by a small group of countries in Asia. For some countries, one or two primary products account for 80 percent of exports (see Table 18.7). As a result, DCs are heavily influenced by fluctuations in the prices of primary products. For this reason, some development proposals have focused on the prices of primary products: it has been suggested that if rich countries paid more for basic goods, poor countries would develop. However, it would be wrong to think that DCs are the only exporters of primary products. Some ACs (such as Australia, Canada, and New Zealand) export large quantities of primary products.

The experience of Uganda illustrates the problem of dependence on a single product: "The price of Ugandan coffee in the international market has declined steadily in recent years, to $0.82 a kilogram in fiscal year 1992/93 from $2.05 a kilogram in 1987/88. Overall, Uganda's terms of trade have

---

[5]Primary products are those in categories 0–4 of the Standard International Trade Classification (SITC).

Table 18.7
Examples of Export Concentration (1990)

		% of Exports
Bangladesh	Jute goods (19), Raw jute (7)	26
Botswana	Diamonds (79), Copper–Nickel (8)	87
Burundi	Coffee (75)	75
Cent. Afric. Rep.	Diamonds (45), Coffee (20)	66
Chile	Copper (46)	46
Costa Rica	Bananas (22), Coffee (17)	39
Côte d'Ivoire[a]	Cocoa beans (36), Coffee (8)	44
Dominican Rep.	Ferro nickel (31), Sugar (22)	53
El Salvador	Coffee (45)	45
Ethiopia	Coffee (44), Hides and skins (21)	65
Fiji	Sugar (32)	32
Ghana	Cocoa (41), Wood (6)	47
Guatemala	Coffee (26), Sugar (13)	39
Guyana	Sugar (32), Bauxite (31)	63
Honduras	Bananas (40), Coffee (20)	60
Jamaica	Alumina (45), Bauxite (13)	58
Kenya	Tea (26), Coffee (18)	45
Malawi	Tobacco (68), Tea (11)	80
Papua New Guinea	Copper conc. (62), Coffee (13)	75
Paraguay	Cotton (32), Soybeans (31)	63
Rwanda	Coffee (66), Tea (22)	88
Uganda	Coffee (93)	93
Zambia	Copper (86)	86

[a]Figures refer to 1989.
Source: IMF International Financial Statistics, May 1992.

deteriorated by about 65 percent over the last six years. As a result, export earnings have been more than halved. . ."[6]

The structure of production in DCs is different from that in ACs (see Table 18.8). Agriculture is more important and services are less important to DCs. Long–term economic growth typically includes a shift from agriculture to other sectors. However, in the early stages of economic development, the size of the agricultural sector makes its performance an important part of economic growth. This sector is also of special concern because many of the

---

[6]*IMF Survey*, January 24, 1994, pp. 21–2.

Table 18.8
The Structure of Production (1989)

	Agriculture	Industry	Construction	Services
Developing countries	14.5	28.4	6.1	51.0
Developed market economies	2.0	24.5	4.9	68.6

Source: United Nations, *UNCTAD Handbook of International Trade and Development Statistics*, *1991*.

poorest people in the world live in agricultural communities. Unfortunately, government policies have often been biased against this sector.[7]

The Terms of Trade Problem

One "explanation" of underdevelopment is so common that it is worth examining in detail. The argument is that DCs suffer from a declining long–term trend in their terms of trade.[8] It is said that DCs are poor because they must export increasing amounts for a given amount of imports. Since DCs are poor, by definition, it may seem unnecessary to evaluate the terms of trade argument. However, if there truly is concern about the plight of DCs, an attempt must be made to identify the true causes of poverty. Faulty diagnosis can lead to incorrect policy prescriptions: at best we might end up treating the symptoms, not the disease; at worst, we could prolong or worsen the disease.

In order to assess the validity and significance of the terms of trade argument, three things must be considered:

1) the products that are important
2) the period over which to examine price changes
3) the implications of these price changes for economic welfare

[7]See Chhibber, A. and J. Wilton, "Macroeconomic Policies and Agricultural Performance in Developing Countries," *Finance and Development*, 23, Sept. 1986, pp. 7–9.

[8]The terms of trade may be defined as the ratio of the price of exports to the price of imports. The following discussion focuses on the long–term trend in the terms of trade. Plans to stabilize or increase primary product prices are discussed in the next section.

The Choice of Products

DCs often export primary products, so it is natural to focus on these products. Some are oil exporters, but oil prices are often excluded as being a special case (either because oil prices rose dramatically during the 1970s, or because oil prices are subject to special influences). It is arguable that products that have experienced abnormal increases in price should be excluded from the analysis because they are not typical of the general problem. The same reasoning would lead one to exclude products which have experienced abnormal decreases in price. (Over some periods oil would again be excluded.)

There is no right answer to the problem of product selection. If some products are excluded as being atypical, the objectivity of the measurement of the terms of trade is brought into question. It may seem that the selection of products is being made to generate the desired result. However, including all products leads to an average picture with little resemblance to the problems of individual countries which often rely on a handful of products.[9]

The Sample Period

The problems of measurement multiply when a sample period is chosen. Ideally, the period should begin with a base year when prices were neither abnormally high or abnormally low, otherwise the return to "normal" prices may be confused with the trend in prices. The terms of trade change continuously, and over a long period some changes average out. But, as Table 18.9 shows, in a single year the terms of trade can change twice as much as over a ten–year period. Therefore, the date one chooses for the beginning of a study is of great significance.

Table 18.9
Percentage Changes in the Terms of Trade

	1974–83	84	85	86	87	88	89	90
Developing countries	5.9	2.0	-2.2	-14.2	1.7	-3.9	1.7	2.1
Oil exporters	14.3	0.7	-4.3	-40.3	8.2	-17.0	9.2	14.4
Non–oil DCs	-2.0	3.2	-0.9	2.7	-0.7	1.1	-0.5	-2.5
Industrial countries	-1.3	0.6	1.2	8.6	1.0	1.3	-0.7	-0.7

Source: IMF *World Economic Outlook*, October 1992.

[9]The dramatic fall in oil prices in 1986 helped the DCs that are oil importers but hurt those that are oil exporters.

Welfare and the Terms of Trade

It is difficult to test empirically the proposition that over the twentieth century as a whole there has been a downward trend in the terms of trade of developing countries, and the evidence supporting the proposition is weak at best.[10] But, assuming a downward trend does exist, a decline in the relative price of the exports of developing countries does not necessarily imply lower welfare. The prices of digital watches, color televisions, and computers have declined relative to prices in general, but these changes are not viewed as an indication of a problem in the economic system. If prices decline because of technological improvements that reduce the costs of producing primary products, DCs may be better off after a price fall than they were before. (In fact, improvements in technology have reduced production costs and increased the supply of many products.) Therefore, lower prices do not necessarily imply lower welfare.

The Issue of Exploitation or Bias

If it could be shown that there is a significant long–run downward trend in the prices of primary products relative to manufactured goods, would this prove that the world trading system is biased against DCs? The answer is simple: no. Changes in the prices of primary products reflect structural changes that have little to do with the international trading system. There are many plausible reasons why commodity prices might decline relative to manufactured goods. Technological progress has reduced the production costs of primary products, provided substitutes for primary products, and enabled producers of manufactured products to economize on the inputs they use. Another influence has been that the rich countries' demand for primary products has weakened as they have shifted away from heavy manufacturing toward light manufacturing and services. Finally, a long–term downward trend in the relative price of primary products can be explained by changes in the nature of manufactured products. The quality of manufactured products is improving and the degree of technological sophistication is increasing continuously. In contrast, primary products have changed little

---

[10]The sample period used is critical to the results. For example, Cuddington and Urzúa (1989) found that: "Primary commodity prices (relative to manufactures) experienced an abrupt drop after 1920. Apart from this one–time structural shift, however, there is no evidence of an ongoing, continual downward trend in the relative price of primary goods" (p. 441). Also, see Barros, A. R. and Amazonas, A., "On the Deterioration of the Net Barter Terms of Trade for Primary Commodities," *UNCTAD Review*, 1993, pp. 99–116.

over the past few decades: sugar is sugar and doesn't change noticeably from one decade to another.

The Significance of the Terms of Trade Issue

The controversy over the terms of trade results from the choice of which facts to present and the interpretation put upon them. The controversy is important because we should attempt to diagnose the trade problems of poor countries correctly, but the question of the terms of trade may have received unwarranted attention. Exports of primary products usually account for less than 10 percent of a country's national income. Doubling the prices of these products would do little to change the disparity between rich and poor countries, even allowing for some generous multiplier effects. Historical experience also suggests that DCs are not likely to get rich exporting such products. Countries that have diversified their economies and exported manufactured goods have grown far more rapidly.

Figure 18.1
The Effects of an Increase in Supply When Demand is Inelastic

When demand is inelastic, the percentage change in quantity is less than the percentage change in price. Thus, when the quantity increases from Q_0 to Q_1, the fall in price (P_0 to P_1) is proportionately larger than the increase in quantity, and producers' revenue falls.

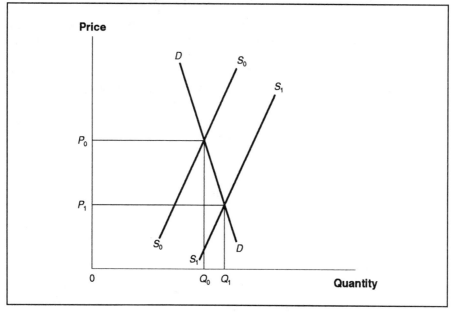

Why are the prospects limited for producers of primary products? Part of the answer is that (in the short run) the demand for primary products is inelastic with respect to price. Therefore, when the supply of primary products increases, the price of primary products falls so much that producers receive less revenue than they did initially.[11] This is illustrated in Figure 18.1. Also, as real incomes rise over time, consumers demand more manufactured goods incorporating the latest technology; they do not demand more primary products. Thus, the demand for primary products does not increase with income as much as the demand for manufactured products. The conclusion that suggests itself is that rather than focus on the prices of primary products, it may be more fruitful to encourage exports of manufactured products.

Reform Proposals and the New International Economic Order

In 1964, the first United Nations Conference on Trade and Development (UNCTAD) was convened in Geneva. UNCTAD has since become a permanent part of the United Nations, representing the views of DCs. During the 1960s, the main objectives were to secure lower (preferential) tariffs for DCs' exports and increased aid. Some success was achieved in the pursuit of the first objective. During the early 1970s, the objectives broadened to include fundamental changes in the international economic system.

The New International Economic Order

In 1974, a resolution was passed in the United Nations General Assembly calling for the creation of a **new international economic order (NIEO)**, and plans for the implementation of a NIEO were the subject of the UNCTAD IV conference in Nairobi, Kenya, in 1976. The flavor of the proposed NIEO can be appreciated by considering its four basic recommendations relating to:
1) market access and the trade policies of ACs
2) cartels to maintain and increase commodity prices
3) commodity price stabilization schemes
4) increased flows of aid

Market Access and the Trade Polices of ACs

DCs doubt whether ACs are really serious in their promotion of free trade. Manufacturing in ACs is protected by tariffs that often increase as higher

---

[11]The reverse is also true—a reduction in supply leads to an increase in revenue, as OPEC discovered in 1973–74. See Chapter 14.

stages of production are reached. Escalating tariffs are seen as barriers to development because they prevent DCs from competing in AC markets.[12] **Tariff preferences** are sometimes conceded in the form of a lower tariff on imports from DCs than those from ACs. However, the concessions often include limits on the amount a DC can export. Also, DCs have faced trade barriers in products in which they are competitive. Two of the most glaring examples of trade barriers that hurt DCs are the barriers ACs maintain on imports of textiles and steel, which are particularly odious because these are products that DCs can produce competitively. Production of steel and textiles does not require high technology, and DCs have a competitive advantage in these products because they have lower labor costs.[13]

Participation in GATT

DCs have not always participated fully in GATT. One reason is that they do not accept the principle of reciprocity in GATT negotiations: they feel that tariff concessions by ACs should not be conditional on the removal of their own tariff barriers. Another reason is that some DCs are not convinced that they have a lot to gain from trade. Unfortunately, it seems that the danger DCs face from an escalation of trade barriers is usually ignored. Given that preferential tariffs apply to a limited range of products, and include quantity limits, DCs have probably gained more from the reduction in general barriers to trade under the auspices of GATT than they have from preferential tariffs. However, as tariff barriers fell, non–tariff barriers increased.

Coverage of GATT

The coverage of GATT agreements has been a source of concern. In particular, DCs complain that agricultural products are excluded. This grievance is clearly justified. In general, developed countries have encouraged domestic agricultural production and used trade barriers to separate domestic and international markets. (The common agricultural policy of the European Union is a good example.) The result has been overproduction and a decline in world food prices. Also, dumping surplus output on world markets has sometimes destabilized world food prices. The high cost to rich countries of their agricultural polices has led some countries to express the view that reform is needed in this area. Although gains from lower trade barriers in agriculture are clearly possible, there is a long tradition of government

---

[12]Examples of tariff escalation are shown in Tables 5.1, 5.2, and 15.2.

[13]The Uruguay Round, discussed in Chapter 15, resulted in an agreement which may reduce barriers to textiles and steel imports.

intervention in rich countries to support domestic agriculture. The Uruguay Round addressed the problem of subsidized exports, but it remains to be seen whether the agreement will have much impact on world agricultural markets.[14] Perhaps we should be skeptical about whether poor countries will be allowed to export enough to rich countries to realize large gains from specializing in agricultural products.

Raw Materials and Producer Cooperation

The importance of primary products to DCs is reflected in the NIEO's objectives of stabilizing and increasing primary product prices. Let us begin by considering the objective of increasing primary product prices.

The oil price increase of 1973–74 created problems for DCs but also seemed to offer a solution to their problems, that is, it led some poor countries to hope that they would be able to follow the example of OPEC and push up the prices of their exports. One reason why such action is needed, it is alleged, is because the control of primary products is exercised by companies from ACs and leads to artificially low prices.[15] We need not spend time discussing such allegations of exploitation. The major argument against producer agreements does not concern the underlying motives—it is simply that such agreements are not sustainable.

If the price of a product is to be raised by a cartel agreement, all the major producers of the product must join so that supply can be restricted in order to push up the price. Also, if the higher price is to be maintained, overproduction must be prevented by the allocation of production quotas. It is possible that some major producers may refuse to join, for example, because they want to be able to take advantage of technological developments and do not want their output to be limited by the cartel agreement. Also, some producers may not join because they have different political or economic objectives from the other producers. (Recall that ACs are often major producers of primary products.)

The problems do not end there. If the cartel succeeds in raising the market price, the standard problem which then emerges is that the higher price acts as an incentive to members to "cheat" by overproducing or to withdraw from the agreement. Also, higher prices may eventually lead to competition from alternative sources of supply. Few markets have the

---

[14]The Uruguay Round almost failed due to differences between the United States and the European Union (in particular France) over proposals to cut farm supports.

[15]See Diaz–Alejandro, C. F., "International Markets for LDCs—The Old and the New," *American Economic Review*, (Papers and Proceedings), 68, May 1978, pp. 264–9. Reprinted in Adams (1985), pp. 487–95.

characteristic that allowed OPEC to be successful for so long—an inelastic product demand and a long period needed before alternative sources of supply can be developed. During the 1970s, oil producers were able to increase the price of oil by restricting supply, but even OPEC could not succeed forever. The development of new sources of supply, disputes between OPEC members over their production quotas, and a fall in the rate of growth of demand for oil eventually led to a fall in oil prices during the mid–1980s. In early 1994 oil prices were lower in real terms than they were 20 years earlier.

Cartels may also be undermined by technological advances leading to the development of synthetic substitutes that are cheaper or of higher quality than natural materials. For example, synthetic materials are widely used in the clothing industry, sometimes because they are cheaper and sometimes because they have special desirable properties. Tin was used in canning, but now cans are made of light–weight alloy which is cheaper and performs better than tin. UNCTAD's recommendation that "in cases where natural materials can satisfy the requirements of the market, new investment for the expansion of the capacity to produce synthetic materials and substitutes should not be made" is reminiscent of the calls of the Luddites to stop the spread of mechanization.[16]

Export Prices and Export Earnings

DCs have unstable export earnings because of fluctuations in the price and quantity of exports. Part of the problem is that because DCs often rely on a few commodities, price and quantity fluctuations are not averaged out as much as when exports are diversified. One of the objectives of UNCTAD has been to secure agreement on bufferstock schemes to stabilize the prices of important commodities. This idea seems attractive because a small number of commodities accounts for a large proportion of DC trade. Ten commodities are often the focus of these proposals: cocoa, coffee, tea, sugar, cotton, jute, sisal, rubber, copper, and tin.

Bufferstocks

Essentially, a **bufferstock** can be used to stabilize commodity prices in the same way as international reserves can be used to stabilize an exchange rate. When prices are low, the intervention agency increases the demand for the product and pushes up the price by adding to the bufferstock. When the price is abnormally high, sales are made from the bufferstock.

---

[16]The Luddite riots began in Britain in 1811. Machines were smashed in an attempt to stop the mechanization of the woolen industry.

Attempts to stabilize prices in this way have generally been unsuccessful. The initial problem is that funds must be available for the creation of the bufferstock. DCs do not have the required funds, and ACs have been reluctant to provide the funds needed. A second problem concerns the selection of the target price to be used by the intervention agency. Producers have an incentive to push for a high intervention price. But a price that is set too high results in an excess supply, and the intervention agency must continuously add to the bufferstock. Moreover, the excess supply created by the high price is likely to get worse because high prices attract new producers and lead consumers to look for substitutes. Eventually, the intervention agency runs out of funds and the bufferstock agreement collapses.

Figure 18.2
Bufferstocks and the Stability of Earnings

The demand for a primary product (coffee) is shown by the demand curve $D_0 D_0$. Initially, export revenue is $P_0 \times Q_0$. Assume that the supply of coffee falls from $S_0 S_0$ to $S_1 S_1$ as a result of a bad harvest. In the absence of a bufferstock, the price of coffee increases from P_0 to P_1. The tendency for export earnings to fall because of the fall in quantity is offset (to some extent) by the increase in price. Revenue is $P_1 \times Q_1$ after the fall in supply. Price stabilization prevents this offsetting price effect. Producers sell Q_2 at P_0 and $Q_0 - Q_2$ is sold from the bufferstock. Revenue is only $P_0 \times Q_2$. This price stabilization leads to a greater fall in earnings.

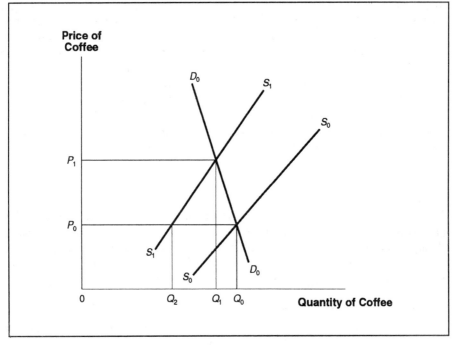

If a bufferstock is to stabilize prices, it must buy when prices are low and sell when prices are high. In other words, leaving storage and operations costs aside, the agreement should run at a profit. Requests by DCs for substantial resources to run such schemes suggests that the object of such schemes is price support, not price stability. If so, the schemes are probably doomed to failure. Also, if price support is the objective of the bufferstock, it is not surprising that ACs have been reluctant to spend money on schemes designed to increase the prices of the products they buy.

Even if a bufferstock can stabilize prices, this does not guarantee that export earnings will be stabilized. The effect on earnings depends on the source of the price change. When price changes result from demand fluctuations, export earnings will be stabilized by a bufferstock that stabilizes market prices. But, when price changes result from supply fluctuations, fixing prices may destabilize export earnings. For example, when there is a fall in supply, prices tend to increase, and this helps maintain export earnings. Price stabilization prevents the price increase and leads to lower export earnings. This is illustrated in Figure 18.2.

Resource Transfers

The United Nations established an AC target for official development aid to DCs of at least 0.7 percent of an ACs GNP, but few countries have reached this goal. In fact, as Table 18.10 shows, over the last two decades aid has declined as a percentage of some donors' incomes.

If past official aid had had a clearly demonstrable effect on income disparities, for many people the case for transfers from rich to poor countries would be overwhelming in view of the large disparities between incomes. In fact, the record of official aid has been patchy at best. Individual projects have sometimes been successful, but foreign aid has not reduced overall disparities between incomes. Whether this is because the aid has been wasted or because it has been too small is a matter of debate. We shall not examine this issue further because there are no signs that a massive increase in aid is likely, and because aid takes so many different forms.[17]

SDR Allocations

One proposal that crops up regularly is that IMF special drawing rights (SDRs) should be allocated to poor countries as a form of aid and not (as at

---

[17]Meier (1984, pp. 281–309), OECD (1985), and Cassen (1986) are useful introductions to the major issues.

present) on the basis of IMF quotas.[18] It is sometimes mistakenly argued that helping DCs in this way is virtually costless because SDRs cost nothing to create. True, SDRs cost nothing to create, but when a country uses SDRs to pay for goods or debts, the recipient in effect accepts SDRs rather than real resources. Thus, there is a resource cost from the acceptance of SDRs even if there is no cost of creation. If ACs are not willing to make direct payments of significant amounts of aid, or to write off debts, why should one expect them to agree to allocations of SDRs that have the same resource cost?

Other Recommendations

Other recommendations include: the development of appropriate technology and its transfer to DCs; the adoption of a set of rules to regulate the behavior of multinational corporations; the cancelling of debts of DCs; the formation of DC customs unions; a share in the profits (if any) of seabed mining; compensation for skilled workers from DCs who choose to remain in ACs; etc.

Table 18.10
Official Development Assistance

	1970	1980	1991	Millions of Dollars 1991
United States	0.32	0.27	0.20	11,362
Japan	0.23	0.32	0.32	10,952
France	0.66	0.63	0.62	7,484
Germany	0.32	0.44	0.41	6,890
Italy	0.16	0.15	0.30	3,352
United Kingdom	0.41	0.35	0.32	3,348
Canada	0.41	0.43	0.45	2,604
Netherlands	0.61	0.97	0.88	2,517
Sweden	0.38	0.78	0.92	2,116
Denmark	0.38	0.74	0.96	1,300
Norway	0.32	0.87	1.14	1,178
Australia	0.59	0.48	0.38	1,050
Belgium	0.46	0.50	0.42	831

Source: World Bank, *World Development Report, 1993.*

---

[18]SDRs are discussed in Chapter 13.

The numerous proposals reflect the plight of DCs. We are left feeling that DCs are asking ACs to do anything, but at least do something.[19] The challenge is to help DCs succeed in the present economic system, if demands for a new order are to be abandoned. Perhaps the most important step for ACs in meeting this challenge is to reduce barriers to trade on imports from DCs. This policy would increase incomes in ACs as well as DCs. One significant difficulty to overcome is the power of AC special interest groups. The next section considers the polices that DCs might adopt to increase economic growth.

Strategies for Trade and Development

Broadly speaking, two types of trade strategy have been used by DCs: a policy of restricting trade in an effort to concentrate on domestic production (import substitution), and increasing exports in an attempt to increase domestic income through international trade (export promotion).

Import Substitution

The rationale for **import substitution** is that the demand for primary products is inelastic with respect to price and income. Therefore, increasing the supply of primary products has an adverse effect on price (as Figure 18.1 shows), and long–term growth of income in ACs does not lead to a significant increase in the demand for these products. DCs also feel that trade barriers and lack of technology prevent them from competing with ACs in manufactured products. Therefore, they need protection to develop an industrial base.

Export Promotion

The proponents of export promotion argue that **export promotion** is preferable to import substitution because production is not limited to the domestic market. (The reader may recall that the benefit of an expanded market is one of the basic arguments in favor of free trade.) Although proponents of expanded trade accept that governments may encourage exports, they take a more market–oriented view of the world than the proponents of import substitution. For example, Krueger (1985b) says "Policies assisting those attempting to export have a high probability of success; policies determining what commodities shall be exported are probably destined to failure" (p. 208). To encourage export–led growth, other

---

[19]The different proposals also reflect differences between the interests of the DCs.

government policies should seek to maintain a stable economy, free trade, and a realistic exchange rate (a rate that changes gradually to reflect differential inflation rates and does not overvalue domestic currency).

What Is Wrong with Import Substitution?

The case for import substitution is a general version of the infant industry argument and has the same weakness: protecting an infant removes the incentive for it to become competitive. Although import substitution has encouraged the growth of the protected sectors, it has not been able to make the protected sectors efficient. Import substitution has also had limited success in establishing manufacturing. Assembly plants have been established, but usually DCs have not been able to manufacture components efficiently. One reason is that DC markets are too small for efficient large–scale production.[20] Another is that manufacturing techniques and machines have been imported from ACs, where a major objective is to economize on the use of labor. These machines required skilled maintenance and skilled operators. Therefore, the technology was not always appropriate for use in DCs.

Another problem is that import substitution has had adverse effects on the export sector. There are three reasons for this. First, import substitution encourages some domestic industries, but other industries that use the products of the protected industries, including exporters, face higher costs. Second, exporters suffer because their costs increase as resources are attracted to the import–competing sector. Third, an overvalued exchange rate is a common characteristic of countries that pursued import substitution. (Exporters suffer because an overvalued exchange rate makes their goods too expensive on world markets.) Capital flight is likely when a currency is overvalued because investors seek the capital gain which will result from the appreciation of foreign currency. In short, the policy of import substitution, which was supposed to reduce the need for foreign exchange, ends up creating a greater shortage of foreign exchange.

Import Substitution versus Export Promotion

The success of export promotion depends on the ability of DCs to penetrate foreign markets. Although a few DCs have pursued export promotion successfully, critics of export promotion suggest that sufficient market access cannot be expected to enable all DCs to pursue this policy: it is argued that

---

[20]Some industries in Brazil, China, and India were exceptions to this generalization because the domestic markets were large enough to sustain large–scale production (IMF, 1987, p. 88).

rich countries will not want or tolerate imports on such a scale. A more optimistic view is that market access will not be a problem because markets will expand. As DCs increase their exports, they will increase their imports from ACs and other DCs. As a result, market penetration by DC products will not be an issue.

The policies of export promotion and import substitution have been extensively studied. The consensus that has emerged from empirical studies is that export promotion is a more effective policy for promoting growth than import substitution. For example, Figure 18.3 shows the results of a World Bank study of the relationship between trade strategies and economic growth for 41 developing countries. Overall, the growth rates of the countries that pursued outward–oriented policies were greater than the growth rates of countries that pursued inward–looking strategies.

Debate continues over the relative merits of the two strategies. For example, advocates of import substitution argue that export promotion often worked because it was preceded by a period of import substitution during which the foundations for growth were established. The low rates of growth when import substitution policies were in place cast doubt on the view that import substitution provided the basis for future growth by encouraging the growth of a manufacturing base. The reason why many countries abandoned import substitution in favor of export promotion was because import substitution was not working. The debate will probably never be settled

Figure 18.3
Outward and Inward Looking Trade Strategies

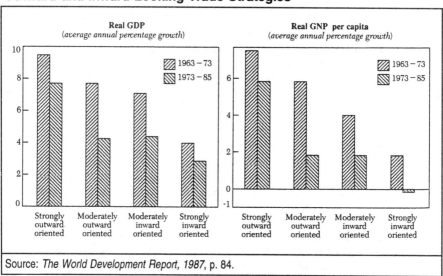

Source: *The World Development Report, 1987*, p. 84.

completely, but most professional economists now feel that export promotion is a more effective policy for economic development than import substitution.[21]

The East Asian Miracle

A small group of economies in East Asia have achieved high growth over a long period. Japan and the "four tigers" (Hong Kong, South Korea, Singapore, and Taiwan) led the way. They have been joined by the three newly industrializing economies: Indonesia, Malaysia, and Thailand. This group of eight countries achieved a growth rate of 5½ percent per year from 1965–90. Their success was the subject of a recent report by the World Bank. Some of the general lessons which emerged were:

1) Their macroeconomic performance was stable: inflation and budget deficits were kept under control. (Action was also taken to stop currencies from becoming overvalued.)
2) They had exceptionally high levels of saving and investment. (In some cases government policies encouraged high savings and investment.)
3) Educational spending concentrated on providing basic skills through primary and secondary education.
4) They started with lower technology than the rich industrialized countries, but they were able to adopt and adapt advanced technology from industrial countries, and thus to increase productivity.
5) Exports were encouraged (but the degree to which the countries were open to imports differed).
6) Per capita incomes were able to grow because growing income was not offset by rapid population growth.

One of the main conclusions which emerged from the report is that in many other ways their experiences differed. Proponents of government intervention can find examples of policy successes, while proponents of free markets can find examples of policy failures and successes achieved without government aid.[22]

---

[21]Official policies do not always reflect this consensus. It is interesting to watch Western diplomats argue that Japan's success is attributable to protectionist policies, while at the same time they preach to poor countries that they should abandon protection.

[22]"Strategies to promote exports and to adapt and improve the technology available in industrial countries have been by far the most generally successful selective approaches used by these economies and hold the greatest promise for other developing countries." (Page, 1994, p. 5.)

Table 18.11
The Growth of Developing Countries' Debt

	1970	1974	1976	1978	1980	1982	1984	1985
Total debt	68.4	141.0	203.8	311.7	428.6	551.1	673.2	727.7
Debt as % of GNP	13.3	14.0	16.6	19.3	20.6	26.3	33.0	35.8
Debt as % of exports	99.4	63.7	79.6	92.9	90.0	117.6	121.2	143.7
Debt service ratio	13.5	9.5	10.9	15.4	16.0	20.6	19.5	21.4

Sources: From *World Development Report 1984* and *1987*. Reprinted by permission of Oxford University Press, Inc. Compiled information from p. 31 (1984) for 1970–78 and from p.18 (1987) for 1980–85.

The International Debt Problem

Some Background to the Problem

The debt crisis began in August 1982 when Mexico announced that it could not meet interest payments on its debt. It soon became clear that other countries were also facing difficulties meeting the payments on the debt they had accumulated. Defaults by one or more of the major debtor nations could have resulted in some large banks going bankrupt. The vulnerable banks were those that had specialized in loans to a small number of the largest debtor countries. In particular, attention focused on the ten largest American banks that had loaned heavily to Argentina, Brazil, and Mexico. Loans to these countries accounted for more than 100 percent of capital for all but two of the banks.

Table 18.11 shows the growth of DC debt. The first row shows the total debt. The second row shows how debt increased as a percentage of GNP. The third and fourth rows are measures of the burden of debt in relation to export earnings (exports provide revenue to make payments on debt); the third row shows how debt has increased relative to exports, and the fourth row shows how debt service payments (interest and principal) have increased relative to exports. The last row is of great importance because, as debt payments increase relative to exports, there is less revenue available for imports. Some imports are consumption goods, but imported goods are often materials or capital goods that are needed in export production. For the major Latin American debtors in particular, export performance was hampered by high debt–service ratios. For example, in 1982 the ratios were Brazil, 89 percent; Argentina, 68 percent; and Mexico, 57 percent.[23]

---

[23]Weisner (1985).

Causes of the Debt Problem

Although the debt problem was recognized in the early 1980s, the origins of the problem go back to the 1970s. One cause of the buildup of DC debt was the 1973–74 oil crisis. Oil importers responded to the oil price increase by borrowing. The alternative, an attempt by many countries to cut back on imports of other goods, would have led to a collapse of world trade. Therefore, it was desirable that loans to oil importers should allow them to adjust gradually to higher oil prices. Unfortunately, adjustment to the adverse change in the terms of trade did not take place. This was partly because the banks did not attach conditions to the loans that they made. They recycled funds from oil exporters to oil importers, but did not ensure that the funds were used productively. In particular, some governments ran large budget deficits financed by money creation. Domestic inflation resulted, and loans were used to finance foreign exchange market intervention to maintain overvalued exchange rates.

Debt continued to increase gradually throughout the 1970s. Some countries needed international loans to finance development projects because there was a shortage of domestic funds due to an outflow of private capital.[24] Some of the projects were of dubious economic value. Allegations have been made that banks were too eager to lend and DCs too eager to borrow. This is too simplistic. It should be remembered that, at the time, DCs seemed to be good growth prospects and they were able to service their debts. Also, governments in lending countries often encouraged banks to make international loans. However, it is difficult to defend the exposure of major American banks in Latin America.

The Debt Problem in the 1980s

There are four reasons why the debt problem became more severe in the early 1980s: an increase in interest rates, an increase in oil prices, a world recession, and an increase in the value of the dollar. These developments are shown in Table 18.12. The reader may recall from Chapter 16 that interest rates on international loans are usually only fixed for short periods. As countries adopted inflation–reduction policies at the end of the 1970s, international loan rates followed domestic loan rates skyward, and interest payments on outstanding debts increased dramatically. The oil price increase of 1979 helped push the debts of oil–importing DCs higher, and this

---

[24]Estimates of private capital outflows by Kahn and Ul Haque (1987) suggest that between 12 percent and 30 percent of debt can be attributed to this cause. For some countries, notably Argentina and Venezuela, capital flight was a much greater problem than for others.

Table 18.12
Factors Contributing to the 1982 Debt Crisis

	3–month Eurodollar Rate	Average Crude Oil Price	Terms of Trade of Non–oil DCs (1975 = 100)	Trade Weighted Value of U.S. Dollar (March 1973 = 100)
1977	6.0	13.01	115.6	93.1
1978	8.8	13.06	108.3	84.2
1979	12.0	18.91	105.9	83.2
1980	14.0	31.39	95.5	84.8
1981	16.8	35.03	90.3	100.8
1982	12.2	34.23	84.6	111.7

Sources: *Barclays Review*, May 1984, p. 32. *Economic Report of the President*, 1986, p. 373.

combined with the anti–inflation policies of the time led to a world recession in 1980-82. During this period, commodity prices collapsed, world trade stagnated, and DC export earnings fell. Finally, because debts are usually denominated in dollars, as the dollar's value rose, the values of debt and interest payments on debt rose relative to the debtors' currencies or earnings in other currencies. The result of these influences was that debtors found they could not meet the interest due on past debts; they were often forced to borrow in order to meet their debt servicing obligations.

The Reduction of the Debt Problems of Banks

One of the major fears for lending countries was that a default by a major borrower, or a series of defaults, would lead to the collapse of the major banks. The banks belatedly recognized the possibility of defaults and the danger of their overexposure. The result was that new private lending virtually dried up in the mid–1980s, and, as a result, there was a substantial net transfer of funds from poor countries to rich countries as poor countries made payments on their past debts. The banks also took measures to reduce the level of their exposures. One method used was to sell off claims against debtor countries. These are now traded at a discount in a secondary market. (The size of a discount reflects the possibility that a loan will not be repaid.)

Banks have been able to reduce the absolute amount of their claims on DCs and have been able to deal with minor defaults and reschedulings.[25]

Why Didn't Debtor Nations Default?

Debtor nations have two things to lose from default: short–term trade credits, and access to future capital. Trade credits bridge the gap between the receipts from sales of a good and having to pay for a good. Having to pay cash for imports, or using barter, severely increases the cost of imports, effectively preventing normal trading relations. This is not a prospect to be taken lightly. The danger of losing future foreign capital may seem a less significant problem if a country already faces difficulties in borrowing additional funds. But, in general, countries which have pursued unilateral policies have generally found that they are unworkable because they need access to international credit. The arrears which built up had to be paid eventually, delaying adjustment did not help the economy, more had to be paid for such credit as was available, and isolationist polices undermined domestic confidence.[26]

Defaults and the Banking System

When debtors default, banks lose some of their assets and could go bankrupt (if their liabilities to depositors exceed their assets). However, the disaster scenario that suggests that if one or more major banks collapses the entire domestic banking system will collapse is unlikely. Domestic monetary authorities (the Federal Reserve in the United States) can ensure that domestic monetary stability is maintained by guaranteeing that liabilities to depositors will be honored. The Federal Reserve has shown that it is capable of handling a far bigger problem than international debt: the collapse of hundreds of savings and loan banks. The savings and loan crisis forced the government to pay hundreds of billions of dollars, but the system did not collapse.

---

[25]Rescheduling agreements are complex and vary greatly. Some common features include: a lower interest rate, spreading payments out over a longer period, and a period during which no payments need be made. See Watson, M., et al., *International Capital Markets: Developments and Prospects*, IMF Occasional Papers No. 43, 1986.

[26]Ahmed and Summers (1992).

The Brady Plan

In March 1989, Treasury Secretary Nicholas Brady suggested a plan based on **voluntary debt reduction**. The main mechanisms for debt reduction have been cash buy–backs of debt (at a discount) by debtors, or the exchange of existing claims for new "enhanced" claims which include a cut in the value of the debt, a cut in interest rates, or an extended repayment period. The "enhancements" which induce the banks to agree have taken the form of deposits of collateral which are held against future payments of interest or principal. The enhancements have been financed either from international reserves, with loans from international financial institutions, or with loans from the governments of creditor countries. The condition for future loans has usually been that countries have in place a credible adjustment program (making future repayments likely).

One of the common problems in debtor countries has been large government deficits. Often inflation has been a problem because new money has been printed to finance excess government spending. Adjustment has entailed getting these deficits under control by cutting government spending, and reducing inflation by cutting the rate of growth of the money supply. Privatization, returning parts of the public sector to private ownership, has also been used to raise money and because inefficient public sector enterprises were a drain on government resources. The countries that have successfully stabilized their economies are again experiencing inflows of private capital. Mexico is an example of how an economy can be transformed.

The Mexican Adjustment

The *1994 Economic Report of the President* describes Mexico's economic reforms as follows:

> "Mexico is one of the outstanding economic success stories of the last decade. After the debt crisis of 1982, the Mexican government began a broad program of economic reform, which has continued through the early 1990s. Fiscal policy changes, which removed the primary budget (that is excluding interest payments) from a deficit of about 7 percent of GDP to a sustained surplus, were the first step. More fundamental reform began in December 1987 when the Mexican government implemented a concerted program that combined macroeconomic stabilization with microeconomic liberalization.
>
> Stabilization efforts in 1989–91 were pursued through a fiscal policy of tight spending controls and tax reform that broadened the tax base and lowered tax rates, while maintaining a roughly stable

level of revenue. Monetary and exchange rate policies were combined to reduce inflation while preventing large exchange–rate movements. Finally, incomes policies were used to reduce expectations of inflation and any inflationary inertia.

The microeconomic reforms were sweeping. More than 80 percent of the 1,155 public sector enterprises in existence in 1982 have already been privatized or liquidated. Privatization has enhanced microeconomic efficiency and reduced the fiscal demands imposed by badly run state–owned enterprises. In addition, Mexico joined GATT in 1986. Tariffs were cut sharply and many nontariff barriers to trade, such as quotas and import licenses, were removed. Finally, a renegotiation and restructuring of Mexico's external debt eased its debt burden and greatly reduced the uncertainty associated with debt service.

The results of these reforms have been impressive. Inflation fell from approximately 160 percent in 1987 to 12 percent in 1992. At the same time, real GDP growth rose from –3.8 percent in 1986 to 4.5 percent in 1990 before slowing somewhat to 2.6 percent in 1992. The recent passage of NAFTA should strengthen the reform effort in Mexico and make a positive contribution to its economic performance in the future." (p. 226.)

The Debt Problem of the 1990s

One view might be that the debt problem does not exist anymore because the stability of the international financial system is no longer threatened. However, while private capital flows have resumed for a few middle income countries, there is a group of very poor countries with severe debt problems. Many of these countries lie in Sub–Saharan Africa, i.e., those countries to the south of the Sahara, excluding Nigeria and South Africa. They have difficulty making payments on their debt, and have little access to private capital markets. The reason for the lack of willingness in the private market to lend to these countries is obvious: banks are reluctant to make new loans to countries that have very limited growth prospects and difficulties making payments on their present debts. There is often no guarantee that the loans will be used productively or that they will ever be repaid. Also, when claims against debtor countries are trading in a secondary market at a discount, lenders face the prospect that new loans will fall immediately to the same discount. Loans from the World Bank and IMF have become more important than private capital for the countries with severe debt difficulties.

Debt Forgiveness

While it would cost money to reduce the debt problems of poor countries, this need not be the end of the story. Freed from the burden of trying to meet interest on foreign debt, DCs could finance new productive investments. In this case, their exports would increase, their economies would grow, and they would increase their imports of foreign goods. Therefore, debt forgiveness is not necessarily a total loss for ACs. In fact, if it could be guaranteed that past mistakes would not be repeated and DCs would undertake productive investments, in the long run forgiving debts might even benefit all countries.

The Future Role of Foreign Investment

It is becoming clear that private capital flows have a positive role to play in economic development, but that not all countries can expect to be beneficiaries. The debt problems of the poorest countries, and the future economic development of these countries, will not be solved by the private market alone. The prospects for meaningful growth are too limited. In some cases, it will be necessary to provide support to save lives.

Summary of Main Points

Developing countries (DCs) have remained poor while taking part in international trade. DCs trade mainly with **advanced countries (ACs)** and mainly export **primary products**. Often, a small number of products accounts for most of a country's exports.

It is often alleged that the poverty of DCs is attributable to a long–term downward trend in their terms of trade. There are methodological problems in assessing whether a significant long–term trend exists: the result is strongly affected by the choice of products and the period used. Also, it is not clear what significance should be attached to the results because welfare changes are not necessarily associated with changes in the terms of trade. Even if a trend could be identified, increasing the terms of trade would do little to increase living standards in DCs.

Many reform proposals have been put forward with the intention of increasing the incomes of poor countries. Some were reflected in the call of the United Nations for the creation of a **new international economic order (NIEO)**. Proposals covered issues such as increased aid to DCs, measures to increase the prices of primary products, and improved access for the exports of DCs in AC markets.

Some countries have succeeded in growing rapidly by adopting policies that encourage exports. Attempts to promote domestic industries by restricting imports (**import substitution**) appear to have failed. Whether

export promotion by DCs in general is a viable development strategy is a matter of debate. Skeptics point out that ACs do not allow market access in the products in which DCs are competitive, for example, agriculture, steel, and textiles. Promotion of exports, it is claimed, would lead to further restrictions. Many economists argue that DCs have suffered not from trade, but from lack of free trade.

The international debt problem can be viewed from the lenders' or the borrowers' perspectives. Some borrowers have built up large debts and have had difficulty meeting their repayments. A few have restructured their economies, have renegotiated loans (under the Brady Plan), and are experiencing renewed capital inflows. Others are still having problems repaying debt. In particular, the poorest countries seem to have few options without international help. The danger of defaults by borrowers and bankruptcy for major lending banks is receding because banks have sold debt in the secondary market and reduced their exposure in high–debt countries.

Study Questions

1. What are the characteristics of DC trade?
2. Increasing exports is often cited as a way of encouraging economic growth. Why might this be counterproductive for producers of primary products?
3. Explain the methodological problems in measuring the long–term trend in the terms of trade of producers of primary products. Assuming that a trend exists, can it be explained by factors other than exploitation?
4. Why has import substitution not encouraged growth?
5. Why might an overvalued exchange rate deter economic development?
6. Why is it unlikely that bufferstocks can increase long–run incomes?
7. Why do bufferstocks and cartels collapse?
8. In what ways can ACs help economic development without transferring resources to DCs?
9. What were the causes of the 1982 debt crisis?
10. In view of your answer to Question 9, is it likely that the international debt problem will escalate in the near future?
11. What is the significance of the international debt problem (a) for the United States and (b) for DCs?
12. Assuming that you were asked to represent a DC at the next UNCTAD meeting, what would you suggest or request?

Selected References

Adams, J., (ed.), *The Contemporary International Economy*, 2e, New York: St. Martin's, 1985.

Ahmed, M. and L. Summers, "A Tenth Anniversary Report on the Debt Crisis," *Finance and Development*, 29, September 1992, pp. 2–5.

Bank for International Settlements, *63rd Annual Report*, Basle: Switzerland, 1993, p. 61.

Bauer, P. T., *Reality and Rhetoric: Studies in the Economics of Development*, Cambridge, MA: Harvard University Press, 1984.

Cassen, R., "The Effectiveness of Aid," *Finance and Development*, 23, March 1986, pp. 11–14.

Cassen, R., et al., *Does Aid Work?* New York: Oxford University Press, 1986.

Corden, W. M., *The NIEO Proposals: A Cool Look*, Thames Essay No. 21, London: Trade Policy Research Center, 1979. Reprinted in Baldwin, R. E. and J. D. Richardson, (eds.), *International Trade and Finance*, 2e, Boston: Little Brown, 1981.

Cuddington, J. T. and C. M. Urzúa, "Trends and Cycles in the Net Barter Terms of Trade: A New Approach," *Economic Journal*, 99, June 1989, pp. 426–42.

Dornbusch, R., "International Debt and Economic Stability," *Economic Review*, Federal Reserve Bank of Kansas City, January 1987, pp. 15–32.

Grubel, H. G., "The Case Against the New Economic Order," *Weltwirtschaftliches Archiv*, 113, 1977, pp. 284–306. Reprinted in Adams (1985).

IMF, *World Economic Outlook*, Washington, DC: International Monetary Fund, 1987.

Kahn, M. S. and N. Ul Haque, "Capital Flight from Developing Countries," *Finance and Development*, 24, March 1987, pp. 2–5.

Krueger, A. O., *Foreign Trade Regimes and Economic Development: Liberalization Attempts and Consequences*, New York: Columbia University Press, 1974.

Krueger, A. O., "The Effects of Trade Strategies on Growth," *Finance and Development*, 20, June 1983, pp. 6–8.

Krueger, A. O., "Import Substitution Versus Export Promotion," *Finance and Development*, 22, June 1985a, pp. 20–23.

Krueger, A. O., "The Experience and Lessons of Asia's Super Exporters," in V. Corbo, (ed.), *Export–Orientated Development Strategies*, Boulder, CO: Westview Press, 1985b, pp. 187–212.

Meier, G. M., *Leading Issues in Economic Development*, 4e, New York: Oxford University Press, 1984.

OECD, *Twenty–Five Years of Development Cooperation*, Paris: OECD, 1985.

Page, J., "The East Asian Miracle: Building a Basis for Growth," *Finance and Development*, March 1994, pp. 2–5.

United Nations, *UNCTAD Trade and Development Report 1993*, New York: 1993.

Weisner, E., "Domestic and External Causes of the Latin American Debt Crisis," *Finance and Development*, 22, March 1985, pp. 22–26.

World Bank, *The East Asian Miracle: Economic Growth and Public Policy*, New York: Oxford University Press, 1993.

World Bank, *World Development Report*, various issues, New York: Oxford University Press.

Nineteen

Multinational Corporations

Introduction

For our purposes, a **multinational corporation** may be defined simply as an enterprise that operates in more than one country. Multinationals have been described by some people as a threat to freedom and welfare, whereas others have suggested that they contribute to the growth of world income and increase economic development. We shall see that it is not possible to say which view is nearer the truth. Multinationals can have many effects, and no two corporations are the same. Thus, critics and defenders of multinationals have no difficultly in finding examples to support their views.

We begin our study by examining the growth and importance of multinationals. The motives for foreign direct investment are examined. Then we consider the economic effects of multinationals at a global level and the economic effects on individual countries. A distinction is drawn between the economic effects of multinationals on host countries and source countries. A **source country** is the country where the multinational has its headquarters; a **host country** is a country where a multinational's foreign operations are located.

The Growth and Importance of Multinational Corporations

Multinationals are not a recent phenomenon. Around 2500 B.C., in the earliest recorded civilization, the merchants of Sumeria found it useful to have foreign representatives handle their products.[1] The British East India Company, a trading company that operated from A.D. 1600 until 1858, is often quoted as an early example of a multinational corporation. The origins of multinational corporations in manufacturing can be traced to the nineteenth century, when American manufacturing companies established foreign subsidies to produce goods embodying new technology. For example, in 1855 Singer licensed a foreign company to produce sewing machines, and in 1867 Singer established its own plant in Glasgow. In 1882 Western Electric

---

[1]This and the following examples are taken from a study by Wilkins (1970) documenting the early growth of American multinationals.

established a plant in Belgium to manufacture telephone equipment. In 1889 George Eastman incorporated a company in London to manufacture film for cameras he was exporting from the United States.

Although multinational enterprise has a long history, it was not until after World War II that multinational corporations became a significant force in the world economy. Their growth can be attributed to improvements in communications and the development of computers, which made it possible to manage foreign subsidiaries. Also, multinationals benefitted as the international market was opened up by falling transport costs and reductions in barriers to trade and investment. Global production and marketing became possible. Multinational enterprises are likely to play an important role in the world economy over the next few years because there are many new opportunities for investment emerging. For example, China is slowly opening up for business, and the countries which made up the Soviet Union are desperately trying to attract foreign companies to help their economic development.

The Importance of Multinational Corporations

There is no doubt that multinational corporations are an important part of the international economic system. It is estimated that at the beginning of the 1990s there were over 37,000 multinational corporations, with over 170,000 foreign affiliates. Fourteen developed countries are home base for 24,000 of these corporations. Multinational corporations had global sales of about $5.5 trillion in 1992.[2] The output of multinationals in the United States accounted for over one quarter of U.S. GDP. Multinational corporations play a very important role in trade—they account for over 75 percent of U.S. merchandise trade. Sales by one part of a company to another part of the same company, intrafirm trade, accounted for about 30 percent of U.S. exports, and 45 percent of U.S. imports, in 1992.[3]

Most of the large corporations shown in Table 19.1 are multinationals. It is often pointed out that the value of the sales of one of these companies is larger than the national income of many small countries. However, although national income is measured as value added, sales figures do not take account of inputs purchased by a corporation. Therefore, sales figures tend to overstate the size of corporations relative to countries. We would have to deduct the value of inputs used by multinationals to have

---

[2]United Nations (1993).

[3]In contrast, 75 percent of U.S. imports from Japan are intra–firm. (Economic Report of the President, 1994, p. 218.)

comparable figures. However, the value added of the largest multinationals would still be larger than some countries' incomes.

A common misconception about multinationals is that they are all or nearly all American. American companies account for only eight of the 25 largest industrial companies in the world (see Table 19.1), and they account for only 14 of the top 50. Multinationals sell both to the domestic market and the world market. Given the size of the domestic market in the United States, it is not surprising that firms based in that market are large. Domestic market size also helps explain why firms from the two other large regional markets, Europe and Japan, account for the majority of large non–American corporations.

Table 19.1
The World's Largest Industrial Corporations (1991–92)

Rank		Corporation		Sales $millions	Assets $millions	Assets rank	Employees Number	Employees rank
92	91							
1	1	General Motors	U.S.	132,774.9	191,012.8	2	750,000	1
2	3	Exxon	U.S.	103,547.0	85,030.0	6	95,000	67
3	4	Ford Motor	U.S.	100,785.6	180,545.2	3	325,333	7
4	2	Royal Dutch Shell	Brit/Neth	98,935.3	100,354.3	4	127,000	41
5	5	Toyota	Japan	79,114.2	76,131.8	8	108,167	54
6	7	IRI	Italy	67,547.4	—		400,000	3
7	6	IBM	U.S.	65,096.0	86,705.0	5	308,010	8
8	11	Daimler Benz	Germany	63,339.5	53,209.9	13	376,467	4
9	8	General Electric	U.S.	62,202.0	192,876.0	1	268,000	12
10	9	Hitachi	Japan	61,465.5	76,667.6	7	331,505	6
11	10	British Petroleum	Brit	59,215.7	52,637.3	14	97,650	64
12	12	Matsushita	Japan	57,480.8	75,645.1	9	252,075	14
13	13	Mobil	U.S.	57,389.0	40,561.0	24	63,700	100
14	17	Volkswagen	Germany	56,734.1	46,480.2	20	274,103	11
15	18	Siemens	Germany	51,401.9	50,752.8	15	413,000	2
16	14	Nissan	Japan	50,247.5	62,978.5	10	143,754	31
17	15	Phillip Morris	U.S.	50,157.0	50,014.0	16	161,000	25
18	19	Samsung	S Korea	49,559.6	48,030.8	19	188,558	19
19	16	Fiat	Italy	47,928.7	58,013.6	11	285,482	9
20	20	Unilever	Brit/Neth	43,962.6	24,267.0	49	283,000	10
21	21	ENI	Italy	40,365.5	54,790.5	12	124,032	46
22	24	Elf Aquitane	France	39,717.8	45,129.4	21	87,900	74
23	26	Nestle	Switzer	39,057.9	30,336.3	39	218,005	15
24	25	Chevron	U.S.	38,523.0	33,970.0	34	49,245	143
25	27	Toshiba	Japan	37,471.6	49,341.6	18	173,000	22

Source: *Fortune*, July 26, 1993, p. 39.

The Geographical Distribution of Foreign Direct Investment

Multinational corporations are established by foreign direct investment. Direct and portfolio investment are similar in that both involve a flow of capital. In the case of **portfolio investment,** there is no attempt to gain control over the operations of the foreign enterprise, which continues to be run by local managers. **Direct investment** entails the acquisition of sufficient capital to exercise a measure of control over an enterprise. The distinction between the two is inevitably arbitrary. What percentage of equity is needed to exercise influence over operations? The U.S. Department of Commerce defines direct investment as the acquisition of 10 percent or more of a company's equity.

Table 19.2 shows the geographical distribution of American direct investment abroad and foreign direct investment in the United States. Most American direct investment abroad (three quarters) is in developed countries. This is significant because, although the activities of multinational companies in developing countries have attracted attention, developing countries are not particularly important to multinationals. Latin America accounts for over half of the stock of American foreign direct investment in developing countries.

The stock of foreign direct investment is not an accurate measure of the current value of foreign direct investment because it is based on historical costs and does not reflect increases in the market value or replacement cost of foreign assets caused by inflation. For example, in 1992 the value of

Table 19.2
Foreign Direct Investment by Regions (1992)

By U.S. firms (outward)	
United Kingdom	77.8
Canada	68.4
Germany	35.4
Switzerland	28.7
Japan	26.2
All Countries	486.7
By foreign firms in the U.S.	
Japan	96.7
United Kingdom	94.7
Netherlands	61.3
Canada	39.0
Germany	29.2
All Countries	419.5

Source: *Economic Report of the President*, 1994, p. 212.

American foreign direct investment based on historical cost was $486.7 billion, whereas the market value was estimated to be $776 billion.[4] A second problem when attempting to use investment figures as a guide to the significance of foreign direct investment is that the figures record the ownership of equity and do not necessarily show the resources controlled.

Reasons for Foreign Direct Investment

In order to understand the operations of multinationals and the problems they are alleged to cause, we must understand why a company undertakes foreign direct investment.

Inputs and Raw Materials

In extractive industries the reason for foreign operations is obvious: oil companies such as Exxon and Royal Dutch Shell locate where there is oil; copper mining companies such as Anaconda and Kennecott locate where there is copper. However, this does not explain why foreign firms exploit resources rather than local firms. A common explanation of this phenomenon is that local firms lack the capital and technology needed to find and develop natural resources.

Manufacturing firms can buy inputs on world markets, but they may have an incentive to acquire control over foreign sources of inputs. For example, a firm can guarantee its source of supply and avoid delays, it can reduce its holding of inventories, and the inputs can be designed or packaged to meet the needs of the corporation. Also, it may be possible to deny competitors access to inputs.

Costs

Companies may invest in other countries to take advantage of lower production costs. Low wages are an important example, as are subsidized capital and low rents. For example, low wages in Mexico have induced some American firms to locate part of their operations there. However, other firms have pulled out of Mexico. One reason is that productivity is so low that, even with the lower wage cost, it is more expensive to produce in Mexico than in the United States. (Also, when firms look at other costs, Mexico appears less attractive: for example, the poor infrastructure leads to high

---

[4]British investments in the United States are much older than those of Japan, so it is probable that the 1992 market value of the United Kingdom's assets in the United States far exceeded the market value of Japan's American assets.

transport costs, and energy costs can be high.) In fact, most of the output of **majority owned foreign affiliates (MOFAs)** is produced in relatively high–wage countries.[5]

Even if production costs are low, this does not necessarily imply that production by a multinational is viable in that country. Multinational corporations incur costs that local firms do not. For example, communication and travel between the parent and foreign subsidiaries can be expensive. Also, a multinational may incur costs because the managers are not familiar with the language, customs, and culture of the society in which they work.

If a multinational is to be able to compete with local firms in a foreign market, it must have some advantages that they do not. These advantages can take many forms. For example, a multinational corporation may possess superior manufacturing technology, managerial experience and methods, and an international distribution network for its products. Also, it may be able to borrow capital more easily than local firms because it has access to international capital markets.

International Subcontracting

Initially, foreign production by multinationals was often destined for local markets. During the late 1960s and 70s there was a growth of foreign production for re–export to the home country or to other foreign markets. One reason for this development was that wage differences between countries exceeded differences in productivity. Components manufactured in the United States are now assembled in developing countries and then re–exported to other markets or back to the United States. In this way, foreign subsidiaries are incorporated into an international production process.[6] Foreign assembly usually takes place in products that have a high value to weight ratio, and when assembly is labor intensive and can be separated from other parts of the production process. American companies are able to use foreign assembly because the United States does not levy a duty on that part of a product's value attributable to the use of components made in the United States. This arrangement is known as the **offshore assembly provision.**

---

[5]"U.S. multinationals do not appear to have shifted manufacturing operations to low–wage countries to any significant degree between 1977 and 1991. In both years, about 85 percent of MOFA gross product in manufacturing was accounted for by relatively high–wage countries." Mataloni and Goldberg (1994, p. 42).

[6]See United Nations (1993).

Technology and Manufacturing

When a company has a secure domestic market position, it may own intangible assets such as managerial skills, patents, and trademarks. The company may be able to use these assets in foreign markets without jeopardizing the home market. Foreign production is sometimes preferable to exporting because minor modifications can be made to suit local specifications and tastes. Also, exporting may be difficult because of high transport costs or barriers to trade.

A choice must be made between setting up foreign manufacturing facilities through foreign direct investment, or selling the right to produce a product to foreign manufacturers. Foreign direct investment may be preferred for a number of reasons. Patents can be sold, but a company cannot easily sell its manufacturing experience. Also, when a company licenses foreign production, it has less control over the product. The company may want to protect its name and keep its manufacturing technology secret. Finally, foreign licensing is not an option if potential foreign licensees do not have adequate capital.

Market Access

Market access is important for companies marketing products worldwide. Market access can be limited by transport costs or by government barriers to trade. The effects of transport costs are obvious: American companies selling in Europe are more competitive if they do not have to ship their goods across the Atlantic. The importance of transport costs depends on the product. For products that have a high value in relation to size and weight, transport costs are less important. For example, American electronics companies have been able to move production to the pacific rim and export the products back to the United States because transport costs are low relative to the value of electronics goods.

Tariff and non–tariff barriers to trade can also be a significant influence on a company's location decision because a company can avoid trade barriers by producing within a country. Automobiles are often affected by barriers to trade, and there are many cases where foreign producers have opened factories within an important export market. For example, the possibility of import restrictions was one of the reasons why foreign automobile manufacturers have set up plants in the United States. Similarly, Japanese automobile manufacturers have opened plants in the European Union. The United Kingdom has benefitted from new foreign companies, in part because wages are lower in the United Kingdom than in most of the other member countries of the European Union. Also, some allege that the health, safety, and pollution standards in the United Kingdom are less stringent than in other member countries.[7]

Dealer Networks

A company's activities do not always end when a product is sold. The availability of services and advice to customers is often an important part of a company's activities. Failure to provide these services can be sufficient reason to prevent a product selling. Would you buy a make of car which is only backed up by one or two dealers in the United States? Foreign direct investment is sometimes needed in order to provide customer services, but the provision of a dealer network does not necessarily imply foreign ownership. Local franchises can be a substitute for a dealer network owned by the company itself. This solution is often adopted in the automobile industry.

Taxes

Finally, companies must consider the range of taxes that countries apply to their activities. Taxes on profits are one important example. States or towns often compete with each other by giving periods of tax exemption to attract a company. Although taxes may influence location, it is unlikely that they are the dominant influence relative to other factors such as market proximity and economic and political stability. (The reason is that multinationals can often find ways to avoid paying taxes.)

The Global Effects of Multinational Corporations

The Allocation and Quantity of Capital

One of the basic effects of multinationals is that they increase global income. They do this by reallocating resources (mainly capital) between countries to take advantage of local production and marketing opportunities. Because of their size, wealth, and global connections, they are better able to recognize and exploit investment opportunities than national companies. In so doing, they increase the world stock of capital and the level of world income. An interesting benefit from international factor mobility is that multinationals

---

[7]The refusal of the British Conservative government to adopt the European Union's social charter, which created and standardized some benefits for workers in the European Union, is an example of a country attempting to attract foreign companies by its low costs.

reduce the welfare losses that might otherwise result from barriers to trade. Companies can produce in foreign markets instead of exporting to these markets. For example, the negative impact on American consumers of restrictions on imports of Japanese automobiles has been somewhat offset by the production of automobiles in Japanese plants in the United States.

Economies of Scale

Multinational corporations also increase world income by taking advantage of economies of scale. Large–scale production is possible when a plant can produce for a number of countries. Also, the average cost per unit of output from overheads such as research and development is reduced if increased output allows the overhead cost to be spread over more units. Another source of lower costs is that large firms may be able to subcontract internationally to take advantage of low production costs.

Monopoly Power

The argument that multinationals improve the global allocation of resources must be qualified to the extent that multinationals are a departure from perfect competition, that is, they have monopoly power. The significance of this observation is difficult to assess. Basic microeconomic theory would lead us to expect that a monopolist will charge a higher price and produce a smaller quantity than a competitive industry with the same costs. However, if large (monopolistic) firms have lower average costs than small (competitive) firms, as seems likely in the case of multinationals, the departure from perfect competition need not reduce welfare. Also, merely because multinationals are large does not mean that they can behave as monopolists: competition between large firms is often intense.

Multinationals and Trade Theory

Standard trade theory is based on the assumption that factors of production are mobile within countries but not between countries. This assumption might lead one to predict that the resources available within a country determine the production possibilities of the country. Multinationals do not fit neatly into standard trade theory because a country's production possibilities change when the stock of capital increases (as a result of a company locating within the country). The policy implication is that countries should not only consider the goods which can be produced from available resources, but the goods that might be produced if suitable companies can be induced to move into the country. Standard trade theory might lead us to place too much emphasis on the availability of local resources.

The Economic Effects of Multinational Corporations on Source Countries

Wages and Employment

It has been suggested that multinationals reduce wages and employment in the source country; for example, in the United States we often hear complaints about an export of American jobs. There are two main ways in which this might happen. First, foreign investment may be undertaken instead of domestic investment. In this case, real wages in the source country are reduced by the export of capital (because the marginal productivity of labor declines as the amount of capital that domestic labor has to work with decreases). Employment may also be reduced if there are imperfections in the labor market that prevent real wages from falling or prevent labor from moving into other activities.

Multinationals may reduce wages and employment in the source country since foreign investment can lead to the growth of foreign companies that compete with producers in the source country. For example, rather than buy from American suppliers, some American firms have established foreign plants to manufacture parts for automobile plants in the United States. American–owned foreign companies also compete with American firms in world markets. This leads to heated allegations that American companies are sacrificing American workers in the pursuit of profit, or that they are undertaking foreign investment because they want to weaken the power of trade unions by reducing the dependency of American factories on American goods.

There are a number of reasons for avoiding generalizations about the effects of foreign investment on wages and employment in the source country. First, the assumption that foreign investment replaces domestic investment is too simplistic. In many cases, domestic and foreign investment are not substitutes. The alternative to foreign investment may be no investment at all. For example, firms may undertake foreign investment to break into markets that cannot be supplied by exports, or to guarantee a source of raw materials. In these examples, foreign investment is likely to increase wages and employment in the source country. Second, foreign direct investment may be financed by foreign earnings or by borrowing abroad, rather than by domestic capital. In these cases there is no reason to suppose that domestic investment will fall. Third, foreign direct investment may lead to an increase in employment in the source country as a result of sales of inputs by the parent company to foreign subsidiaries or because the foreign distribution network can be used to market other products of the parent company.

Historical experience suggests that foreign direct investment does not have an adverse effect on the economy of the source country. During the 1960s, rapid American foreign direct investment was accompanied by high employment in the United States. More recently, the growth of multinationals from Japan and the newly industrialized countries of Southeast Asia took place while the economies of these countries were growing rapidly. High foreign investment seems to be a sign of success, not a cause of weakness.

Loss of Tax Revenue

In principle, the source country can gain from taxes levied on the profits of multinationals. In fact, the gain to the United States and other source countries is usually small because of the way in which source countries tax the profits of multinationals. First, multinationals are allowed to defer taxes on foreign profits that are reinvested abroad. This acts as an incentive to foreign investment. Reinvested earnings are one of the main factors behind the growth of foreign direct investment. Second, if a company chooses to repatriate profits to the United States, it can deduct the taxes it has paid in the host country from its American tax liability. For example, if a company has earned $100 million in profits, at a tax rate of 35 percent it would be liable for $35 million in the United States. If it has already paid $30 million to the host country, its American tax liability is only $5 million. The method of taxing multinationals is designed to avoid double taxation. It has an important effect: the total tax rate applied to domestic and foreign earnings of a company is the same. Thus, the procedure reduces the possibility that worldwide investment will be distorted by taxes.

In practice, multinationals are usually taxed as though transactions between different parts of the same corporation take place as if they were between separate companies. But different parts of a corporation are so closely linked that companies can alter revenues and costs within the corporation to ensure that profits are not earned. **Transfer pricing** is one way that a company can avoid local taxes. For example, assume that a French company wants to transfer funds to an American company. It can do so by paying an abnormally high price for purchases from the American company. The excess payment over the normal cost is in effect a capital transfer. Alternatively, the transfer can be achieved by the French company selling goods to the American company for less than their true value.[8]

The problem is that, as a result of reinvestment abroad, the deduction of foreign tax payments, and transfer pricing, many large companies seem to be able to avoid paying taxes completely. This led California to introduce a

---

[8]Transfer pricing also enables multinationals to avoid import duties by undervaluing imports.

"unitary tax" which taxes companies on their global earnings. The problem with this approach is that firms operating in California could be liable for taxes in California even if they never make a profit there. Also, companies could be liable for double taxation. The California tax was challenged in court by Barclays Bank (a British bank), but the U.S. Supreme Court ruled (in June 1994) that government does have the right to tax corporations on global income. In response to protests from multinationals, the fear that California would lose business, and the danger of foreign retaliation, California passed a law in 1993 allowing corporations to choose between unitary taxation and the normal system of taxation (which exempts foreign profits from taxation as long as they are not repatriated to California).

Perhaps global corporations create a need for a global tax system, but there is no sign of this being a likely development. While governments would like to be able to collect tax from multinationals, individual countries which unilaterally adopt their own solutions are likely to lose business and be faced with foreign retaliation. This could lead to a tax war. If governments decide to tackle the issue, the debate about how best to tax multinationals promises to be very interesting.

The Economic Effects of Multinationals on Host Countries

Although most foreign direct investment is from one developed country to another, in the following discussion of the effects of multinationals on host countries we shall often assume that the host country is a developing country. There are two reasons for this. First, individual multinationals are less significant in economies with high levels of income and diversified production than they are in poor countries. Second, investment flows between developed countries are offsetting to some extent. Although multinationals from developing countries have emerged, foreign direct investment in developing countries is much larger than foreign direct investment by developing countries.

Output and Employment

An inflow of capital increases real income because additional capital increases the productivity of labor. If there is high unemployment, which is common in developing countries, the level of employment will also increase. A commonly accepted view is that developing countries lack the capital and technology to be competitive producers. Multinationals can provide capital and technology that developing countries lack, and can help them increase exports without first having to develop a manufacturing base. Drucker (1974) offers a slightly different explanation of the gains to developing countries. He attributes underdevelopment to the low productivity, not the limited availability, of resources. He suggests that multinationals help channel local resources into productive uses, which sets off multiple repercussions in the economy, so the gains in one sector spread out to other sectors.

The general argument that multinationals increase income and employment must be qualified. The total output of a multinational is not always an accurate representation of the scale of a company's activities in a particular market, because multinationals often use imported inputs. Particularly in the case of assembly operations, the domestic value added may be quite small relative to total output. The smaller the domestic value added, the smaller will be the contribution of a multinational to income and employment. Even if employment increases by a large amount, not all local people gain. For example, domestic employers who compete with the multinational for inputs find that their costs increase.

An indication of the benefits from direct investment is the fierce competition between American cities for firms. Local officials try many gimmicks to attract companies, and all major areas have people working to attract companies. Countries also gain from direct investment, and they too compete fiercely for new plants. For example, European Union countries have been competing to attract Japanese automobile companies. In Wales and Northeast England, where mines closed and people were unemployed, Japanese companies provided desperately needed employment. Northern Mexico has seen similar benefits.

Balance of Payments

Some countries are concerned about the effects of multinationals on the balance of payments. If a country has a balance of payments deficit (on the sum of the current account and net private capital) which is financed by official borrowing or reserves, the country may be anxious to increase its foreign exchange earnings. In other words, countries may want to see an increase in credit items in the balance of payments.[9] The initial effect of a multinational on the balance of payments of a host country is ambiguous: when a multinational locates in a country, there is a capital inflow that is a credit in the balance of payments. When a company's operations have begun, there are other effects. Exports by the multinational are a credit item, whereas debit items include imported materials and payments to the parent company (such as fees, royalties, and profits).

---

[9]The balance of payments effects of multinationals may be particularly important to countries with overvalued exchange rates. While multinationals do affect the balance of payments, the damage done to an economy by an overvalued exchange rate is potentially much more serious.

A company that produces primarily for export will probably result in an overall credit for the host country. A company that uses imported inputs and sells in the domestic market will probably lead to an overall debit. (However, the debit resulting from a multinational producing and selling in the domestic market will be smaller than if the goods were imported instead.) To complicate matters, in some years financial transfers may outweigh the effects of a multinational's trading operations. It is impossible to say whether the overall effect on the balance of payments in any year will be a credit or a debit. Each multinational corporation must be examined separately, and the effects of each may change through time.

Taxation

One "problem" encountered by host countries is that multinationals do not willingly pay high taxes. For example, transfer pricing enables companies to avoid earning profits in areas where taxes are high. In order to control transfers of funds, governments may require companies to use world market prices for intracompany trade. However, in some cases international prices for comparable products are not available, for example, when the company is the sole producer of a particular type of product. Also, there are no standards for fees and royalties or for services such as management.[10] These considerations mean that it is difficult for governments to control transfer pricing. Companies have difficulty fixing appropriate prices when world prices for similar products or services are not available. If a company's prices are not challenged, then the company may assume that they were appropriate.

Ultimately, if a company is forced to pay high taxes, it may decide to leave a country. This is understandable. If a company locates in a country because it has low taxes, no one should be surprised if it leaves when taxes are increased. The possibility that the conditions facing a multinational in a host country will change lies behind the interesting idea of obsolescing contracts.

Obsolescing Contracts

Early critics of multinationals suggested that developing countries inevitably faced one–sided contracts when they acted as hosts to multinationals. Partly this notion seemed to derive from the observation that large companies were rich, and therefore powerful, while some small countries were poor, and therefore weak. A more rational explanation is that there are substantial costs

---

[10]One simple way to transfer money out of a country is to send a management team on a visit (holiday) and then charge a large amount for their services.

and risks associated with locating in developing countries. Thus, in order to attract multinationals, developing countries often had to give concessions. For example, countries were induced to give tax concessions or access to duty–free imports.[11]

Once the initial costs have been paid and the risks overcome, the company has a potentially much more profitable investment. Because companies want to protect their investments and avoid reallocation costs, developing countries have sometimes been able to renegotiate contracts on much more favorable terms than were possible initially. In other words, in some cases, the initial agreement became obsolete. Recognition of this possibility marked an important step forward in understanding the relationship between host countries and multinationals.[12]

The extraction of natural resources examplifes the **obsolescing contract**. In the case of the extraction of natural resources, the returns from the development of deposits are often uncertain. Companies were induced to undertake exploration and development by concessions such as low taxes. When these projects were successful, resentment was felt in the host country because foreign companies were making large profits from extraction of the country's resources. As a result, tax rates were increased, and in some cases foreign firms were nationalized. Oil companies are an obvious example. To avoid losing capital, many companies now prefer joint ventures or licensing of technology to foreign direct investment.

Nationalization of foreign assets is an extreme example of the obsolescing contract. In some cases compensation has been paid at the time of nationalization, such as in 1970 when Peru took over the 51 percent interest of Chase Manhattan in the Peruvian Banco Continental. In other cases, compensation has not been paid. An early example of the expropriation of foreign assets without compensation was the seizure of foreign assets in the Soviet Union following the revolution of 1917. The confiscation of foreign assets by the Cuban government in 1960 was a similar case. Other examples where compensation was not paid include Peru's seizure of the assets of the International Petroleum Company in 1968, and Chile's seizure of the copper mining interests of Anaconda and Kennecott in 1971.[13]

---

[11]In cases where host countries were induced to guarantee a company a domestic monopoly, the gains to the host country have often been less than where host countries were able to maintain competition. See Moran (1985) for examples.

[12]The theory of obsolescing contracts was put forward by Vernon (1971).

[13]In the last two cases the American government eventually reached settlements with the governments of Chile and Peru.

Technology Transfer

It has been suggested that multinationals are a means of transferring technology from developed countries to developing countries. For example, local firms can copy the technology of the multinational or obtain it under license. Although multinationals may produce in developing counties using technology that was not locally available, the extent to which this technology is transferred to other sectors of the host's economy, and the usefulness of the technology to the developing country, are often limited. Part of the problem is that multinationals use high technology originally designed for use in developed countries. This technology is not appropriate for local companies in a developing country. Also, multinational companies have little incentive to use low technology because this technology is more easily copied than high technology.

Another factor limiting the transfer of technology is that research and development is usually based in the source country. Host countries might like research and development to be carried out in their countries, but it is unrealistic to assume that research staff and research facilities can be moved from the source country to a host country, especially in cases where the host country is a poor country. Multinational corporations may even reduce the research capacity of host countries by attracting employees back to the source country. For example, Canadians often leave Canada for the United States. This problem has been dubbed the "brain drain." Although the brain drain can be a serious problem, it is not the result of multinational enterprise, since employment opportunities with foreign companies can induce people to emigrate. For example, universities often employ foreign academics (though universities are not usually multinational corporations).

An example of the gain which can be experienced from technology transfer is the modernization of the American automobile industry. Japanese firms operating in the United States showed that efficient production could be achieved using American workers. American firms learned from Japanese firms and copied production and management techniques. Also, joint ventures between American and Japanese firms helped spread technology and management techniques (and have blurred the distinction between what is domestic and what is foreign).

Externalities and Safety Problems

It is often alleged that multinationals operate in an undesirable manner, by polluting the environment or exploiting natural resources at too great a rate. Companies in advanced countries are subject to many controls to prevent such problems, but in developing countries the controls are much weaker or even nonexistent. Thus, it has been said that foreign direct investment is a way for the company to avoid controls at home. In the host country, multinationals may be no better or worse than local firms, but because of their size, one company may do greater harm.

The Union Carbide Case

Unfortunately, examples of harm are easily found. One of the worst occurred in 1984 when 2,000 people died in Bhopal, India, following the emission of poison gas from a factory owned by the American company Union Carbide. More people died later of their injuries: the *New York Times* (February 15, 1989) reported over 3,500 dead and 200,000 injured.

The Union Carbide case is interesting because in February 1989 the Indian Supreme Court ordered Union Carbide to pay $470 million as a result of the accident.[14] This amount may seem small given the size of the tragedy. Leaving aside the question of whether Union Carbide was negligent or legally responsible (the plant was operated by an Indian subsidiary), the case shows the problem of holding a multinational company liable for damages. Union Carbide's Indian assets at the time were only worth about $30 million; thus a larger settlement could not have been enforced by seizing assets. Perhaps a larger settlement might eventually have been reached by proceeding through Indian and then American courts, but India's Supreme Court felt that immediate relief was needed rather than prolonged legal wrangling.[15]

The actions of companies can never be wholly regulated, so countries must rely on the social responsibility of firms. The failure of individual firms to recognize their responsibilities is not confined to multinational corporations. Local companies can behave irresponsibly. One of the reasons why multinationals are criticized less now than in the past is that they recognize that their long-term interests are served by generating goodwill.

Nationality and Allegiance

Early critics of multinational corporations suggested that multinationals would reduce international competition, and that the power of corporations would weaken and replace the power of national states. These fears have proved to be largely unfounded. Some of the criticism was because the multinationals were seen as part of American power. In this context, because

---

[14]The company subsequently also agreed to pay 650 million rupees, about $22 million, to fund a hospital for victims of the disaster.

[15]The settlement is described in the *New York Times*, February 15, 1989, and *The Economist*, February 18, 1989.

many of the multinationals in the early years were American, and the United States was and is an important military and economic power, multinationals were sometimes described as being instruments of American domination. The emergence of multinationals from Europe, Japan, and some developing countries makes it difficult to characterize multinationals as instruments of American neocolonialism.

Sovereignty

The sovereignty of a host country can be reduced because a multinational has the option of reducing or curtailing its activities in a country. This option is not open to national firms. Also, some multinationals have attempted to exert political influence on the host country. For example, the United Fruit Company (later called United Brands) was criticized for conspiring to topple the government of Guatemala in 1954 (and for its abuse of monopoly power from the early part of this century until the 1950s). It now prefers to work with the governments of host countries, has given up most of its land, and concentrates on distribution and marketing. However, it still has considerable influence in Latin America. In 1971, the International Telephone and Telegraph Company (ITT) attempted to change the policies of the Allende government in order to avoid losing its telephone and hotel interests in Chile. ITT also sought help from the American government. Although the American government officially refused, it is generally believed that ITT and the Central Intelligence Agency (CIA) helped bring about the overthrow of the Allende government in 1973. This incident adversely affected the position of other American companies in Latin America. Fortunately, examples of direct political interference are less common now.[16]

The sovereignty of a host country may be reduced because a multinational may respond to pressures from the source country. For example, in 1982 the American government attempted to stop completion of a natural gas pipeline from the Soviet Union to Western Europe.[17] American firms, and European firms doing business with American firms, were instructed not to sell products for use in this project. This action was seen by European governments as an infringement of their sovereignty. European countries responded by ordering companies to honor contracts. What little sympathy there might have been for the American position was eroded when the United States signed an agreement to sell grain to the Soviet Union. Eventually, the action was abandoned. Canada has experienced similar

---

[16]Other examples of "imperialist" behavior by multinationals are given by Hood and Young (1979).

[17]The pipeline fiasco is discussed by Hufbauer and Scott in Moran (1985).

problems as a result of American embargoes on sales to countries that Canada has friendly relations with. Although these issues are mainly political, the problem is economic to the extent that the host country is not compensated for losses resulting from these actions.

Culture and the Quality of Life

It is alleged that multinationals are responsible for the breakdown of traditional cultural values in developing countries and the spread of what is sometimes called "Coca–Cola culture." The influence of Western culture can be seen throughout the world, but is the influence due to multinationals or due to improved communications? An what, if anything, should be done about it? These are not economic questions, but economists can point out the costs of attempting to cure these problems by economic isolationism. Poor countries are not the only countries affected. A clash between the United States and the European Union over trade in audio visual products almost prevented agreement in the Uruguay round. One of the major issues behind the debate was foreign ownership of media, the influence of foreign productions on European culture and language, and the number of foreign productions that are presented in Europe.

Conclusion

The main conclusion that emerges from studying the effects of multinationals on host countries is that we cannot say with certainty whether any particular multinational will increase welfare. We cannot even say that a particular country will always benefit from multinationals. It may by reasonable to conclude that multinationals increase world income, and the individual host countries can gain from multinationals if appropriate policies are enacted. In particular, policies are needed to prevent the creation and abuse of monopoly power. While negative effects are possible, it seems that most countries believe that they will gain if they can attract multinationals. Therefore, while some countries may restrict foreign ownership, we can expect multinationals to continue as a feature of the world economic system.

Summary of Main Points

A **multinational corporation** is a company with operations in more than one country. The growth of multinationals was facilitated by falling transport costs and improvements in communications. In the postwar period, the first multinationals to attract attention were usually American, but American corporations now account for less than half the largest companies in the world. Many multinationals are from Europe or Japan. Although attention has often focused on the effects of multinationals on developing countries, host countries are usually developed markets.

Multinational corporations are established by **direct foreign investment.** This investment is usually from one developed country to another. A company may decide to set up a foreign branch for many reasons: control over inputs, lower operating costs, access to markets, or lower taxes. Foreign companies often face higher costs than local firms that are familiar with the local language, culture, and business practices. In order to be able to compete, multinationals must have other advantages. These may include: patents and brand names, superior technology, production or management expertise, access to global capital markets, or an established global marketing network.

Multinational corporations lead to a more efficient global allocation of capital, and because they may have easier access to funds than national companies, they may increase global investment. Also, they benefit from economies of scale in both production and marketing. Thus, we would expect multinationals to increase global income. Because multinationals are large, they are sometimes criticized as examples of monopoly inefficiency. This criticism presumes that multinationals do not face competition or benefit from lower costs.

Multinationals influence welfare in the **source country** where the company has its headquarters, and in the **host country** where the company invests. Although attention has often focused on the effects of multinationals on developing countries, host countries are usually developed markets.

Multinationals are often attacked as reducing income and employment in the source country. This criticism presumes that the alternative to foreign investment is greater domestic investment. The relationship between foreign and domestic investment is not necessarily close; for example, foreign investment may be financed by funds raised in foreign markets. Also, foreign investment may increase domestic employment by establishing foreign companies that use the products of the parent company, by establishing distribution networks for exports, or by developing sources for low–cost inputs.

The effect of foreign investment on domestic income and employment in the host country is also unclear. Multinationals increase the available capital and thus add to income and employment in the host country. Domestic producers may lose if the products of the multinational compete with their products, and because they must compete for labor with the multinational. When there is unemployment, competition for labor is not usually a serious problem. The effect of multinationals on the balance of payments of host countries cannot be predicted. Although the effects of the trading activities of multinationals may be clear, the overall effect of multinationals also depends on transfers of profits, fees, and royalties.

Neither source countries nor host countries gain much from taxes on multinationals. If a host country attempts to tax a multinational heavily, the company may move. **Transfer pricing** can also be used to reduce a company's tax liability in a high tax area. Source countries do not gain significantly from taxes levied on multinationals because foreign taxes reduce a company's domestic taxes. Also, because reinvested profits are not subject to tax, multinationals can often avoid taxes altogether.

Some developing countries offered favorable contracts to companies in order to induce them to undertake large investments. After the investment had been made, these contracts could be renegotiated on terms more favorable to the host country (because the companies did not want to lose their investments). As a result, many companies now prefer to engage in joint ventures with local producers.

Other criticisms of multinationals include allegations that they do not transfer appropriate technology to developing countries and that they avoid health and safety regulations by producing in the least regulated markets. Also, examples of multinationals intervening in the politics of the host countries are used by critics who allege that they undermine the sovereignty and culture of host countries.

Examples of good and bad behavior by multinationals can always be found. However, because multinationals and countries differ so widely, one cannot generalize about the effects of multinationals: each multinational must be examined separately in order to identify its effects.

Study Questions

1. Describe briefly the importance of multinational corporations within the international economic system.
2. What were the factors that contributed to the rise of multinational corporations after World War II?
3. Why might a multinational corporation prefer foreign direct investment to a) exporting or, b) licensing foreign producers?
4. Why might multinational corporations be expected to increase world income?
5. Source countries and host countries complain that they do not receive taxes from multinational corporations. How can multinationals avoid paying taxes?
6. Describe the nature of the obsolescing contract.
7. Would American employment increase if American corporations were prevented from investing abroad?
8. What are the effects of multinational corporations on the balance of payments of host countries?
9. What benefits do multinational corporations bring to host countries?
10. Why do developing countries often try to attract multinational corporations?

11. Under what conditions would a multinational reduce the welfare of the host country?

Selected References

Abraham C. M. and S. Abraham, "The Bhopal Case and the Development of Environmental Law in India," *International and Comparative Law Quarterly*, April 1991, pp. 334–65.

Baldwin, R. E. and J. D. Richardson, (eds.), *International Trade and Finance*, 2e, Boston: Little Brown, 1981.

Barnet, R. J. and J. Cavanagh, *Global Dreams: Imperial Corporations and the New World Order*, New York: Simon & Schuster, 1994.

Drucker, P. F., "Multinationals and Developing Countries: Myths and Realities," *Foreign Affairs*, 53, Oct. 1974, pp. 121–34. Reprinted in Adams, J., *The Contemporary International Economy*, 2e, New York: St. Martin's Press, 1985.

Grunwald, J. and K. Flamm, *The Global Factory: Foreign Assembly in International Trade*, Washington, DC: Brookings Institution, 1985.

Hood, N. and S. Young, *The Economics of Multinational Enterprise*, New York: Longman, 1979.

Howenstine, N. G. and W. J. Zeile, "Characteristics of Foreign Owned U.S. Manufacturing Establishments," *Survey of Current Business*, January 1994, pp. 34–59.

Hymer, S., "The Efficiency Contradictions of Multinational Corporations," *American Economic Review*, 60, May 1970, pp. 441–53. Reprinted in Baldwin and Richardson (1981).

Mataloni, R. J. and L. Goldberg, "Gross Product of U.S. Multinational Companies," *Survey of Current Business*, February 1994, pp. 42–63.

Moran, T. H., (ed.), *Multinational Corporations: The Political Economy of Foreign Direct Investment*, Lexington, MA: DC Heath, 1985.

Robock, S. F. and K. Simmonds, *International Business and Multinational Enterprise*, 4e, Homewood, IL: Richard D. Irwin, 1989.

Sigmund, P. E., *Multinationals in Latin America: The Politics of Nationalization*, Madison, WI: University of Wisconsin Press, 1980.

Streeten, P., "Multinationals Revisited," *Finance and Development*, 16, June 1979, pp. 39–42. Reprinted in Baldwin and Richardson (1981).

United Nations, *World Investment Report 1993: Transnational Corporations and Integrated International Production*, New York: United Nations, 1993.

Vernon, R., *Sovereignty at Bay: The Spread of U.S. Enterprises*, New York: Basic Books, 1971.

Vernon, R., *Storm over the Multinationals: The Real Issues*, Cambridge, MA: Harvard University Press, 1977.

Wilkins, M., *The Emergence of Multinational Enterprise: American Business Abroad from the Colonial Era to 1914*, Cambridge, MA: Harvard University Press, 1970.

Index

A

Absolute advantage, 5-7, 26
    labor inputs as basis for, 14
Absorption, 166, 189-91, 198, 227
Abundant factor, 55
Accounting balances, 162-63
Adams, J., 434n
Adjustment
    costs of, 209-10
    lags in, 205-6
    as problem in Bretton Woods system, 305-6
Administrative obstructions to trade, 91-92
Ad valorem tariff, 76, 348
Advanced countries (ACs), 420, 449
    attempt to foster growth in developing countries, 425
    market access and trade policies of, 433-34
Aggregate demand, 79, 178, 180, 198
    increase in, 230
Aggregate supply, 178, 198
Agriculture. *See also* Common agricultural policy (CAP)
    in developing countries, 427-28
    under GATT, 360
        in Uruguay Round, 433-34
    policy on, in European Union, 400-4
Ahmed, M., 446n
Amazonas, A., 430n
Annual Report on Exchange Arrangements and Exchange Restrictions, 299n
Apartheid, 424
Appreciation, 122, 151
Arbitrage
    covered interest, 145, 146-47
    in spot market, 122-23
    triangular, 124
Argentina, inflation and exchange rates in, 144

Asset markets, and exchange rates, 128-29
Assets, and exchange rate, 132-34
Austria, collapse of gold standard in, 286
Autonomous consumption, 178

B

Bahamas, 381n
Balance of international indebtedness, 169-70
Balance of payments, 155, 172-73
    adjustment in, and gold standard, 265
    deficit in, 161-62, 226-27, 231
        and inflation, 243
        and unemployment, 242
    definition of, 155
    and fiscal policy, 207-11
    and foreign exchange market, 162
    influences on, 234
    monetary approach to, 206
    and national income, 165-72
    surplus in, 231
        and inflation, 243
        and unemployment, 242-43
    of United States, 156, 168-69
Balance of payments accounting, 155
    accounting balances in, 162-63
        basic balance, 164
        current account and net foreign assets, 163
        current account balance plus net private capital flows, 164-65
    capital flows in, 157
    credits and debits in, 155-56
    deficits and surpluses in, 161-62
    double-entry bookkeeping in, 159-60
    measurement problems in, 158-59
    merchandise trade, services, and investment income in, 156-57